Trade Policy Review

Colombia
2012

World Trade Organization
Geneva, August 2012

WTO/GATT TRADE POLICY REVIEWS CURRENTLY AVAILABLE

Albania	2010
Antigua and Barbuda	2001
Angola	2006
Argentina	1999, 2007
Armania	2010
Australia	1989, 1994, 1998, 2002, 2007, 2011
Austria	1992
Bahrain	2000, 2007
Bangladesh	1992, 2000, 2006
Barbados	2002, 2008
Belize	2010
Belize and Suriname	2004
Benin	1997
Benin, Burkina Faso and Mali	2004, 2010
Bolivia	1993, 1999, 2005
Brazil	1992, 1995, 2000, 2004, 2009
Brunei Darussalam	2001, 2008
Bulgaria	2003
Burundi	2003
Cambodia	2011
Cameroon	1995, 2001
Cameroon and Gabon	2007
Canada	1990, 1992, 1994, 1996, 1998, 2000, 2003, 2007, 2011
Central African Republic	2007
Chad	2007
Chile	1991, 1997, 2003, 2009
China	2006, 2008, 2010, 2012
Colombia	1990, 1996, 2006, 2012
Congo	2006, 2010
Costa Rica	1995, 2001, 2007
Côte d'Ivoire	1995
Croatia	2010
Cyprus	1997
Czech Republic	1996, 2001
Djibouti	2006
Dominica	2001
Dominican Republic	1996, 2002, 2008
East African Community	2006
Ecuador	2005, 2011
Egypt	1992, 1999, 2005
El Salvador	1996, 2003, 2010
European Communities (European Union)	1991, 1993, 1995, 1997, 2000, 2002, 2004, 2007, 2009, 2011
Fiji	1997, 2009
Finland	1997
Gabon	2001
Gambia	2004, 2010
Georgia	2009
Ghana	1992, 2001, 2008
Grenada	2001
Guatemala	2002, 2009
Guinea	1999, 2005, 2011
Guyana	2003, 2009
Haiti	2003
Honduras	2003, 2010
Hong Kong, China	1990, 1994, 1998, 2002, 2006, 2010
Hungary	1991, 1998
Iceland	1994, 2000, 2006
India	1993, 1998, 2002, 2007, 2011
Indonesia	1995, 1998, 2003, 2007
Israel	1995, 1999, 2006
Jamaica	1998, 2005, 2011
Japan	1992, 1995, 1998, 2000, 2002, 2005, 2007, 2009, 2011
Jordan	2008
Kenya	1993, 2000
Kyrgyz Republic	2006
Liechtenstein	2000, 2004
Macao, China	1994, 2001, 2007
Madagascar	2001, 2008
Malawi	2002, 2010
Malaysia	1993, 1997, 2001, 2006, 2010
Maldives	2003, 2009
Mauritania	2002, 2011
Mauritius	1995, 2001, 2008
Mexico	1993, 1997, 2002, 2008
Mongolia	2005
Morocco	1990, 1996, 2003, 2009
Mozambique	2001, 2009
Nepal	2012
New Zealand	1990, 1996, 2003, 2009
Nicaragua	1999, 2006
Niger/Senegal	2003, 2009
Nigeria	1991, 1998, 2005, 2011
Norway	1991, 1996, 2000, 2004, 2008
Oman	2008
Pakistan	1995, 2002, 2008
Panama	2007
Papua New Guinea	1999, 2010
Paraguay	1997, 2005, 2011
Peru	1994, 2000, 2007
Philippines	1993, 1999, 2005, 2012
Poland	1992, 2000
Qatar	2005
Republic of Korea	1992, 1996, 2000, 2004, 2008
Romania	1992, 1999, 2005
Rwanda	2004
Saint Kitts and Nevis	2001
Saint Lucia	2001
Saint Vincent and the Grenadines	2001
Separate Customs Territory of Taiwan, Penghu, Kinmen, and Matsu	2006, 2010
Sierra Leone	2005
Singapore	1992, 1996, 2000, 2004, 2008
Slovak Republic	1995, 2001
Slovenia	2002
Solomon Islands	1998, 2009
Southern African Customs Union	1998, 2003, 2009
Sri Lanka	1995, 2004, 2010
Sweden	1995
Switzerland and Liechtenstein	1991, 1996, 2000, 2004, 2008
Tanzania	2000
Thailand	1991, 1995, 1999, 2003, 2007, 2011
The Kingdom of Saudi Arabia	2012
The State of Kuwait	2012
Togo	1999, 2006
Trinidad & Tobago	1998, 2005, 2012
Tunisia	1994, 2005
Turkey	1994, 1998, 2003, 2007, 2012
Uganda	1995, 2001
United Arab Emirates	2006, 2012
United States	1990, 1992, 1994, 1996, 1999, 2001, 2004, 2006, 2008, 2010
Uruguay	1992, 1998, 2006, 2012
Venezuela	1996, 2002
Zambia	1996, 2002, 2009
Zimbabwe	1995, 2011

Co-Published by the World Trade Organization and Bernan Press. Printed in the U.S.A.

ISBN 13: 978-1-59888-598-9
ISSN: 1556-2050

All reports are available in English, French, and Spanish.

For more information, please contact:

WTO PUBLICATIONS
Centre William Rappard
Rue de Lausanne 154
1211 Geneva 21, Switzerland
Telephone: (41 22) 739 5208, 5308
Fax: (41 22) 739 5792
Email: publications@wto.org
www.wto.org

BERNAN PRESS, a wholly owned subsidiary of
The Rowman & Littlefield Publishing Group, Inc.
4501 Forbes Boulevard, Suite 200
Lanham, MD 20706, U.S.A.
Telephone: (301) 459-7666 (Washington, D.C. area)
(800) 865-3457 (toll-free)
Email:customercare@bernan.com
www.bernan.com

PREFACE

The Trade Policy Review Mechanism (TPRM) was first established on a trial basis by the GATT CONTRACTING PARTIES in April 1989. The Mechanism became a permanent feature of the World Trade Organization under the Marrakesh Agreement which established the WTO in January 1995.

The objectives of the TPRM are to contribute to improved adherence by all WTO Members to rules, disciplines and commitments made under the Multilateral Trade Agreements and, where applicable, the Plurilateral Trade Agreements, and hence to the smoother functioning of the multilateral trading system, by achieving greater transparency in, and understanding of, the trade policies and practices of Members. Accordingly, the review mechanism enables the regular collective appreciation and evaluation of the full range of individual Members' trade policies and practices and their impact on the functioning of the multilateral trading system. It is not intended to serve as a basis for the enforcement of specific obligations under the Agreements or for dispute settlement procedures, or to impose new policy commitments on Members.

The assessment carried out under the TPRM takes place, to the extent relevant, against the background of the wider economic and developmental needs, policies and objectives of the Member concerned, as well as its external environment. However, the function of the review mechanism is to examine the impact of a Member's trade policies and practices on the multilateral trading system.

Under the TPRM, the trade policies of all Members are subject to periodic review. The four largest trading entities in terms of world market share, counting the European Union as one, are reviewed every two years, the 16 next largest trading entities every four years, and other Members every six years; a longer period may be fixed for least-developed countries.

The reviews are conducted by the Trade Policy Review Body (TPRB) on the basis of two documents: a policy statement by the Member under review and a comprehensive report drawn up by the WTO Secretariat on its own responsibility.

TABLE OF CONTENTS

Note: The documents that comprise this publication are available online at: http://www.wto.org/english/tratop_e/tpr_e/tp_rep_e.htm.

PART A

CONCLUDING REMARKS BY THE CHAIRPERSON

OF THE TRADE POLICY REVIEW BODY,

H.E. MR SHAHID BASHIR (PAKISTAN),

AT THE TRADE POLICY REVIEW

OF COLOMBIA

26 AND 28 JUNE 2012

CONCLUDING REMARKS BY THE CHAIRPERSON

1. I commend the Vice Minister and the Disccusant to make very pertinent remarks this morning and many issues which Members had, have been touched on briefly but comprehensively. Chairing the meeting for the fourth Trade Policy Review of Colombia was personally a rewarding experience. The Trade Policy Review of Colombia has provided an opportunity for us to improve our understanding of recent developments in Colombia's trade and trade related policies. I would like to thank Vice Minister Duque of Colombia, Ambassador Eduardo Muñoz and the rest of the delegation of Colombia for their constructive engagement in this meeting. My thanks also go to Ambassador Tim Yeend for his excellent participation as discussant, and to the Members for their numerous interventions. I would further like to commend the authorities of Colombia for the effort made to answer the questions received prior to this meeting.

2. Members generally congratulated Colombia for weathering the global crisis well by using countercyclical fiscal policies, instead of resorting to protectionist trade measures. Colombia has a relatively open trade and investment regime with few restrictions. Members urged Colombia to continue to deepen the liberalization process that had been so beneficial to the country.

3. Members also praised Colombia for having used trade policy to promote sustainable growth and for implementing the National Development Plan 2010 2014 with the caption "Prosperity for All" which focusses on ensuring that the different levels of society would benefit from growth. Further poverty reduction remained a challenge, but the results achieved so far were impressive.

4. Members expressed their appreciation for Colombia's active participation in the WTO, particularly in the Doha negotiations; they acknowledged that Colombia was a strong supporter of the multilateral system. They noted with satisfaction Colombia's participation as an observer in the Agreement on Government Procurement, and urged Colombia to accede to it. Members also urged Colombia to improve its compliance with its WTO notification obligations.

5. Members noted that Colombia's trade policy thrust since the last Review has focused on the negotiation of preferential trade agreements so as to secure a stable preferential market access for its products. The authorities expect this to continue to diversify exports and attract more foreign investment. Several Members were especially interested in the steps Colombia had taken to implement the U.S.-Colombia FTA.

6. Similarly, there was a positive assessment of the legal and institutional reforms introduced to Colombia's competition and government procurement framework; however, Members highlighted a number of areas for further improvement, such as the application of SPS and TBT measures.

7. A close examination of the observations made by the delegations during this Review would suggest that there are reasons to recommend that the authorities of Colombia consider introducing further improvements in certain areas, some of which have been already mentioned by the Vice-Minister this morning. The main areas are:

- Customs procedures for imports (including rules of origin) and customs valuation: Members commended Colombia for its efforts to facilitate trade through the single window. Nevertheless, they raised questions regarding documentation requirements and the use of customs agents. In this regard, Members urged Colombia to continue to streamline its customs procedures through the implementation of further trade facilitation measures. Regarding Colombia's customs valuation system, concerns were raised with respect to the continued use of reference and indicative prices as a parameter for checking the reported value during customs inspection, and the criteria to calculate them.

- Tariffs and other import duties: Members expressed their satisfaction with the sharp reduction in Colombia's MFN applied tariffs, one of the most important trade policy developments since Colombia's last review in 2006. Members, however, noted that the most recent tariff reduction, which took place in August 2011, was only temporary. Members urged Colombia make the temporary reduction permanent. They sought more information on the application of the CAN Common External Tariff and on the functioning of the Andean Price Band System.

- Non-tariff measures: Some Members noted Colombia's use of non-tariff measures, including import prohibitions, restrictions and licensing. They urged Colombia to simplify and clarify its licensing system. In general, Members suggested that Colombia may reduce non-tariff restrictions.

- SPS and TBT: A number of Members questioned the procedures to establish sanitary and phytosanitary measures and technical regulations and pointed out that certain sanitary and phytosanitary measures adopted by Colombia could constitute a barrier to trade. Members urged Colombia to eliminate measures that impeded trade and to introduce a clear notification mechanism so that trading partners could be kept informed of all the measures that are in force.

- Government procurement: Members noted the reforms made by Colombia on certain aspects of its government procurement regime and sought more information on the impact of these changes on procurement procedures, and on the possibility of putting in place a mechanism to deal with procurement-related challenges. Colombia was urged to reconsider the costs to its economy of using preferences for domestic suppliers and was invited to join the WTO Plurilateral Agreement on Government Procurement as soon as it is possible.

- Incentives: Pointing out that Colombia had a series of incentive schemes to attract investment, promote exports, and protect agriculture and other less advantaged sectors, such as micro and small enterprises, Members asked whether Colombia had assessed the impact of these programmes and determined whether they were WTO consistent.

- Intellectual property rights: Members sought additional information on several aspects of the Colombia's intellectual property rights regime. Members were also interested in knowing the steps taken by Colombia to implement the IPR commitments negotiated in the various trade agreements in which Colombia participates. Noting the actions undertaken to strengthen the enforcement of intellectual property rights, including through administrative reforms, Members urged Colombia to continue stepping up efforts in this area.

- Agriculture: Members, while recognizing the importance of agriculture for Colombia, also noted the support and protection received by that sector. Mention was made of the fact that tariff protection for agricultural products was substantially higher than for industrialized goods. Members encouraged Colombia to continue liberalizing the agricultural sector by reducing tariffs, reducing the gap between applied and bound tariff rates, and eliminating incentive and any unnecessary sanitary and phytosanitary measures.

- Services: Members commended Colombia on its continuous efforts to liberalize trade in services and highlighted the restructuring of telecommunications regime as a significant measure. Members encouraged Colombia to continue in this path, for instance, by lowering the nationality requirements and relaxing the requirements for commercial presence in certain services sectors, especially finance, logistics and transport.

- Investment and FDI: Members observed that Colombia had been successful in seeking to attract FDI to boost economic growth and employment, and that most sectors were at least partly open to foreign direct investment. A number of Members emphasized the importance of FDI for Colombia's future development in view of its infrastructure and technological requirements and urged Colombia to eliminate remaining investment barriers.

8. In conclusion, Members encouraged Colombia to continue with its domestic, regional and multilateral efforts to facilitate trade, increase investment and promote sustainable economic growth. This successfully concludes our fourth Review of Colombia. The detailed nature of the questions submitted and the numerous interventions attest to Members' interest in Colombia's trade policies and practices. I would like once again to thank the delegation of Colombia, the discussant and the Members for contributing to an enlightening Review of Colombia's trade policies and practices.

9. I may also mention the efforts of the Secretariat to compile a very comprehensive report and to organize this Review in a very befitting manner.

PART B

REPORT BY THE WTO SECRETARIAT

This report was drafted by Mr Angelo Silvy and Mrs Eugenia Lizano.

CONTENTS

CHARTS

TABLES

APPENDIX TABLES

Page

SUMMARY

(1) INTRODUCTION

1. Since the last Trade Policy Review conducted in 2006, Colombia has continued steering its trade policy towards greater openness, setting its sights on closer integration with Latin America and the Caribbean, as well as with the rest of the world, through the negotiation of preferential agreements to increase external trade and foreign investment flows. To this end, Colombia has participated in various negotiations to consolidate existing bilateral and regional agreements, and has signed and continues actively negotiating new agreements with the aim of ensuring preferential access to strategic markets. This does not detract from the particular importance that Colombia attaches to participation in the WTO as part of its trade policy strategy. Colombia therefore places great emphasis on maintaining an open trade regime in the framework of a transparent multilateral system complemented by regional and bilateral efforts.

2. Colombia has a substantially open trade regime, with an average tariff which declined considerably during the period under review. Although the general trend is towards greater openness and reduced obstacles to foreign trade, some non-tariff restrictions remain in place, mainly related to registration and import licensing requirements. The trade regime is also somewhat complex, owing to the large number of regulations.

(2) ECONOMIC ENVIRONMENT

3. During the period under review, Colombia's GDP grew at an annual average rate of 4.8 per cent. Economic growth picked up speed between 2005 and 2007, but the global financial crisis caused a loss of momentum in 2008 and 2009. However, given the combination of countercyclical policies and the strong performance of some export products, Colombia did not fall into recession and the economy rebounded again, reaching 4 per cent growth in 2010 and 5.9 per cent in 2011.

4. As a result of solid economic performance, per capita GDP grew rapidly, from US$3,417 in 2005 to US$7,236 in 2011. Despite this improvement, poverty levels, although they have reduced, remain high and there is a continued lack of equity in income distribution. In addition, despite trending downwards, the unemployment rate in 2011 was still some 9.8 per cent.

5. During the financial crisis, Colombia used fiscal policy as an instrument to boost medium-term growth and reduce unemployment, and this led to an increase, albeit a modest one, in expenditure and fiscal deficit levels. At the same time, however, Colombia has committed itself to maintaining fiscal discipline, a commitment enshrined in the Constitution. Accordingly, 2011 saw the introduction of a fiscal regulation to enhance public sector discipline and a reform of the system of royalties to improve their management and distribution. This countercyclical fiscal policy was also accompanied by an expansive monetary policy, resulting in a sharp decline in the intervention interest rate between late 2008 and mid-2010. With the rise in inflation in 2011, however, a contractionary monetary policy was adopted.

6. Colombia maintains a floating exchange rate. During the period under review and partly because of substantial capital inflows into Colombia, a real appreciation of the peso took place which, while lowering the cost of imports, made exports less competitive. To address that situation, the Bank of the Republic intervened repeatedly on the exchange markets and adopted measures to deal with exchange-rate pressures.

7. International trade in goods and services in the review period showed dynamic growth: imports, in US dollar terms, increased at an annual average rate of 17.1 per cent between 2005 and 2011, and exports at an annual average rate of 17.9 per cent, with both indices practically doubling during the period. Colombia's trade is relatively concentrated, both geographically and in terms of export products. The United States continues to be the main market for Colombian goods and mining products accounted for approximately 65 per cent of Colombian exports in 2011.

8. Colombia's current account balance has traditionally been in deficit, owing to the negative balances in income and services. Nevertheless, the balance of trade in goods remained in surplus for most of the period under review, and more particularly as from 2008, because of strong export growth. Colombia has also benefited from improved terms of trade and strong demand for raw materials. The continuous increase in investment flows has also played a major role and reflects greater investor confidence in the country.

(3) TRADE AND INVESTMENT POLICY

9. During the period under review, Colombia's trade policy focused mainly on the negotiation of preferential agreements. The Trade Promotion Agreement between Colombia and the United States, signed in November 2006, was incorporated in Colombian legislation in 2007 and approved by the United States Congress in 2011; it is currently at the stage of implementation. Nevertheless, as a founding Member of the WTO, Colombia recognizes the importance of having a multilateral trading system with clear and transparent rules that support the integration of developing countries into the global economy. Colombia supported the swift and balanced conclusion of the Doha Development Agenda, which it considers necessary in order to achieve more open, undistorted markets and to strengthen the multilateral system. Colombia continues to have observer status in the Committee on Government Procurement and recently acceded to the Information Technology Agreement.

10. Colombia grants national treatment to foreign investment in all but a few sectors where it maintains limitations or prohibitions. In addition, the State may determine that only one enterprise may exclusively provide services in a particular sector for a specified period of time. No prior authorization is required for foreign investment, subject to some exceptions (financing in the hydrocarbons and mining sectors, and portfolio investment); such investment must be registered with the Bank of the Republic in order to make it possible for earnings to be repatriated and/or reinvested. Both domestic and foreign direct investors may sign a legal stability contract with the State, which guarantees that, for the duration of the contract, there will be no change in the legal rules under which the investment was made.

(4) TRADE POLICY BY MEASURE

11. Colombia has a substantially open trade regime, and the average tariff rate has been decreasing. Some non-tariff restrictions still remain in place, however, mainly related to import registration and licensing requirements. The regime is also somewhat complex on account of the large number of regulations.

12. During the review period, Colombia simplified its customs and administrative procedures by establishing a single window for imports and exports and a system of risk analysis, which has reduced the frequency of inspection. But further efforts are needed to facilitate trade, including the improved functioning of the single window. Colombia continues to use reference prices as parameters for checking the value reported by importers during the customs inspection process.

13. Since its last review, Colombia has considerably reduced tariff protection. It has implemented a tariff reform aimed at reducing the levels and dispersion of tariffs, which also addresses the anti-export bias manifest in the Colombian tariff. As a result of this reform, the average tariff has fallen to 6.2 per cent, compared with 12 per cent in 2006. Apart from tariff reductions effected in late 2010 and early 2011, in August 2011 Colombia lowered its applied tariffs on a large number of products (mainly industrial inputs and capital goods) for a period of 12 months. In general, the tariffs applied by Colombia are *ad valorem*. Colombia continues to use the Andean Price Band System (SAFP) to apply import duties on a number of agricultural products; the duties vary according to the international prices of the products concerned.

14. Imports are also subject, as a rule, to value added tax (VAT). Both domestic and imported products attract VAT which is applied at the same rates in both cases. However, certain imports not produced in Colombia are exempted or excluded from the payment of VAT. In order for an importer to be eligible for VAT exemption, the Ministry of Commerce, Industry and Tourism (MCIT) must certify, prior to import, that the product to be imported is not produced domestically. A consumption tax is also applied to some imported and domestic products. The various import procedures or customs regimes and the different export promotion programmes provide, under certain conditions, for relief from the payment of customs duties and other taxes applicable to goods imports.

15. As regards non-tariff measures, Colombia prohibits imports of certain goods on grounds of public health or morality, as well as to protect the environment or national security and to meet the commitments contained in international agreements to which it is a signatory. Colombia also applies an automatic ("free import") and non-automatic ("prior licence") licensing system. During the period under review, the import licensing system, as notified to the WTO by Colombia, underwent no substantial changes. The number of tariff lines subject to automatic and non-automatic licensing has increased since 2006 due to a change in the tariff classification in the case of automatic licensing, and in the case of non-automatic licensing to the fact that, as from 2010, a non-automatic licence is required to import certain precursors for the production of narcotic drugs.

16. Colombia continued having recourse to anti-dumping measures during the period reviewed. Between 2006 and 2011, Colombia initiated 25 anti-dumping (AD) investigations and applied ten new definitive measures; provisional measures were imposed in 13 of the 25 investigations initiated. Most of the measures were applied in 2007. As at 31 December 2011, Colombia had 12 AD measures in force, all of which were applied to imports from China. In the same period, no countervailing or safeguard measures were applied and no related investigations were initiated.

17. The task of preparing technical regulations is not centralized in a specific body; such regulations may emanate from the standardization institute ICONTEC, or from ministries, regulatory commissions and decentralized bodies. Although each entity has its own internal procedure for the establishment of technical regulations, since 2009 a procedure for elaborating and issuing them has been agreed, on the basis of good practice recommendations. Most technical regulations reflect or are based on international standards. During the period 2006-2011, Colombia made 207 notifications to the WTO Central Registry, including notifications of draft technical regulations and their implementation, amendment or rejection. Important changes have taken place in the accreditation process since the last review. The responsibility for formulating policy on sanitary and phytosanitary (SPS) measures in Colombia is shared by various ministries. The SPS system operates on the principle of the harmonization of policy in the different sectors. SPS measures are adopted by the body responsible for risk assessment, where appropriate.

18. Export freedom is the general rule in Colombia, subject to the limitations or prohibitions established by laws or international agreements in force. However, the Government may issue standards to regulate trade, so as to enable the economy to overcome any external or internal circumstances that are adverse to Colombia's trade interests. Consequently, during the period under review, Colombia applied temporary quotas for exports of cattle (female) on the hoof in order to guarantee national herd replenishment and thereby improve the exportable supply of meat and meat products. Colombia maintains special charges on the exportation of certain products (including mild coffee, unset emeralds and coal) to finance development funds.

19. Colombia continues to run a number of export support and promotion programmes. The free zone programme was reviewed to bring it into line with the provisions of the Agreement on Subsidies and Countervailing Measures (SCM Agreement). The new regime is designed to promote the production of goods and services intended primarily, but not exclusively or necessarily, for foreign markets. Exporters of goods and services are also eligible for the total or partial refund of indirect taxes, charges and contributions through applications for the tax reimbursement certificate (CERT). In addition, exporters may be eligible for other export support and promotion programmes such as the special export programmes (PEX) and the Vallejo Plan.

20. In 2009, with a view to updating the rules on protection of competition, Colombia adopted a new law on the subject. The Supervisory Authority for Industry and Trade (SIC), which was restructured in 2011, is now the National Authority for the Protection of Competition; its function is to conduct investigations, impose fines and adopt other decisions concerning infringements of the competition protection regulations. During the period reviewed, the SIC made considerable progress with regard to the average duration of the investigation and decision-making process. The Special Administrative Unit for Civil Aviation (air transport) and the Financial Supervisory Authority currently deal only with business mergers in their respective sectors. There is a special competition regime for the agricultural sector, considered a sector of basic importance to the economy, in which some anti-competitive agreements are therefore allowed for stabilization purposes. Similarly, the following are exempted from the application of the competition law: price stabilization funds, parafiscal funds for agricultural development, establishment of minimum guaranteed prices, regulation of domestic markets for agricultural products, supply chain agreements in the agricultural sector and the agricultural safeguard regime.

21. Colombia continues using fiscal incentives as an instrument to promote national and foreign investment, as well as other support programmes to promote development in specific sectors and to contribute to social and political equality. Colombia has observer status in the context of the Plurilateral Agreement on Government Procurement. During the period under review, Colombia strengthened the legal and institutional framework for government procurement, particularly for the purpose of increasing transparency, through the introduction, in 2007, of legal changes in the public procurement regime. However, procurement is also used as a tool to boost domestic industry and employment, mainly through the use of preferences.

22. During the period under review, Colombia made no important changes to the legal framework of its intellectual property protection regime; changes were, however, made in the regulatory area to facilitate formalities through automation and, at the institutional level, through the establishment of the Intersectoral Commission on Intellectual Property (CIPI), with a view to coordinating the policies, activities and programmes of public and private institutions relating to intellectual property.

(5) Trade Policy by Sector

23. The period under review saw the introduction of some changes in the sectoral composition of the Colombian economy. The mining sector substantially increased its share of GDP, from 6.3 per cent in 2005 to 10.3 per cent in 2011. This was due partly to increased oil and coal production and the rise in international prices. The share of the agricultural and manufacturing sectors contracted, reflecting a relative increase which, though solid, was less pronounced than for the more dynamic sectors of the economy. The contribution of financial and real estate services to GDP declined only slightly in spite of the financial crisis, while the share of the construction sector increased, partly under the impetus of increased public spending.

24. The agricultural sector is of key importance to the Colombian economy on account of its contribution to GDP, employment and exports. The current focus of agricultural policy is on promoting development in rural areas, increasing competiveness and market diversification. Colombian agricultural policy is also aimed, albeit not explicitly, at contributing to food security. Agricultural products (WTO definition) have a higher tariff protection level (14.5 per cent) than other sectors such as manufacturing (4.9 per cent), and this has been accentuated by the recent tariff reduction. The agricultural sector also benefits from programmes of domestic support, preferential access to credit and debt refinancing programmes, subsidization of agricultural insurance and mitigation of exchange rate risk. Colombia also uses other mechanisms to help producers cope with fluctuating world prices, such as price stabilization funds.

25. Colombia's mining policy is geared to guaranteeing supplies of hydrocarbons and electric power, and to generating the resources needed to promote national development. Colombia grants national treatment to foreign investment in the mining and hydrocarbons sectors, as well as in other sectors. Foreign enterprises must establish a subsidiary domiciled in Colombia in order to be granted exploration concessions. In the hydrocarbons sector, a significant earner of foreign exchange, the State-owned company ECOPETROL S.A. continues to play a predominant role in the extraction, refining, trade, distribution and transportation of petroleum and petroleum products. Colombia continues to grant a sales subsidy on fuel in the domestic market, which, despite having been reformed, still represents a substantial fiscal burden. Private sector participation in the electricity sector accounts for 45 per cent of total generation. Although the State retains a major stake in the sector, reforms have been introduced to promote the functioning of market mechanisms. Thus, during the period under review, Colombia established the Wholesale Electricity Market as an entity responsible for granting concessions for electricity generation, interconnection and transmission networks between regions. The Wholesale Electricity Market has also been used for the adoption of mechanisms to address possible electricity shortages. A subsidy regime is applied to residential users in the most vulnerable sections of society, in accordance with the level of core or subsistence consumption.

26. The manufacturing sector's contribution to GDP declined during the period under review, albeit largely as a result of the accelerated growth of mining. The authorities are seeking to implement a Productive Transformation Programme, by identifying and developing emerging sectors and defining a new industrial strategy structured around sectoral committees. The aim is to promote the development of human capital and improve management and infrastructure, as well as to attract greater foreign investment and to formalize the activities of the informal sector.

27. Services accounted for some two thirds of Colombian GDP in 2011. The main contributors were financial and trade services. Colombia is a net importer of services. However, both imports and exports grew during the period under review.

28. The Constitution characterizes financial, stock exchange and insurance activities as being in the public interest; these activities can therefore only be exercised with prior State authorization. The financial sector is open to foreign investment and there are no legal limitations on foreign capital holdings in commercial banks or insurance companies. Nevertheless, special authorization is required to take out insurance with companies domiciled abroad. During the review period, the financial institutions' prudential indicators remain sound, on account of the reforms introduced in the regulatory framework and in prudential criteria. Colombia satisfactorily weathered the global financial crisis of 2008 and 2009 through increased surveillance and the application of specific measures to increase reserves in order to meet any deterioration in the financial status of institutions.

29. Foreign companies are required to establish a subsidiary in Colombia in order to operate in the national telecommunications market. In 2009, Colombia introduced a new law to promote investment in the sector, which established a general approval regime and abolished the subsidy regime for low-income populations, subject to a transition period. Suppliers of telecommunications services are allowed to set their tariffs freely, except in cases where competition is deemed inadequate or where the quality or supply of services is not acceptable. However, some tariffs are monitored and a tariff ceiling is currently imposed on calls from fixed to mobile telephones.

30. Air transport policy is aimed at providing flexible market access in order to promote competition. Air cabotage services are the preserve of Colombian aircraft, and a nationality requirement is applied, whereby 90 per cent of the staff employed by Colombian airlines and agencies/subsidiaries of foreign airlines established in Colombia must be Colombian nationals. This restriction is applied on a basis of reciprocity. Airports are operated under a concession regime or by the departments/municipalities where they are located.

31. Access to the maritime transport market is based on the principle of reciprocity. In the area of maritime transport, cabotage is reserved for Colombian-flagged ships, although the chartering/hire of a foreign-flagged ship may be authorized if no Colombian vessels are available or suitable for the purpose. The captain, officers and 80 per cent of the crew on ships registered in Colombia must be Colombians. International maritime transport and cabotage companies set their own tariffs and freight rates but must notify them to the authorities, which may review them and raise objections. The construction, maintenance and administration of ports are entrusted to port companies under a 20-year concession regime.

32. The provision of certain types of tourism services is subject to registration requirements. Providers of certain tourist services must pay a parafiscal contribution for the promotion of tourism, which has also been applied to commercial centres since 2011. A range of incentives are offered for investment in the sector, mainly for the renovation or construction of hotels and the provision of ecotourism services.

I. ECONOMIC ENVIRONMENT

(1) Overview

1. Colombia's GDP grew at an average annual rate of 4.8 per cent between 2005 and 2011. After a period of rapid economic expansion between 2005 and 2007, growth slowed in 2008 and 2009 owing to the international financial crisis. Nevertheless, thanks to a combination of countercyclical policies and the buoyancy of some of its export products, Colombia was able to stave off recession during the crisis and growth regained momentum in 2010 to reach 4 per cent. The estimated real GDP growth for 2011 is close to 6 per cent. As a result of the acceleration in economic growth, the review period saw a significant increase in per capita GDP, which stood at US$7,236 in 2011 versus US$3,417 in 2005. However, although poverty was reduced somewhat during the review period, it does remain high and income distribution is uneven. Besides, although unemployment has been falling over this review period owing to the strong performance of the economy in recent years, the rate still stood at a high 9.8 per cent in 2011.

2. In response to the international financial crisis, the Colombian authorities adopted a countercyclical fiscal policy designed to spur economic growth. It led to moderately higher spending and fiscal deficit levels. The present administration regards fiscal policy as a useful tool for stimulating sustainable medium-term growth and reducing unemployment. At the same time, however, it has placed emphasis on the commitment to fiscal sustainability, which is now enshrined in the Constitution. Three important fiscal policy changes occurred in 2011, impacting the economy as a whole as well as various individual sectors. They were: (i) the introduction of a Fiscal Rule; (ii) the incorporation of the principle of fiscal sustainability into the Constitution; (iii) the reform of the system for the distribution of royalties generated by natural resources. The Fiscal Rule is intended to strengthen fiscal discipline and thereby reduce the public debt burden and facilitate the use of countercyclical fiscal policies. The reform of the royalty distribution system is meant to improve the management and distribution of royalties across the national territory. The authorities also implemented a tariff reform aimed at reducing the levels and dispersion of tariffs, as well as tackling the anti-export bias that is present in Colombia's tariff structure.

3. The implementation of the countercyclical fiscal policy went hand-in-hand with an expansionary monetary policy that translated into a substantial and extensive reduction in the intervention interest rate between end-2008 and mid-2010, amounting to 650 basis points. Not only was the interest rate reduction intended to pump-prime the economy but also to send positive signals to the market by guaranteeing liquidity. In response to a modest uptick in inflation, a tight money policy was introduced in 2011, as borne out by the seven increases in the intervention rate during the year.

4. Colombia maintains a floating exchange rate. During the review period and partly as a result of significant capital inflows to Colombia, the peso appreciated in real terms by more than 20 per cent, which, whilst lowering the cost of imports, made manufactures export less competitive. The *Banco de la República* (Bank of the Republic - the central bank) intervened repeatedly on the foreign exchange market to deal with this situation. The Government further announced a series of measures in October 2010 to relieve exchange rate pressures and cushion the impact of the revaluation and hence protect jobs.

5. International trade in goods and services represented some 36.5 per cent of GDP and merchandise trade 32 per cent. Colombia's current account balance traditionally shows a deficit stemming mainly from the deficits in the income and services balances. The 2011 current account

deficit is estimated at 3 per cent of GDP. The balance of trade in goods has shown a surplus for most of the review period. The surplus increased mainly as of 2008 on the back of highly dynamic exports in a context of rapid import growth. Colombia has benefited from the improved terms of trade and from strong demand for commodities. The steady expansion of investment flows has also played a significant role and reflects the increased investor confidence in Colombia.

(2) Structure of the Economy, Growth and Employment

6. Some changes could be observed during this review period in the sectoral make-up of the Colombian economy (Table I.1). The share of the mining sector in GDP increased substantially, moving from 6.3 per cent in 2005 to 10.3 per cent in 2011. This is due in part to the increased output of hydrocarbons and coal as well as rising international prices. The share of the agricultural and manufacturing sectors contracted, indicating relative growth which, though solid, was below that of the more dynamic sectors of the economy. The share of financial and real estate services in GDP declined only slightly despite the financial crisis, whilst that of the construction sector increased, driven in part by higher public spending.

Table I.1
Basic economic indicators, 2005-2011

	2005	2006	2007	2008	2009[a]	2010[a]	2011[a]
Gross domestic product (GDP)[b]							
Current GDP (billion pesos)	340,156	383,898	431,072	480,087	504,647	543,747	615,772
Current GDP (US$ billion)	147	163	207	244	234	286	333
Real GDP, growth rate (%)	4.7	6.7	6.9	3.5	1.7	4.0	5.9
Per capita GDP (current US$)[c]	3,417	3,751	4,722	5,493	5,203	6,295	7,236
By branch of economic activity			(percentage of current GDP)				
Agriculture, livestock farming, hunting, forestry and fishing	7.7	7.4	7.1	6.9	6.9	6.5	6.4
Mining and quarrying	6.3	6.6	6.0	7.9	7.3	6.5	6.4
Manufacturing industries	14.1	14.3	14.5	13.9	13.1	12.9	12.7
Electricity, gas and water supply	4.0	3.9	3.8	3.7	3.6	3.5	3.4
Construction	5.6	6.0	6.4	7.0	7.7	7.0	6.9
Trade, repairs, restaurants and hotels	11.9	11.9	12.1	11.6	11.6	11.6	11.2
Transport, storage and communications	6.8	6.9	7.1	6.6	6.6	6.4	6.2
Financial institutions, insurance, real estate activities and business services	19.1	18.8	18.8	18.8	19.4	19.2	18.3
Community, social and personal service activities	15.9	15.4	15.2	15.0	15.7	15.8	15.0
Total taxes	8.5	8.9	9.1	8.6	8.1	8.4	8.6
Employment							
Total national employment (thousands of persons)[d]	18,057	17,897	18,215	17,472	18,490	19,279	20,774
Unemployment rate (% of economically active population (EAP)), end of period[c, d]	10.3	11.8	9.9	10.6	11.3	11.1	9.8
Underemployment rate (% of EAP), end of period	31.4	35.9	34.3	27.1	29.8	30.5	30.3
Memorandum items							
EAP (thousands)[d]	19,803	18,884	19,378	19,738	21,535	21,979	23,024
Working-age population (thousands)[d]	39,190	32,744	33,305	33,867	34,423	34,961	35,491
Total population (thousands)[c, d]	42,889	43,405	43,926	44,450	44,978	45,509	46,044

a Preliminary figures.
b Seasonally adjusted GDP series.
c Data provided by the Bank of the Republic.
d Colombian National Administrative Department of Statistics.

Source: National Administrative Department of Statistics; Bank of the Republic; Ministry of Social Welfare; and information provided by the Colombian authorities.

7. Colombia witnessed a period of accelerated growth between 2005 and 2007. The international financial crisis led to a slowdown in 2008 and 2009, though mainly in this latter year. Thanks to a combination of countercyclical policies and the buoyancy of some export products, however, Colombia was able to avert recession during the crisis. Economic growth accelerated in 2010 and 2011, driven by dynamic domestic demand, and in particular by investment. Real GDP growth is estimated at almost 6 per cent in 2011 as compared to the 2010 figure of 4 per cent.

8. The main driver of economic growth during this review period continued to be private domestic demand, and more specifically investment, as well as public and private consumption (except for 2009 in the latter case, the year of the crisis). In general, public consumption has been used as a countercyclical tool to stimulate economic growth. This can be seen clearly from the example of 2009 when government spending counteracted the impacts on GDP of a significant slowdown in private consumption and a contraction of gross capital formation. The rate of investment as a percentage of GDP expanded further during the review period, increasing from 20.2 per cent of GDP in 2005 to 24.5 per cent of GDP in 2010 and an estimated 27.1 per cent of GDP for 2011 (Table I.2).

9. The authorities expect GDP growth over the coming quarters to be based largely on dynamic household consumption.[1] Household spending will continue to be influenced by three factors that have been present since 2010: (i) a buoyant labour market; (ii) low real interest rates combined with an ample supply of credit; and (iii) soaring consumer confidence. On the labour market front, the number of employed persons has increased and demand for work (measured by the rate of employment) has outstripped the supply of work (measured by the overall rate of participation, which led to a fall in the unemployment rate to 9.8 per cent in December 2011, as compared to the 11.1 per cent recorded for the same month in 2010.

10. Consumer credit was granted at historically low real interest rates (except for credit cards), and this has generated double-digit growth in the real consumer credit portfolio (21.6 per cent annually for the third quarter of 2011).[2] The authorities have pointed out that this trend in the real sector is still a recurrent feature of brokerage activities, which remain dynamic.[3] Finally, household confidence has remained above the average recorded since 2001, being comparable to that of years of highly dynamic consumption.

Table I.2
Structure of GDP by expenditure, 2005-2011

	2005	2006	2007	2008	2009[a]	2010[a]	2011[a]
Percentage of constant GDP (at 2005 prices)							
Total consumption	81.7	81.4	81.5	81.4	81.4	82.2	82.1
Household consumption	65.7	65.5	65.8	65.7	65.0	65.7	66.0
Final government consumption[b]	16.0	15.8	15.7	15.7	16.3	16.6	16.0
Gross capital formation[c]	20.2	22.6	23.9	25.2	23.7	24.5	27.1
Gross fixed capital formation	19.7	21.8	23.3	24.7	24.0	24.1	26.6
Inventory changes	0.6	0.8	0.5	0.4	-0.3	0.4	0.5
Total exports	16.8	17.2	17.2	17.3	16.5	16.1	16.9
Total imports	18.8	21.1	22.5	24.0	21.5	22.8	26.2

[1] Bank of the Republic (2011a).

[2] Although the real consumer interest rate has remained below its average since 1998, the levels are relatively high. The average interest rate for the third quarter of 2011 was 15.2 per cent, which is equivalent to a real interest rate above 10 per cent.

[3] Bank of the Republic (2011b) and (2011c).

	2005	2006	2007	2008	2009[a]	2010[a]	2011[a]
Real annual growth (%)							
Total consumption	4.3	6.3	7.0	3.5	1.6	5.1	5.8
Household consumption	4.0	6.4	7.3	3.5	0.6	5.0	6.5
Final government consumption[b]	5.2	5.6	6.0	3.3	5.9	5.5	2.6
Gross capital formation[c]	12.8	19.2	13.0	9.2	-4.1	7.3	17.2
Gross fixed capital formation	13.2	18.1	14.4	9.9	-1.3	4.6	16.6
Inventory changes	-4.2	58.8	-29.0	-26.9	-172.5	-235.3	53.8
Total exports	5.7	8.6	6.9	4.5	-2.8	1.3	11.4
Total imports	11.9	20.0	14.0	10.5	-9.1	10.5	21.5

a Provisional figures.
b Final government consumption includes final consumption expenditure by private non-profit institutions that provide household services (IPSFH).
c Gross fixed capital formation plus inventory changes.

Source: National Administrative Department of Statistics.

11. Although the contribution of net exports to GDP continues to be negative primarily due to strong import growth combined with dynamic domestic demand, itself being fuelled by an ample supply of credit, Colombian exports have grown rapidly despite the unfavourable international environment. Measured in US dollars, Colombian exports grew at an annual rate of 43 per cent in 2011, chiefly on the back of higher sales of mineral-based commodities (crude petroleum and its derivatives, coal, ferronickel and gold), which rose at an annual rate of 56 per cent.[4] Imports still consist mainly of intermediate and capital goods, which represent 80 per cent of the total. In the case of these two groups as in that of consumer goods, the annual growth rate for 2011 surpasses 34 per cent when measured in US dollars.[5]

12. The review period witnessed substantial per capita GDP growth bound up with the growth of the economy and in part generated by the strengthening of the peso against the US dollar. Per capita GDP was US$7,236 in 2011 as against US$3,417 in 2005. Yet despite some reduction of poverty during the review period, it does remain high, and income distribution is uneven. According to the World Bank, the poverty headcount ratio was 37.2 per cent in 2010, which is still a high level, albeit less than the 45 per cent seen in 2005.[6]

13. Although unemployment has been declining during the review period thanks to the sound performance of the economy in recent years, it is still at a relatively high level (9.8 per cent in 2011). This is partly because recent growth in employment has been skewed towards informal work, although the authorities point out that there has also been net job creation based on the entry of skilled and highly qualified people into the workforce.[7] The present government's economic strategy, laid out the National Development Plan 2010-2014: "Prosperity for All", aims to step up job creation, reduce poverty and promote economic growth. The economic strategy is based on a system of "engines" or key sectors that will drive sustainable economic growth.

[4] Bank of the Republic (2011a).
[5] Bank of the Republic (2011a).
[6] The national poverty rate is the percentage of the population living below the national poverty line. National estimates are based on population-weighted subgroup estimates from household surveys. (World Bank online information, "Countries: Colombia". Viewed at: http://datos.bancomundial.org/pais/colombia).
[7] Bank of the Republic (2011a).

14. In May 2011, the IMF approved a new two-year arrangement for Colombia under the Flexible Credit Line (FCL), in an amount equivalent to SDR 3.870 million (about US$6.220 million).[8] The Colombian authorities stated that they intend to treat the arrangement as precautionary, and do not intend to draw on the line. Colombia's first FCL arrangement was approved in May 2009 and a successor one-year arrangement was approved in May 2010.[9] Despite the favourable short-term economic outlook, the authorities thought it prudent to request a new FCL arrangement, as they see Colombia as still exposed to downside risks, for example from severe commodity price fluctuations and other adverse developments. The new precautionary agreement is therefore being seen as insurance against external shocks.[10] In the discussions for the approval of the arrangement, the Executive Directors underlined Colombia's strong economic performance underpinned by a sound institutional framework and skilful macroeconomic management. They also stressed that countercyclical policy support had paved the way for the recovery, that a credible inflation targeting regime had anchored inflation expectations, and that exchange rate flexibility had cushioned the impact of external shocks and large capital inflows. Additionally, the IMF pointed out that strong supervisory and regulatory oversight has underpinned the soundness of the domestic financial system.[11]

(3) FISCAL POLICY

15. The responsibility for formulating and managing the implementation of fiscal policy in Colombia rests with the Ministry of Finance and Public Credit, in virtue of Decree No. 246 of 2004. During the early years of this review period, fiscal policy was geared towards achieving a primary surplus. Between 2006 and 2008 the non-financial public sector (SPNF) posted primary surpluses ranging between 0.2 and 0.9 per cent of GDP (Table I.3). Owing to the international financial crisis, however, this approach was abandoned in favour of a countercyclical fiscal policy designed to spur economic growth.

Table I.3
Central Government finances, 2005-2011
(Percentage of current GDP)

	2005	2006	2007	2008	2009	2010	2011[a]
I. Total income	**13.5**	**14.7**	**15.0**	**15.6**	**15.2**	**13.7**	**16.3**
1. Current national revenue	12.5	13.4	13.5	13.5	12.9	12.3	14.7
Tax revenue	12.4	13.4	13.4	13.4	12.8	12.2	14.6
DIAN Administered internal	8.6	9.1	9.2	8.9	9.1	8.4	10.1
Revenue	5.3	5.7	5.7	5.2	5.6	4.7	6.1
Domestic VAT	3.4	3.5	3.5	3.7	3.5	3.7	4.0
DIAN Administered external	2.6	3.1	3.0	2.8	2.4	2.5	2.5
Foreign VAT	1.8	2.2	2.0	2.0	1.6	1.7	1.9
Tariff	0.8	0.9	1.0	0.9	0.8	0.8	0.7
Tax on financial movements	0.7	0.7	0.7	0.7	0.6	0.6	0.8
Petrol	0.3	0.3	0.3	0.3	0.3	0.3	0.3
Democratic security	0.1	0.1	0.3	0.7	0.4	0.4	0.9
Remainder	0.0	0.0	0.0	0.0	0.0	0.0	0.0
Non-tax revenue	0.1	0.1	0.1	0.1	0.1	0.1	0.1

[8] IMF, Press Release No. 11/165 of 6 May 2011. Viewed at: http://www.imf.org/external/np/sec/pr/2011/pr11165.htm.

[9] IMF, Press Releases No. 09/161 of 11 May 2009 and No. 10/186 of 7 May 2010. Viewed at: http://www.imf.org/external/np/sec/pr/2009/pr09161.htm; and http://www.imf.org/external/np/sec/pr/2010/pr10186.htm.

[10] IMF, Press Release No. 11/165 of 6 May 2011. Viewed at: hhttp://www.imf.org/external/np/sec/pr/2011/pr11165.htm.

[11] IMF, Press Release No. 11/165 of 6 May 2011. Viewed at: http://www.imf.org/external/np/sec/pr/2011/pr11165.htm; and IMF (2011).

	2005	2006	2007	2008	2009	2010	2011[a]
Contribution of hydrocarbons	0.0	0.0	0.0	0.0	0.0	0.0	0.0
Remainder	0.1	0.1	0.1	0.1	0.1	0.1	0.1
Special funds	0.1	0.2	0.1	0.2	0.2	0.2	0.2
Other capital resources	0.8	1.1	1.3	1.9	2.0	1.2	1.4
Total financial returns	0.2	0.3	0.2	0.2	0.1	0.1	0.1
Financial surpluses	0.5	0.8	1.1	1.1	1.7	1.0	1.1
Ecopetrol	0.4	0.5	0.8	0.9	1.6	0.6	0.8
ISA and ISAGEN	0.0	0.0	0.0	0.1	0.0	0.0	0.0
Bancóldex	0.0	0.0	0.0	0.0	0.0	0.0	0.0
Estapúblicos	0.0	0.0	0.0	0.0	0.0	0.1	0.1
Remaining companies	0.1	0.2	0.2	0.1	0.0	0.2	0.2
Recovery of financial public sector portfolio (interest and capital repayments)	0.0	0.0	0.0	0.0	0.0	0.0	0.0
Refunds and unallocated funds	0.1	0.0	0.1	0.6	0.2	0.1	0.2
II. Total payments	**17.4**	**17.6**	**17.8**	**17.4**	**18.8**	**17.1**	**15.8**
Total payments without interest	14.5	14.1	14.3	14.5	16.0	14.5	13.2
Current national payments	16.1	16.2	15.9	15.2	16.6	15.0	14.1
Interest	2.9	3.5	3.5	2.9	2.9	2.6	2.6
Interest external debt	1.3	1.0	0.9	0.8	0.8	0.7	0.6
Interest domestic debt	2.5	2.7	2.8	2.4	2.3	2.1	2.3
Difference between issue and placement of treasury securities (TES)	-0.9	-0.2	-0.2	-0.2	-0.2	-0.2	-0.3
Operations	13.2	12.7	12.4	12.3	13.7	12.4	11.5
Personal services	2.2	2.2	2.0	2.0	2.2	2.1	1.9
Transfers	10.2	9.6	9.4	9.5	10.8	9.5	9.0
General Revenue Sharing System *(Sistema General de Participaciones)*	4.3	4.1	3.9	3.9	4.2	4.2	3.8
Pensions	3.4	3.4	3.5	3.5	3.5	3.1	3.2
Other	2.5	2.1	2.0	2.2	3.1	2.2	1.9
Overheads and other expenditure	0.8	0.9	0.9	0.8	0.7	0.8	0.6
Military	0.2	0.3	0.2	0.2	0.1	0.1	0.6
Remainder	0.6	0.7	0.7	0.6	0.6	0.7	0.0
Investment	1.3	1.4	1.9	2.2	2.2	2.1	1.7
III. Cash deficit or surplus	**-3.9**	**-2.9**	**-2.8**	**-1.8**	**-3.7**	**-3.4**	**0.5**
Net loan	0.1	0.1	0.1	0.0	0.0	0.0	0.0
Accrued revenues	0.0	0.0	0.0	0.0	0.0	0.0	0.0
Accrued expenditure	0.2	0.2	0.2	0.3	0.1	0.1	0.2
Floating debt	-0.2	0.2	-0.4	0.2	0.3	0.3	-1.1
IV. Total deficit or surplus	**-4.0**	**-3.4**	**-2.7**	**-2.3**	**-4.1**	**-3.8**	**1.3**
V. Cost of the financial restructuring	**0.4**	**0.3**	**0.3**	**0.3**	**0.2**	**0.1**	**0.1**
Capitalization of FOGAFIN interest	0.0	0.0	0.0	0.0	0.0	0.0	0.0
Indexation of TES Law No. 546	0.0	0.0	0.0	0.0	0.0	0.0	0.0
Indexation of Debt Reduction Securities (TRD)	0.0	0.0	0.0	0.1	0.0	0.0	0.0
Interest Law No. 546	0.0	0.0	0.0	0.0	0.0	0.0	0.0
FOGAFIN interest	0.1	0.1	0.0	0.0	0.0	0.0	0.0
Amortization TRD	0.0	0.0	0.0	0.0	0.0	0.0	0.0
Amortization Law No. 546	0.1	0.1	0.1	0.1	0.1	0.0	0.0
Winding up Caja Agraria	0.1	0.1	0.0	0.0	0.0	0.0	0.0
VI. Deficit to be financed	**-4.3**	**-3.7**	**-3.0**	**-2.6**	**-4.3**	**-3.9**	**1.2**
Primary balance	**-0.9**	**0.2**	**1.0**	**0.9**	**-1.1**	**-1.1**	**1.3**
Memorandum items							
Consolidated public sector results	0.0	-0.7	-0.6	-0.1	-2.7	-3.2	..
Central Government gross domestic debt[b, c]	28.5	26.6	25.5	24.8	26.0	27.6	32.5
Central Government gross domestic and external debt[b, c]	42.5	40.3	36.6	36.2	37.7	38.4	46.0
Gross domestic debt, non-financial public sector	34.4	32.4	30.7	29.3	31.3	33.4	39.5
Net domestic debt, non-financial public sector[d]	22.7	20.9	19.3	18.4	21.0	22.9	28.4
Gross external debt, non-financial public sector	15.7	15.1	13.1	13.3	13.5	12.4	15.8

	2005	2006	2007	2008	2009	2010	2011[a]
Net external debt, non-financial public sector[e]	12.9	11.6	9.9	12.4	12.2	11.8	15.0

.. Not available.

a Data for the first three quarters of 2011.

b Since the first quarter of 2008, Ecopetrol and ISAGEN assets have not been included. These entities were withdrawn from the sample at that time.

c Adjusted internal debt. Not including indexed bonds. Includes floating debt.

d The SPNF gross domestic debt less remaining SPNF debt to the Central Government, Central Government promissory notes, FOGAFIN capitalization bonds held by the SPNF, bonds held by the Social Security Institute (ISS), bonds held by Ecopetrol, bonds held by Cajanal, bonds held by the rest of the SPNF and Carbocol bonds held by the Central Government and Ecopetrol.

e SPNF gross external debt less treasury stock, FAEP assets and assets of decentralized entities.

Source: Ministry of Finance and Public Credit; and information provided by the Colombian authorities.

16. The primary balance became negative between 2009 and 2010, and the central government deficit increased from 2.3 per cent of GDP in 2008 to 4.1 per cent in 2009. This was the result of increased spending, which moved from 17.4 per cent of GDP in 2008 to 18.8 per cent in 2009, whilst revenue fell from 15.6 to 15 per cent of GDP.

17. Taxes on foreign trade represented 2.5 per cent of GDP in 2010, of which 1.7 per cent was value added tax, and 0.8 per cent customs duties. This represents 19.2 per cent of the value of goods imports in 2010, of which VAT represented 13 per cent of the overall value of goods imports and customs duties 6.2 per cent. The contribution of foreign trade taxes in 2012 will be an estimated 2.3 per cent of GDP.

18. The present Colombian Government views the administration of public finances as a crucial contributing factor in the pursuit of macroeconomic stability. Therefore, without disregarding the commitment to fiscal sustainability, fiscal policy is deemed to be a useful instrument for spurring sustainable medium-term growth and reducing unemployment. Consequently, some of the fiscal targets proposed in 2010 and in the 2011 Financial Plan were revised, mainly to support employment-generating sectors with linkages to other production sectors. The new administration has implemented a fiscal policy for the period 2010-2014 as part of a series of reforms designed on the one hand to guarantee fiscal sustainability through macroeconomic stability and job creation, and on the other, to stimulate growth in the economy and bolster productivity.[12]

19. Four important fiscal policy changes occurred in 2011, impacting the economy as a whole as well as various individual sectors: (i) the introduction of a Fiscal Rule; (ii) the incorporation of the principle of fiscal sustainability into the Constitution; (iii) the reform of the system by which royalties generated by natural resources are distributed; and (iv) the implementation of a tariff reform.

20. In June 2011 the Congress approved the Fiscal Rule, a quantitative rule governing Central Government finances aimed at enhanced fiscal discipline to reduce the public debt and pave the way for the use of countercyclical fiscal policies, mainly through the improved management of royalties.[13] Amongst the main features of the Fiscal Rule are: (i) it determines a policy of fiscal consolidation designed to reduce the central government's structural deficit to 2.3 per cent of GDP in 2014 and to

[12] Ministry of Finance and Public Credit (2010).

[13] The Fiscal Rule contains supplementary rules on limits to the growth of spending, considering that structural spending must be consistent with the evolution of structural revenue. Furthermore, the Investment Plan of the National Development Plan, the Medium-Term Spending Framework and the General Budget of the Nation must be compatible with the fiscal rule.

1.5 per cent of GDP in 2015, and to hold it below 1 per cent as of 2022; (ii) it allows for fiscal expansion (countercyclical policy) when the expected GDP growth rate is at least two percentage points below the long-term growth rate (also in cases of emergency or major shocks affecting macroeconomic stability); and (iii) it creates a Macroeconomic Stability Fund for managing the savings generated by the application of the Rule; this Fund must guarantee the resources necessary to implement a countercyclical policy if need be.[14] It is hoped that the Fiscal Rule will help to consolidate the adjustment process carried out over the past decade and serve to anchor expectations regarding the country's fiscal sustainability.

21. The fiscal policy framework was buttressed by amendments to the Constitution in June and July of 2011. Legislative Act No. 3 of 1 June 2011 amended the Constitution to introduce the principle of fiscal sustainability.[15] Legislative Act No. 5 of 18 July 2011 amended the Constitution and created the General System of Royalties.[16] The second constitutional amendment aims to revamp the royalty distribution system so that the resources can be distributed throughout the entire country on the basis of social, regional and inter-generational equity, with priority being given to the country's poorest regions (Box I.1).

22. The amount of funds entering the General System of Royalties was an estimated US$7.500 million for 2010, which is expected to reach some US$12.000 million by 2020.

[14] Under the Fiscal Rule, in periods of marked economic downturn, the government will be able to implement countercyclical spending in order to stabilize the economy and avoid major spikes in unemployment and poverty.

[15] This Legislative Act enshrines the duty of all branches and organs of government to ensure that their decisions are in keeping with fiscal sustainability, in that way achieving the aims of the Social State Guided by the Rule of Law. The text may be viewed at: http://wsp.presidencia.gov.co/Normativa/Leyes/Documents/ActLeg0301072011.pdf.

[16] The text may be viewed at: http://wsp.presidencia.gov.co/Normativa/ActoLeg/Documents/ActLeg0518072011.pdf.

Box I.1: The General System of Royalties

Legislative Act No. 5 of 18 July 2011 amended the Constitution to create the General System of Royalties, intended to ensure the more equitable and rational distribution of royalties.

Revenue accruing to the General System of Royalties will go towards: the funding of social, economic and environmental development projects in the territorial units, savings for their pension liabilities, investment in education, science, technology and innovation, the generation of public savings, the monitoring of the exploration and exploitation of mineral deposits and the surveying and geological mapping of the subsoil, and boosting the overall competitiveness of the economy so as to improve social conditions for the population. Departments, municipalities and districts in whose territory non-renewable natural resources are being exploited, as well as municipalities and districts with sea and river ports used to transport those resources or products derived from them, are entitled to a share of the royalties.

Various funds were created in pursuit of the aims and objectives of the General System of Royalties, namely the Science, Technology and Innovation Fund, the Regional Development Fund, the Regional Compensation Fund, and the Savings and Stabilization Fund.

The revenues accruing to the General System of Royalties will be distributed as follows:

- 10 per cent for the Science, Technology and Innovation Fund;
- 10 per cent for territorial pension savings; and
- up to 30 per cent for the Savings and Stabilization Fund.

The remainder will be distributed as follows: 20 per cent for direct allocations and 80 per cent for the Regional Compensation Fund and the Regional Development Fund (of this latter percentage, 60 per cent will go to the first fund and 40 per cent to the second).

- In addition, 2 per cent of the revenues of the General System of Royalties will be allocated for the monitoring of the exploration and exploitation of mineral deposits, and the surveying and geological mapping of the subsoil. This percentage will be deducted proportionally from the total abovementioned amounts to be distributed from revenues of General System of Royalties. The deductions will be determined by the Ministry of Mines and Energy or an entity appointed by it.

- Any difference between the total revenues of the General System of Royalties and the abovementioned allocations will go to the Savings and Stabilization Fund.

The Regional Compensation Fund will finance development projects that will impact the country's poorest territorial units at the regional or local level. The duration of the Regional Compensation Fund will be 30 years as from the effective date of the law. At the end of that period, those funds will go to the Regional Development Fund. The Savings and Stabilization Fund and the returns on its resources will be managed by the Bank of the Republic.

The Savings and Stabilization Fund will serve to smooth out fluctuations in the value of royalties and thereby reduce the income volatility of beneficiaries. In other words, it will generate savings in times of increased revenues, which will then serve to stabilize spending when there are less royalties. Through this Fund, the royalties would therefore play a significant role in financing territorial pension savings. This would help cover the pension liabilities of local authorities, which were estimated by the Ministry of Finance and Public Credit at 82.4 trillion pesos (some US$45 million) at the end of 2009, and for which provisions currently stand at 30 per cent, by official estimates.

The General System of Royalties will have its own budget system, and its funds will not be part of the General National Budget.

Source: WTO Secretariat.

23. One important element of the fiscal reform is the reform of the tariff system introduced at the end of 2010, which lowered the average tariff from 12.2 per cent to 8.2 per cent (Chapter III)(2)(iv)). The authorities stated that the aim of the tariff reform is to overcome many of the problems associated with the tariff structure that are affecting competitiveness and exports. The view is that prior to the changes introduced in 2011, Colombia's tariff structure had a distorting effect and displayed a high degree of dispersion. This gave rise to an average tariff higher than that of other countries in Latin America and an anti-export bias as well as negative effective protection in the case of some industries, which had to be partly offset by means of export promotion schemes.[17] The authorities deemed it necessary to undertake a tariff reform in the light of the regulatory changes introduced by Decision No. 669 of the Andean Community, which temporarily restored tariff-setting autonomy to Member Countries. The upshot was tariff dispersion amongst the countries that negatively impacted the competitiveness of Colombia's production sector on account of the tariff reductions instituted by other countries such as Peru and Ecuador.

24. In this context, the Government undertook a structural reform that entailed reducing the nominal tariff in force per subheading by as much as ten percentage points at the most. The reform is intended to modernize the tariff scheme to enhance its simplicity, efficiency and transparency and to boost competitiveness and thereby generate positive spin-offs in the form of job creation, economic growth and improved well-being for the population.[18] The tariffs on raw materials and capital goods were reduced to 5 and 10 per cent respectively, depending on whether they correspond to the industrial or agricultural sector (WTO definition); the tariff on consumer goods was lowered to 15 per cent. The tariff reductions did not include some agricultural products regarded as sensitive in terms of production and employment, amongst which were corn (maize), rice, meat, milk and barley, though the tariffs on other products such as sugar, cotton and wheat were reduced by five percentage points. The tariff cuts of April 2011 were followed by fresh cuts in August that temporarily lowered the tariffs on capital goods and inputs not produced in Colombia from 5 per cent to 0 per cent, bringing the average tariff down to 6.2 per cent (Chapter III)(2)(iv)).

25. In the light of the tariff reductions the Government reviewed its fiscal targets. It was announced in September 2011 that the 2011 Financial Plan submitted to Congress in June would be revised, and a new 2011 target set for the central government deficit - 4.1 per cent of GDP - which was higher than that announced in June by almost 0.2 per cent of GDP. The projected deficit would result from a greater imbalance between revenue (14.4 per cent of GDP) and expenditure (18.5 per cent of GDP) due in particular to an increase in investment spending as a result of the injection of additional funds to shore up the five strategic sectors of mining, housing, infrastructure, agriculture and technological innovation. The estimated deficits were 1 per cent of GDP in the primary balance, 3.4 per cent of GDP for the non-financial public sector, and 3.2 per cent for the consolidated public sector deficit.[19] The authorities report that 2011 results were better than projected, with a central government deficit of 2.9 per cent of GDP and a consolidated public sector deficit of 2.2 per cent of GDP.

26. The 2012 Financial Plan was formulated on the basis of the Legislative Act on Fiscal Sustainability, the General System of Royalties and the adoption of the Fiscal Rule. Bearing in mind the positive effects expected from these reforms, the Financial Plan foresees a reduction in the consolidated public sector deficit between 2011 and 2012 from 2.2 to 1.8 per cent of GDP.

[17] Ministry of Finance and Public Credit (2010).

[18] It is also hoped that the increased imports resulting from the tariff cuts will increase demand for dollars, which will have the effect of devaluing the currency, thereby counteracting the uptrend in the exchange rate that has been observed in recent quarters.

[19] Information provided by the authorities; and Ministry of Finance and Public Credit (2010).

That result would be consistent with a primary surplus in the non-financial public sector of 1.2 per cent of GDP. It is anticipated that the Central Government deficit will be 2.8 per cent of GDP in 2012, including additional spending to deal with the extreme winter weather in 2011. As regards deficit financing, it is expected that government borrowing will be reduced and replaced with privatisations. The authorities expect funds worth almost 0.6 per cent of GDP to accrue to the government in 2011 from the reduction of its stake in the *Empresa de Petróleos de Colombia*, Ecopetrol (Colombia Oil Company).[20] Similarly, net non-financial public sector debt is expected to the decline in 2012.

27. As a percentage of GDP, the non-financial public sector debt diminished slightly between 2006 and 2011, despite the costs deriving from capital injections into the banking system during the financial crisis and the deterioration of the fiscal situation as of 2008 (Table I.3). This was partly caused by the devaluation of the external debt induced by the appreciation of the peso. Indeed, the net debt of the non-financial public sector declined from 47.5 per cent of GDP at the end of 2006 to 34.7 per cent of GDP at the end of 2010 and estimates are that it closed 2011 at 32.4 per cent.

(4) MONETARY AND EXCHANGE RATE POLICY

28. The Bank of the Republic is the body responsible for formulating and implementing monetary and exchange rate policies. The management and execution of the tasks of the Bank of the Republic are undertaken by its Board of Directors, which comprises seven members including the Minister of Finance and Public Credit, who chairs it. The Bank of the Republic also acts as Government banker, fiscal agent and trustee.[21]

29. The primary aim of monetary policy is to achieve and maintain low, stable inflation and ensure growth of the national product consistent with its long-term trend. To carry out its mandate, the Board of Directors of the Bank of the Republic sets quantitative inflation targets based on the annual variation in the consumer price index (CPI) produced by the National Administrative Department of Statistics (DANE).

30. Monetary policy decisions are based on an analysis of the current state and outlook of the economy and an evaluation of inflation forecasts *vis-à-vis* the targets. If the evaluation suggests that under the current monetary policy conditions inflation will deviate from the target over the policy timeline and that the deviation will not be the result of temporary shocks, the Board will modify it its policy position.[22] In this regard, the Bank of the Republic implements monetary policy by changing the intervention interest rates (monetary policy and open market operations) at which it injects liquidity into the economy or mops up excess liquidity.[23] These intervention rates are the main instruments of monetary policy and through them, the Bank influences market interest rates. Another

[20] Ministry of Finance and Public Credit, Press Release No. 63 of 20 December 2011. Viewed at: http://www.minhacienda.gov.co/portal/page/portal/MinHacienda/elministerio/prensa/Comunicados/COMUNICADO%20DE%20PRENSA%2063%20PLAN%20FINANCIERO%202012f.pdf.

[21] Bank of the Republic online information. "*Funciones*". Viewed at: http://banrep.gov.co/the_bank/funct.htm.

[22] Bank of the Republic (2011a).

[23] The main monetary policy intervention mechanism used by the Bank of the Republic to influence the amount of money in circulation and economy is the alteration of the minimum interest rate charged to financial entities for loans to them, or of the maximum interest rate paid to receive excess money from them. These operations are also known as open market operations, and take place over very short terms (1, 7 and 14 days). The loans are granted in sessions known as "expansion auctions" and the surplus funds are received in sessions called "contraction auctions". The minimum rate for 1-day expansion auctions is called the monetary policy intervention rate of the Bank of the Republic. There is also a maximum expansion rate.

significant monetary instrument is the buying and selling of foreign currency on the foreign exchange market.

31. Both an annual inflation target and a long-term inflation target are set, ranging between 2 and 4 per cent. For 2012, the Board of Directors of the Bank of the Republic agreed that this year's inflation target would be the same as the long-term target (i.e. ranging between 2 and 4 per cent), with 3 per cent as the ad hoc target for legal purposes. In its decision, the Board took the view that the economic situation was such that inflation would fall within the long-term range going forward, and that this was helping to anchor inflation expectations at that level.[24]

32. In response to the global financial crisis, the Bank of the Republic maintained a highly expansionary monetary policy, involving a substantial and extensive reduction in the intervention interest rate between the end of 2008 and in mid-2010. The rate was cut by 650 basis points from 9.5 per cent in December 2008 to 3 per cent in May 2010. This level was maintained until December 2010. The authorities have pointed out that the interest rate cuts were intended not just to pump-prime a slowing economy, but also to send positive signals to the market by guaranteeing liquidity, and that the cuts were possible because inflation was continuing to fall owing to diminished inflationary pressures and the international financial crisis.[25]

33. In the early months of 2011 the Board of Directors of the Bank of the Republic decided that given the recovery in domestic demand, the good credit indicators and inflation expectations consistent with the dynamism of the economy, the monetary stimulus should be gradually reduced. Besides, this was thought to be particularly timely considering that inflation had accelerated beyond the midpoint of the target band. Hence, between February and December 2011 there were seven increases in the intervention rate totalling 175 basis points (Table I.4).

34. After a period of relatively high inflation between 2006 and 2008, price increases slowed substantially in 2009 as a result of slower growth in domestic demand and falling raw materials prices. Inflation remained low in 2010 despite the maintenance of an expansionary monetary policy. In 2011, the consumer price index (CPI) posted a further annual rise of 3.73 per cent, which was more than anticipated and largely attributable to rising food prices. Despite some acceleration, the rise in the CPI remained within the inflation target band of 2 to 4 per cent. As seen above, the authorities responded to the uptick in inflation by tightening the monetary policy through repeated increases in the monetary policy intervention rate in 2011.

---

[24] Bank of the Republic online information. "*Politica monetaria*". Viewed at: http://banrep.gov.co/monetary_policy/index.html.

[25] Ministry of Finance and Public Credit (2011), Chapter 2: *Balance Macroeconómico 2010 y Perspectivas para 2011.*

Table I.4
Main monetary indicators, 2005-2011

	2005	2006	2007	2008	2009	2010	2011
Monetary aggregates							
Monetary base (billion pesos, end of the period)	22,804	27,032	32,415	37,040	39,545	44,875	51,339
M1 (variation over 12 months)	17.8	18.2	11.9	8.2	7.5	17.7	10.8
M3 (variation over 12 months)	16.0	17.0	18.1	17.8	7.1	11.4	18.1
Interest rates							
Bank of the Republic monetary policy intervention rate (%)[b]	6.0	7.5	9.5	9.5	3.5	3.0	5.75[a]
Intervention rate for open market operations (maximum expansion rate)	7.0	8.5	10.5	10.5	4.5	4.0	5.75
Term deposit certificates (CDTs), total, 90 days	7.0	6.2	7.9	9.6	6.1	3.6	4.17[c]
One-day inter-bank interest rate (December)	5.5	7.5	9.3	8.8	3.0	3.0	4.8
Inflation (variation over 12 months)[d]							
Consumer Price Index[e]	4.9	4.5	5.7	7.7	2.0	3.2	3.7
Producer Price Index[f]	2.1	5.5	1.3	9.0	-2.2	4.4	5.2
Exchange rates							
Representative market rate (annual average: pesos/US$)	2,321	2,358	2,078	1,966	2,156	1,898	1,848
Exchange rate variation (December-December[g]	-4.4	-2.0	-10.0	11.4	-8.9	-6.4	1.5
Real exchange rate index (total trade, December) (increase = depreciation) (1994=100)[h]	104.0	104.7	97.0	98.2	90.3	81.9	81.4

a End of November 2011.
b Bank of the Republic intervention rates, end of period.
c 2011 average.
d Data from the National Administrative Department of Statistics (DANE).
e Between October 2006 and September 2007, a survey of income and expenditure was conducted in the framework of the *Gran Encuesta Integrada de Hogares* (Major Integrated Household Survey) covering 42,733 households in the country's 24 principal cities. It was thus possible to identify changes in the consumption habits and spending patterns of the Colombian population. On the basis of the findings of the survey, a new CPI calculation method was developed by an interdisciplinary team of specialists, with the advice of the statistics entity of Canada, and has been in use since January 2009. A new two-tier basket was created with a fixed and a flexible level, making it possible to update the basket of goods and services to reflect changes in final consumption. Besides expanding the basket, the new CPI-08 expanded its geographical coverage to 24 cities.
f Since December 2006 the DANE has been responsible for calculating the producer price index (PPI). It includes goods produced and consumed domestically as well as imported goods.
g A minus quantity indicates appreciation, a positive quantity, depreciation.
h ITCRIPC (T): real exchange rate index, uses the CPI as deflator and total weightings. Total weightings correspond to the moving share of each country in Colombia's foreign trade (imports and exports) with its 20 main partners.

Source: Bank of the Republic of Colombia; and Colombian National Administrative Department of Statistics (DANE).

35. Colombia has maintained a floating exchange rate system since 1999. The Bank of the Republic intervenes in the foreign exchange market in order to: (i) maintain an adequate level of international reserves for reducing the economy's vulnerability to external shocks in both the current and capital accounts; (ii) limit excessive short-term exchange rate volatility; and (iii) regulate excessive appreciation or depreciation that may jeopardize the attainment of future inflation targets and the external and financial stability of the economy.[26]

36. The Bank of the Republic may intervene in the foreign exchange market to head off fluctuations, in the following ways: (i) intervention through automatic auctions to buy or sell foreign exchange options whenever the exchange rate deviates by more than 5 per cent from the moving average for the previous 20 business days; (ii) intervention at its discretion through auctions for the sale (purchase) of foreign exchange options, in order to increase (reduce) international reserves; (iii) discretionary intervention through direct purchases or sales of foreign exchange on the foreign

[26] Bank of the Republic online information, "*Politica cambiaria*". Viewed at: http://banrep.gov.co/exchange_policy/index.html.

exchange market; and (iv) intervention through competitive auctions for the purchase of dollars on the foreign exchange market. Foreign exchange market interventions are done in a manner consistent with the inflation target. Thus for example, no foreign exchange purchases are made when the Bank of the Republic is raising its intervention rates, nor are there sales when those rates are being lowered. If the projected inflation is below the target, foreign exchange is bought in order to increase the money supply and attenuate any appreciation; if on the other hand projected inflation is above the target, the Bank of the Republic must sell foreign exchange on the market to reduce the money supply.[27]

37. During the review period and owing in part to significant capital inflows to Colombia, the peso appreciated in real terms by more than 20 per cent. That real appreciation made imports cheaper but rendered Colombia's exports less competitive, more particularly exports of manufactures.

38. Considering that during the first half of 2010 Colombia's nominal and real revaluation was the most pronounced in the region, the Bank of the Republic intervened in the currency market to make direct purchases through auctions, worth US$400 million per month between March and June. Those purchases were resumed in September and continued until mid-June 2011, so that between March 2010 and May 2011 the Bank of the Republic had made purchases to the tune of some US$5.080 million.[28]

39. Moreover, in October 2010 the Government announced a series of measures to relieve exchange rate pressures and thereby diminish the impact of the revaluation and protect jobs. Those measures were: (i) the decision not to monetize US$1.500 million in assets, of the amount projected for 2010; (ii) the modification of the 2011 Financial Plan so as to balance external funding sources with debt service, which meant a US$384 million reduction in the assets monetized by the Central Government in 2011; (iii) the implementation by the Ministry of Finance of the strategy of foreign currency hedging for external debt service payments, of up to US$3.700 million; (iv) the opening by the Ministry of Agriculture, through FINAGRO, of a facility of up to Col$50 billion to support currency hedging by export-oriented agricultural sectors (Chapter IV(2)); and (v) the elimination of the exemption from income tax on interest payments on credit contracted with foreign entities.

(5) BALANCE OF PAYMENTS

40. Colombia's current account balance has traditionally shown a deficit, owing mainly to the large income balance deficit, which partly reflects remittances abroad for royalties and other payments related to the mining and energy sector. It also reflects the customary deficit in the services balance. There was a substantial increase in the current account deficit coinciding with the period of economic growth from 2006 to 2008. Thereafter, it declined to 2.1 per cent of GDP in 2009 as a result of the international financial crisis, which slowed down Colombia's GDP growth and depressed imports. The current account balance deteriorated further in 2010 when economic growth again accelerated, bringing the deficit to 3.1 per cent of GDP for that year (Table I.5). The 2011 current account deficit is estimated at 3.0 per cent of GDP.

---

[27] Bank of the Republic online information, "*Politica cambiaria*". Viewed at: http://banrep.gov.co/exchange_policy/index.html.

[28] Ministry of Finance and Public Credit (2011), Chapter 2: *Balance Macroeconómico 2010 y Perspectivas para. 2011.*

Table I.5
Balance of payments, 2005-2011[a]
(US$ million)

	2005[b]	2006[b]	2007[b]	2008[b]	2009[b]	2010[b]	2011[b]
Current account	**-1,886**	**-2,988**	**-5,978**	**-6,699**	**-4,960**	**-8,760**	**-9,980**
A. Goods	**1,595**	**323**	**-584**	**971**	**2,545**	**2,240**	**5,514**
General trade	1,387	-45	-707	775	2,053	2,038	5,487
Exports	20,818	23,930	29,381	37,095	32,563	39,546	56,216
Imports f.o.b.	19,431	23,975	30,088	36,320	30,510	37,508	50,728
Special foreign trade operations	208	368	122	196	493	202	27
Exports	911	1.251	1.195	1.439	1.462	1.322	1.524
Imports	703	883	1.073	1.243	969	1.120	1.497
B. Services	**-2,102**	**-2,118**	**-2,647**	**-3,072**	**-2,821**	**-3,623**	**-4,621**
Exports	2,668	3,377	3,636	4,137	4,202	4,446	4,907
Imports	4,770	5,495	6,283	7,210	7,023	8,070	9,528
C. Factor income	**-5,461**	**-5,935**	**-7,962**	**-10,110**	**-9,298**	**-11,851**	**-15,820**
Income	1,070	1,519	1,895	1,925	1,479	1,444	2,284
Interest	872	1,121	1,423	1,218	568	447	533
Profits and dividends	166	359	441	665	877	963	1,714
Employee remuneration	32	38	30	42	35	34	34
Expenditure	6,531	7,454	9,857	12,035	10,777	13,296	18,104
Interest	2,927	2,820	3,160	3,284	3,079	3,376	3,763
Profits and dividends	3,585	4,615	6,667	8,721	7,666	9,879	14,302
Employee remuneration	19	19	29	29	33	40	39
D. Current transfers	**4,082**	**4,743**	**5,216**	**5,512**	**4,613**	**4,475**	**4,948**
Income	4,342	5,037	5,642	5,898	5,253	5,343	5,673
Workers' remittances	3,314	3,890	4,493	4,842	4,145	4,023	4,168
Other transfers	1,029	1,147	1,149	1,056	1,107	1,319	1,505
Expenditure	260	294	426	386	640	868	726
Capital and financial account	**3,236**	**2,890**	**10,347**	**9,515**	**6,254**	**11,770**	**13,322**
A. Financial account	**3,236**	**2,890**	**10,347**	**9,515**	**6,254**	**11,770**	**13,322**
Long-term financial flows	4,367	7,183	11,466	9,960	12,598	6,733	12,673
Assets	4,659	1,097	912	2,253	3,079	6,560	8,288
Colombian investment abroad	4,662	1,098	913	2,254	3,088	6,562	8,289
Direct	4,662	1,098	913	2,254	3,088	6,562	8,289
Portfolio	0	0	0	0	0	0	0
Loans	-2	0	0	0	0	0	0
Trade credit	0	0	0	0	0	0	0
Other assets	-1	-1	-1	-1	-9	-2	-1
Liabilities	9,074	8,328	12,398	12,214	15,686	13,301	20,979
Foreign investment in Colombia	10,085	7,113	9,436	10,425	11,959	7,813	18,537
Direct	10,252	6,656	9,049	10,620	7,137	6,899	13,234
Portfolio	-167	457	387	-195	4,822	913	5,303
Loans	-1,165	1,248	2,736	1,336	1,781	5,486	2,015
Trade credit	49	-88	116	182	242	-13	-108
Financial leasing	105	55	110	272	727	16	535
Other liabilities	0	0	0	0	976	0	0
Other long-term financial movements	-48	-47	-20	-1	-8	-8	-18
Short-term financial flows	-1,131	-4,293	-1,120	-445	-6,345	5,038	648
Assets	1,823	4,019	3,186	-83	4,518	1,567	5,388
Liabilities	692	-274	2,066	-528	-1,826	6,604	6,036
Errors and omissions	**378**	**120**	**328**	**-193**	**54**	**126**	**402**
Variation in gross international reserves (balance-of-payments methodology)	**1,729**	**23**	**4,698**	**2,623**	**1,347**	**3,136**	**3,744**
Balance of gross international reserves[c]	**14,957**	**15,440**	**20,955**	**24,041**	**25,365**	**28,464**	**32,303**
Balance of net international reserves [c]	**14,947**	**15,436**	**20,949**	**24,030**	**25,356**	**28,452**	**32,300**
Variation in net international reserves (balance-of-payments methodology)	**1,723**	**27**	**4,696**	**2,618**	**1,349**	**3,133**	**3,754**
Memorandum items							
Current account (as percentage of GDP)	-1.3	-1.8	-2.9	-2.7	-2.1	-3.1	-3.0

	2005[b]	2006[b]	2007[b]	2008[b]	2009[b]	2010[b]	2011[b]
Net external debt, non-financial public sector (as percentage of GDP, December)	12.9	11.6	9.9	12.4	12.2	11.8	15.0[d]

a In accordance with the methodology set out in the Fifth Edition of the IMF *Balance of Payments Manual*.
b Preliminary data.
c Includes contributions by the Bank of the Republic to the Latin American Reserve Fund (FLAR) and cash balances under international agreements (ALADI).
d First three quarters of 2011.

Source: Bank of the Republic, *Estudios Económicos* [Economic Studies].

41. The goods trade balance has shown a surplus for most of the review period. That surplus has been growing, though mainly since 2008. It peaked in 2009 largely because imports fell more sharply than exports. The favourable trade balance has remained high in 2010 and 2011, above all given the dynamic performance of exports (Table I.5). The balance of services has shown a deficit throughout the review period, reflecting a large deficit in the transport and business and construction services, as well as financial services accounts (Table I.6).

42. Outflows for profits and dividends abroad have more than doubled during the review period. They surpassed US$14.000 million in 2011 to become the second largest source of foreign currency outflows after goods imports. Given the significant increase in recent years, this item is now three times as large as interest payments on the external debt, which amounted to US$3.763 million in 2011 (Table I.5). At over US $4.100 million in 2011, workers' remittances from abroad are still one of the main sources of current account revenue.

43. Once again there were substantial direct investment flows during the review period despite considerable fluctuations from year to year. The flow was particularly strong in 2007 and 2008. It declined during the 2009-2010 financial crisis and rose again in 2011 (see below).

44. During the review period, the share of the external debt in GDP continued to contract significantly, partly owing to the real appreciation of the peso. The net external debt of the non-financial public sector therefore represented 11.8 per cent of GDP in 2010 and is estimated at 11.2 per cent of GDP for 2011. Total external debt is estimated at 21.6 per cent of GDP for 2011.[29]

45. At the end of September 2011, net international reserves stood at roughly US$32.300 million, or the equivalent of some 8 months of goods and services imports.

(6) TRADE AND INVESTMENT FLOWS

(i) Developments in the trade in goods[30]

46. Foreign trade recorded highly dynamic growth during this review period. Expressed in United States dollars, imports grew at an average annual rate of almost 17.1 per cent between 2005 and 2011 and exports at an average annual rate of 17.9 per cent, and both practically doubled in US dollar terms over the period. Total 2011 imports and exports amounted to US $54.675 million and US$56.954 million respectively (Tables AI.1 and AI.2).

[29] Ministry of Finance and Public Credit (2011), Chapter 2: *Balance Macroeconómico 2010 y Perspectivas para 2011.*

[30] Data in this section are from the Commodity Trade Statistics Database (Comtrade) of the United Nations Statistics Division.

(a) Breakdown of trade in goods

47. Mining products represented some 65 per cent of Colombian exports in 2011 (Table AI.1 and Chart I.1). Crude oil and coal made up the bulk of mining exports. The share of the agricultural sector has contracted further, although agricultural products still make up just over one fifth of exports. The main agricultural exports are coffee, flowers and bananas.

48. The manufacturing sector accounted for 17.5 per cent of exports in 2011, which was considerably below the 34.7 per cent recorded in 2005 (Table AI.1). Chemicals are still the main manufacture exported by Colombia.

49. Manufactures accounted for almost 80 per cent Colombia's imports for 2011 (Table AI.2). The main categories of imported manufactures are machinery and transport equipment and chemicals. Agricultural imports made up 10.5 per cent of total imports in 2011.

(b) Direction of the trade in goods

50. Colombia's trade continues to be relatively concentrated geographically and is still highly dependent on developments in the North American market. The United States is still the main source of imports, with 25 per cent of the total in 2011 (Table AI.3). Next in line are China, the European Union and Mexico. The China's share has increased substantially since the last review.

51. The United States is the main destination for exports and accounts for 38.5 per cent of the total for 2011 (Table AI.4 and Chart I.2). It is followed by the European Union with almost 15.6 per cent and the Andean Community countries with 7 per cent.

Chart I.1
Trade in goods by product, 2005 and 2011

2005 | **2011**

(a) Exports (f.o.b.)

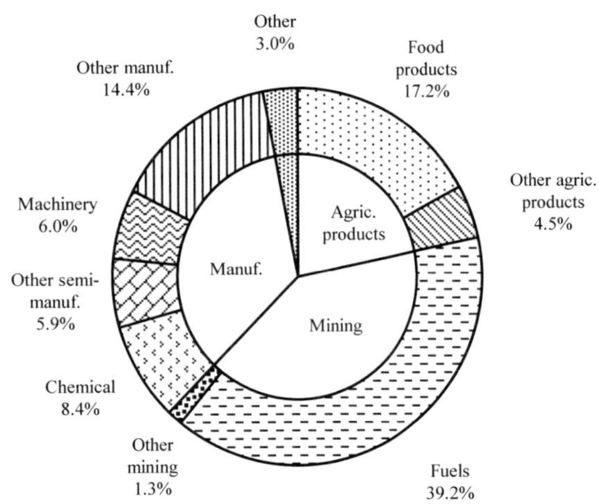

Total: US$21,190 million

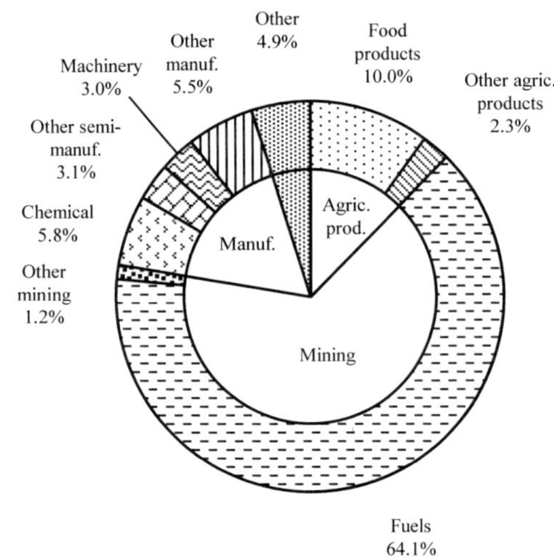

Total: US$56,954 million

(b) Imports (c.i.f.)

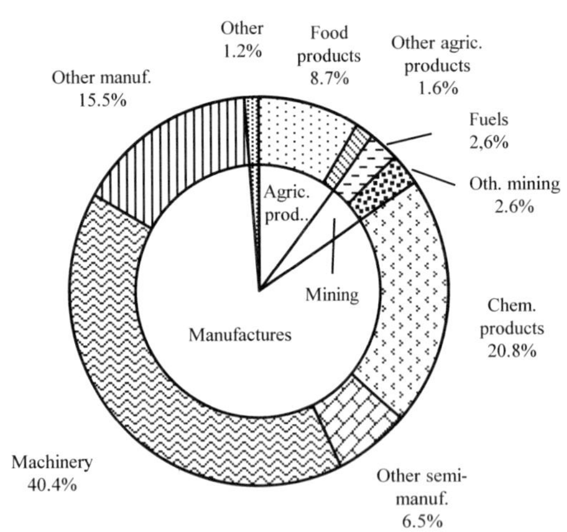

Total: US$21,204 million

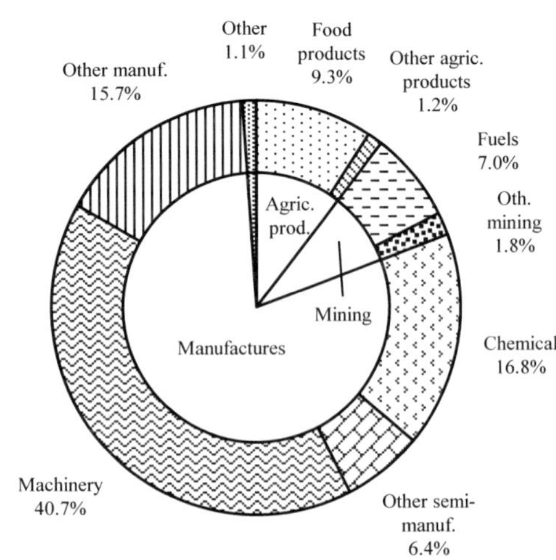

Total: US$54,675 millon

Source: Comtrade database of the United Nations Statistics Division and data provided by the Colombian authorities.

Chart I.2
Trade in goods by trading partner, 2005 and 2011

2005 | **2011**

(a) Exports (f.o.b.)

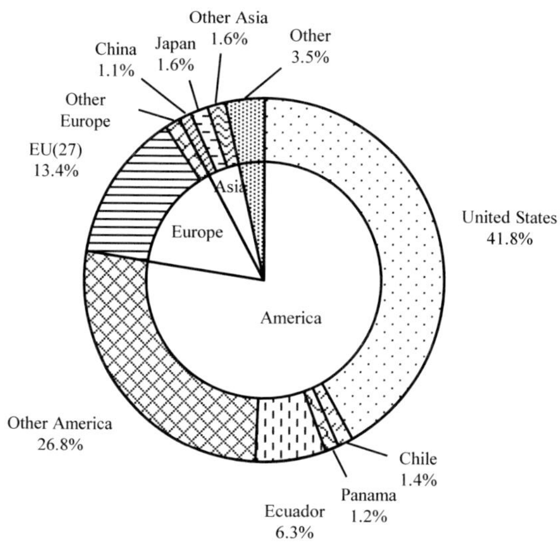

Total: US$21,190 million

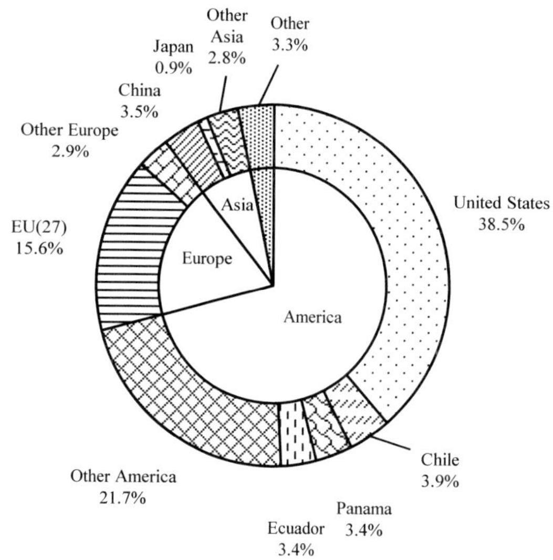

Total: US$56,954 million

(b) Imports (c.i.f.)

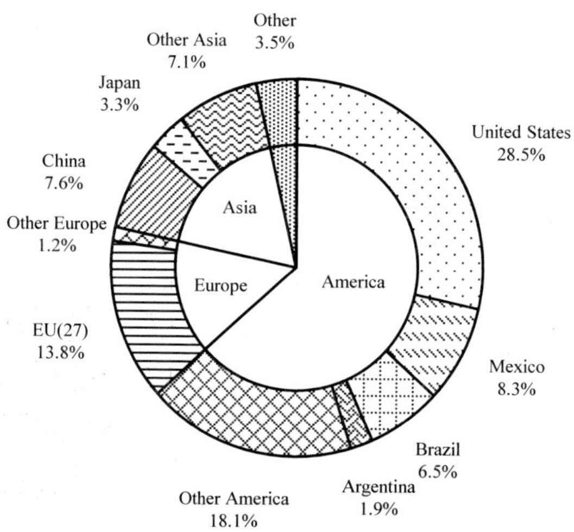

Total: US$21,204 million

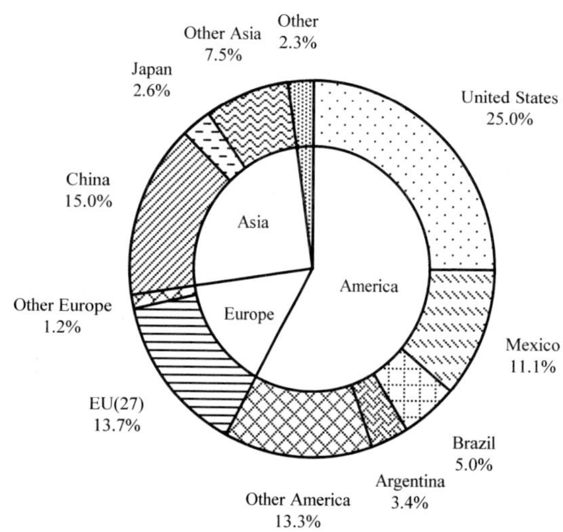

Total: US$54,675 million

Source: Comtrade database of the United Nations Satistics Division and data provided by the Colombian authorites.

(ii) Trade in services

52. Colombia has traditionally shown a trade-in-services deficit stemming from the large deficit in the transport and business and construction services, and to a lesser extent the financial services deficit (Table I.6). The transport services deficit again accelerated during this review period owing to the expansion in the goods trade. The travel balance also continued to show a deficit between 2006 and 2011, as did the average balance of communications, data and information technology, except in the year 2007. Trade in services fared better than trade in goods during the 2008-2010 international financial crisis. Income increased further, whilst expenditure contracted, though only in 2009.

Table I.6
Trade in services, 2005-2011
(US$ million)

	2005[a]	2006[a]	2007[a]	2008[a]	2009[a]	2010[a]	2011[a]
Services balance	**-2,102**	**-2,118**	**-2,647**	**-3,072**	**-2,821**	**-3,623**	**-4,621**
Total income	**2,668**	**3,377**	**3,636**	**4,137**	**4,202**	**4,446**	**4,907**
Transport	780	899	1,104	1,239	1,136	1,207	1,378
Travel	1,222	1,554	1,669	1,844	1,999	2,083	2,201
Communications, data and information technology	238	287	291	302	317	277	334
Insurance and finance	31	59	68	70	48	45	55
Business and construction	272	445	372	528	546	603	722
Other services	125	133	132	154	157	230	238
Total expenditure	**4,770**	**5,495**	**6,283**	**7,210**	**7,023**	**8,070**	**9,528**
Transport	2,107	2,253	2,623	3,008	2,329	2,823	3,094
Travel	1,130	1,332	1,537	1,739	1,752	1,826	2,238
Communications, data and information technology	270	342	273	320	388	361	442
Insurance and finance	435	480	541	580	558	700	868
Business and construction	600	836	994	1,178	1,599	1,798	2,290
Other services	228	253	315	383	398	561	596

a Preliminary data.

Source: Bank of the Republic, *Estudios Económicos*.

(iii) Foreign direct investment

53. Net annual foreign direct investment flows fluctuated considerably during the period of this review. They surpassed US$10.000 million in 2005, 2008 and 2011 and posted their lowest level in 2006. The effect of the international financial crisis was to reduce flows in 2009 and 2010, but 2011 brought a renewed upturn.

54. For this review period, the oil and mining sectors were the main recipients of foreign investment, representing 6 and 23.3 per cent of total foreign direct investment respectively for the period (Table I.7). The other sectors receiving foreign direct investment included manufacturing (18.4 per cent of the total), largely on account of acquisitions of national enterprises by multinationals, as well as commerce, restaurants and hotels (9.3 per cent), the financial sector (8.5 per cent), and transport and storage and communications (7.3 per cent).

Table I.7
Net foreign direct investment by economic sector, 2005-2011
(US$ million)

	2005[a]	2006[a]	2007[a]	2008[a]	2009[a]	2010[a]	2011[a]
Total	**10,252**	**6,656**	**9,049**	**10,620**	**7,137**	**6,899**	**13,234**
Petroleum sector	1,125	1,995	3,333	3,428	2,428	2,781	5,083
Agriculture, forestry, hunting and fishing	6	8	40	41	28	67	131
Mining and quarrying (includes coal)	2,157	1,783	1,100	1,798	3,025	1,755	2,621
Manufacturing	5,513	803	1,867	1,748	621	656	533
Electricity, gas and water	-251	-141	-79	156	-977	36	585
Construction	146	156	210	380	262	298	454
Commerce, restaurants and hotels	305	523	803	1,049	594	370	2,264
Transport, storage and communications	1,021	1,061	414	853	348	-425	1,421
Financial institutions	246	464	1,319	1,095	720	1,252	343
Community services	-16	4	40	72	88	110	-201

a Preliminary data.

Source: Bank of the Republic.

55. The European Union is still the main source of foreign direct investment in Colombia, accounting for some 29 per cent of the total from 2005 to 2011 (Table I.8). The United States is also a major source of investment, with some 25.2 per cent in total, followed by Panama with 11.2 per cent.

Table I.8
Net foreign direct investment by country of origin, 2005-2011[a]
(US$ million)

	2005[b]	2006[b]	2007[b]	2008[b]	2009[b]	2010[b]	2011[b]
European Union	4,727	699	-319	801	152	137	1,829
Germany	11	2	4	52	-100	-27	25
Austria	2	1	1	10	31	24	21
Belgium	1	1	2	3	3	0	6
Cyprus	0	0	0	1	5	8	2
Spain	599	492	289	564	-327	44	733
Finland	0	0	0	0	0	0	0
France	18	4	139	70	113	48	46
United Kingdom	0	0	0	0	0	0	0
Greece	0	0	0	8	3	3	0
Holland	319	25	-818	-130	-109	-158	810
Hungary	0	0	0	0	0	0	0
England	3,747	17	35	200	386	194	390
Ireland	14	38	4	2	2	7	1
Italy	2	9	11	11	11	18	15
Lithuania	0	0	0	0	0	0	0
Luxembourg	0	109	11	2	100	-30	34
Netherlands	0	0	0	0	0	0	0
Portugal	2	0	1	3	2	2	1
Sweden	1	0	1	0	32	3	-255
Denmark	9	0	0	5	0	3	-1
Scotland	0	0	0	0	0	0	0
Panama	208	240	477	760	337	426	650
Anguilla	0	0	1,195	1,111	790	257	184
Bermuda	222	8	12	31	287	-31	9
Canada	2	18	8	52	78	163	174
Bolivarian Republic of Venezuela	16	59	34	1	51	42	20
Cayman Islands	31	159	131	0	23	34	-1
Barbados	0	0	0	4	5	19	61
United States	1,410	1,524	1,064	1,215	1,198	401	507
Costa Rica	3	4	2	10	21	10	7

	2005[b]	2006[b]	2007[b]	2008[b]	2009[b]	2010[b]	2011[b]
Aruba	3	0	16	1	2	9	0
Chile	6	2	46	45	54	20	583
Mexico	1,063	31	340	412	-647	-624	80
MERCOSUR	47	32	549	141	75	74	341
Other European countries	38	17	43	57	67	48	109
Andean Community	15	6	10	18	18	17	39
Other	347	375	136	231	87	29	-173
Subtotal (new investment less repayments of capital)	**8,140**	**3,174**	**3,745**	**4,891**	**2,598**	**1,033**	**4,419**
Reinvestment of profits [c]	988	1,487	1,971	2,301	2,111	3,086	3,732
Petroleum sector	1,125	1,995	3,333	3,428	2,428	2,781	5,083
Total	**10,252**	**6,656**	**9,049**	**10,620**	**7,137**	**6,899**	**13,234**

a Not including capital inflows arising from reinvestment of profits and investments in the oil sector, as the breakdown per country is not available.
b Preliminary data.
c Not including the oil sector.

Note: A negative flow means that capital repayments exceed new investments.

Source: Bank of the Republic, Economic Studies.

II. TRADE AND INVESTMENT REGIME

(1) OVERVIEW

1. Colombia's trade policy continues to be geared towards Latin American and Caribbean integration as well as the strengthening of trade and investment flows with the rest of the world. It is vitally important to Colombia to maintain an open trade regime in the framework of a transparent, predictable and inclusive multilateral system that is complemented by regional and bilateral endeavours. Colombia has therefore participated in a range of negotiations to deepen the existing bilateral and regional agreements (Cuba, Chile, Mexico, Northern Triangle of Central America) in the framework of the Latin American Integration Association (LAIA) and has signed new agreements (Canada, EFTA, the United States and the European Union) so as to secure stable preferential access to strategic markets. In addition, Colombia is currently negotiating free trade agreements with the Republic of Korea, Panama and Turkey.

2. However, within its trade policy strategy, Colombia attaches special importance to its participation in the WTO, with a view to creating a multilateral system with clear and transparent rules that support the integration of the developing countries into the international economy. Colombia is a founding member of the WTO and took part in the negotiations on telecommunications and financial services following the Uruguay Round; it signed the Fourth and the Fifth Protocols to the General Agreement on Trade in Services. Colombia is an observer in the Committee on Government Procurement. During the period under review, Colombia participated in 20 disputes within the framework of the WTO Dispute Settlement Body: once as a complainant, twice as a respondent and 17 times as a third party. Colombia has supported the swift and balanced conclusion of the Doha Round, which it considers necessary to achieve more open, undistorted markets and to strengthen the multilateral system. Colombia attaches the utmost importance to the reform of agriculture.

3. Colombian legislation accords national treatment to foreign investment. Most sectors are open to foreign investment, barring a few in which Colombia maintains limitations or prohibitions. Besides, the State may determine areas in which only one company may provide services exclusively for a specified period of time. All foreign investment must be registered with the Bank of the Republic. Registration is necessary to enable investors to repatriate and/or reinvest the profits on their investment. Foreign investments do not require prior authorization, except for direct investments in the financial and hydrocarbons and mining sectors, as well as portfolio investments, which fall under a special investment regime. Colombian or foreign direct investors may sign a legal stability contract with the State, which guarantees that the legal provisions under which the investment was made will continue to apply for the duration of the investment, regardless of any amendments to those provisions.

(2) TRADE POLICY FORMULATION AND IMPLEMENTATION

(i) Institutional and legal framework

4. Colombia is a social state guided by the rule of law, organized in the form of a unitary republic.[1] Colombia's territorial organisation consists of departments, municipalities, districts and indigenous territories. In principle, those territorial entities have the following rights: to govern themselves under their own authority; to administer their resources; to establish the taxes necessary for their operation; to participate in national revenues; and to exercise the jurisdictions appropriate to

[1] Article 1, Political Constitution of Colombia (1991).

them.[2] The distribution of powers between the central government and the territorial authorities was determined in 2011 in a basic law, which prescribes that international trade is the purview of the central government.[3]

5. The Legislature is the Congress, which comprises the Senate of the Republic and the Chamber of Representatives.[4] The 102 senators and 166 representatives are elected simultaneously by universal suffrage for a term of four years and may be re-elected.

6. The Executive comprises the National Government and the Departmental Entities. The National Government consists of the President, the ministers[5] and the directors of administrative departments.[6] The President of the Republic is the Head of State, Head of Government, and the supreme administrative authority.[7] The President is elected by universal suffrage for a four-year term and may be re-elected once.[8]

7. The Judicial Branch comprises the Supreme Court of Justice, the Council of State, the Constitutional Court, the Higher Council of the Judiciary, the Office of the Prosecutor General and the courts. The Constitution also assigns judicial duties to the authorities of indigenous peoples.[9]

8. The Constitution takes precedence over any other law. In the event of incompatibility between an agreement - including trade and economic integration agreements - and the Constitution, the political authorities must amend the agreement or reform the Constitution so as to eliminate that incompatibility.

9. Laws are issued by the Congress and then ratified and promulgated by the executive. Bills must be approved by both Houses of Congress, after which they go to the executive for ratification. In the absence of any objection to a bill, the executive orders its enactment as a law. The President may object to bills on the grounds that they are "unconstitutional" or "unsuitable" and return them to Congress in keeping with the timeframes stipulated in the Constitution.[10] If a bill is rejected as unconstitutional, it is submitted to the Constitutional Court for its decision. If the Court approves it, the President must ratify and enact it into law. Bills returned as "unsuitable" may become law, however, if the Congress approves them a second time.[11] Should the President of the Republic not

[2] Article 287, Political Constitution of Colombia.

[3] Organic Law No. 1,454 of 2011.

[4] Article 114, Political Constitution of Colombia.

[5] There are currently 16 ministries: Interior; Labour; Justice and Law; Foreign Affairs; Finance and Public Credit; National Defence; Agriculture and Rural Development; Health and Social Welfare; Mining and Energy; Commerce, Industry and Tourism; National Education; Environment and Sustainable Development; Housing, Urban and Territorial Affairs; Information Technologies and Communications; Transport; and Culture (online information from the Office of the President of the Republic of Colombia, "*Gobierno*". Viewed at: http://wsp.presidencia.gov.co/Paginas/Presidencia.aspx).

[6] In accordance with Article 115 of the Constitution, governorates and mayoralties as well as supervisory authorities, public establishments, and state-owned industrial or commercial enterprises are part of the executive branch.

[7] Article 115, Political Constitution of Colombia.

[8] Re-election was introduced by means of a constitutional reform implemented through Legislative Act No. 2 of 2004, Article 2.

[9] Article 246, Political Constitution of Colombia.

[10] Article 199, Law No. 5 of 1992. The Executive shall have a six-day time-frame for returning, together with its objections, any bill consisting of 20 articles or less; a ten-day time-frame for a bill containing 21 to 50 articles; and up to 20 days if it comprises more than 50 articles.

[11] Articles 166-168, Political Constitution of Colombia.

ratify the laws in the terms and in accordance with the stipulations of the Constitution, they will be ratified and promulgated by the President of the Congress.

10. The Congress may invest the President of the Republic for up to six months with extraordinary powers to issue decrees with the force of law for reasons of public necessity or convenience.[12] This power must be requested expressly by the Government and its approval requires the vote of an absolute majority of the members of both Houses. The Congress may nonetheless amend such decrees at any time and on its own initiative. These powers may not be conferred for the purpose of issuing codes, statutes, basic laws or of levying taxes.[13]

11. The management of Colombia's international relations and the conclusion of international treaties are the responsibility of the President of the Republic. International treaties must be approved by the Congress, which has no authority to amend them. Once a treaty has been approved, the Constitutional Court reviews its constitutionality as well as that of the law approving it and issues the judgement approving the treaty. This judgement is forwarded to President of the Republic for ratification. The Constitution allows for the provisional approval of treaties of an economic and commercial nature agreed upon in the realm of international bodies, pending their approval by the Congress.[14] International treaties have the status of law.[15] Citizens may therefore rely on WTO Agreements and Andean Community rules in Colombian courts.

(ii) Trade policy formulation and objectives

12. The Ministry of Commerce, Industry and Tourism (MCIT) is still the institution principally responsible for formulating and applying trade policy in Colombia. To formulate foreign trade policy, the MCIT consults with various public sector entities involved with trade, as well as with private sector and civil society representatives (Table II.1).

Table II.1
Institutions responsible for formulating and applying trade policy

Institution	Trade-related function
Ministry of Finance and Public Credit	Formulates policy concerning the levy and collection of customs duty and other taxes.
Ministry of Agriculture	Determines the requirements for importing and exporting agricultural products. Lays out the sanitary requirements for the importation of plants and animals.
Higher Council for Foreign Trade	Advisory body comprising the President and various Ministers. Advises the Government on general and sectoral foreign trade policy.
Committee on Customs	Advisory body consisting of various Vice-Ministers. Advises the Higher Council for Foreign Trade on: the customs and tariff regime, tax refunds relating to foreign trade operations and the adoption of provisional safeguard measures.
Joint Committee on Foreign Trade	Entity attached to the Ministry of Foreign Trade, Industry and Tourism. It comprises the members of the Higher Council, the representatives of the economic sectors, two representatives of the labour sector and two representatives of academia. Advises the President of the Republic on matters pertaining to the improvement of quality, productivity and the competitiveness of the country.

Source: WTO Secretariat.

13. Colombia uses trade policy as an instrument for attaining its overall economic policy objectives of growth, job creation and development in general. Colombia continues to encourage

[12] Article 18 of Law No. 1,444 of 2011.
[13] Article 150, Political Constitution of Colombia.
[14] Article 224, Political Constitution of Colombia.
[15] Article 93, Political Constitution of Colombia.

integration processes and bilateral and multilateral trade agreements that expand and facilitate Colombia's external transactions with a view to promoting exports.

14. Colombia's trade policy continues to be geared towards Latin American and Caribbean integration as well as the strengthening of trade and investment flows between Colombia and the rest of the world. The country has therefore participated in a range of negotiations to improve the existing bilateral and regional agreements and to sign new agreements to secure stable preferential access to strategic markets. Another important goal of Colombia's trade policy is to continue its participation in the WTO with a view to creating a multilateral system with clear and transparent rules that support the integration of developing countries into the international economy.

(3) International Trade Relations

(i) WTO

15. Colombia has been a member of the WTO since 30 April 1995.[16] Colombia took part in the negotiations on telecommunications and financial services following the Uruguay Round and signed the Fourth and the Fifth Protocols to the General Agreement on Trade in Services.[17] Colombia has been an observer in the Committee on Government Procurement since 2006. Colombia acceded to the Information Technology Agreement on 28 March 2012.

16. Colombia attaches great importance to the multilateral trading system and the WTO, especially in the light of the world economic situation. For Colombia, the antidote to the crisis is an open trade regime in the framework of a transparent, predictable and inclusive multilateral system that is complemented by regional and bilateral endeavours. Colombia believes in strengthening the system in such areas as the operation of the regular bodies, the monitoring and review of trade policies and practices, compliance with notification commitments and the dissemination and use of the information notified.[18]

17. Colombia has supported the early and balanced completion of the Doha Round, maintaining the reform of agriculture as the central plank. To that end Colombia stands ready to explore areas of negotiation in which we can advance towards provisional or definitive agreements. Colombia considers it necessary to conclude the negotiations so as to achieve more open, undistorted markets, to strengthen the multilateral system and ensure that markets that are now open continue to be so. The results of the Round should embody the needs of developing countries. For Colombia, this means better market access conditions for both services and agricultural goods, as well as eliminating distortions in agriculture and strengthening the rules-based system.

18. In accordance with its assumed commitments, Colombia has continued to submit notifications to the WTO since the last review (Table II.2).

[16] Law No. 170 of 1994.

[17] WTO documents GATS/SC/20/Suppl.2 of 11 April 1997 and GATS/SC/20/Suppl.3 of 26 February 1998.

[18] WTO document WT/MIN(11)/ST/54 of 16 December 2011.

Table II.2
Principal notifications submitted pursuant to the WTO Agreements, 1 January 2006-29 February 2012

Agreement	Requirement	WTO document (date) (latest document if submitted regularly)
Agreement on Trade-Related Aspects of Intellectual Property Rights (TRIPS)		
Article 63.2	Legislation	IP/N/1/COL/3 (30/01/2012)
Article 69	Information Services	IP/N/3/Rev.10/Add.3 (14/07/2008)
Agreement on Agriculture		
Articles 10 and 18.2 (ES.1 and ES.2)	Export subsidies for the years 2008, 2009 and 2010	G/AG/N/COL/44/Add.1 (25/11/2011) G/AG/N/COL/45 (25/11/2011)
Article 18.2 (DS.1)	Domestic support for 2010	G/AG/N/COL/48 (25/11/2011)
Article 18.2 (MA.1)	Administration of tariff quota commitments for 2009	G/AG/N/COL/35/Add.1 (13/01/2011)
Article 18.2 (MA.2)	Volume of imports under tariff quotas for calendar year 2010	G/AG/N/COL/47 (25/11/2011)
Articles 5.7 and 18.2 (MA.5)	Special safeguard provisions during 2010	G/AG/N/COL/46 (25/11/2011)
General Agreement on Trade in Services (GATS)		
Article III:3	Legislation	S/C/N/576 (05/10/2010)
Article III.4 and/or IV.2	Information Services	S/ENQ/78/Rev.9 (01/12/2006)
Article V.7(a)	Regional trade agreements (RTAs): Colombia and Canada	S/C/N/602 WT/REG301/N/1 (10/11/2011)
	RTAs: Colombia and Switzerland and Liechtenstein	S/C/N/600 WT/REG299/N/1 (15/09/2011)
	RTAs: Colombia and Mexico	WT/REG289/N/1/Add.1 (15/12/2011) S/C/N/563 WT/REG289/N/1 (14/09/2010)
	RTAs: Colombia and Chile	S/C/N/509 WT/REG272/N/1 (25/08/2009)
GATT 1994		
Article XVII.4(a) (State trading)	State trading enterprises	G/STR/N/13/COL (01/07/2010)
Article XXIV:7(a) (Free trade areas)	RTAs: Colombia and Canada	S/C/N/602 WT/REG301/N/1 (10/11/2011)
	RTAs: Colombia and Switzerland and Liechtenstein	S/C/N/600 WT/REG299/N/1 (15/09/2011)
	RTAs: Colombia and Mexico	S/C/N/563 WT/REG289/N/1 (14/09/2010)
	RTAs: Colombia and Chile	S/C/N/509 WT/REG272/N/1 (25/08/2009)
Article XXVIII:3	Modification of schedules (retaliatory withdrawal of concessions)	G/SECRET/20/Add.3 (03/07/2006)
Article XXVIII:5	Modification of schedules (reserve the right to modify schedules for a three-year period)	G/MA/276 (09/01/2012)
Agreement on Implementation of GATT Article VI (Anti-dumping)		
Article 16.4 (semi-annual)	Anti-dumping measures (taken in the preceding six months)	G/ADP/N/216/COL/Corr.1 (30/08/2011)
Article 16.5	Competent authorities	G/ADP/N/14/Add.23 G/SCM/N/18/Add.23 (24/04/2007)
Article 18.5	Laws/regulations and changes thereto	G/ADP/N/1/COL/3 (12/08/2010)
Agreement on Import Licensing Procedures		
Articles 5.1-5.3	Import licensing procedures or modifications thereto	G/LIC/N/2/COL/1/Corr.1 (13/10/2011)
Article 7.3	Replies to questionnaire	G/LIC/N/3/COL/9 (10/10/2011)
Article 8.2(b)	Laws/regulations (and changes thereto, including changes in the administration of such laws)	G/LIC/N/1/COL/2 (08/10/2007)
Agreement on the Application of Sanitary and Phytosanitary Measures		
Article 7, Annex B	Sanitary/phytosanitary regulations	G/SPS/N/COL/215 (26/01/2011)

Agreement	Requirement	WTO document (date) (latest document if submitted regularly)
Agreement on Technical Barriers to Trade		
Article 2.10	Technical regulations (urgent)	G/TBT/N/COL/126/Add.1 (15/03/2010)
Article 2.9	Technical regulations	G/TBT/N/COL/115/Add.2 (06/02/2012)
Articles 2.9 and 5.6	Technical regulations; conformity assessment procedures	G/TBT/N/COL/156/Add.1 (06/02/2012)
Article 5.6	Conformity assessment procedures	G/TBT/N/COL/163/Add.2 (20/01/2012)
Articles to be determined	Technical regulations	G/TBT/Notif.00/579/Add.2 (18/12/2009) G/TBT/N/COL/103 (03/10/2007)
Article 15.2	Administrative arrangements; laws/regulations	G/TBT/2/Add.18/Rev.1/Suppl.1 (09/01/2012)
Agreement on Subsidies and Countervailing Measures		
Article 27.4, Part VIII: developing country Members	Special and differential treatment for developing country Members: the developing country Members shall phase out their export subsidies within the eight-year period, preferably in a progressive manner.	G/SCM/N/160/COL (31/05/2011)
Article 25.1 GATT Article XVI.1	Subsidies	G/SCM/N/186/COL G/SCM/N/220/COL (30/05/2011)
Article 25.11	Countervailing measures (taken in the preceding six months)	G/SCM/N/228/Add.1 (19/10/2011)
Article 25.12	Competent authorities	G/ADP/N/14/Add.23 G/SCM/N/18/Add.23 (24/04/2007)

Source: WTO Secretariat.

19. During the period of this review, Colombia has participated in 20 disputes under the WTO Dispute Settlement Body: once as a complainant, twice as a respondent and 17 times as a third party (Table II.3).

20. On 21 March 2007, Colombia requested consultations with the European Union (formerly the EC) concerning its regime for the importation of bananas.[19] When those consultations failed to produce a satisfactory result, Colombia submitted the matter to Director-General, asking him to use his good offices to facilitate a solution of its dispute with the EU. Consultations took place in 2008 and 2009 under the Colombia EU good offices procedure. These direct consultations finally yielded two agreements between the EU and its MFN banana suppliers - one with all Latin American MFN suppliers and the other with the United States. The parties initialled the two agreements on 15 December 2009.[20]

21. In 2007 Panama initiated a dispute settlement procedure against Colombia regarding the use of indicative prices and restrictions on ports of entry. The Panel concluded that Colombia had acted inconsistently with the provisions of the Customs Valuation Agreement and the GATT 1994 and recommended that Colombia should bring its measures into conformity with the said Agreements. In February 2010, Colombia notified having taken the requisite steps to comply with the recommendations and rulings of the DSB.[21]

---

[19] WTO online information, "Dispute settlement: Dispute DS361". Viewed at: http://www.wto.org/english/tratop_e/dispu_e/cases_e/ds361_e.htm.

[20] The text of the agreement between the European Union and its Latin American MFN suppliers - the "Geneva Agreement on Trade in Bananas" - was then circulated to the General Council for its information (WT/L/784) WTO document WT/DS361/2 WT/DS364/2 of 22 December 2009.

[21] WTO online information, "Dispute settlement: Dispute DS366". Viewed at: http://www.wto.org/english/tratop_e/dispu_e/cases_e/ds366_e.htm.

Table II.3
Situation regarding dispute settlement cases, 1 January 2006-29 February 2012

Subject of dispute:	Against/ raised by	Status as at 29 February 2012 (date)	WTO document series
Colombia as complainant			
Regime for the Importation of Bananas	EU (formerly the EC)/ Colombia	At the consultation stage (21 March 2007)	WT/DS361
Colombia as respondent			
Customs measures on the importation of certain goods from Panama	Colombia/ Panama	Settled or terminated (withdrawn, mutually agreed solution) (1 December 2006)	WT/DS348
Indicative prices and restrictions on ports of entry	Colombia/ Panama	Implementation by respondent notified (18 February 2010)	WT/DS366
Colombia as third party			
Certain country-of-origin labelling requirements	USA/ Canada	Report of the Panel circulated (18 November 2011)	WT/DS384
	USA/ Mexico		WT/DS386
Measures related to the exportation of various raw materials	China/ USA	Report adopted with the recommendation to bring measures into conformity (22 February 2012)	WT/DS394
	China/ EU		WT/DS395
	China/ Mexico		WT/DS398
Definitive anti-dumping measures on certain iron or steel fasteners from China	EU/ China	Report adopted with the recommendation to bring measures into conformity (28 July 2011)	WT/DS397
Measures prohibiting the importation and marketing of seal products	EU/ Canada	Panel established, but not yet composed (21 April 2011)	WT/DS400
	EU/ Norway		WT/DS401
Taxes on distilled spirits	Philippines/ USA	Report adopted with the recommendation to bring measures into conformity (20 January 2012)	WT/DS403
	Ukraine/ Moldova	Panel established, but not yet composed (20 July 2011)	WT/DS423
Anti-dumping measures on certain footwear from China	EU/ China	Report adopted with the recommendation to bring measures into conformity (22 February 2012)	WT/DS405
Measures affecting the production and sale of clove cigarettes	USA/ Indonesia	Panel report under appeal (5 January 2012)	WT/DS406
Safeguard measures on imports of polypropylene bags and tubular fabric	Dominican Republic/ Costa Rica	Report adopted with the recommendation to bring measures into conformity (22 February 2012)	WT/DS415
	Dominican Republic/ Guatemala		WT/DS416
	Dominican Republic/ Honduras		WT/DS417
	Dominican Republic/ El Salvador		WT/DS418

Source: WTO Secretariat.

(ii) Regional trade agreements

(a) Andean Community

22. Together with the Plurinational State of Bolivia, Ecuador and Peru, Colombia is a member of the Andean Community, founded with the signing of the Cartagena Agreement in 1969.

On 20 September 2006, Chile was granted the status of Associate Member Country.[22] The MERCOSUR countries (Argentina, Brazil, Paraguay, Uruguay) have also been Associate Members since 7 July 2005.[23] Member countries are free to negotiate trade agreements with third countries or groups of countries.[24] One of the requirements is that they notify the Andean Community Commission before signing the agreement.[25]

23. In 2006 the Bolivarian Republic of Venezuela denounced the Cartagena Agreement.[26] During that same year, however, the Bolivarian Republic of Venezuela signed a Memorandum of Understanding with the member countries of the Andean Community agreeing to respect fully the trade advantages received and granted under the Andean Liberalization Programme, which must be maintained amongst the parties.[27] Finally, in 2011, Colombia and the Bolivarian Republic of Venezuela signed a partial scope agreement in the LAIA framework to maintain those preferences.[28] This agreement will take effect once its six annexes have been agreed upon.[29]

24. A free trade area has existed since 1993 between the Plurinational State of Bolivia, Colombia and Ecuador, and covers the entire tariff universe (Peru became a full member of the free trade area in January 2006).[30] In 1995, the Common External Tariff was adopted by Colombia, the Plurinational State of Bolivia and Ecuador (Decision No. 370).[31] In August 2007 it was decided through Decision No. 669 to create a High Level Working Group on Tariff Policy in order to formulate an Andean Community tariff policy that would apply to all member countries by 31 January 2008 at the latest.[32] Decision No. 669 temporarily restored tariff policy control to member countries, thus freeing them from the obligations imposed by Decision No. 370, which lays out the Andean common tariff policy. Decision 671 of 13 July 2007 provided for the harmonization of the customs regimes of Andean Community member countries. In December 2011, however, the obligation to apply the Community's common external tariff regulations and the supplementary provisions, including the Andean price band system, was suspended until 31 December 2014 (Decision No. 771 of 7 December 2011).[33]

---

[22] Decision No. 645, and CAN online information, "*Relaciones Externas: Chile*". Viewed at: http://www.comunidadandina.org/exterior/Chile.htm.

[23] Decision No. 613. Viewed at: http://www.comunidadandina.org/normativa/dec/D613.htm.

[24] Decision No. 598 of 2004.

[25] CAN online information, "*Política Arancelaria*". Viewed at: http://www.comunidadandina.org/comercio/union.htm.

[26] Andean Community, Press Release "*Secretaría General de la CAN recibió comunicación oficial del retiro de Venezuela*", 22 April 2006. Viewed at: http://www.comunidadandina.org/prensa/notas/np22-406a.htm.

[27] Article 135 of the Cartagena Agreement (Decision No. 641).

[28] Online information, People's Ministry of Communication and Information, "*Noticias: NoticiasMinCI: Establecido nuevo acuerdo comercial entre Venezuela y Colombia*". Viewed at: http://www.minci.gob.ve/noticias/1/208784/establecido_nuevo_acuerdo.html

[29] The six annexes are: preferential tariff treatment, sanitary and phytosanitary standards, technical standards, rules of origin, trade protection and dispute settlement mechanism. To date (14 February 2012), two of the annexes have been agreed on, and are now at the legal review stage.

[30] Andean Community Decision No. 414 of 30 July 1997.

[31] CAN online information, "*Política Arancelaria*". Viewed at: http://www.comunidadandina.org/comercio/union.htm.

[32] CAN online information, "*Comercio de bienes*". Viewed at: http://www.comunidadandina.org/comercio/comercio_bienes.htm.

[33] This notwithstanding, the General Secretariat of the Andean Community (SGCAN) continues to set the reference prices of the products in that system every 15 days.

25. As regards services, it was decided in December 2006 to liberalize services in the Andean area and to identify those sectors in which sectoral norms would be harmonized. Those sectors included financial and professional services as well as radio and television and transport services, for which regulations were agreed in order to encourage the participation of subregional investors.[34] It was decided in 2011 that financial as well as free to air television services would not be liberalized until 2014.[35]

26. In 2007 the Andean Community Presidents agreed to promote more balanced integration that would take account of the social, cultural, economic, political, environmental and trade dimensions.[36] In 2010, the Andean Council of Foreign Ministers approved the new guiding principles for the Andean integration process and the Strategic Agenda, which sets out the areas in which the Andean Community member countries are resolved to move forward together.[37] In that same year the Council, through Decision 741, adopted the notion of Andean Community Observer Country, thereby allowing non-member countries to support the Andean Community's integration endeavours through the policy and cooperation mechanisms they deem appropriate. In 2011, Spain formally requested observer status with the Andean Community, thus becoming entitled to participate with a voice in the meetings of Andean Community bodies and to promote joint programmes and activities.[38]

(b) Partial-scope agreements negotiated in the framework of the Latin American Integration Association (LAIA)

27. In the LAIA framework, Colombia has signed agreements with Costa Rica, Chile, Cuba, Mexico, Nicaragua and Panama[39] and the Bolivarian Republic of Venezuela[40], as well as with the member countries of the Caribbean Community (CARICOM)[41], the Northern Triangle of Central America (El Salvador, Guatemala and Honduras) and MERCOSUR.[42] Since 2006, Colombia has been renegotiating and strengthening the agreements with Cuba, Chile, Mexico, and the Northern Triangle of Central America.

---

[34] Decision No. 659 of 14 December 2006; CAN online information, "*Cronología temática*". Viewed at: http://www.comunidadandina.org/quienes/tematica.htm.

[35] Decision No. 772 of 7 December 2011.

[36] CAN online information, "*Reseña histórica*". Viewed at: http://www.comunidadandina.org/quienes/resena.htm.

[37] CAN online information, "*Reseña histórica*". Viewed at: http://www.comunidadandina.org/quienes/resena.htm.

[38] CAN online information, "*Cronología por fechas*". Viewed at: http://www.comunidadandina.org/quienes/crono.htm.

[39] Partial-Scope Agreement under Article 25 of the Treaty of Montevideo of 1980, between the Republic of Colombia and the Republic of Panama, AAP.A25TM No. 29 of 9 July 1993, incorporated into Colombian Law by Decree No. 2781 of 1994; First Protocol Amending AAP.A25TM No. 29 of 28 April 2003, incorporated into Colombian Law by Decree No. 1845 of 2003; and Second Protocol Amending AAP.A25TM No. 29 of 15 February 2005, incorporated into Colombian Law by Decree No. 1138 of 2005.

[40] The Partial-Scope Agreement signed in the LAIA framework on 28 November 2011 has not entered into force.

[41] Partial Scope-Agreement on Trade and Economic and Technical Cooperation between the Republic of Colombia and the Caribbean Community (CARICOM) AAP.A25TM No. 31 of 24 July 1994, incorporated into Colombian law by Decree No. 2.891 of 1994 and Decree No. 973 of 1998.

[42] Economic Complementarity Agreement AAP.CE No. 59 of 18 October 2004, incorporated into Colombian law by Decree No. 141 of 2005. The Agreement incorporates the tariff preferences laid down in the partial scope agreements concluded previously ("historical heritage") between Colombia and MERCOSUR members (online information, Ministry of Commerce, Industry and Tourism, "CAN MERCOSUR". Viewed at: http://www.tlc.gov.co/publicaciones.php?id=13228).

28. Economic Complementarity Agreement No. 49 between Colombia and Cuba was signed in 2000 in the LAIA framework and took effect on 10 July 2001. The agreement was deepened in 2008 with the signing of two protocols: the first addressed the existing preferences and the second incorporated topics that go beyond market access (Table AII.1).[43]

29. Colombia and Chile signed Economic Complementarity Agreement (ECA) No. 24 on 6 December 1993, establishing a reciprocal tariff reduction programme covering all trade.[44] On 27 November 2006 the two countries signed a free trade agreement that took effect on 8 May 2009. That agreement consists of an Additional Protocol to ECA No. 24 that further buttresses it by liberalizing the entire tariff universe of both parties as well as trade in services excluding financial and air services.[45] In 2012, products not yet covered by the tariff reduction programme will be liberalized, including rice, sugar and meat, dairy and oilseed products (Table AII.1).[46]

30. Although the Bolivarian Republic of Venezuela denounced the Free Trade Agreement between Colombia, Mexico and the Bolivarian Republic of Venezuela (FTA G-3) in May 2006, that instrument still governs trade between Colombia and Mexico. In August 2009, Colombia and Mexico concluded negotiations on an Amending Protocol to the Treaty, which took effect in August 2011.[47] One of the main achievements of the negotiation was the inclusion of some agricultural and industrial products that had been excluded from the original tariff reduction programme, as well as the incorporation of provisions on rules of origin.

31. In 2006, Colombia and the countries of the Northern Triangle of Central America (El Salvador, Guatemala, Honduras) began negotiations on a trade agreement[48], which was signed on 9 August 2007 and ratified by the Colombian Congress in June 2008.[49] That agreement covers market access, investment, services, e-commerce, cooperation, dispute settlement, government procurement, trade facilitation, sanitary and phytosanitary measures, technical standards, rules of origin and trade protection measures (Table AII.1).

(iii) Other agreements and preferences in force

32. The Trade Promotion Agreement between Colombia and Canada was signed in November 2008 and became effective in August 2011. It consists of three separate but interrelated agreements: the Free Trade Agreement, which contains provisions on trade in goods, trade in services and investment; the Labour Cooperation Agreement, which formulates obligations regarding the protection of labour rights and compliance with internal standards; and the Agreement on the

---

[43] Online information, Ministry of Commerce, Industry and Tourism, "*Acuerdo Colombia Cuba*". Viewed at: https://www.mincomercio.gov.co/publicaciones.php?id=1888.

[44] Economic Complementarity Agreement between Colombia and Chile for the establishment of an extended economic area, AAP.CE No. 24 of 6 December 1993, incorporated into Colombian law by Decree No. 2717 of 1993, as amended by Decree No. 1.741 of 1994 and extended by Decrees No. 2,172 of 1995, No. 2.181 of 1996, No. 2.178 of 1997 and No. 617 of 2002.

[45] WTO document WT/REG272/1/Rev.1 of 21 December 2010.

[46] Online information, Ministry of Commerce, Industry and Tourism, "*Resumen del Acuerdo*". Viewed at: http://www.tlc.gov.co/publicaciones.php?id=1425.

[47] This Amending Protocol was approved by Decrees No. 2,676 and No. 2,677 of 2011.

[48] Colombia's trading relations with Guatemala, El Salvador and Honduras have been governed by partial-scope agreements signed in 1984 in the LAIA framework (Partial-scope agreement between the Republic of Colombia and the Republic of Costa Rica, AAP.A25TM No. 7 of 2 March 1984).

[49] Besides, the President approved that agreement on 30 July 2008 through Law No. 1.241 and it was declared constitutional by the Constitutional Court on 8 July in Judgement No. C 446 of 2009, which was notified on 23 September 2009.

Environment, which lays out the obligations of both parties regarding environmental protection (Table AII.1).[50]

33. The free trade agreement between Colombia and the EFTA countries (Switzerland, Liechtenstein, Norway and Iceland) was signed on 25 November 2008 and approved in 2010.[51] In 2011 that agreement took effect between Colombia and Switzerland and Liechtenstein, which ratified it in 2009. Norway and Iceland have not yet ratified it, however. Not only does the agreement contemplate the liberalization of trade in agricultural and industrial goods, rules of origin, customs procedures and trade facilitation, it also includes commitments regarding trade in services, the transit of persons, e-commerce, technical standardization, investment measures, competition policy and intellectual property (Table AII.1).[52]

34. Under the Generalized System of Preferences (GSP) Colombia is still a beneficiary of schemes established by Canada, Japan, Norway, New Zealand, Russia, Turkey and Switzerland.[53]

35. The EU accords tariff preferences to Colombia under the "GSP plus" regime, and these will be valid until 31 December 2013. The regime grants tariff preferences of 100 per cent for 6,600 products, 4,037 sensitive products and 2,563 non-sensitive ones, except for shrimp, which will be subject to a preferential tariff.[54]

36. Since 1992 Colombia has enjoyed tariff preferences accorded by the United States under the Andean Trade Preferences Act (ATPA). In August 2002, these preferences were renewed through the Andean Trade Promotion and Drug Eradication Act (ATPDEA), which renewed the ATPA regime until 2006 and extended the benefits thereunder.[55] As of 2006, the preferences granted under the ATPDEA were renewed on a year-by-year basis until February 2011, when they were suspended.[56] Nevertheless, the preferences were reintroduced on 5 November 2011 with retrospective effect, and will be valid until July 2013.[57]

---

[50] Online information, Ministry of Commerce, Industry and Tourism, "*Resumen del tratado de libre comercio entre Colombia y Canadá*". Viewed at: https://www.mincomercio.gov.co/tlc/publicaciones.php?id=721.

[51] Law No. 1.372 of 7 January 2010.

[52] Online information, Ministry of Commerce, Industry and Tourism, "*Resumen del tratado de libre comercio entre Colombia y los Estados AELC (EFTA)*". Viewed at: https://www.mincomercio.gov.co/tlc/publicaciones.php?id=702.

[53] UNCTAD online information, "GSP Handbooks: Canada, Japan, Switzerland and Turkey". Viewed at: http://archive.unctad.org/Templates/Page.asp?intItemID=1421&lang=1; document UNCTAD/TAP/258/Rev. 3 of April 1998 (New Zealand); and Ministry of Commerce, Industry and Tourism (2003).

[54] Online information, Ministry of Commerce, Industry and Tourism, "*Sistema Generalizado de Preferencias*". Viewed at: https://www.mincomercio.gov.co/publicaciones.php?id=10158.

[55] A limited number of products, including certain textiles, articles of apparel, rum and canned tuna do not enjoy preferences. The United States is also maintaining its tariff quotas for imports of certain agricultural products.

[56] ATPDEA preferences were suspended from February to October 2011.

[57] Online information, Ministry of Commerce, Industry and Tourism, "APTA ATPDEA". Viewed at: https://www.mincomercio.gov.co/publicaciones.php?id=10542.

(iv) Trade agreements signed and under negotiation

37. The Trade Promotion Agreement between Colombia and the United States was signed in November 2006.[58] Both the Agreement and its "Amending Protocol" were incorporated into Colombian Law in 2007.[59] The United States Congress approved the Agreement in October 2011, and the President ratified it that same month. Colombia is now at the stage of implementing the new regulations pertaining to the Agreement, which entails making the necessary legal adjustments so as to guarantee that it is consistent with the Colombian legal order. Once this stage is complete, there will be an exchange of notes between the two Governments, and the agreement will take effect 60 days thereafter.[60]

38. Colombia and Peru completed negotiations on a trade agreement with the EU on 19 May 2010. In March 2011, the legal review process was completed, giving way to the translation stage (the agreement must be translated into the 21 official EU languages), after which it will be signed, approved and ratified. This Agreement includes commitments in all the areas of the trade in goods and services.[61]

39. Colombia is currently negotiating free trade agreements with the Republic of Korea (since December 2009), Panama (since March 2010), and Turkey (since June 2011). In 2012, Colombia will begin negotiations with Israel. Similarly, Colombia has started exploratory talks with Japan on the possibility of negotiating an economic partnership agreement.

(4) Investment Regime

40. The foreign investment regime, which includes foreign direct investment (FDI) and portfolio investments by natural and legal persons not resident in Colombia, is regulated by Decree No. 2080 of 2000. Colombia grants national treatment to foreign investment.[62] Upon request, investments originating in an Andean Community member country are considered as national investments.[63]

41. Within the framework of the Andean Community's common investment regime, Colombia freely determines its investment policy.[64] That policy is formulated by the Ministry of Commerce, Industry and Tourism in coordination with the Ministry of Finance and Public Credit, and bearing in mind the recommendations of the National Economic and Social Policy Council (CONPES).[65] Until 2007, CONPES had been empowered to identify those sectors that were not open to foreign capital;

---

[58] The agreement covers market access, rules of origin, customs procedures, sanitary and phytosanitary measures, technical barriers to trade, trade protection, government procurement, investment, cross-border services, financial services, telecommunications, e-commerce, intellectual property, competition policy, labour aspects, environment, transparency and dispute settlement.

[59] Law No. 1,143 of 2007, Constitutional Court Judgements No. C 750/08 and No. C 751/08.

[60] Online information, Ministry of Commerce, Industry and Tourism, "*TLC Colombia Estados Unidos*". Viewed at: http://www.tlc.gov.co/publicaciones.php?id=14853.

[61] MCIT online information, "*Resultados de la Negociación con la Unión Europea*". Viewed at: https://www.mincomercio.gov.co/publicaciones.php?id=17495.

[62] Decree No. 2.080 of 2000, Article 2.

[63] Decree No. 2.080 of 2000, Article 13.

[64] CAN, Decision No. 291 of 1991.

[65] Law No. 210 of 2003, Article 2.

that power was never exercised, however, and was therefore eliminated.[66] Proexport is the entity responsible for promoting investments and advising investors.[67]

42. Foreign investment is permitted in most sectors, except for some in which Colombia maintains limitations or prohibitions (Table II.4). Similarly, domestic and foreign investment in the provision of certain household public services[68] are subject to restrictions. Besides, the State may determine areas in which only one company may provide services exclusively for a specified period of time.[69] The acquisition of land in border areas, coastal areas and island territory is restricted for foreigners.[70] Andean multinational enterprises are entitled to participate in the sectors reserved for domestic enterprises.[71]

43. All foreign investments must be registered. The investor effects the registration directly with the Bank of the Republic.[72] There are several registration procedures depending on the type (direct or portfolio) and the form (foreign exchange or other) of the investment.[73] Registration is necessary to enable investors to repatriate and/or reinvest the profits on their investment.[74] Foreign investments do not require prior authorization, except for direct investments in the financial and hydrocarbons and mining sectors, as well as portfolio investments, which fall under a special investment regime.[75] Foreign investments in the financial and hydrocarbons and mining sectors require prior authorization from the competent ministry/supervisory authority. Portfolio investments may be made only through stockbrokers, trust companies or investment management companies.[76]

Table II.4
Prohibitions and restrictions on foreign investment

Sector	Legal framework	Prohibition	Limitation
Activities pertaining to national defence and security	Decree No. 2.080 of 2000, Article 6	Yes	
Processing, disposal and elimination of toxic, hazardous or radioactive waste not produced in Colombia.		Yes	
Surveillance and Personal Security Companies	Decree No. 3,564 of 1994	Yes	Only companies organized under Colombian law as private limited companies or private security and surveillance cooperatives may provide private security and surveillance services in Colombia. The partners or members of these companies must be Colombian nationals. Companies established before 11 February 1994 with foreign partners or capital may not increase the participation of the foreign partners. Cooperatives established before that date may retain their legal status.

[66] Decree No. 2,466 of 2007.
[67] Proexport online information. Viewed at: http://www.inviertaencolombia.com.co.
[68] Water supply and sewage services, sanitation, gas distribution and electricity.
[69] Law No. 142 of 1994, Article 40.
[70] Article 100 of the Political Constitution and Decree Law No. 1.415 of 1940.
[71] CAN, Decision No. 292 of 1991. Andean companies are defined as companies in which: at least 60 per cent of the capital is owned by investors from two or more member countries; or at least 30 per cent of the capital is owned by investors from two member countries only.
[72] Decree No. 2.080 of 2000, Article 8.
[73] The procedures are detailed in External Regulatory Circular No. DCIN 83 dated 28 January 2011 issued by the Bank of the Republic. Viewed at: http://www.banrep.gov.co/documentos/reglamentacion/cambiaria/2011/4.pdf.
[74] Proexport online information, "*Registrar la Inversión*". Viewed at: http://www.inviertaencolombia.com.co/como invertir/pasos para instalarse/registrar la inversion.html.
[75] Decree No. 2.080 of 2000, Article 7.
[76] Decree No. 2.080 of 2000, Title III.

Sector	Legal framework	Prohibition	Limitation
Companies providing free-to-air television services	Law No. 680 of 2001, Article 1		40% of the capital. The investor's country of origin must offer reciprocity with respect to Colombian investments. The investment must be made by companies dedicated to the television industry in the country of origin.
Geological consulting services	Law No. 9 of 1974 Article 10		Associate with a Colombian firm.

Source: WTO Secretariat.

44. Colombian or foreign direct investors may sign a legal stability contract with the State, guaranteeing that the legal provisions under which the investment has been made will continue to apply for the duration of that investment, regardless of any amendment of those provisions. Foreigners wishing to make portfolio investments in Colombia are not entitled to sign this type of contract, however.[77] Legal stability contracts nevertheless do not cover changes to the regulations governing certain areas such as the harmonization of international treaties with national regulations; the social security system; investments made by the Government during a state of emergency, indirect taxes, rules which, during the execution of the legal stability contract, are declared to be illegal or unconstitutional, regulations issued by the Bank of the Republic, prudential regulations for the financial sector, the tariff regime for public services, and the obligation to declare and pay taxes.[78]

45. To sign a legal stability contract, the investor must submit an application to the MCIT Technical Secretariat.[79] This application is assessed by the Legal Stability Committee, which is chaired by the Minister of Commerce, Industry and Tourism.[80] Legal stability contracts are granted only if a minimum amount is invested, whether in new or existing projects. The minimum amount of investment is expressed in terms of the *Salario Minimo Mensual Legal Vigente* (SMMLV) (minimum legal monthly wage) and must be equivalent to 7,500 SMMLVs.[81] In addition, upon signing the legal stability contract, the investor must pay the State a stability "premium" (rate) the amount of which, as of 2011, has been set "on the basis of tax regulations that the government decides should be subject to stabilization".[82] Previously, the amount was equivalent to 1 per cent of the value of the annual investment, and in periods of low profitability, to 0.5 per cent only. The legal stability contracts are signed for periods ranging from 3 to 20 years and must be registered with the National Planning Department.[83]

46. To date, Colombia has negotiated 15 international investment agreements. They include reciprocal investment promotion and protection agreements (APPRIs) as well as free trade agreements (FTAs) that contain stipulations regarding investment.[84] Colombia has eight agreements in force, seven of which became effective during this review period: they are with Spain (APPRI), Canada (FTA), Chile (FTA), Peru (APPRI) and Switzerland (APPRI), and at the regional level, with the European Free Trade Association (EFTA)(FTA), and the Northern Triangle of Central America (FTA). Colombia has signed an APPRI with Switzerland, which has been in effect since October 2009, but has also concluded a free trade agreement containing investment related provisions

[77] Law No. 963 of 2005.
[78] PricewaterhouseCoopers and Proexport (2010).
[79] For more information on the procedures, see Decree No. 2,950 of 2005.
[80] Legal Stability Committee, Resolution No. 1 of 2005, Article 1.
[81] Law No. 1.111 of 2006, Article 51.
[82] Law No. 1.450 of 2011, Article 48.
[83] Law No. 963 of 2005, Article 10.
[84] National Economic and Social Policy Council (2010a).

with EFTA member countries, in force since July 2011 for Switzerland and Liechtenstein.[85] The agreements signed since 2006 but still in the process of approval are the APPRIs signed by Colombia with China, India, the United Kingdom and Japan.[86]

47. Colombia is a member of the Multilateral Investment Guarantee Agency and of the International Centre for the Settlement of Investment Disputes.[87]

---

[85] Laws No. 1,198 of 2008 and No. 1,372 of 2010; and online information, Ministry of Commerce, Industry and Tourism, "*Tratado de Libre Comercio*". Viewed at: http://www.tlc.gov.co/; and "*Acuerdos Internacionales de Inversión*". Viewed at: https://www.mincomercio.gov.co/mincomercioexterior/publicaciones.php?id=1847.

[86] National Economic and Social Policy Council (2010a); and information provided by the authorities.

[87] Online information, Ministry of Commerce, Industry and Tourism, "*Acuerdos Internacionales de Inversión*". Viewed at: https://www.mincomercio.gov.co/mincomercioexterior/publicaciones.php?id=1847.

III. TRADE POLICIES BY MEASURE

(1) OVERVIEW

1. Since the last review in 2006, Colombia has continued to liberalize its trading arrangements, both unilaterally and through free trade agreements. Colombia's trade regime is now basically open, and its average tariff rate has been falling. Nonetheless, a number of non-tariff barriers persist, mainly involving import registration and licensing requirements; and the large number of regulations also makes the regime somewhat complex.

2. During the review period, Colombia has simplified its customs and administrative procedures, setting up a single-window facility for imports and exports, together with a risk analysis system that has reduced the frequency of inspection. Further trade facilitation measures are needed, however, and the functioning of the single window needs to be improved. Colombia has not applied minimum prices since 2003, but it continues to use reference prices as parameters for checking the value declared by importers during the customs inspection process. Colombia continues to apply licensing systems - both automatic (free importation) and non-automatic (prior licence). The licensing process is applied irrespective of the origin of the imported product.

3. Since the last trade policy review, Colombia has substantially reduced its level of tariff protection; and its average tariff is currently 6.2 per cent, down from 12 per cent in 2006. In addition to lowering tariffs generally in late 2010 and early 2011, it also reduced duties on a large number of products (mainly industrial inputs and capital goods) for a 12-month period as from August 2011. Nonetheless, these tariffs are expected to return to their previous levels in August 2012, which would raise the average tariff by nearly 2 percentage points (8.2 per cent). Colombia continues to use the Andean Price Band System (SAFP), which is applied to various agricultural imports.

4. Colombia taxes the consumption of certain goods, both imported and domestically produced. The consumption tax base varies between products, and may be the retail sale price or the price of sale to the public. The different importation modalities or customs regimes, and the different export-promotion programmes, provide for relief from the payment of duties and other taxes on goods imports under certain conditions.

5. Between 2006 and 2011, Colombia initiated 25 anti-dumping (AD) investigations and applied ten new definitive measures; provisional measures were applied in 13 of the 25 investigations launched - most of them in 2007. As of 31 December 2011, Colombia had 12 AD measures still in force, all of which were applied to imports from China. No countervailing measures or safeguard measures were adopted between 2006 and 2011, nor were any investigations launched in this regard.

6. Colombia continues to levy surcharges on three export products (mild coffee, unset emeralds and coal) to promote the development of these sectors; and it also maintains several export-development programmes. These include the duty-free zone programme, which was revamped in 2005 to bring it into line with the provisions of the WTO Agreement on Subsidies and Countervailing Measures (SCM). The new regime seeks to promote the production of goods and services primarily for external markets, although not exclusively and not necessarily. Goods and services exporters can obtain a full or partial refund of indirect taxes, charges and contributions, by applying for the Tax Reimbursement Certificate (CERT); and they can also benefit from special export programmes (PEX) and from the Vallejo Plan, which grants total tariff and VAT exemption for certain imports.

7. Technical regulations can be drafted by the Standardization Institute (ICONTEC) or by ministries, regulatory commissions or decentralized bodies. Each entity has specific internal procedures for issuing technical regulations. Nonetheless, since 2009, a procedure has been agreed upon for preparing and issuing them, abiding by recommendations on good technical regulation practices. Most technical regulations reflect international standards, or are based on them. During the period 2006-2011, Colombia made 207 notifications to the WTO Information Centre concerning draft technical regulations and their amendments, rejections and implementation. Since the last review, major changes have been made to the accreditation process. Various ministries share responsibility for policy on sanitary and phytosanitary (SPS) measures in Colombia, although the SPS system operates on the basis of harmonizing policies in the different sectors. SPS measures are adopted by the risk assessment agency, where relevant.

8. In 2009 Colombia passed a new law to update regulations governing the protection of competition. It continues to use tax incentives to promote both domestic and foreign investment, along with other programmes to support the development of specific sectors and to improve social and regional equality. Colombia has observer status in the Plurilateral Agreement on Government Procurement. During the review period, it has strengthened its legal and institutional framework for government procurement, in particular by improving transparency, with legal amendments to the public procurement regime being introduced in 2007. Nonetheless, procurement is used as a means to promote domestic industry and employment, mainly through preferences.

9. No major changes were made to the legal framework governing intellectual property during the review period. However, regulatory changes were made to facilitate automated procedures; and at the institutional level the Intersectoral Commission on Intellectual Property (CIPI) was created to coordinate the policies, activities and programmes of public and private institutions dealing with intellectual property.

(2) MEASURES AFFECTING IMPORTS

(i) Customs documentation and procedures

10. Customs procedures are regulated by Decree No. 2.685 of 1999 (and amendments thereto)[1] and by Resolution No. 4240 of 2000. The Directorate of Taxes and National Customs (DIAN) is the institution responsible for customs administration in Colombia.[2]

11. Importers must be enrolled in the Single Tax Register; and if their imports require prior registration, they must also be enrolled as users of the Single Window for Foreign Trade (VUCE). When the f.o.b. value of the import is more than US$1,000, the importer needs the services of a customs agency or a bonded warehouse, which can act as customs agents, to bring the imported merchandise into the country.[3] According to the authorities, customs agents ensure that importers and exporters fulfil existing legal regulations on imports, exports and customs transit, thus minimizing the risks inherent in the activity and avoiding information errors. Importers considered "regular customs users" do not have to use a customs agent and their imports can be cleared immediately (automatic clearance). In the first five working days of each month, regular customs users must submit a consolidated payments statement through the Single Income and Automated Control Services Form (MUISCA) and pay, through a bank or other authorized financial institution, the total amount of

[1] Amended by Decrees Nos. 2.101 of 13 June 2008 and 1.039 of 1 May 2009.

[2] Decree No. 1.071 of 1999.

[3] Title II, Chapter I, Article 10 of Decree No. 2.685 of 26 December 1999 (and amendments thereto).

customs duties and/or penalties specified in the import declarations filed with customs, on which clearance has been obtained during the immediately preceding month.

12. To be recognized and enrolled as a regular customs user, the importer must file an application with the DIAN, subject to the following requirements: (i) in the 12 months prior to the presentation of the application, the applicant must have made imports with an f.o.b. value of at least US$5 million, or imports with this annual average value in the three years preceding the application; (ii) have filed at least 100 import declarations during the 12 months immediately preceding the submission of the application; or (iii) benefit from the development programmes associated with special import-export systems (defined in Decree Law No. 444 of 1967), in which case they must show that during the three years immediately preceding the submission of the application for enrolment (as a regular customs user) they have developed programmes of this nature. They must also show that they had made exports with an f.o.b. value of at least US$2 million in the 12 months immediately preceding the application.[4]

13. Imported goods remain in the customs warehouse while import procedures are being completed.[5] The customs agent must submit the import declaration, accompanied by the following documents: commercial invoice; freight manifest; transport document[6]; shipment list; Andean Value Declaration; and mandate, in the absence of a customs endorsement authorizing a person to carry out the customs procedure and the import declaration is submitted through a customs agent. The following may also be required in certain cases: import registration or permit; certificate of origin; health certificate; prior authorization from the DIAN for the importation of certain goods[7]; and an export declaration or a document accrediting the export operation in the country of origin of the goods in question, in cases where the merchandise will enter under the modality of "re-importation in the same state" or "re-importation for inward processing". Sanitary approval or clearance must be obtained prior to the documentary or physical inspection and before the merchandise clearance decision. This procedure is performed online through the VUCE.[8] Strictly on a contingency basis (when the online system is down), the manual procedure is authorized and the documentation is delivered in person. Once this process has been completed, the customs duties are paid, which can also be done online. Importers can also use the advance import declaration, which streamlines the customs clearance process. Use of the advance declaration is optional, except for imports of footwear, textiles and garments (HS Chapters 50-68), which always require an advance import declaration.[9]

14. Customs duties payable are assessed on the date on which the respective import declaration is presented and accepted. Once the duties have been paid and accredited, a risk analysis is performed

---

[4] Title II, Chapter II, Article 29 of Decree No. 2.685 of 26 December 1999 (and amendments thereto).

[5] The goods may remain in a customs warehouse for one month, renewable for one further month (Article 115 of Decree No. 2.685 of 26 December 1999 (and amendments thereto)).

[6] The transport document could be the bill of lading (maritime transport), the airway bill (air transport), and the freight bill (land transport).

[7] Under Decree No. 1.299 of 2006, individuals or legal entities intending to import textiles, clothing, footwear and accessories (Chapters 50 to 64 of the Customs Tariff) and alcoholic beverages (tariff line 2208, apart from sub-item 2208.90.10.00) must obtain authorization from the DIAN. The permit remains valid for two years, provided the accounting and property requirements are fulfilled as required. The authorization is processed through the Subdirectorate of Customs Registration Management of the Customs Management Directorate, and is decided on within 15 days from the day following the date on which the application is received.

[8] Online information from the Ministry of Trade, Industry and Tourism, "*Ventanilla Única de Comercio Exterior*". Viewed at: http://www.vuce.gov.co.

[9] Information provided by the authorities.

to decide whether the goods can be immediately dispatched (automatic clearance) or whether a documentary inspection (yellow channel) or a physical inspection (red channel) is necessary. The risk analysis system is based on several criteria, taking account of the category of user, the type of merchandise, and the customs post in question. Levels of inspection are established for each customs post through which the importation is effected.[10] The DIAN Selectivity Committee (Resolution No. 2.118 of 1999) defines selectivity criteria and risk profiles.

15. The import regime in Colombia includes the following modalities in addition to ordinary importation: duty-free importation; re-importation for inward processing; re-importation in the same state; importation to fulfil a guarantee; temporary admission for re-exportation in the same state; temporary admission for outward processing; importation involving postal traffic and urgent shipments; urgent deliveries and travellers (Table AIII.1).

16. Goods in customs transit status require an international customs transit declaration (ICTD). This is a standard customs document used by member countries of the Andean Community, containing all the data and information needed for the international customs transit operation. Goods entering Colombia under the international customs transit regime are transported from one customs post to the other, under customs control, without paying any duty. Goods under national customs transit - i.e. goods transported under customs control from one customs post to another in the same country - require a transit declaration. In principle, goods can be received under the transit regime in all Colombian ports, but the DIAN may prohibit or restrict access for reasons of public safety, health, sanitary, zoo-sanitary, phytosanitary or environmental security, pursuant to a request made by the competent authorities, or else when for this is deemed appropriate control reasons. In addition, customs transit is expressly prohibited, among other things, for any merchandise for which importation is prohibited by law[11]; imports of textile material and its manufactures, footwear, garters and similar articles and parts thereof (HS Chapters 50 to 64); and goods that cannot be inviolably sealed, unless a physical inspection of the goods is performed by the customs authority.

(ii) Customs valuation

17. In Colombia imported goods are valued pursuant to Articles 1 to 7 of the WTO Customs Valuation Agreement and Article 6 of Andean Community (CAN) Decision No. 571.[12] Colombia specifies the dutiable base as the c.i.f. value of the transaction.[13] The order of application of Articles 5 and 6 of the WTO Customs Valuation Agreement may be reversed whenever the importer so requests and provided the DIAN gives its consent. Colombia has not used minimum prices since 2003.[14]

18. Colombia continues to use reference prices as control parameters when checking the values declared by importers. Currently there are reference prices for some 50 products, which are updated periodically by the DIAN. Reference prices are used as a basis for calculating the customs value only when the imported merchandise cannot be valued in accordance with Articles 1 to 7 of the WTO Customs Valuation Agreement.[15]

---

[10] Resolution No. 2.118 of 1999.

[11] For example, weapons and explosives, precursors for the manufacture of drugs or narcotics not authorized by the Ministry of Health, and nuclear or toxic waste.

[12] Articles 247 and 248 of Decree No. 2.685 of 1999 and Article 192 of Resolution No. 4.240 of 2000.

[13] CAN Decision No. 571.

[14] WTO document G/VAL/N/4/COL/4 of 21 May 2003.

[15] CAN Resolution No. 846, Community Regulation of Decision No. 571 - Customs value of imported merchandise. Viewed at: http://www.comunidadandina.org/normativa/res/R846sg.pdf.

19. During the review period, the estimated and indicative prices introduced by Colombia as a subcategory of reference prices in 2002 and 2004, respectively[16], were eliminated.[17] These prices were applied to various products as from 2006 (Table III.1). Since 2007, however, the use of indicative prices has been mandatory for certain textile, garment and footwear imports originating from any country, except those which Colombia has signed free trade agreements.

Table III.1
Estimated and indicative prices

Products	Resolution No./date	Origin of the goods	Price		Status as of March 2012
			Est.	Indic.	
Vehicle piston rings, NPR brand	1.576/21.02.2006 2.820/28.03.2006	Japan		X	Repealed[a]
Footwear	7.509/26.06.2007 7.512/26.06.2007 11.414/28.09.2007 11.415/28.09.2007 6.635/24.07.2008	All countries[b]		X	Repealed[a]
	13.565/18.11.2006		X		..
CD-R, CD-RW, DVD-R for the recording of sound and/or image	433/19.11.2008	All countries[b]		X	Repealed[a]
	5.657/16.05.2007	All countries	X		..
Manufactured goods made of textile materials, stockings and socks	7.511/26.06.2007 7.412/12.08.2008 8.812/17.09.2008	All countries[b]		X	Repealed[a]
Exercise/note books	8.761/27.07.2007	All countries[b]	X		Repealed[a]
Electrical appliances	11.413/28.09.2007	All countries[b]		X	Repealed[a]
	5.658/16.05.2007	All countries	X		..
Sunglasses	11.199/16.10.2009	All countries[b]		X	Repealed[a]
Toys, stuffed and unstuffed	4.953/18.05.2006	China; North Korea; Philippines; Hong Kong (Special Administrative Region of China); India; Indonesia; Malaysia; Pakistan; Panama; Republic of Korea; Singapore; Thailand; Chinese Taipei; and Viet Nam		X	Repealed[c]
	4.953/18.05.2006		X		Repealed[d]
Toys, stuffed and unstuffed	434/19.11.2008	All countries[b]		X	Repealed[a]
	13.871/21.11.2006		X		..
Inner tubes and treads for tyres	11.400/28.09.2007 2.671/18.03.2008	All countries[b]		X	Repealed[a]
Manufactures of plastic and other synthetic products	1.907/19.12.2008 3.499/03.04.2009 7.779/24.07.2009 12.110/09.11.2009	All countries[b]		X	Repealed[a]
Leather goods	7.411/12.10.2008 8.568/11.11.2008 781/27.11.2008	All countries[b]		X	Repealed[a]
Water scooters	2.672/18.03.2008	All countries[b]		X	Repealed[a]

[16] Decrees Nos. 1.161 of 2002 and 4.431 (Article 2) of 30 December 2004, amending paragraph 5 of Article 128 of Decree No. 2.685 of 1999.
[17] Decree No. 111 of 2010.

Products	Resolution No./date	Origin of the goods	Price		Status as of March 2012
			Est.	Indic.	
Outboard motors, Yamaha brand, two-stroke	6.645/06.06.2007	All countries	X		Repealed[a]
Paper	3.218 / 06.04.2006	Indonesia and Panama		X	Repealed[c]
	3.218 / 06.04.2006		X		Repealed[d]
Paper	7.513/26.06.2007	All countries[b]		X	Repealed[a]
Batteries	2.866/28.03.2008	All countries[b]	X		Repealed[a]
Expandable polystyrene and its products of polyethylene and polypropylene	6.891/31.07.2008 8.976/22.09.2008	All countries[b]		X	..
Polyethylene and polypropylene	4.449/20.05.2008	All countries[b]		X	..
Textiles	7.510/26.06.2007 11.412/28.09.2007 7.413/12.08.2008 5.516/22.05.2009	All countries[b]		X	Repealed[a]

.. Not available.

a DIAN Resolution No. 000870 of 3 of February 2010.
b Except for countries with which Colombia has signed free trade agreements.
c DIAN Resolution No. 12.956 of 30 October 2006.
d DIAN Resolution No. 12.950 of 30 October 2006.

Source: WTO document WT/DS366/R of 27 April 2009; online information from DIAN, "*Normatividad: normas técnicas: resoluciones*". Viewed at: http://www.dian.gov.co/dian/13Normatividad.nsf/formResoluciones?openform; online information from DIAN, "*Servicio al ciudadano: datos de interés: circulares precios de referencia*". Viewed at: http://www.dian.gov.co/content/servicios/solicitados.htm; and information provided by the Colombian authorities.

20. Estimated and indicative prices were introduced by administrative order as a way of controlling the f.o.b. value declared on imported merchandise.[18] They were applied according to the type of goods, and were calculated on the basis of average international production costs when data on this were available, or else on the basis of the lowest price at which the product had previously been traded or supplied for importation into Colombia.[19] Estimated or indicative prices could be imposed in the following situations: (i) at the request of domestic producers or importers of similar products who considered themselves damaged by unfair competition; (ii) when the customs authorities detected unfair competition practices; or (iii) when the DIAN decided that they were necessary, based on sector studies, risk profiles, or specific policies.[20] Estimated or indicative prices are used for control purposes during the inspection process. When the declared value of the merchandise is called into question, the importer has either two days to submit documents accrediting the declared price, or up to five days to correct the declared value and pay the corresponding customs duties and sales tax. If the importer does not correct the declared value or pay the customs duties and sales tax based on the indicative price, the goods in question have to be reshipped within one month, or else be declared

[18] The "reference price" is defined in Article 237 of Decree No. 2.685 of 1999 as "the price established by the DIAN, used on an indicative basis during the inspection process to check the value declared on identical or similar goods".

[19] The difference between estimated and indicative prices is that the former provide a range of prices and would be applied irrespective of the origin or place of departure of the goods, whereas an indicative price is a single value applicable to goods of a specific origin.

[20] The methodology used to calculate reference prices is described in detail in sections 2.1, 2.2, 2.3 and 3.1 of Article 237 of Decree No. 2.685 of 1999.

"legally abandoned".[21] Should the importer choose to correct the import declaration and pay the customs duties and sales tax based on the indicative prices, the goods will obtain clearance and the relevant documents will be sent to the Customs Inspection Division.[22] This initiates the "subsequent verification" process.[23] If subsequent verification shows that the declared prices were correct, any excess duty paid is refunded. Where the importer does not agree with a DIAN ruling, he may lodge an administrative appeal.

21. In 2005, the DIAN issued the first of several resolutions setting indicative prices for selected products originating in Panama, China and other countries, including certain textiles, garments and footwear classified in HS Chapters 50 to 64. In mid-2005, it also introduced a measure requiring the textiles, garments and footwear in question, originating in or arriving from Panama or China, to be imported exclusively through Bogotá airport or Barranquilla seaport.[24] According to the authorities, this measure was necessary to reduce contraband and under-invoicing. The two measures were the subject of a dispute under the Dispute Settlement Understanding (DSU)[25]; and the first consultation between Panama and Colombia led to the signing of a Customs Cooperation Protocol to prevent customs violations in the two countries.[26] Nonetheless, in 2007 Colombia again introduced indicative prices for textiles, garments and footwear from any country of origin, except those with which it had signed free-trade agreements; and it introduced port restrictions on the importation of textiles, garments and footwear from the Colón Free Zone (ZLC) and Panama. In response to these measures, in 2007 Panama requested consultations with Colombia, thereby launching a dispute settlement process in the WTO, which resulted in the measures being rejected by the Panel that heard the dispute in 2009. Colombia notified the WTO that in 2009 it had repealed the measures restricting the entry of products from Panama to the Bogota and Barranquilla customs posts, authorized goods clearance even when there were doubts about the declared value, and put mechanisms in place to guarantee the payment of customs duties, following the valuation dispute[27]; and that in 2010 it had set up a new risk control system in the customs to implement the Panel rulings.[28] The new system aims to identify the risks and find ways to counteract or prevent them. High-risk operations will be inspected and monitoring mechanisms will be implemented for this purpose. In terms of customs valuation, the system identifies, among other things, distortions in the value of imported goods, either independently or in the context of other irregularities arising during the importation process.

(iii) Rules of origin

22. Colombia does not apply non-preferential rules of origin.[29]

---

[21] Article 115 of Decree No. 2.685 of 1999.

[22] Article 128 of Decree No. 2.685 of 1999.

[23] Article 172 of Resolution No. 4.240 of 2000.

[24] Resolutions Nos. 05796 of 7 July 2005, 12.465 of 21 December 2005 and 06691 of 22 June 2006.

[25] WTO documents WT/DS366/1 of 17 July 2007, WT/DS366/R of 27 April 2009, WT/DS366/R/Corr.1 of 6 May 2009 and WT/DS366/13 of 2 October 2009.

[26] "Protocol on Procedures for Customs Cooperation and Information Exchange between the Customs Authorities of the Republic of Panama and the Republic of Colombia (*Protocolo de Cooperación Aduanera*).

[27] DIAN Resolution No. 13.518 of 11 December 2009 (WTO document WT/DSB/M/279 of 31 March 2010).

[28] Decree No. 111 of 21 January 2010, published in Official Journal (*Diario Oficial*) No. 47.599 of 21 January 2010, Ministry of Finance and Public Credit (WTO document WT/DSB/M/279 of 31 March 2010).

[29] The non-preferential rules of origin contained in Decree No. 2.666 of 1984 of the Ministry of Finance and Public Credit (Article 282-285) notified to the WTO in 1995 (WTO documents G/RO/N/1 of 9 May 1995 and G/RO/N/1/Add.1 of 22 June 1995), are not in force because Decree No. 2.666 of 1984 was repealed by Decree No. 2.685 of 1999.

23. Colombia applies preferential rules of origin in the framework of the regional and bilateral free trade agreements and other preferential agreements it has signed. The general criteria include the value of regional content and change in tariff classification (Table III.2).

Table III.2
Rules of origin criteria

Agreement	Criteria		*De minimis*	Specific requirements of origin
	Value of regional content	Change in classification		
Regional free trade agreement				
Latin American Integration Association (LAIA)	50% of the f.o.b. value. (40% of the f.o.b. value for less developed countries)	Yes		Yes
Andean Community (CAN)	50% of the f.o.b. value.	Yes		Yes
Bilateral free trade agreement				
European Free Trade Association (EFTA)	Between 47% and 67% of the factory gate price[a]	Yes	10% of the factory price or of the weight of fibres or yarns in the case of garments	Yes
Canada	Formula[a] (between 5% and 65% of the transaction price. Between 65% and 70% of the net cost (automotive sector) 45% of the transaction value[b])	Yes	10% of the transaction price; 15% of the weight of fibres or yarns in the case of garments	Yes
Chile	Formula[a] (between 35% and 70% of the f.o.b. value)	Yes	10% of the f.o.b. value, or of the weight of fibres or yarns in the case of garments	Yes
United States	Formula[a] (between 20% and 65% of the f.o.b. value.; 35% of the net cost (automotive sector)	Yes	10% of the adjusted value, or of the weight of fibres or yarns in the case of garments	Yes
Mexico[c]	Formula[d] (between 35% and 55% of the f.o.b. value)	Yes	7% of the f.o.b. value, or of the weight of fibres or yarns in the case of garments	Yes
Northern Triangle of Central America (El Salvador, Guatemala and Honduras)	Formula[d] (between 30% and 50% of the f.o.b. value)	Yes	10% of the f.o.b. value	Yes
European Union	Between 30% and 50% of the factory price depending on the product	Yes	10% of the factory price; 8% of the factory price or 10% of the weight of fibres or yarns in the case of garments	
Partial scope agreement				
CARICOM	50% of the f.o.b. value	Yes		
Costa Rica	50% of the f.o.b. value	Yes		
Nicaragua	50% of the f.o.b. value	Yes		
Panama	40% of the f.o.b. value	Yes		
Economic complementarity agreement				
CAN-MERCOSUR	50% of the f.o.b. value. Until 2012; 55% of the f.o.b. value. As from 2013[e]	Yes		Yes

Agreement	Criteria		De minimis	Specific requirements of origin
	Value of regional content	Change in classification		
Cuba	50% of the f.o.b. value. (40% of the f.o.b. value for less developed countries)	Yes		Yes

a Sets or assortments of goods qualify as originating if the value of the non-originating goods does not exceed 15 per cent of the f.o.b. value.
b Alternative classification criterion except for agricultural products, plastics and plastic manufactures, and textiles and garments.
c Previously the Group of Three. The Bolivarian Republic of Venezuela denounced the free trade agreement and has not been part of it since November 2006.
d Sets or assortments of goods qualify as originating provided the value of the non-originating goods does not exceed 7 per cent of the f.o.b. value.
e The regional content percentage will be 50 per cent of the f.o.b. value, applicable until the seventh year following the entry into force of the Agreement (1 February 2005), and 55 per cent of the f.o.b. value as from the eighth year. Sets or assortments of goods qualify as originating provided the value of the non-originating goods does not exceed 6 per cent of the f.o.b. value.

Note: The agreements signed with the United States and the European Union are not yet in force.

Source: WTO Secretariat on the basis of online information from the Ministry of Trade, Industry and Tourism, "*Comercio Exterior: TLC*". Viewed at: https://www.mincomercio.gov.co/mincomercioexterior/index.php; online information from the Organization of American States (OAS), "*Información sobre Colombia: Acuerdos comerciales*". Viewed at: http://www.sice.oas.org/ctyindex/COL/COLAgreements_s.asp#Inforce; online information from LAIA, "*Integración y Comercio: Acuerdos: Colombia*". Viewed at: http://www.aladi.org/nsfaladi/textacdos.nsf/vpaises/colombia; Ministry of Trade, Industry and Tourism (2007), *Normas de origen, preferencias arancelarias y registro de productores nacionales*. Viewed at: http://www.mincomercio.gov.co/eContent/documentos/comercio/CartillaNormasOrigen.pdf; Commission Regulation (EU) No.1063/2010 of 2010; Plazas Peralta, G.S. (2009), *Normas de origen y acuerdos comerciales*, 2 March, Bogotá Chamber of Commerce. Viewed at: http://camara.ccb.org.co/documentos/5694_normasdeorigeny_acuerdoscomerciales.pdf; and information provided by the Colombian authorities.

24. Colombia has notified the WTO of its preferential rules of origin as specified in the agreements with the Andean Community and LAIA.[30]

25. Specific Requirements of Origin (SROs) can be revised in the different regional agreements. In the Andean Community Framework, the CAN Secretariat can establish and revise them, either at the request of the party or on its own initiative, provided they constitute a tool for economic and technological development of the subregion. When the Secretariat acts on its own initiative, it informs the parties of its motives and requests comments within 20 days.[31] The LAIA Committee of Representatives establishes and modifies SROs at the request of the parties. The Committee may also establish, at the request of parties, SROs for goods produced with materials originating in the participating countries but produced in third parties, provided the value of regional content is 50 per cent of the f.o.b. value.[32] The CAN-MERCOSUR Administration Commission agrees, modifies, or repeals SROs when this is considered justified.[33]

26. As of December 2011, SROs were being applied to some 160 products in the CAN framework[34], and 624 within the LAIA.[35] In addition, specific requirements were being applied

[30] WTO documents G/RO/N/1 of 9 May 1995, G/RO/N/1/Add.1 of 22 June 1995 (CAN) and G/RO/N/12 of 1 October 1996 (LAIA).

[31] For further information, see CAN Decision No. 417 of 1997.

[32] LAIA Resolution No. 252 of 1999.

[33] For further information, see CAN-MERCOSUR Economic Complementarity Agreement No. 59, Annex IV.

[34] For further information on SROs, see Andean Community online information, "*Normas de origen: Requisitos específicos de origen vigentes en la Comunidad Andina*" [Rules of origin: Specific requirements of

to 769 items in trade with Argentina (NALDISA 2007), 1,009 with Brazil, 21 with Paraguay and 48 with Uruguay under the CAN-MERCOSUR Agreement. In the framework of LAIA, Colombia has signed several regional market opening agreements with the Plurinational State of Bolivia, Ecuador and Paraguay. These do not contain any rules-of-origin clause, but encompass products for which member countries unilaterally lift all tariffs and other restrictions, when they are originating. Each Agreement has its own rules of origin regime.[36]

(iv) Tariffs

(a) MFN tariff structure and levels

27. Tariff policy is defined according to the Andean Community framework and guidelines. Colombia applies the CAN Common External Tariff, with certain exceptions; and it uses the Andean countries' Common Tariff Nomenclature (NANDINA), which is based on the Harmonized Commodity Description and Coding System (HS). Colombia only applies *ad valorem* tariffs, for which the duties are calculated on the basis of the c.i.f. value of the goods in question. It implements the Andean Price Band System (SAFP) on imports of various agricultural products, including: palm oil, soybean oil, white rice, white sugar, raw sugar, pigmeat, barley, whole milk, yellow maize, white maize, yellow soya, wheat, and chicken cuts. In 2010, the SAFP was being applied to 163 tariff lines (0.9 per cent of the tariff universe) (Chapter IV(1)).

28. In 2010, the Colombian Tariff contained 7,273 lines at the 2007 HS ten-digit level, compared to 6,993 lines at the time of the last trade policy review in 2006. By April 2011, the number of tariff lines had grown to 7,285; and in August that year, when Colombia implemented its latest tariff reform, the number was 7,292 (Table III.3). The average MFN applied tariff rate rose slightly by 0.2 percentage points from 12 per cent in 2006 to 12.2 per cent in 2010. Nonetheless, following the tariff reform, the average tariff dropped to 8.2 per cent in the first seven months of 2011; and in August that year, the arithmetic mean fell further to 6.2 per cent, as a result of the temporary reduction on certain tariff items (Table III.3).

Table III.3
MFN tariff structure, 2006, 2010 and 2011
(Percentage)

		2006	2010[a]	2011	
				January-July[b]	August-December[b]
1.	Total number of lines	6,993	7,273	7,285	7,292
2.	Non-*ad valorem* tariffs (% of tariff lines)	0.0	0.0	0.0	0.0
3.	Non-*ad valorem* tariffs with no AVEs (% of tariff lines)	0.0	0.0	0.0	0.0
4.	Tariff quotas (% of tariff lines)	0.3	0.1	0.1	0.1
5.	Duty-free tariff lines (% of tariff lines)	3.0	4.2	4.8	47.5
6.	Average lines above zero (%)	12.3	12.7	8.6	11.8
7.	Arithmetic mean	12.0	12.2	8.2	6.2
8.	Agricultural products (WTO definition)	16.5	18.3	14.8	14.5

origin in force in the Andean Community]. Viewed at: http://www.comunidadandina.org/origen.htm; and LAIA Resolution No. 252 of 1999.

[35] For further information on these products see LAIA Resolution No. 252 of 1999, Annex 2.

[36] Online information from LAIA, "*Integración y Comercio: Acuerdos: Disposiciones de Internalización, Sumarios y Textos: Acuerdos Actuales: Colombia*" [Importation provisions, summaries and texts: Current agreements: Colombia]. Viewed at: http://www.aladi.org/nsfaladi/textacdos.nsf/vpaises/colombia.

		2006	2010[a]	2011	
				January-July[b]	August-December[b]
9.	Non-agricultural products (excluding oil)	11.3	11.3	7.2	4.9
10.	Agriculture, hunting, forestry and fishing (ISIC 1)	11.7	11.7	10.1	9.9
11.	Mining (ISIC 2)	5.2	5.2	5.0	1.3
12.	Manufacturing (ISIC 3)	12.1	12.3	8.1	6.0
13.	Raw materials	11.6	11.8	9.9	8.5
14.	Semi-processed products	10.0	9.7	5.2	2.5
15.	Finished products	13.2	13.8	9.6	7.9
16.	Domestic tariff peaks (% of tariff lines)[c]	0.4	0.8	1.4	1.4
17.	International tariff peaks (% of tariff lines)[d]	24.7	25.0	1.6	1.6
18.	Overall standard deviation of applied rates	7.5	9.4	8.6	9.3
19.	Nuisance applied rates (% of tariff lines[e]	0.0	0.0	0.0	0.7
20.	Bound tariff lines (% of tariff lines)	100.0	100.0	100.0	100.0

a Includes the annual average tariffs of the Andean Price Band system (SAFP).
b Includes the six-monthly SAFP averages.
c Domestic tariff peaks are defined as rates exceeding three times the overall simple average of applied rates.
d International tariff peaks are defined as rates exceeding 15 per cent.
e Nuisance rates are above zero, but no more than 2 per cent.

Source: WTO Secretariat calculations, based on data provided by the Colombian authorities.

29. In 2010, Colombia applied 36 different tariff rates, ranging from 0 to 119.11 per cent, when the rates produced by price bands are taken into account; if the latter were not included, the tariff would have 13 different rates, ranging from 0 per cent to 98 per cent. In 2011, both the number of tariff rates applied and the range remained unchanged. Despite the liberalization process, the maximum applied rate actually rose during the review period, from 80 per cent in 2006 to 98 per cent in August 2011. Although only a few tariff lines have applied rates of over 20 per cent, their proportion has increased since 2006. Nonetheless, there has also been a significant increase in the percentage of duty-free tariff lines, from 3 per cent of the total in 2006 to 47.3 per cent in August 2011. This mainly reflects the temporary reduction in tariffs implemented in August 2011, which included a zero rate of duty on raw materials and capital goods not produced in Colombia, which in normal circumstances pay a tariff of 5 per cent Chart III.1).

Chart III.1
Frequency distribution of MFN tariff rates, 2006, 2010 and 2011

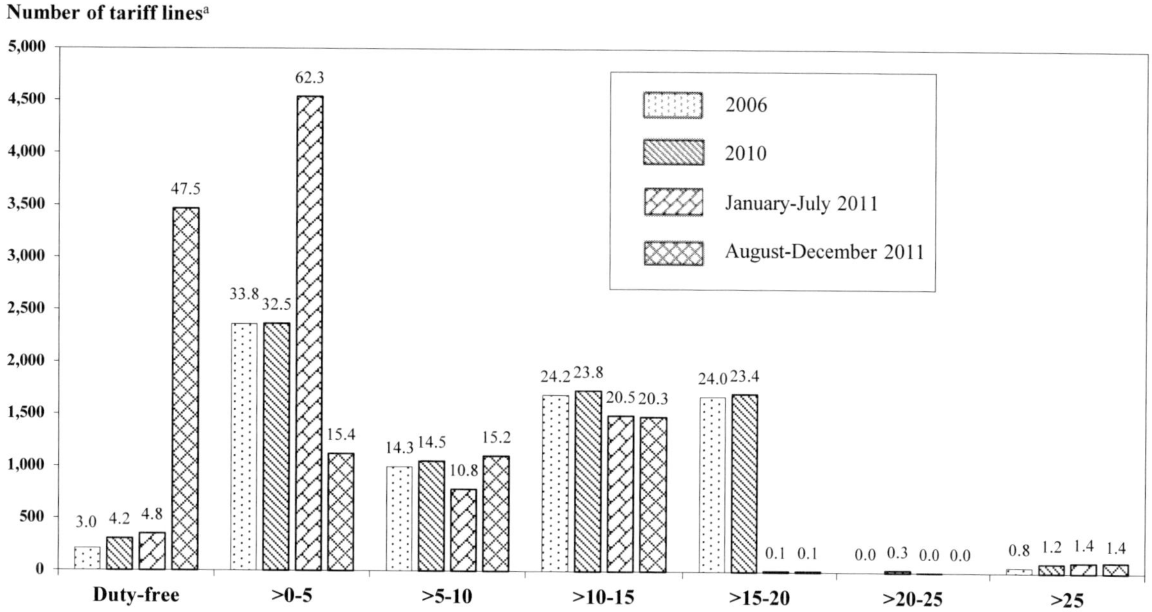

a Total number of tariff lines: 6,993 in 2006; 7,273 in 2010; 7,285 in April 2011 and 7,292 in August 2011.
Note: Figures indicate the percentage of the number of tariff lines.

Source: WTO Secretariat calculations, based on data provided by the Colombian authorities.

30. Agricultural products (WTO definition) continue to enjoy greater protection than non-agricultural goods, and the disparity has widened as a result of the temporary tariff reduction, which mainly affected the industrial sector (Table III.4). The average tariff for agricultural products (WTO definition), which in 2010 was 18.3 per cent, dropped to 14.5 per cent in August 2011, while the average tariff on non-agricultural products fell sharply from 11.3 per cent to 4.9 per cent. Also in August 2011, the highest average tariff per WTO category was applied to agricultural products, specifically animals and products of animal origin, and dairy products, with tariffs of 25.2 per cent and 55.5 per cent, respectively, compared to 32.4 per cent and 58.9 per cent in 2010. This represents a substantial increase on the tariffs applied in 2006, which were 23.6 per cent and 21.2 per cent, respectively. The highest tariff in 2010 was 119.1 per cent, applied to seven lines of HS heading 02.07 (meat and edible offal, of poultry), whereas the maximum tariff in 2011 was 98 per cent (both in the first seven months of the year and after August), applied to 14 lines of the HS heading 04.02 (concentrated milk and cream).

31. The tariff applied by Colombia was until 2008 based on the Andean tariff structure, under which tariffs rise according to the level of processing of the good in question (Decisions Nos. 370, 371 and 465) - except in the case of specific raw materials, imports and capital goods not produced in the Andean subregion. Until a common tariff policy is defined in the CAN framework, Colombia has departed from the negotiated common tariffs and the level-of-processing criterion on which the Andean policy was based. As a result, raw material imports are currently subject to a higher average tariff than semi-processed products.

Table III.4
Summary analysis of the MFN tariff, 2006, 2010 and 2011

Product description	2006		2010[a]		January-July 2011[b]		August-December 2011[b]		Bound tariff
	No. of lines	Average (%)	No. of lines	Average (%)	No. of lines	Average (%)	No. of lines	Average (%)	Range (%)
Total	**6,993**	**12.0**	**7,273**	**12.2**	**7,285**	**8.2**	**7,292**	**6.2**	**15-227**
HS 01-24	989	17.5	1,042	19.2	1,045	15.3	1,045	15.0	15-227
HS 25-97	6,004	11.0	6,231	11.0	6,240	7.0	6,247	4.7	30-180
By WTO category									
Agricultural products	943	16.5	959	18.3	966	14.8	966	14.5	15-227
Animals and products of animal origin	106	23.6	111	32.4	111	28.5	111	25.2	70-209
Dairy products	34	21.3	35	58.9	35	56.2	35	55.5	90-159
Coffee and tea, cocoa, sugar, etc.	171	17.2	180	16.0	181	11.1	181	11.3	70-195
Cut flowers, plants	53	8.4	52	8.7	52	7.5	52	7.5	70-90
Fruit and vegetables	213	17.7	221	17.7	227	15.7	227	15.7	15-178
Cereals	36	20.8	39	19.1	39	14.8	39	15.4	90-194
Oilseeds, oils and fats and products thereof	106	15.0	103	12.1	103	3.8	103	4.1	75-227
Beverages and spirits	52	18.8	54	18.9	54	14.4	54	14.4	70-137
Tobacco	12	16.7	12	16.7	12	12.9	12	12.9	70-70
Other agricultural products n.e.s.	160	10.0	152	9.1	152	8.5	152	8.4	35-151
Non-agricultural products (including petroleum)	6,050	11.3	6,314	11.3	6,319	7.2	6,326	4.9	30-104
Non-agricultural products (excluding petroleum)	6,021	11.3	6,284	11.3	6,289	7.2	6,296	4.9	30-104
Fish and fishery products	138	18.8	168	18.5	164	13.9	164	13.7	35-104
Mineral products, precious stones and precious metals	374	10.0	377	10.1	377	6.1	377	3.6	35-35
Metals	706	10.0	727	10.1	728	5.7	734	3.0	35-35
Chemicals and photographic goods	1,421	7.4	1,525	7.3	1,519	5.1	1,519	2.0	30-70
Leather, rubber, footwear and travel goods	211	13.1	211	13.1	211	8.1	211	6.5	30-35
Wood, wood pulp, paper and furniture	325	12.9	329	12.8	329	7.9	329	6.2	35-35
Textiles and clothing	943	18.3	950	18.3	949	9.7	949	8.7	35-40
Transport equipment	193	14.2	218	14.8	239	13.1	239	11.1	35-40
Non-electrical machinery	759	9.1	800	9.0	793	5.6	794	2.6	35-35
Electrical machinery	406	10.2	410	10.3	410	6.4	410	3.7	35-35
Non-agricultural products n.e.s.	545	10.9	569	11.6	570	9.1	570	7.5	35-35
Petroleum	29	10.0	30	9.7	30	5.0	30	1.0	35-35
By ISIC sector[c]									
Agriculture and fishing	399	11.7	408	11.7	413	10.1	413	9.9	20-194
Mining	110	5.2	108	5.2	108	5.0	108	1.3	35-35
Manufacturing	6,483	12.1	6,756	12.3	6,763	8.1	6,770	6.0	15-227

Product description	2006		2010[a]		January-July 2011[b]		August-December 2011[b]		Bound tariff
	No. of lines	Average (%)	No. of lines	Average (%)	No. of lines	Average (%)	No. of lines	Average (%)	Range (%)
By HS Section									
01 Live animals; animal products	268	20.7	305	27.5	302	23.7	302	22.6	35-209
02 Vegetable products	378	14.6	380	14.4	386	12.3	386	12.5	15-195
03 Fats and oils	62	17.3	64	13.9	64	3.9	64	4.3	75-227
04 Prepared foodstuffs, etc.	281	18.4	293	18.1	293	13.1	293	12.9	35-151
05 Mineral products	194	6.2	192	6.1	192	5.0	192	1.0	35-35
06 Products of the chemical or allied industries	1,340	6.6	1,423	6.3	1,419	4.9	1,419	1.8	30-180
07 Plastic and rubber	298	13.2	317	13.1	315	6.7	315	4.9	30-35
08 Raw hides and skins	80	12.1	78	12.4	78	8.5	78	7.7	35-70
09 Wood and articles of wood	98	12.3	107	12.5	107	6.5	107	5.0	35-35
10 Pulp of wood, paper, etc.	204	12.6	202	12.5	202	8.2	202	6.3	35-35
11 Textiles and textile articles	930	18.1	936	18.1	935	9.6	935	8.6	35-99
12 Footwear, hats and other headgear	58	18.8	56	18.8	56	12.8	56	12.9	35-40
13 Articles of stone	163	13.8	168	13.9	168	6.6	168	5.0	35-35
14 Precious stones, etc.	57	11.1	57	11.1	57	7.1	57	4.2	35-35
15 Base metals and articles of base metal	690	10.4	713	10.5	714	5.9	720	3.4	35-35
16 Machinery and mechanical appliances	1,199	9.4	1,236	9.3	1,229	5.9	1,230	3.1	35-35
17 Transport equipment	205	14.1	230	14.6	251	12.8	251	10.7	35-40
18 Precision instruments	303	6.9	285	7.1	285	5.6	285	2.8	35-40
19 Arms and ammunition	28	18.2	69	17.5	69	14.9	69	14.9	35-35
20 Miscellaneous manufactured articles	150	17.9	155	18.0	156	13.1	156	13.0	35-40
21 Works of Art	7	20.0	7	20.0	7	15.0	7	15.0	35-35
By state of processing									
First stage of processing	810	11.6	843	11.8	845	9.9	845	8.5	15-194
Semi-processed products	2,348	10.0	2,429	9.7	2,425	5.2	2,431	2.5	30-195
Fully processed products	3,835	13.2	4,001	13.8	4,015	9.6	4,016	7.9	35-227

a Includes the annual average tariffs of the Andean Price Band System (SAFP).
b Includes the semi-annual tariffs of the SAFP.
c ISIC (Rev.2), except for electricity (one line).

Source: WTO Secretariat estimates, based on data supplied by the Colombian authorities.

(b) Tariff quotas

32. During the review period, Colombia notified some products subject to tariff quotas in 2006-2010 to the WTO, including meats, dairy products, grains and cereals, soya, oils and fats, and cotton.[37] Apparently, Colombia does not make use of these quotas because the applied tariff is below the in-quota tariff.

[37] WTO documents G/AG/N/COL/37 of 9 October 2009, G/AG/N/COL/41 of 13 January 2011 and G/AG/N/COL/47 of 25 November 2011.

33. In 2010-2011, Colombia opened quotas for five products, of which all except whey (HS sub-category 0404.10.10.00) are covered by the Government Mechanism for Administering Agricultural Quotas (MAC) (Table III.5) (Chapter IV). This mechanism was established in 2004 for imports from non-CAN member countries and is applicable to 11 tariff lines including the following agricultural products: yellow flint maize, white flint maize, rice, sorghum, soybeans and cotton.[38] Although the mechanism cannot be applied in a way that is incompatible with the free trade agreements currently in force in Colombia[39], the importer is required to also purchase national output if the imports are processed within the quota.

34. Most products subject to tariff quotas are also covered by the price band system: 157of the 163 tariff lines covered by the price band are also subject to a tariff quota. In addition, of the four products for which Colombia opened a tariff quota under the MAC in 2010 and 2011, three of them (yellow flint maize, white flint maize, and soybeans) are also covered by the price band (Table III.5). Following application of the price band system, the applied tariffs were zero in some cases in 2011 which made the quota redundant, since the imports were made at that tariff rate. Moreover, in the case of white flint maize (HS line 1005.90.12.00), the SAFP was suspended in 2011, and the out-of-quota MFN tariff was applied. For other products (yellow flint maize and beans), although the price band system continues to be used, it was decided in 2011 that if the tariff calculated by the SAFP was below the maximum tariff (5 per cent in 2011), then the latter would be used.

Table III.5
Tariff quotas, 2010-2011

Tariff line	Description	Year	Volume (tonnes)		In-quota tariff	Out-of-quota tariff			
			Quota	Imports[a]		Excl. SAFP	Incl. SAFP		
							2010[b]	Jan-Jul 2011[c]	Aug-Dec 2011[d]
0404.10.10.00	Whey partly or totally de-mineralized, whether or not concentrated or containing added sugar or other sweetening matter	2010[e] 2011[e]	3,000 3,000	600 597	20 20	94 94	94	 94	 94
1005.90.11.00	Flint maize, yellow	2010[f] 2011[g]	2,600,000 2,040,000	1,719,448 1,152,040	5 0	15 5[h]	11.5	 5	 5[i]
1005.90.12.00	Flint maize, white	2010[f] 2011[g]	123,000 80,000	65,500 51,831	0 0	40 40	37.9	 40[j]	 40[j]
1201.00.90.00	Other beans (*poroto, frijol, frejol* beans) soybeans, whether or not broken	2010[f] 2011[g]	300,000 300,000	232,890 166,154	2 0	12 5[h]	10.1	 5	 5[i]

[38] Decree No. 430 of 2004.

[39] Information provided by the authorities.

Tariff line	Description	Year	Volume (tonnes)		In-quota tariff	Out-of-quota tariff			
			Quota	Imports[a]		Excl. SAFP	Incl. SAFP		
							2010[b]	Jan-Jul 2011[c]	Aug-Dec 2011[d]
5201.00.30.00	Cotton, not carded or combed, of yarn length greater than 22.22 mm but not longer than 28.57 mm	2010[k] 2011[g]	52,000 0	57,229 32,920	0 0	10 5	10	5	5

a Corresponds to total imports made.
b Tariffs subject to the SAFP are calculated on the basis of the MFN tariff of 2010.
c Tariffs subject to the SAFP are calculated on the basis of the MFN tariff of July-August 2011.
d Tariffs subject to the SAFP are calculated on the basis of the MFN tariff of August-December 2011.
e Decree No. 2.112 of 2009 suspends the SAFP.
f Decree No. 4.551 of 2009 establishes the annual quotas and in-quota tariffs.
g Decree No. 4.662 of 2010 establishes the annual quotas and in-quota tariffs.
h The tariff for this product is subject to the SAFP.
i Decree No. 14 of 2010 establishes in-quota tariffs and Decree No. 4.900 of 2011 establishes the annual quotas and in-quota tariffs.
j The SAFP was suspended in 2011.
k Decree No. 760 of 2009 sets cotton quotas and the in-quota tariff.

Source: Ministry of Agriculture and Rural Development; and information provided by the Colombian authorities.

35. Colombia has also negotiated tariff quotas for agricultural products under several preferential agreements (Table III.6).

Table III.6
Preferential agricultural quotas, 2006-2011
(Tonnes, unless indicated otherwise)

Tariff line	Product	Year	Quota volume	Country subject to the quota	Import volume[a]	Tariff quota		Decree No.
						In	Out	
0201.30.00.10	Meat of bovine animals, fresh or chilled, boneless, thin cut	2006 2007 2008 2009 2010 2011	3,713 3,825 3,939 4,057 4,179 4,305	MERCOSUR	40 223 111 228 181 59	14 13 11 10 8	55 50 46 41 37 32	141 of 2005
0201.30.00.90 0202.30.00.10 0202.30.00.90 0206.10.00.00 0206.21.00.00 0206.22.00.00 0206.29.00.00 0210.20.00.00 0504	Meat of bovine animals, frozen, bovine offal and intestines	2006 2007 2008 2009 2010 2011	2,601 2,653 2,706 2,760 2,815 2,872	MERCOSUR	2,081 2,603 2,291 3,224 2,795 671	13.8[b]-16[c] 12.6[b]-14.6[c] 11.4[b]-13.2[c] 10.2[b]-12[c] 9.2[b]-10.6[c] 8[b]-9.2[c]	64[b]-67.9[c] 64[b]-67.2[c] 65[b]-66.5[c] 66[b]-65.8[c] 67[b]-65.3[c] 64[b]-64.7[c]	141 of 2005
0402	Milk	2006 2007 2008 2009 2010 2011	3,606 3,716 3,827 3,942 4,060 4,182	MERCOSUR	22 0 74 325 200 1,601	15 5.6 0 34 14.6 8.2	98 98 98 98 98 98	141 of 2005
1602.10.00.00 1602.49.00.00 1602.50.00.00, 1602.90.00.00	Prepared or preserved meat	2006 2007 2008 2009 2010 2011	7,427 7,649 7,880 8,114 8,358 8,610	MERCOSUR	40 365 316 545 366 119	16[d]- [e] 15[d]-13[e] 13[d]-11[e] 12[d]-10[e] 11[d]-9[e] 9[d]-8[e]	16[d]; Br[e] 15[d]; 13[e] 13[d]; 11[e] 12[d]; 10[e] 11[d]; 9[e] 9[d]; 8[e]	141 of 2005

Tariff line	Product	Year	Quota volume	Country subject to the quota	Import volume[a]	Tariff quota		Decree No.
						In	Out	
1704[f]	Sugar confection (incl. white chocolate), no cocoa	2006	137	MERCOSUR	184	10	20	141 of 2005
		2007	140		188	7	20	
		2008	143		115	3.4	20	
		2009	146		196	0	20	
		2010	146		159	0	20	
		2011	146		430	0	20	
1806[f]	Chocolate and other food products containing cocoa	2006	241	MERCOSUR	202	10	20	141 of 2005
		2007	246		230	7	20	
		2008	251		206	3.4	20	
		2009	256		148	0	20	
		2010	256		119	0	20	
		2011	256		98	0	20	
1901.10.10.00	Food preparations for infant use, prepared for retail sale; milk formulas for infants	2006	300	MERCOSUR	673	0	16	141 of 2005
		2007	300		1,445	0	15	
		2008	300		1,105	0	13	
		2009	300		1,125	0	12	
		2010	300		1,275	0	11	
		2011	300		906	0	9	
2208.90.10.00 (millions of litres)	Other Ethyl Alcohol (Strength of Less than 80 degrees), Liqueurs	2010	12.0	Northern Triangle of Central America	0	0	20	4.768 of 2009
		2011	12.6		0	0	15	
2309.10.90.00	Other dog or cat food for retail sale	2010	2,400	Guatemala	0	0	16	4.768 of 2009
		2011	2,448					
		2010	1,000	Honduras	0	0	5	
		2011	1,000					

a Corresponds to total imports made from countries subject to the quota.
b Bovine meat and offal.
c Bovine intestines. The tariff is calculated on the basis of the tariff reduction programme contained in Economic Complementarity Agreement No. 59 between MERCOSUR States parties and members of CAN.
d Argentina, Paraguay and Uruguay. The tariff is calculated on the basis of the tariff reduction programme contained in Economic Complementarity Agreement No. 59 between MERCOSUR States parties and members of CAN.
e Brazil. The tariff is calculated on the basis of the tariff reduction programme contained in Economic Complementarity Agreement No. 59 between MERCOSUR States parties and members of CAN.
f For Argentina only.

Source: Ministry of Agriculture and Rural Development; and information provided by the Colombian authorities.

(c) Tariff bindings

36. Colombia bound all of its tariffs in the Uruguay Round at rates varying between 15 per cent and 227 per cent (Table III.4). Roughly 81 per cent of the tariff universe is bound at rates between 30 per cent and 35 per cent, while 6.3 per cent is bound at higher levels varying between 85 and 227 per cent. Bound tariffs on agricultural products range between 15 per cent and 227 per cent, whereas the rates for non-agricultural products are between 30 per cent and 104 per cent. The highest bound rate of 104 per cent is levied on fish and fish products.

(d) Preferential tariffs

37. Colombia grants preferential treatment to all imports from the Plurinational State of Bolivia, Ecuador and Peru, provided they fulfil the Andean Community's origin requirements.[40] Colombia also grants preferential treatment to imports from countries with which it has signed agreements in the LAIA framework and under other bilateral agreements (see Chapter II). The preferences granted to the Bolivarian Republic of Venezuela as a former CAN member were extended by Colombia until the partial-scope agreement being negotiated within LAIA comes into force.[41]

38. The average of preferential tariffs applied per country varies from 0.2 per cent (August version), for its Andean Community partners, to 4.6 per cent for CARICOM member countries, with average rates of 6 per cent for Panama and 6.3 per cent for countries such as Costa Rica and Nicaragua. In these three cases, the preferences cover a very small proportion of the tariff universe - 221 tariff lines in the case of Panama, 46 in the case of Costa Rica, and just 34 tariff lines for Nicaragua. The preferential tariffs applied on agricultural products are nearly always substantially higher than those applied to non-agricultural products, except for CAN countries (Table III.7).

Table III.7
Summary of preferential tariffs, August 2011

		Total		WTO categories			
				Agricultural products		Non-agricultural products (excl. oil)	
	Preferential lines[a] (% of total tariff lines)	Average (%)	Tariffs with preference (%)	Average (%)	Tariffs with preference (%)	Average (%)	Tariffs with preference (%)
MFN		6.2	47.5	14.5	2.9	4.9	54.2
Regional agreements[b]							
CARICOM	17.5	4.4	61.1	8.9	41.2	3.8	64.0
Andean Community	74.9	0.3	97.8	0.8	96.2	0.2	98.0
Northern Triangle of Central America							
El Salvador	73.3	3.7	71.9	9.1	48.2	2.9	75.4
Guatemala	73.4	3.6	72.0	9.1	47.7	2.8	75.5
Honduras	85.7	2.5	80.7	8.5	48.7	1.6	85.5
LAIA agreements[b]							
Argentina	98.1	2.1	55.2	5.0	43.8	1.6	56.8
Brazil	99.6	2.2	59.7	5.0	41.7	1.8	62.3
Chile	98.7	0.4	97.1	2.9	81.4	0.0	99.6
Cuba	82.2	4.5	53.9	10.7	14.7	3.6	59.8
Mexico	97.7	0.9	94.8	6.2	64.3	0.1	99.4
Paraguay	99.6	1.3	57.6	4.1	40.6	0.9	60.1
Uruguay	97.2	1.7	60.8	5.3	42.5	1.2	63.4
Bilateral agreements[b]							
Costa Rica	0.6	6.2	47.5	14.3	2.9	4.9	54.2
Nicaragua	0.5	6.2	47.6	14.4	3.1	4.9	54.3

[40] CAN, Press communiqué, "*Perú completó su plena incorporación a la zona of libre comercio andina*" [Peru completes full integration into the Andean Free Trade Zone], 10 January 2006. Viewed at: http://www.comunidadandina.org/prensa/notas/np10-1-06.htm.

[41] CAN Decision No. 746 of 27 April 2011.

		Total		WTO categories			
				Agricultural products		Non-agricultural products (excl. oil)	
	Preferential lines[a] (% of total tariff lines)	Average (%)	Tariffs with preference (%)	Average (%)	Tariffs with preference (%)	Average (%)	Tariffs with preference (%)
Panama	3.0	5.9	49.6	13.9	6.1	4.7	56.2

a The August 2011 MFN contains 7,292 tariff lines.
b In cases where a country has several preferential agreements with Colombia, and different preferential tariffs are applied to the same product under the different agreements, the highest preference was used in each case to calculate the average preferential tariff.

Source: WTO Secretariat estimates, based on data provided by the Colombian authorities.

(e) Tariff concessions

39. Colombia offers tariff concessions to importers under the various export promotion programmes (Special Import-Export Systems, Free Zones, and Special Economic Export Zones (see section (3)(iv)) and the various import procedures or customs regimes (Table AIII.1). These regimes provide for relief from payment of duties and other taxes on goods imports under certain conditions.

40. Decree No. 4.743 of 2005 made it possible to grant tariff exemptions, for a five-year period (2005-2010), on imports of machinery, equipment and spare parts intended for the extraction, treatment, processing and transport of minerals and the recovery, pipeline transport and refining of hydrocarbons. The decree lists the products that are subject to tariff exemptions.[42] Although these exemptions were repealed as originally envisaged, a 50 per cent exemption was applied to the current tariff for imports of 21 tariff lines at the ten-digit level from 2011 to 2015, including machinery, equipment, and spares intended for the extraction, treatment, processing and transport of minerals and the recovery, pipeline transport and refining of hydrocarbons.[43] Under Andean Community regulations, Colombia is only authorized to grant these exemptions having previously confirmed a shortage of subregional supply, and only when the imports were made by government entities or enterprises that directly engage in activities of exploration, extraction, treatment, processing and transport, or refinery of products from the coal and hydrocarbons industry.[44]

41. The CAN Economic Complementarity Agreement for the Automotive Sector, in force from 2000 to 2011, granted a suspension of import duties on spares and parts intended for use in vehicle production and assembly, for automobile manufacturers requesting this.[45] This enabled assembly firms to incorporate subregional and imported material, and allowed the vehicle produced to circulate in the subregion duty-free. The agreement is currently being renegotiated.[46]

[42] Decree No. 4.743 of 30 December 2005 (viewed at: http://www.presidencia.gov.co/prensa_new/Decreeslinea/2005/diciembre/30/dec4743301205.pdf), and Decree No. 260 of 2005 (Tariff exemption for the activities of mining and oil companies).

[43] Decrees Nos. 562 of 2 March 2011 and 1.570 of 13 May 2011.

[44] CAN Resolution No. 969 (Authorization for Colombia to grant tariff exemptions in the hydrocarbons). Viewed at: http://www.comunidadandina.org/normativa/res/r969sg.htm.

[45] Complementarity Agreement in the Automotive Sector. Viewed at: http://www.comunidadandina.org/normativa/tratprot/conv_automotor.htm.

[46] Information provided by the authorities.

(v) Other charges on imports

(a) Value added tax (VAT)

42. Value-added tax, also known as "sales tax" in Colombia[47], is charged on the value of the imported product including tariffs.[48] Nonetheless, when the import value also includes the provision of a service, the tax base is determined pursuant to the provisions of the WTO Customs Valuation Agreement.[49] In the specific case of beer, VAT is charged on the "retail price" and not on the customs value. The "retail price" is calculated differently depending on whether the beer is produced in Colombia or imported. Whereas the retail price of imported beer is the customs value, including tariffs plus a 30 per cent profit margin, the retail price of domestically produced beer is the price invoiced to the distributor.[50]

43. Since 2006, the general VAT rate has been 16 per cent, with a number of exceptions.[51] Certain products are taxed at rates between 10 per cent and 35 per cent (Table III.8). During the review period, these rates, and the products to which they apply, have changed.[52] For example, VAT on beer was raised from 11 per cent in 2006 to 14 per cent between July and December 2010; and since 2011, it has been subject to the general rate of 16 per cent (Table III.8).[53] In addition, the 2 per cent rate charged on live animals (HS headings 01.02, 01.03, 01.04, 01.05, 01.06, 03.01) was repealed December 2006[54], and VAT on these products is currently charged at 16 per cent.

44. Both national and imported products are liable for VAT; and since 2006 the same rates have charged on domestic and imported products alike (Table III.8).[55] In the case of beer, however, there could be a difference in VAT incidence since the tax base for imported beers is calculated differently from that applicable to domestically produced beers.[56]

Table III.8
Other VAT rates

HS Code	Description	Rate	
		Imports	National production
0901	Coffee, whether or not roasted or decaffeinated; coffee husks or skins; coffee substitutes containing coffee in any proportion, including soluble coffee	10%	10%
1001	Wheat and meslin		
1005	Maize for industrial use		
10.06	Rice for industrial use		
1101	Wheat or meslin flour		
11.02	Other cereal flours		
1209.99.90.00	Seeds for sugar cane		

47 DINA (2009).
48 Tax Statute, Article 459.
49 Tax Statute, Article 459.
50 Tax Statute, Article 475 and Law No. 223 of 1995, Article 189.
51 Tax Statute, Article 468.
52 For further information on the rates in force in 2006, see WTO (2006).
53 Tax Statute, Article 475.
54 Tax Statute, Article 468-2 and Law No. 1.111 of 2006, Article 78.
55 Tax Statute, Articles 468-1, 471, 473 and 475 and WTO (2006).
56 Tax Statute, Articles 468-1, 471, 473 and 475.

HS Code	Description	Rate	
		Imports	National production
1601	Sausages and similar products, of meat, meat offal or blood, food preparations based on those products		
1602	Other prepared and preserved meat, meat offal or blood		
1701	Cane or beet sugar		
1702.30.20.00	Glucose syrups		
1702.30.90.00	Other		
1702.40.20.00	Glucose syrups		
1702.60.00.00	Other fructose, fructose syrup (fructose content in dry state more than 50% by weight)		
1703	Molasses from the extraction or refining of sugar		
1803	Cocoa paste, defatted or not		
1805	Cocoa powder, not sweetened		
1806	Chocolate & other food products containing cocoa, except chewing gum, sweets, candy, toffees and chocolate bars		
1902.11.00.00	Pastas uncooked, without filling, not otherwise prepared, containing egg		
1902.19.00.00	Other		
1905	Bakery, pastry, cakes, biscuits and other bakers' wares, whether or not containing cocoa; except bread		
5201	Cotton fibre		
2203	Beer	16%	16%
8703	Camper vehicles with an f.o.b. value or equivalent thereof, as the case may be, of less than US$30,000, including bodywork, chassis and cabins	20%	20%
8903	Vessels for pleasure or sport		
8703	Vehicles with an f.o.b. value or equivalent thereof, as the case may be, of less than US$30,000, including bodywork, chassis and cabins, except camper vehicles	25%	25%
8711.30.00.00 8711.40.00.00 8711.50.00.00	Motorcycles and scooters, with cylinder capacity exceeding 185 cc		
2208	Ethyl alcohol, un-denaturalized, of less than 80% alcohol strength by volume; "*aguardientes*", liqueurs, and other spirits; mixed alcoholic preparations of a kind used to manufacture beverages, other than "*sabajaones*", cream punches and aperitifs of less than 20° strength	35%	35%
8802	Private aircraft		
8703	Automobiles and pick-up trucks with an f.o.b. value or equivalent thereof, as the case may be, of less than US$30,000, including bodywork, chassis and cabins		

Source: Tax Statute, Articles 468-1, 471, 473 and 475.

45. Certain imported products that are not produced in Colombia are exempt or excluded from the payment of VAT (Table III.9).[57] For an importer to be able to be excluded from VAT payment, the Ministry of Trade, Industry and Tourism (MCIT) must certify that there is no domestic production of the product it is intended to import, before the importation takes place.[58] Also excluded from VAT payment are imported products covered by programmes aimed at supporting exports or basic industries (Table III.9).[59] Beer imports in the departments of San Andrés, Providencia and

[57] Tax Statute, Article 482-1.
[58] Tax Statute, Articles 428 and 482-1.
[59] Tax Statute, Article 428.

Santa Catalina are VAT-exempt[60], as are imports of consumer goods from firms based in Leticia (department of Amazonas).[61]

Table. III.9
VAT-exempt imports

Materials to be processed under special import and export programmes or under the Vallejo Plan
Articles intended for use by the official foreign diplomatic or consular service and foreign technical missions
Weapons and ammunition for national defence
Temporary imports of heavy machinery for basic industries[a]
Machinery or equipment for the recycling and processing of garbage or waste, and for purifying or treating wastewaters, atmospheric emissions or solid wastes, provided they form part of a programme approved by the Ministry of the Environment
Equipment for environmental control and monitoring, including that needed to comply with the Montreal Protocol
Industrial machinery intended for use in the processing of raw materials, when imported by "high export users" (ALTEX)[b]
Goods and equipment under the framework of agreements, treaties, or international agreements destined for the national government or a national public entities, excluding state industrial and commercial firms, and semi-public companies
Machinery and equipment intended for use in activities that help reduce greenhouse gas emissions

a Mining, hydrocarbons, heavy chemicals, iron and steel, extractive metallurgy, electricity generation and distribution and catchment, purification and transport of water.

b ALTEX users have to show that their annual exports represent 30 per cent of their total sales value. In addition, the imported machinery must remain in their ownership for a period of not less than its useful life, and may not be transferred for third party use, except in the case of transfer to a leasing company, with the aim of obtaining financing through a leasing contract. Failure to comply with these obligations by ALTEX results in the reassessment of unpaid VAT plus overdue interest, and the payment of a fine of 5 per cent of the f.o.b. value of the imported machinery.

Source: Tax Statute, Article 428.

(b) Other taxes

46. Colombia also taxes the consumption of certain products, both imported and domestic. Consumption tax is charged on: beer (bottled or draught), shandy and mixtures of alcoholic and non-alcoholic beverages; spirits, wines and similar aperitifs.[62] Although the consumption tax on beers is collected nationally, the central government transfers the revenue collected to the departments, on condition that it is used to finance public health.[63]

47. The consumption tax base varies by product and may be the retail price or the price of sale to the public (Table III.10).[64] In general, the tax base and rates do not vary according to the product's origin.[65] Nonetheless, when the tax base is the retail price, as in the case of beer, the calculation depends on whether it is an imported variety or not. The retail price of imported beer is defined as the customs value, including tariffs, plus a marketing margin of 30 per cent; whereas the retail price of domestically produced beer is the amount invoiced to the distributor.[66] In the case of wines and spirits of an alcohol strength of 20° to 35°, the National Administrative Department of Statistics (DANE) specifies the retail price. The DANE also sets the retail price and price of sale to the public each

[60] Tax Statute, Article 475. Excluded goods are not liable for VAT, while exempt goods are zero-rated (DINA, 2009).

[61] Law No. 488 of 1998, Article 112 and DINA (2009).

[62] Law No. 223 of 1995, Chapters VII, VIII and IX.

[63] Law No. 223 of 1995, Article 185, 202 and 207 and Instituto de Ciencia Política (2009).

[64] Law No. 223 of 1995, Articles 189 and 205 and Law No. 1.111 of 2006, Article 76.

[65] Law No. 223 of 1995, Articles 189 and 205 and Law No. 1.111 of 2006, Article 76.

[66] Law No. 223 of 1995, Articles 189 and 205.

semester.[67] The price of sale to the public for cigarettes and manufactured tobacco is calculated according to a formula, depending on brand and type of product (filtered, etc.).[68]

Table III.10
Consumption tax, 2007 and 2011

Products	Tax base	Rates	
		2007	2011
Beers, aerated waters, shandies, and mixtures of alcoholic and non-alcoholic beverages			
Beers and shandies	Retail price	48%	48%
Shandies and mixtures	Retail price	20%	20%
Spirits, wines and similar aperitifs			
Alcohol strength 2-5° to 15°	Retail price	20%	Col$256
Alcohol strength 15° to 20°	Retail price	25%	Col$256
Alcohol strength 20° to 35°	Retail price	35%	Col$256
Alcohol strength over 35°	Retail price	40%	Col$386
Cigarettes and manufactured tobacco			
Cigarettes, tobaccos, cigars and "cigarritos" (pack of 20)	Price of sale to the public	..	Col$570
Chewing tobacco (gramme)	Price of sale to the public	..	Col$36

.. Not available.

Source: Law No. 223 of 1995, Articles 190 and 206; Law No. 1.393 of 2010, Articles 5 and 8, and information provided by the Colombian authorities.

48. Since 2010, cigarettes and manufactured tobacco, both foreign and domestic, have been subject to a consumption surcharge - equivalent to 10 per cent of the price of sale to the public (as defined by the DANE), for cigarettes, and 10 per cent of the consumption tax per gramme of chewing tobacco.[69] Colombia's departments mainly use the revenue obtained from the tax to finance public health-care services.[70]

49. Colombia also levies a global tax on petrol (gasoline) and engine fuel oils, whether domestic or imported. The tax is levied on petrol (regular and extra) and engine fuel oils, and on any other type of petroleum derivative that is used as a motor fuel.[71] It is a specific tax charged per gallon (Table III.11).[72] Petrol and engine fuel oils, whether imported or domestically produced, are also subject to a consumption surcharge of 25 per cent, based on the monthly price of sale to the public defined by the Ministry of Mines and Energy, which mainly takes account of production costs and producers' profit margins, together with international prices.[73]

---

[67] Law 2 No. 23 of 1995, Article 205 and Law No. 1.111 of 2006, Article 76.

[68] For further information on the formula, see Decree No. 4.676 of 2006, Article 1. Also see online information from DANE on cigarette and tobacco prices "*Información DANE: Económicas: Precios: Cigarrillos y Tabaco*". Viewed at: http://www.dane.gov.co/index.php?option=com_content&view=article&id=347&Itemid=76.

[69] Law No. 1.393 of 2010, Article 6.

[70] Law No. 1.393 of 2010, Article 7.

[71] Law No. 223 of 1995, Article 58.

[72] Law No. 681 of 2001, Article 6.

[73] Online information from the District Finance Secretariat of Bogotá, "*Impuesto Sobretasa a la Gasolina*". Viewed at: http://www.Bogotá.gov.co/portel/libreria/php/frame_detalle_scv.php?h_id=23651.

Table III.11
Global tax on petrol (gasoline) and fuel oils for motors, 2006 and 2011
(Col$/gallon)

	2006	2011
Petrol, "Regular"	651.97	785.52
Petrol, "Extra"	749.77	903.36
ACPM	432.11	484.17

Source: WTO (2006), *Trade Policy Review: Colombia* and information provided by the Colombian authorities.

(vi) Import prohibitions

50. Colombia continues to prohibit the importation of certain goods on grounds of public health or morals, for environmental protection and national security reasons, and to fulfil commitments under the international agreements to which Colombia is a signatory, such as the Montreal Protocol of 1987. In particular, there is a ban on the importation of chemical, biological and nuclear weapons, and on nuclear and toxic waste[74], and warlike toys.[75] Colombia can impose temporary import bans to eliminate the risks to affect human, animal and plant health.

(vii) Licences, registration and other requirements

51. Colombia applies an automatic licensing system, referred to as "free importation", as well as a non-automatic licensing system, known as "prior licensing". Licences are applied irrespective of the origin of the product in question. Colombia informed the WTO that the import licensing regime did not change significantly during the review period. Nonetheless, changes have been made in terms of the locations through which goods can be imported, the cost of the procedure, extensions of licence validity, and the products subject to non-automatic licensing.[76]

52. According to information provided by the authorities, in 2011 there were 2,939 tariff lines subject to automatic licensing, and 188 subject to non-automatic licensing, compared to 2,844 and 185, respectively in 2006. These increases are explained by the fact that a non-automatic licence has been required since 2010 to import certain precursors for narcotics production[77], while the number of tariff lines subject to automatic licensing requirements has increased owing to a change in tariff classification.[78]

(a) Automatic licences

53. Automatic licences are used to implement regulations which, among other things, protect animal and plant health, security and the environment. An automatic licence (also referred to as import registration), is required for imports requiring prior approval by government authorities.[79] Any

[74] Article 81 of the Political Constitution.

[75] Laws Nos. 18 of 1990 and 42 of 1985.

[76] WTO documents G/LIC/N/3/COL/9 of 10 October 2011, G/LIC/N/2/COL/1 of 6 October 2011, G/LIC/N/3/COL/8 of 19 April 2010, G/LIC/N/3/COL/7 of 17 March 2009 and G/LIC/N/1/COL/2 of 8 October 2007.

[77] Decree No. 3.990 of 27 October 2010.

[78] Information provided by the authorities.

[79] An automatic licence (import registration) is needed to import goods subject to quota in respect of quantitative safeguards; fishery resources, private surveillance and security equipment, radioactive isotopes and radioactive material; clothing and accessories for exclusive use by law enforcement agencies; hydrocarbons and petrol; and for products subject to sanitary controls aimed at preserving human, plant and animal health, the

authorization or permit required for the goods to be imported, such as sanitary or phytosanitary certificates, must be obtained before applying for the import licence.

54. The MCIT Foreign Trade Directorate is the authority responsible for processing licences (import registration). These can be applied for at any time of the year and must be processed online through the VUCE. This process must be carried out at least two days before the goods are collected. If the goods arrive at port without a licence (import registration) the importation can still be processed. If the licence is not issued owing to the lack of an approval or justifying document, the goods have to be re-exported or abandoned. At the present time, these licences (registrations) are issued within the space of one day and cost roughly US$15.

55. Automatic import licences are valid for six months from the date of their issuance, except for those needed to import capital goods, which last for 12 months. The validity of the licences can be extended for three months, except for those covering specially manufactured capital goods or products that are hard to obtain on the international market owing to a supply shortage. In such cases, further extensions can be granted for successive periods of up to three months each, but not exceeding six months in total.[80] The licences can be modified, and there is no penalty if they are not used.

(b) Non-automatic licences

56. Colombia maintains a system of non-automatic import licences (or prior licences) for the purpose of controlling imports of a kind that need special import controls. Decree Law No. 444 of 1967, Law No. 7 of 1991 and Decree No. 3.803 of 2006, *inter alia*, constitute the legal basis for licensing.[81] However, the authorities have noted that some criteria and conditions listed in Decree Law No. 444 of 1967 are not currently being applied due to changed economic and commercial circumstances.[82] The Higher Council for Foreign Trade draws up a list of these products.[83] Imports subject to the prior licensing regime include: goods classified for national security reasons; chemical products used in the manufacturing and processing of narcotic drugs; defective, used or remaindered goods and wastes; goods exempt from customs duties, where the annual licensing system is used and in the case of non-refundable imports[84], and if the imports are made by official entities, with the exception of petrol and urea (Table III.12).

fulfilment of technical regulations, dynamic test emission certification, legalization of vehicles, and controls to ensure environmental protection under international treaties, conventions or protocols (Decrees Nos. 4.406 of 2004 and 1.846 of 2005).

[80] WTO document G/LIC/N/3/COL/8 of 19 April 2010.

[81] WTO document G/LIC/N/3/COL/6 of 27 of October 2008.

[82] Article 7 of Decree No. 444 of 1967 reads as follows: "By requiring a prior licence the Government will regulate imports to the extent that it deems necessary to achieve the following objectives: to gauge the demand for foreign exchange, to restrict superfluous consumption, and to coordinate import policy with economic development plans". The authorities have pointed out that even though this law is still in force, these criteria have remained unused since the economic and commercial circumstances have changed (Ministry of Commerce, Industry and Tourism, 2008a).

[83] Ministry of Commerce, Industry and Tourism (2008a).

[84] Solely in the cases specified in Article 15 of Decree No. 3.803 of 2006.

Table III.12
Non-automatic licences

Products	Authorized entity	Type of products covered	Number of tariff subheadings[a]	Justification	Legal measure
Products included in the list drawn up by the Higher Council for Foreign Trade	INVIMA or ICA for imports of food and chemical products, if for human or animal use	Poultry cuts. Arms. Chemicals. Precursors. Narcotic drugs. Detonators and explosives. Rags. Used tyres. Bandages	188	National security; health protection; absorption of production	Resolutions No. 1 of 1991, No. 12 of 1993, No. 4 of 1998 and No. 4 of 2004; and Decree No. 2.303 of 2002
Products imported by the National Narcotic Drugs Council	National Narcotic Drugs Directorate	Narcotic drug precursors	31	National security; health protection	Resolution No. 012 of 2003; and Decrees No. 1.097 of 2004 of the MCIT and No. 3.990 of 2010
Products imported through INDUMIL	INDUMIL	Defence industry inputs	153	National security	External Circulars No. 045 of 2005 and No. 06 of 2010
Products imported through the National Narcotic Drugs Fund	National Narcotic Drugs Fund	Can only be imported by the National Narcotic Drugs Fund	105	Security	Circular No. 60 of 2006
Non-refundable imports	Depends on the nature of the product	Goods imported as foreign capital investment. Donations in favour of persons or entities of public or private law. Goods purchased in free zones by making foreign payments. Imports of goods in payment of a debt owed by a foreign to a Colombian enterprise. Household effects, traveller's baggage, accompanied or unaccompanied. Certification of goods as required by the customs regulations	n.a.	To improve control of these operations	Decree No. 3.803 of 2006
Imports with tariff exemption	Ministry of Mining and Energy and Colombian Institute of Geology and Mining for goods for exploring for minerals and hydrocarbons. ICA for imports of inputs needed to produce vaccines; Ministry of Health for the exemption of drugs, vaccines, etc., if imported by the private sector[b]	Donations to the official sector; technical, educational and laboratory equipment for the education sector. Drugs, serums vaccines, equipment for medical and dental treatments and laboratory equipment for the health sector. Raw materials and products for the fertilizer industry; paper for printing scientific and cultural journals and reviews. Vehicles imported by returning Colombian diplomats. Fire-extinguishing equipment imported by fire brigades. Imports for the country's prison system; goods for exploring for minerals or petroleum	n. a	Sectors having priority and strategic importance for national economic and social development	Decrees No. 255/92, No. 1.659 of 1964, No. 2.148 of 1991, No. 540 of 2004, No. 562 and No. 1.570 of 2011 and Laws No. 322 of 1996, No. 74 of 1958 and No. 633 of 2000
Defective, used, rebuilt, remaindered or surplus goods, waste and scrap	Imports Committee[c]	Any defective, used or rebuilt goods, and remaindered or surplus goods, waste and scrap	n.a.	Environmental security and public health	Decrees No. 3.803 of 2006 and No. 2.680 of 2009
Imports by official entities, except for petrol and urea	Imports Committee	Any goods	n.a.	Purchases for State entities	Decree No. 3.803 of 2006

Products	Authorized entity	Type of products covered	Number of tariff subheadings[a]	Justification	Legal measure
Imports under annual licences for the mining and petroleum industry, for the armed forces and for the Colombian Aviation Industry (CIREC)	Ministry of Mining and Energy and the Colombian Institute of Geology and Mining[e]	..	2.309	National security	Decree No. 1.573 of 2002[d]
Goods imported under the temporary admission procedure and finally imported outright	..	Capital goods	n.a.	In accordance with the customs regulations. Taking into account that at the end of temporary admission the goods will generally be used	Decree No. 4.136 of 2004 amending Decree No. 2.685 of 1999

.. Not available.
n.a. Not applicable.

a The tariff lines are ten-digit.
b In the case of these goods the presence or absence of domestic production is verified, in order to determine whether an exemption should be approved or refused.
c In the case of used goods the presence or absence of domestic production registered with the Ministry is verified, to determine whether a licence should be approved or refused.
d Regulates licences for products imported by the armed forces Satena and CIAC.
e Regulate licences for products imported by mining and petroleum enterprises.

Note: INVIMA: Institute for the Surveillance of Food and Drugs. ICA: Colombian Agricultural Institute.

Source: Compiled by the WTO Secretariat, on the basis of information published by the Ministry of Commerce, Industry and Tourism (2008), *Manual de Licencia Previa.* Viewed at: https://www.mincomercio.gov.co/descargar.php?id=24459.

57. The MCIT issues non-automatic import licences in accordance with the criteria established by its Imports Committee (Table III.13).[85] The authorities have notified the WTO that non-automatic licences are not intended to restrict the quantity or value of imports. However, according to the legislation, in some cases the MCIT has to verify whether there is any domestic production before it can decide whether to approve or refuse a licence. According to the authorities, this criterion, although stipulated in the law, is not currently being applied. A non-automatic licence can be granted even if there is domestic production, but in this case a tariff exemption will not be granted, even if it has been requested.[86] The origin of the imported goods is of no consequence as far as the application of non-automatic licences is concerned, unless there is a measure that specifically determines some exclusion.

58. Non-automatic licences are processed electronically, through the VUCE, subject to due notice. For the goods to be released, they must be covered by a valid non-automatic import licence. These licences can be processed at any time, except in the case of narcotic drugs, for which applications must be made during the first 25 days of each month and approved during the last five days. It currently takes approximately 5 days to issue import licences. There is a charge of about

[85] Decree Law No. 444 of 1967 and Resolution No. 0612 of 2005.
[86] Ministry of Commerce, Industry and Tourism (2008a).

US$15 for issuing non-automatic licences. The issuing of a licence is not subject to any prior deposit or advance payment.

Table III.13
Criteria for approving, postponing, refusing and amending the quantity of a non-automatic (prior) licence

The importance of the goods to which the application relates for the satisfaction of consumption requirements and the maintenance or raising of the level of employment
Their contribution to export promotion and diversification
The net savings in foreign currency obtainable from import substitution
Whether there is domestic production that is supplying the demand in the region of destination of the goods and the need to protect the consumer from abuse relating to price or quality
The urgency of the need to provide, with timely imports, for the development of areas that are particularly depressed or economically and socially underdeveloped, even if the imported goods are produced in the country
Where the importation of used, faulty, clearance and waste or surplus goods is concerned, the existence of domestic production that is adequate and competitive in terms of price, quality and availability

Source: Decree Law No. 444 of 22 March 1967; Resolution No. 0612 of 2005 and information provided by the Colombian authorities.

59. The importer of goods subject to a prior or non-automatic licence which have arrived in port without having met this requirement may file, for his own account and at his own risk, a prior licence application with the Imports Committee of the MCIT. If it is granted, he may proceed to have the goods cleared through customs, within the month following their arrival. Otherwise he will have to choose either to re-ship or to abandon the goods, in accordance with the customs legislation (Decree No. 2.685 of 1999).

60. Non-automatic import licences may be refused for non-compliance with the legal requirements for their authorization, or if the data provided by the importer are false or inaccurate. If a licence is refused, the applicant is informed of the reason for the refusal and may apply for reconsideration under the Administrative Disputes Code. If administrative channels have been exhausted, the applicant may take his case before the administrative courts.

61. Non-automatic licences are valid for six months from their date of approval. Those that cover capital goods on the list that the Higher Council for Foreign Trade also maintains for the purpose are valid for 12 months, starting from the date of approval, while those that cover imports of substances classified as narcotic drug precursors are valid for three months.

62. Non-automatic import licences may be extended once only, for up to three months, if the extension is requested before the licence expires. In exceptional cases, duly evidenced, in particular cases of specially manufactured capital goods or products difficult to obtain in the international market owing to shortage of supply, the Imports Committee may grant further extensions for successive periods of up to three months each, without exceeding 12 months of extension. Approved licences can be used within their period of validity for any or all of the goods covered. No sanctions are imposed for the non-utilization or partial utilization of a non-automatic licence.

63. Non-automatic import licences may be amended, except for the purpose of covering larger quantities where narcotic drug precursor substances are concerned.

(viii) Anti-dumping, countervailing and safeguard measures

(a) General provisions

64. There are legal texts that regulate the various aspects of trade protection measures at both national and Andean Community levels. In the Colombian national legislation the main provisions relating to trade protection measures can be found in: Decree No. 2.550 of 2010, which repealed Decree No. 991 of 1998 on anti-dumping (AD) measures; Decrees No. 152 of 1998 and No. 1480 of 2005 on multilateral safeguards and Decree No. 1.820 of 26 May 2010 on bilateral safeguards under free trade agreements; and Decree No. 299 of 1995 on countervailing measures against subsidies. Within the Andean Community, the main trade protection measures are: Decisions No. 283 of 1991 and No. 456 of 1999 relating to dumping and third-country subsidies; Decision No. 457 of 1999 for intracommunity subsidies; Decision No. 452 of 1999 for third-country safeguards; and Chapter XI of the Cartagena Agreement and Decision No. 563 of 2003 for intracommunity safeguards.

65. The Colombian authority competent for investigating dumping, subsidy and safeguard cases is the Foreign Trade Directorate of the MCIT through its Trade Practices Subdirectorate.[87] No imported product may be subjected to both AD and countervailing duties at the same time. At subregional level, applications for the investigation of dumping, subsidies and safeguards relating to products originating in the Andean countries are dealt with by the CAN General Secretariat. Applications for the initiation of investigations may be submitted both by domestic producers and by the governments of CAN countries.

(b) Countervailing measures

66. During the period 2006-2011, Colombia did not adopt any countervailing duties, nor did it initiate any subsidy investigations.[88]

(c) Anti-dumping measures

67. The initiation of AD investigations and the application of AD measures are regulated by Decree No. 2.550 of 2010. The MCIT can initiate an investigation on written application by the domestic industry or ex officio. The MCIT is legally authorized to accept undertakings from exporters to revise export prices or stop exporting at dumped prices. These undertakings, originating in expressions of intent, can be initiated by the exporter or by the MCIT. If initiated by the exporter, expressions of intent can only be submitted during the two months following the date of publication of the resolution adopting the preliminary determination.

68. The MCIT can decide to apply provisional duties if it reaches the preliminary conclusion that imports are being dumped and are causing injury to the domestic industry. Their application must be announced by resolution. Both provisional and definitive anti-dumping duties are expressed as an *ad valorem* percentage or by establishing a base price.

---

[87] Ministry of Commerce, Industry and Tourism online information: "*Comercio exterior*". Viewed at: http://www.mincomercio.gov.co.

[88] WTO documents G/SCM/N/144/Add.1/Rev.1 of 1 May 2007, G/SCM/N/153/Add.1 of 18 April 2007, G/SCM/N/162/Add.1/Rev.1 of 15 November 2007, G/SCM/N/170/Add.1/Rev.1 of 21 October 2008, G/SCM/N/178/Add.1/Rev.1 of 28 April 2009, G/SCM/N/185/Add.1 of 27 April 2009, G/SCM/N/195/Add.1 of 14 October 2009, G/SCM/N/203/Add.1/Rev.1 of 20 October 2010, G/SCM/N/212/Add.1 of 20 October 2010 and G/SCM/N/219/Add.1 of 26 April 2011.

69. Decisions to initiate investigations or impose anti-dumping duties, whether provisional or definitive, may form the subject of direct reconsideration proceedings before the MCIT to seek the revocation of the administrative measure which initiated the investigation or imposed a provisional or definitive anti-dumping or countervailing duty.

70. Between 2006 and 2011, Colombia initiated 25 anti-dumping investigations. During this same period, it applied ten new definitive measures and two in connection with sunset reviews (Table III.14). Fifteen of the new investigations resulted in the non-application of definitive measures. A majority of the measures were applied in 2007; no new AD measures were applied in 2010. According to the notification made to the WTO, as of 31 December 2011, Colombia was maintaining 12 existing definitive AD measures, all applied to imports from China. The products affected by the measures are: hoes, bars and mattocks; link chains, polished, galvanized; hosiery; staples in strips; curtains; bed linen; other textiles and made-up goods (fashion, pre-dyed and mixed fabrics); table linen; towels; screws and bolts; and tableware and kitchenware sets and loose articles, of earthenware and porcelain.

Table III.14
Anti-dumping measures in force, 2006-2011

Country	Product (HS code)	Identification number of the investigation	Measure	Date of imposition (OJ No.)
China	Hoes, bars and mattocks (8201.30.00.00)	D-215-14-48	Duties: difference between the f.o.b. base price of US\$1.32/kg and the f.o.b. price declared by the importer, provided that this is less than the base price	29.07.09 (47.425)
	Link chains, polished galvanized (7315.82.00.00)	D-215-05-39	Duties: difference between the f.o.b. base price of US\$1.82/kg and the f.o.b. price declared by the importer, provided that this is less than the base price	20.04.07 (46.605)
	Hosiery (6115.10.10.00; 6115.30.10.00, 6115.10.90.00; 6115.30.90.00, 6115.95.00.00, 6115.96.00.00 and 6115.99.00.00)	D-215-06-40	Duties: difference between the f.o.b. base price of US\$0.79/pair and the f.o.b. price declared by the importer, provided that this is less than the base price	14.05.07 (46.628)
	Staples in strips (8305.20.00.00)	D-215-12-46	Duties: difference between the f.o.b. base price of US\$1.661/kilo and the f.o.b. price declared by the importer, provided that this is less than the base price	07.05.09 (47.342)
	Textiles and made-up goods (curtains) (6303.12.00.00)	D-215-07-41/curtains	Duties: difference between the f.o.b. base price of US\$6.74/kg and the f.o.b. price declared by the importer, provided that this is less than the base price	26.07.07 (46.701)
	Textiles and made-up goods (fashion, pre-dyed and mixed fabrics) (5208.42.00.00; 5208.49.00.00; 5210.41.00.00; 5210.49.00.00; 5407.42.00.00; 5407.44.00.00; 5407.61.00.00; 5513.11.00.00; 5513.21.00.00; 5513.31.00.00; 5513.41.00.00; 5514.22.00.00; 5515.11.00.00; 5515.12.00.00)	D-215-07-41/fashion, pre-dyed and mixed fabrics	Duties: difference between the f.o.b. base price of US\$0.75/m^2 and the f.o.b. price declared by the importer, provided that this is less than the base price	26.07.07 (46.701)
	Textiles and made-up goods (bed linen) (6302.22.00.00, 6302.32.00.00)	D-215-07-41/bed linen	Duties: difference between the f.o.b. base price of US\$5.29/unit and the f.o.b. price declared by the importer, provided that this is less than the base price	19.10.07 (46.786)
	Textiles and made-up goods (table linen) (6302.51.00.00, 6302.53.00.00)	D-215-07-41/table linen	Duties: difference between the f.o.b. base price of US\$6.64/unit and the f.o.b. price declared by the importer, provided that this is less than the base price	19.10.07 (46.786)

Country	Product (HS code)	Identification number of the investigation	Measure	Date of imposition (OJ No.)
	Textiles and made-up goods (towels) (6302.60.00.00)	D-215-07-41/towels	Duties: difference between the f.o.b. base price of US$5.13/kg and the f.o.b. price declared by the importer, provided that this is less than the base price	08.06.07 (46.653)
	Screws and bolts (7318.15.90.00)	D-215-10-44	Duties: difference between the f.o.b. base price of US$1.31/kg and the f.o.b. price declared by the importer, provided that this is less than the base price	26.02.09 (47.275)
	Tableware and kitchenware sets and loose articles, of earthenware (6912.00.00.00)	RD-215-01-39/ earthenware	Duties: difference between the f.o.b. base price of US$1.71 /kg and the f.o.b. price declared by the importer, provided that this is less than the estimated base price	17.11.06 (46.455). Extension 20.06.11 (48.106)
	Tableware and kitchenware sets and loose articles, of porcelain (6911.10.00.00)	RD-215-01-39/porcelain	Duties: difference between the f.o.b. base price of US$2.88/kg and the f.o.b. price declared by the importer, provided that this is less than the estimated base price	17.11.06 (46.455). Extension 20.06.11 (48.106)

Source: WTO Secretariat.

71. Between 2006 and 2011, provisional measures were applied in 13 out of the 25 investigations initiated. The investigations terminated during the same period without proceeding to the application of definitive duties include: four different investigations into imports of low-carbon steel wire rod for drawing` and rubber strips for retreading tyres from Brazil and Mexico; two investigations into blenders from China, in which, however, provisional duties were first applied; two investigations into casing or tubing imported from China; two into men's and women's underwear, respectively, from China; three investigations into textiles from Chinese Taipei; and two investigations into shovels and ceramic electrical insulators and ceramic insulating parts from China. Three investigations into products from China, namely, screws and bolts; nuts; and staples in strips, resulted in the application of provisional and definitive duties for staples in strips and definitive, but not provisional duties for screws and bolts, and in the non-application of provisional or definitive duties for nuts. In two cases the duties were extended (Table III.14).

(d) Safeguard measures

72. The Colombian national legislation on safeguards is set out in Decree No. 152 of 1998, which authorizes the application of safeguard measures if imports of a particular product have increased substantially and the product is being imported under such conditions as to cause or threaten to cause serious injury to the domestic industry that produces like or directly competitive products. The measures are applied to all imports of the product under investigation irrespective of origin. Within the Andean Community context, there is a special safeguards regime that applies to goods originating in the CAN. The rights and obligations of Article XIX of the GATT 1994 are maintained with respect to Colombia's preferential agreements with Mexico (formerly G-3) and with MERCOSUR.

73. In accordance with the WTO Agreement on Safeguards, the application of a general safeguard measure usually consists in the imposition of a tariff levy for not more than four years, including the period of application of any provisional measure; if it is extended, the total period of application may not exceed eight years. The Colombian legislation states that if a measure is adopted for an initial period of more than three years, the situation is reviewed at mid-term to determine whether it is necessary to maintain the measure. Likewise, there is a requirement to evaluate the adjustment programme.

74. Also in force is the safeguards rule laid down in Decree No. 1.480 of 2005, which regulates the application of safeguard measures to the imports of products originating in the People's Republic of China envisaged in the Protocol of Accession of the People's Republic of China and in the report of the WTO Working Group. Under this Decree, the measure to be applied will usually consist of an increase in the tariff levy in force, a quantitative restriction or some other measure aimed at withdrawing concessions or limiting imports. This measure will be applied for up to four years, including a possible one-year extension.

75. Decree No. 1.820 of 2010 also forms part of Colombia's safeguards legislation; this decree regulates the adoption of bilateral safeguard measures within the context of the international trade agreements to which Colombia is a contracting party.

76. Since its last review, in 2006, Colombia has not notified the WTO of any new safeguards investigation within the context of the Agreement on Safeguards and section 16 of China's Protocol of Accession to the WTO. Nor has it notified any extension of duties.

77. Colombia still reserves, but has not used[89], the right to apply the special safeguard under the WTO Agreement on Agriculture to 57 four-digit tariff lines.[90]

(ix) Standards and technical regulations

(a) Institutional and legal framework

78. The Ministry of Commerce, Trade, Industry and Tourism (MCIT), through its Regulation Directorate, is the body that defines standardization, quality, certification and accreditation and metrological policies and practices. The MCIT coordinates the National Quality System (SNC), whose basic objectives are to promote in the markets the safety, quality and competitiveness of the sector producing or importing of goods and services and to protect the interests of consumers. This work is carried out mainly through the Supervisory Authority for Industry and Trade (SIC) and the National Institute of Metrology (INM), which establish, coordinate, direct and oversee the national industrial quality control, weights, measures and metrology programmes and organize the quality control and metrological laboratories considered indispensable to the proper performance of their functions. Decree No. 4.175 of 2011 split off the SIC's scientific and industrial metrology functions and transferred them to the INM. The SIC continues to perform its legal metrology functions, while the INM's objectives are to coordinate scientific and industrial metrology and to carry out activities that make possible innovation and support economic, scientific and technological development, through research, the provision of metrological services, support for metrological control activities and the dissemination of measurements traceable to the International System of Units.

79. Decree No. 4.738 of 2008 abolished the SIC's accreditation functions and made the National Accreditation Organization of Colombia (ONAC), created in November 2007, the national accreditation body. In February 2009, ONAC issued the first accreditations and in 2010 the SIC ceased its accreditation activities. ONAC is a non-profit semi-public entity; as of 31 December 2010, 67 per cent of the equity was being contributed by the public sector and the remaining 33 per cent by the private sector. ONAC's activities and programmes are under the administrative supervision of the

[89] WTO documents G/AG/N/COL/27 of 4 May 2005, G/AG/N/COL/25 of 28 May 2001, G/AG/N/COL/22 of 21 August 2000, G/AG/N/COL/17 of 30 April 1999, G/AG/N/COL/9 of 7 July 1998 and G/AG/N/COL/5 of 30 June 1997.

[90] Schedule LXXVI: Colombia, Part I: Most Favoured Nation Tariff, Section I: Agricultural products, Section I-A: Tariffs.

MCIT. In Colombia, standardization is the exclusive responsibility of the Colombian Technical Standards Institute (ICONTEC), the national standardization body. ICONTEC has also been accredited for technical regulation certification tasks.

80. The following entities participate in the SNC: (i) the MCIT; (ii) the entities authorized to issue technical regulations; (iii) ICONTEC, which is responsible for coordinating the drafting and dissemination of technical standards; (iv) the Sectoral Standardization Units; (v) the SIC; (vi) ONAC; (vii) the Technical Advisory Council for Accreditation; (viii) the Sectoral Technical Committees; (ix) the accredited Certification and Inspection Organizations; (x) the accredited Testing and Calibration Laboratories; and (xi) other entities with accreditation and control functions, such as the National Institute for the Surveillance of Food and Drugs (INVIMA) and the Colombian Agricultural Institute (ICA).

81. Colombia has notified the WTO that the Regulation Directorate of the MCIT is responsible for applying the Agreement on Technical Barriers to Trade (TBT) and for administering the enquiry point for standardization, technical barriers to trade, sanitary and phytosanitary measures and conformity assessment procedures. Colombia has also notified that ICONTEC has accepted the Code of Good Practice for the Preparation, Adoption and Application of Standards.

82. The legislation on standards and technical regulations is comprised of a body of national laws and Andean Decisions (Table III.15). The main legal instruments governing policy in this area include Decrees No. 2.269 of 1993 and No. 1.112 of 1996.

83. The Colombian legislation currently uses four categories of standards and technical regulations, which are defined in Decree No. 2.269 of 1993: the Technical Standard (NT), the Colombian Technical Standard (NTC), the Sectoral Technical Standard (NTS) and Technical Regulations (RT). NTs are voluntary, based on consensus and approved by a recognized body.[91] NTCs, which are also voluntary, are those approved by the national standardization body. NTSs correspond to technical standards of voluntary application drafted by a Sectoral Standardization Unit for a specific sector. RTs are mandatory and issued by the competent authority.[92]

Table III.15
Legal framework for standards and technical regulations

Instrument	Description
Andean Decision No. 562	Guidelines for the preparation, adoption and application of technical regulations
Andean Decision No. 376	Andean system of standardization, accreditation, testing, certification, technical regulations and metrology
Andean Decision No. 506	Recognition and automatic acceptance of certificates of product conformity with technical regulations issued by accredited or recognized certification bodies
Andean Decision No. 419	Procedure for reporting technical barriers to trade and notifying technical regulations, conformity assessment procedures or other measures of a mandatory nature to be adopted
Andean Decision No. 615	The Notification and Technical Regulation Information System of the Andean Community (SIRT)
Decree No. 2.269 of 1993	National standardization, certification and metrological system

[91] Decree No. 2.269 of 1993 defines the NTC as a "document based on consensus and approved by a recognized body, which sets out, for common and repeated use, rules, guidelines and characteristics for activities or their outcomes, aimed at achieving the optimal degree of order in a given context". Technical standards must be based on the consolidated results of science, technology and experience and their objective must be to ensure the optimum benefits for the community.

[92] Decree No. 2.269 of 1993 defines the RT as a "regulation of a mandatory nature, issued by the competent authority, with a basis in law, which sets out technical requirements, whether directly or by referring to or incorporating the contents of a national, regional or international standard, technical specification or code of good practice".

Instrument	Description
Decree No. 1.112 of 1996	Created the National Standardization Measures and Conformity Assessment Procedures Information System, established rules for harmonizing the issuing of technical regulations
Decree No. 4.738 of 2010	Abolished the accreditation functions of the Supervisory Authority for Industry and Trade (SIC) and designated ONAC as the national accreditation body
Decree No. 323 of 2010	Follow-up assessments of the conformity assessment bodies accredited by the SIC
Decree No. 4.175 of 2011	Split off some functions of the Supervisory Authority for Industry and Trade, created the National Metrology Institute and established its objectives and structure
Resolution No. 25.391 of 2002	Established the mandatory registration of controlled products, i.e., those subject to compliance with technical regulations

Source: Ministry of Commerce, Industry and Tourism.

(b) Standardization

84. Standardization in Colombia is the responsibility of ICONTEC, the national standardization body and the only entity authorized to issue Colombian Technical Standards (NTCs). ICONTEC is a Colombian multinational enterprise formed as a result of the voluntary linkup of representatives of the National Government, the private production, distribution and consumption sectors, and the various branches of the technology sector. ICONTEC also does global conformity assessment (certification) work through its ties with the International Certification Network (IQNet) and quality management work in Colombia, Central America and South America.[93]

85. As the national standardization body, ICONTEC represents Colombia in international and regional standardization organizations such as the International Standards Organization (ISO), the International Electrotechnical Commission (IEC) and the Pan American Standards Commission (COPANT). It is also a member of regional and international standardization bodies, which enables it to participate in the definition and development of international and regional standards.

86. Standardization leading to the drafting of NTC standards is done by ICONTEC through 236 Technical Committees.[94] In January 2012, the ICONTEC database contained 5,659 current NTCs, of which 1,160 were identical with ISO, IEC, CODEX, OIML or ITU standards.

87. In parallel with the work done by ICONTEC in relation to NTCs, there are Sectoral Standardization Units (USN) that draft sectoral standards (NTS). Responsibility for approving the creation of USNs lies with the Regulation Directorate of the MCIT, in conformity with Article 28.9 of Decree No. 210 of 3 February 2003. The function of the USNs is to draw up a sector's own standards, within the international parameters established for that activity, with the possibility of their being submitted to ICONTEC for the NTC adoption and publication process. As of January 2012, there were 14 USNs approved, but only 11 were active.[95] On the same date, there were 61 NTSs, of which four were adopted unchanged from ISO standards.

[93] ICONTEC online information: "*Quienes somos*". Viewed at: http://www.icontec.org.co/index.php?section=18.

[94] The complete list can be viewed on the INCONTEC website at: http://www.icontec.org.co/.

[95] Colombian Safety Council (occupational medicine, industrial hygiene, industrial safety, fire protection and ergonomics); GS1 COLOMBIA (bar code, electronic information exchange); Hotel Association of Colombia (labour skills, operating quality, services and environmental impact, star rating, quality); MCIT (human resource skills, quality of agency operation and social development services and policies); MCIT (quality of service, skills of tourist guides); Colombia Association of the Gastronomic Industry (skills

(c) Technical regulations

88. There are two main sources for the preparation of RTs: (i) ICONTEC, which issues the NTCs that can serve as a basis for preparing RTs; and (ii) the ministries, regulatory commissions and decentralized bodies that issue RTs. In the latter case, each entity has an internal procedure for preparing technical regulations. However, the authorities have noted that, since 2009, there has been an agreed procedure for preparing and issuing technical regulations that embodies recommendations on good technical regulation practices (PEERT).[96] This procedure is described in Table III.16.

89. The legal status of an RT is established by decrees and resolutions, and exceptionally by laws. Most RTs reflect or are based on international standards, although there are no relevant official statistics.

Table III.16
Procedure for preparing and issuing technical regulations

Step	Description
1	Application for a technical regulation (RT): (a) from a sector or a user or (b) government initiative
2	Determination of legal competence for the subject matter
3	Check for duplication in the technical regulation of the same product
4	Identification of the legitimate objective it is intended to fulfil and the level of risk (TBT Agreement 2.2)
5	Determination of relevant standards (TBT 2.4)
6	Determination of the appropriateness of a technical regulation
7	Notice published at an early appropriate stage (TBT 2.9.1 and 5.6.1)
8	Determination of the scope of the RT (tariff subheadings, exclusions)
9	Choice of the definitions to be included in the RT
10	Determination of the labelling or marking requirements, printing, and relevant general and specific techniques, in accordance with the numbered requirements in technical standards
11	Determination of reference technical standards and establishment of guidelines on equivalences between technical standards and between technical regulations
12	Establishment of Conformity Assessment Procedure (PEC) policy
13	Determination of the conformity documents that will be accepted
14	Determination of the surveillance and control entities
15	Determination of the penalty regime
16	Determination of the date of entry into force
17	Determination of transitional provisions
18	Determination of derogations

and aptitudes of human resources, quality of operation of gastronomic establishments and service); Productive Development Centre for Jewellery (quality of precious metals, gems and jewellery-related processes); Externado University of Colombia (sustainability of tourism services provided by lodging establishments, travel agencies, restaurants, and tourist guides); Ministry of Social Welfare (health care quality standards); National Registry of Valuers (preparation, provision, review, auditing and control of valuations); Ministry of National Education (quality of job training); Colombian Federation of the Software Industry (design, development, marketing, installation and implementation of IT products and technologies); Colombian Time Share Association (quality of service and skills and aptitudes of human resources); and Fedelonjas (provision of estate agent services, rental property, developer-marketer of off-plan real estate projects and horizontal property manager) (CONTEC online information: "*Unidades Sectoriales de Normalización*". Viewed at: http://www.icontec.org.co/index.php?section=47).

[96] This procedure was introduced by Resolution No. 1.715 of 2005. In 2009, the procedure was updated internally within the MCIT's Integrated Management System (SIG). Although there is no general standard that makes its application by other regulatory bodies compulsory, this mechanism is being implemented voluntarily through the recommendations issued by the Intersectoral Quality Commission.

Step	Description
19	Preparation of the complete text of the preliminary draft RT
20	Publication on the Web of the preliminary draft RT and dispatch to the sector for at least ten working days of public consultation
21	Analysis and adoption of relevant comments. Meeting with the sector if necessary and preparation of the draft
22	International notification (WTO) of the draft RT (with 90 days for comments) (TBT 2.9.2 and 5.6.2)
23	Opinion on Competition Law (under Law No. 1.340 of 2009, before RTs are published, entities must first seek the opinion of the SIC to establish whether the measure to be issued could affect free competition)
24	Analysis and adoption of relevant national and international comments (meeting with sector if necessary)
25	Preparation of the definitive text of the draft RT and request for legal opinion prior to issuance
26	Issuance of the technical regulation (signature, numbering and dating of the administrative instrument)
27	Certification issued by the WTO enquiry point (Article 72 of Law No. 1.480 of 12 October 2011)
28	Publication in the Official Journal (OJ) and on the Web, dispatch to the sector and updating of the notification to the WTO
29	Entry into force

Source: MCIT, Regulation Directorate.

90. During the period 2006-2011, Colombia made 207 notifications to the WTO Information Centre, having notified the technical regulations in their various stages (draft, approval, etc.), as well as their amendments, rejections and implementation. Since 2001, Colombia has notified the WTO of the application of 72 technical regulations. The Ministries of Health and Social Welfare, Transport and Mining and Energy, the MCIT and the Colombian Agricultural Institute (ICA) are among the main entities responsible for these RTs. Since 2001, Colombia has been applying the recommended period of 60 days or more for commenting on notifications.[97] The criteria most used in the preparation of RTs include the protection of human life and health, consumer protection and the protection of the environment. The sectors in which most drafts were prepared were: industrial products, especially those with an environmental impact, chemical products, and processed and unprocessed foods.

91. At Andean Regional Community level, Decision No. 562 of 2003 established guidelines for the preparation, adoption and application of RTs in the member countries and at Community level. Decision No. 376 established the Andean Standardization, Accreditation, Assays, Certification, Technical Regulations and Metrology System and Decision No. 615 of 2005 created the CAN Notification and Technical Regulation Information System (SIRT), which operates an exporter alert system to warn exporters of mandatory technical requirements.[98] Through the SIRT, the CAN maintains a procedure for receiving and commenting on draft RTs and facilitating the regional harmonization process; however, the focal points of the Andean countries are the only ones authorized to notify their countries' draft and definitive technical regulations.[99] At the end of 2011, the Andean Community had produced two technical regulations: that which regulates the trade in cosmetic products in the Andean Community, by virtue of Decision No. 516 of 2002, and the Andean Technical Regulation on requirements and guidelines for inspection of the operation of establishments that manufacture domestic hygiene products and absorbent personal hygiene products, by virtue of Decision No. 721 of 27 November 2009.

[97] WTO document G/TBT/18 of 17 February 2006.

[98] Decision No. 615. Viewed at: http://www.comunidadandina.org/normativa/dec/D615.html and CAN online information: "Andean Exporter Alert System". Viewed at: http://www.comunidadandina.org/reglamentos/sirt.htm.

[99] CAN online information: "Andean Exporter Alert System". Viewed at: http://www.comunidadandina.org/reglamentos/sirt.htm.

(d) Conformity assessment and certification

92. In the case of products subject to an RT, conformity assessment is mandatory. In accordance with Article 8 of Decree No. 2.269 of 1993, as amended by Article 1 of Decree No. 3.144 of 2008, prior to marketing, manufacturers, importers and marketers must demonstrate compliance with the RT through a certificate of conformity issued by an accredited or designated body. The mechanisms and methods for assessing and demonstrating conformity may be contained in the RT itself and depend on the level of risk involved.[100] These methods include certification, inspection and testing carried out by bodies accredited or designated by the regulatory authority. All regulations lay down a conformity assessment procedure; in those cases in which it is not mentioned explicitly, it is understood that for the products imported the inspection or testing certificates will be granted "homologation" and be accepted at the time of importation of the product.

93. At the end of February 2012, there were 21 bodies accredited for product certification (11 by ONAC and 10 by the SIC); 15 accredited for the certification of management systems (11 by ONAC and four by the SIC); and 13 accredited for the certification of persons (11 by ONAC and two by the SIC).[101] As an example of the mandatory certification process, ICONTEC audits the manufacturer's quality system and has the product tested in laboratories considered reliable. If the product satisfies the requirements of the RT, ICONTEC grants a certificate valid for between one and three years. Once a certificate has been granted, the manufacturer must mark the certified product with the appropriate logo. Later, there will be follow-up audits to confirm that the conditions which enabled a certificate to be granted are still in place.

94. In general, the accredited certification bodies subcontract the services of accredited laboratories for assessing the conformity of a product. If there are no accredited laboratories in Colombia, the certification body must assess the technical competence of a non-accredited laboratory in accordance with standard NTC-ISO/IEC 17025.

95. Despite institutional reform, the SIC still maintains surveillance and control over technical regulations. Moreover, the SIC continues to be responsible for verifying compliance with the requirements relating to the labelling of products, whether domestic or imported, but only if the labelling requirements form part of technical regulations placed under SIC control. This applies to the labelling of: zinc-carbon and alkaline batteries; made-up goods; footwear and leather goods; toys; ceramic tableware and kitchenware; refrigerators; freezers; pressure cookers for domestic use and their accessories; gas-fuelled domestic appliances; and stations for the supply of compressed natural gas for use in vehicles. ICONTEC has developed voluntary Colombian labelling standards.

96. The ministries and agencies lack a unified policy on certification abroad. The MCIT accepts certificates issued abroad, provided that a homologation or validation procedure is followed. For most other ministries and agencies, the certification of a foreign good by bodies accredited abroad is accepted in Colombia provided that the country in question has a mutual recognition agreement with Colombia or is an Andean Community country and the certifying body is registered with the CAN General Secretariat, in accordance with Decision No. 506. ICONTEC has developed recognition agreements with certification bodies in Argentina, the Bolivarian Republic of Venezuela, Brazil, Chile, Mexico and the United States. The authorities have noted that, as of October 2011,

[100] Thus, in the case of lower-risk products, such as textiles or footwear, only a mark or label is required. In the case of higher-risk products, for example, car parts such as brakes or safety belts, inspection or test certificates are required.

[101] ONAC online information: "*Listado de Organismos de Certificación de Producto Acreditados*". Viewed at: http://www.onac.org.co/modulos/contenido/default.asp?idmodulo=172&pagina=2.

work was proceeding on a draft decree for amending and updating the provisions contained in Decree No. 2.269 to create general guidelines on the results of conformity assessment from abroad.

(e) Accreditation

97. Since the last review there have been major changes in the process of accreditation in Colombia. Decree No. 4.738 of 2010 abolished the accreditation powers of the SIC and allowed accreditation to be developed under market conditions by entities established under the rules of private law, in accordance with requirements laid down by the MCIT. This Decree also incorporated provisions for a transitional accreditation regime for conformity assessment bodies accredited by the SIC, which up to then had been coordinating the Accreditation Commission and the Technical Advisory Council for Accreditation, in which consumers, government, businessmen and accredited bodies were participating.

98. Decree No. 4.738 of 2008 designated as the national accreditation body the National Accreditation Organization of Colombia (ONAC), created in November 2007, whose activities and programmes are subject to the administrative control of the MCIT. ONAC issued the first accreditations in February 2009 and in 2010 the SIC ceased its accreditation activities. ONAC is the only official source of information about accreditation in Colombia. ONAC is responsible for granting, maintaining, broadening, restricting, suspending and withdrawing accreditations.

99. ONAC's accreditation work is done through Accreditation Committees composed of four members: two members of ONAC (the Technical Director of ONAC and an official from the technical staff without the right to vote) and two outside experts, who must be unconnected with the ONAC establishment.

100. Nevertheless, some other entities have accreditation powers within their sphere of competence such as, for example, the Institute of Hydrology, Meteorology and Environmental Studies (IDEAM), the National Institute for the Surveillance of Food and Drugs (INVIMA), the National Institute of Forensic Medicine and Forensic Sciences, and the ICA. At present, only the IDEAM is engaged in this activity, in connection with testing laboratories.

101. At the end of February 2012, ONAC had completed 542 accreditations of certifying organizations; of these organizations 11 certify products; 11 certify management systems; 11 certify persons; 23 are inspection bodies; 56 are calibration laboratories; 72 are testing laboratories; two are clinical laboratories; 118 are Accredited Driver Recognition Centres (CRCs); and 238 are Automotive Diagnostic Centres (CDAs). On the same date there were 158 bodies with SIC accreditations still in force: ten organizations certifying products; four certifying management systems; two certifying persons, 23 inspection bodies; 39 calibration laboratories; and 80 testing laboratories.[102]

(x) Sanitary and phytosanitary measures

102. To guide and coordinate policy on sanitary and phytosanitary measures (SPS), Colombia has an Intersectoral Sanitary and Phytosanitary Measures Commission, created by Decree No. 2.833 of 2006. This Commission serves as the National SPS Committee and is composed of the Ministries of Health and Social Welfare; Agriculture and Rural Development (MADR); Environment and Sustainable Development; and Trade, Industry and Tourism (MCIT), together with the

[102] ONAC online information: "*Listado de Organismos de Certificación de Producto Acreditados*". Viewed at: http://www.onac.org.co/modulos/contenido/default.asp?idmodulo=172&pagina=2.

Colombian Agricultural Institute (ICA) and the National Institute for the Surveillance of Food and Drugs (INVIMA), which are regularly invited to participate.

103. Policy implementation is the task of the various institutes and agencies assigned to each Ministry, mainly the Colombian Agricultural Institute (ICA), the National Institute for the Surveillance of Food and Drugs (INVIMA), the Supervisory Authority for Industry and Trade (SIC) and the National Institute of Health (INS). In Colombia, responsibility at national and local level for the operational work of surveillance and control is allocated as follows: plant and animal health to the ICA, which at local level relies on its local offices; public health and food and drug safety (including at importation) to INVIMA, which at local level relies on territorial working groups (GTT). In the case of public health and food safety, in the marketing stage the area health authorities are responsible for surveillance and control. In environmental matters, surveillance is the responsibility of the autonomous regional corporations.

104. The sanitary and phytosanitary system, composed of the above-mentioned entities, operates on the principle of harmonizing policies in the various sectors, in particular, agriculture, public health, environment, trade, regional authorities and the private sector. The decision on the adoption of an SPS measure is taken by the body responsible for risk assessment, as appropriate.

105. The Colombian Agricultural Institute (ICA) is a public body with legal status, administrative autonomy and independent resources, belonging to the National Science and Technology System and assigned to the Ministry of Agriculture and Rural Development. The ICA was established by Decree No. 1.562 of 1962 and restructured by Decree No. 4.765 of 18 December 2008. Decree No. 4.765 includes among the functions of the ICA the adoption, in accordance with the law, of the SPS measures necessary in order effectively to control animal and plant health and guard against biological and chemical risks. The ICA is in charge of risk assessment analysis in primary production and responsible for regulating, preventing, detecting, monitoring and eradicating phytosanitary and animal health problems. The ICA is also responsible for negotiating bilateral and multilateral sanitary and phytosanitary agreements which make it possible to market agricultural products abroad and guarantee the quality of agricultural inputs and seeds used in Colombia, while regulating and controlling the use of living organisms modified by genetic engineering in the agricultural sector. The ICA maintains import and export checkpoints at 127 local offices in as many municipalities spread over 32 departments, as well as at eight airports, eight seaports and five border crossings. The ICA has 55 laboratories and a quarantine station.

106. The main function of INVIMA, a public agency attached to the Ministry of Health and Social Welfare, is to safeguard public health in Colombia, by carrying out inspection, surveillance and sanitary control tasks of a technical and scientific nature, within its sphere of competence. INVIMA, in coordination with the regional health authorities, is responsible for certifying products of public health interest as fit for human consumption. It also makes proposals to the Ministry of Health and Social Welfare for the formulation of policies and regulations concerning quality control and sanitary surveillance in relation to the products mentioned in Law No. 100 of 1993 and other pieces of legislation and controls and monitors the quality and safety of the products specified in that law.[103] Within these functions, INVIMA can prepare, propose, disseminate and update SPS measures applicable in connection with inspection, sanitary surveillance, quality control, assessment and sanctioning procedures and procedures relating to sanitary registrations. INVIMA is represented throughout the national territory by nine regional offices known as territorial working groups (GTT).

[103] INVIMA online information: "*Funciones Generales*". Viewed at: http://web.invima.gov.co/portal/faces/index.jsp?id=54194.

107. INVIMA is the body charged with issuing sanitary registrations, as well as with their renewal, amplification, amendment and cancellation, as appropriate, and with directing and coordinating measures with the national network of laboratories in relation to the products specified in Article 245 of Law No. 100 of 1993 and in other relevant laws and regulations and with promoting their development and modernization; INVIMA is authorized to delegate these functions to certain regional bodies. INVIMA is also responsible for sanitary approval of imports and exports of the products for which it is competent. Moreover, it is entrusted with administering the public functions of quality control and sanitary and epidemiological surveillance of the results and adverse effects of the products for which it is competent and with assessing the risk factors and taking sanitary measures relating to foodstuffs and the raw materials used in their production.

108. INVIMA has exclusive competence for the inspection, surveillance and control of food production and processing, slaughterhouses, milk collection centres, milk and milk product processing plants, and the means of transport associated with these activities. It also has exclusive competence for the inspection, surveillance and control of the safety of imports and exports of foodstuffs and the raw materials used in their production, at ports, airports and border crossings, without prejudice to the powers assigned by law to the ICA.

109. Decree No. 2.323 of 12 July 2006 organized the National Network of Laboratories and regulates its management. The Decree stipulates that the Network is to be supervised by the Ministry of Health and Social Welfare and defines the policies, programmes, plans and projects required for it to function properly. The National Network of Laboratories consists of clinical, cytohistopathological, food science, and reproductive medicine laboratories, blood and organ banks and other laboratories that carry out analyses of significance for the monitoring of public health and for sanitary surveillance and control. The INS and INVIMA are designated national reference laboratories and are jointly responsible for coordinating the National Network.

110. SPS measures are regulated by an extensive body of legislation. The basic norms that govern the application of SPS measures are Law No. 101 of 1993 (agricultural and fisheries development) and Decrees No. 1.840 of 1994, No. 2.141 of 1991 and No. 4.765 of 2008 (functions of the ICA). Animal and plant health and primary food production are dealt with in Law No. 9 of 1979 and its regulatory decrees, Law No. 100 of 1993, which established INVIMA, and Decrees No. 1.290 of 1994 and No. 211 of 2004, which determine its structure and function. Other relevant provisions include Resolution No. 1.277 of 2004 on the analysis of the risks posed by pests and diseases; and Decree No. 3.075 of 1997 on food inspection, surveillance and control.

111. The MCIT is responsible for notifying the WTO of SPS measures. Between April 1997 (date of the first notification) and December 2011, Colombia submitted 231 different notifications relating to SPS measures, as well as a series of additions to those notifications. During the review period, 122 notifications were made and of these 102 related to animal health, 17 to plants and three to other areas (Table III.17). Between April 1997 and the end of September 2011, Colombia made 159 regular and 73 emergency notifications.[104]

Table III.17
SPS notifications to the WTO, 2006-2011

Year	Total	Animals	Plants	Other areas
2006	23	20	3	
2007	16	14	2	

[104] WTO document G/SPS/GEN/804/Rev.4 of 13 October 2011.

Year	Total	Animals	Plants	Other areas
2008	9	6		
2009	23	20	2	1
2010	35	30	5	
2011	16	9	5	2
Total	**122**	**102**	**17**	**3**

Source: Information provided by the Colombian authorities.

112. Table III.18 summarizes the subject matter of the main notifications made between 2006 and 2011 concerning both livestock and plants. The main provisions relating to SPS measures issued in recent years can be consulted in Table AIII.2. Some of the measures adopted have remained in force for years.

Table III.18
Subject matter of the main notifications relating to livestock and plants

Livestock
Prevention of the introduction into Colombia of bovine spongiform encephalopathy and avian influenza
Epidemiological surveillance of brucellosis and bovine tuberculosis
Issuing of livestock sanitary permits or internal movement passports
Declaration of free zones, high-alert zones, containment zones and enclosures for officially controlled diseases
Self-declaration as a country free of certain diseases
Programmes for the prevention and monitoring of avian influenza and for the control and eradication of Newcastle disease
Registration of veterinary diagnostic laboratories
Sanitary and safety conditions in the primary production of bovine cattle, buffalos and swine, and in the production of animal feed
BPM, BPG and biosecurity conditions
Prohibition of use of olaquindox and diethylstilbestrol
Plants
Areas of low prevalence and eradication of diseases of African palm, ornamental plants, cotton, fruit and vegetables, rice, maize, plantain and banana
Declaration of free and low-prevalence areas for fruit fly and chrysanthemum white rust
Provisional procedure for expanding the temporary use of agricultural chemical pesticides on crops of exotic fruit, aromatic and culinary herbs, minor crops, and ornamental plants
Regulation and control of agricultural chemical pesticides, physiological regulators and coadjuvants
BPM, BPA
Natural rubber and coffee plant propagation material
Requirements for registering the operation of fumigation chambers using methyl bromide in quarantine treatments
Requirements and procedures for the production and distribution of fruit tree propagation material in the national territory and other provisions
Quarantine pests subject to official control, absent from and present in the national territory
Requirements concerning the registration of technical departments for testing effectiveness and producers and importers of bio-inputs for agricultural use and other provisions
Living modified organisms (LMOs)

Source: Information provided by the Colombian authorities.

113. To import animals (including aquatic animals) and products of animal origin it is necessary to obtain an Animal Health Import Document (DZI), which is granted by the ICA under

Resolution (ICA) No. 1.558 of 7 May 2010.[105] If the product is not exempt from the issuance of a DZI, the establishment of origin must be registered. If the product is being imported for the first time from a country with which trade has not been established, a prior risk analysis must be carried out, in accordance with Resolution No. 1.277 of 9 June 2004 and Resolution No. 004 of 2005. The result of the risk analysis study is evaluated by the ICA's Livestock Imports Committee, which determines whether or not to approve the importation. If registration is approved, importation is authorized and it is possible to apply for a DZI. This document must be certified by the sanitary authority of the country of origin and is valid for a maximum of 90 days and for a single shipment, so that a prior application must be made for each importation. The risk assessment procedure is based on the guidelines contained in the Terrestrial Animal Health Code of the World Organization for Animal Health (OIE) and in the Andean Community regulations.

114. Where animal health is concerned, the ICA also imposes requirements relating to zoosanitary export certificates, sanitary inspection at the point of exit or entry, registration of genetic material production centres, import and export registration of inputs, temporary internment of equine animals and intra-subregional trade in animals and animal products.[106] Before animals can be imported they must also pass through a quarantine procedure, either in an official quarantine station or on premises specially equipped for the purpose authorized by the ICA.

115. To qualify for importation all plant materials, products and by-products must meet certain phytosanitary requirements, except for those which because of their physical constitution or the processing they have undergone do not represent a phytosanitary risk. Imports of plant products require a Phytosanitary Requirements Import Document (DRFI), issued by the ICA and indicating the phytosanitary requirements which must be met and which the exporting country must certify for it to be possible to export the product to Colombia.[107] Both the plant health and the animal health requirements are set out in ICA Joint External Circular No. 037 of 16 September 2011. To import raw materials, cake, and protein and energy supplements for animal consumption it is necessary to obtain the approval of the Sanitary and Phytosanitary Regulation Division and of the Safety and Veterinary Inputs Directorate of the Animal Protection Division of the ICA. To import wild flora, the application must be accompanied by a clearance document issued by the Ministry of the Environment, Housing and Regional Development. Importers of seed for sowing and fruit-tree and ornamental plant propagation material must be preregistered with the ICA.

---

[105] The following animals and animal products do not require a DZI to enter Colombia: oils and fats, together with broths and soups, tinned or preserved forms, extracts and juices, of fish, marine mammals, crustaceans and molluscs; shark fins, cartilage and meat; ambergris; antiserums; wool tops; casein and its derivatives; caviar; animal glue; tortoiseshell; coral; completely tanned hides; microbial rennet; cultures of microorganisms for non-veterinarian use; spermaceti from whales and other cetaceans; natural sponges of animal origin; fish fillets and deboned fish meat; glands, other organs and their extracts for use in human organotherapy; meal, powder or pellets of fish or molluscs suitable for human consumption; cochineal and its products; silkworms and their products; lactose; whalebone hair and ivory of marine mammals; culture media for growing microorganisms for non-veterinary use; fish roe for human consumption; peptones from fish and shellfish suitable for human consumption; preparations for sauces, sauces and condiments in powder form, made from animals other than bovine animals, sheep and goats; diagnostic reagents for non-veterinary use and for *in vitro* use in human medicine; animal foetal serums for *in vitro* diagnosis in human medicine; vaccines for human medicine; valves and shells of cooked crustaceans, molluscs or echinoderms and cuttle-bone (ICA, 2005).

[106] Andean Community Resolution CMC No. 1.153 of 2008 defined livestock risk categories, rating them from 1 (low risk) to 5 (high risk). Colombia requires a DZI for products classified in categories 3, 4 and 5.

[107] Andean Community Resolution CMC No. 1.008 of 2006 defined phytosanitary risk categories, rating them from zero (no risk) to 5 (high risk). Colombia requires a DRFI for products classified in categories 2, 3, 4 and 5.

116. As a first step, before obtaining a DRFI, the importer must lodge with the ICA's Quarantine Technical Directorate a written preshipment application for each import operation using a standard form. This process can also be carried out on the ICA's website. After examining the application, the ICA issues the corresponding document, which contains the Colombian import requirements. Once the importer receives the document setting out the phytosanitary requirements for importing the plant material, he can ask the MICT for an import registration and send a copy of the document issued by the ICA to the exporting country, so that the phytosanitary authority can issue a phytosanitary certificate in accordance with the Colombian requirements. The document containing the phytosanitary requirements is issued per species and per shipment, is valid for 90 days and must accompany the imports when they enter Colombia, as must the originals of the phytosanitary certificate of the country of origin. The importer must request the ICA's Quarantine Technical Directorate at the place of entry for a phytosanitary inspection. When the documentation has been checked and the inspection carried out, it is decided whether or not to issue the corresponding phytosanitary clearance certificate, a document which must be handed in to the Directorate of Customs (DIAN) in order to obtain the release of the product into free circulation.

117. In accordance with Resolution No. 2.950 of 2001, the ICA is responsible for analysing the biological and chemical risks which could affect animal and plant species due to international and domestic trade in agricultural goods, tourism and means of transport. Resolution No. 1.277 of 2004 defines the situations in which a risk analysis has to be carried out. In general, the ICA makes risk assessments of animal and plant species, products, by-products and biologicals which form the subject of an import application by taking into account the following: whether their importation has been previously authorized; whether they have been imported from the country of origin in the past; and whether the sanitary or phytosanitary situation has changed or new information has emerged concerning a disease or pest outbreak in the country of origin or in Colombia.[108]

118. During the review period, the ICA made a serious effort to improve transparency through the Health Information System for Agricultural and Livestock Imports and Exports (SISPAP), a tool that provides information and makes possible direct participation in the process of importing/exporting agricultural and livestock products into/from Colombia. SISPAP enables the importer/exporter to familiarize himself in advance with the ICA's import/export phyto- and zoosanitary requirements. It is also possible to file online applications to obtain the documents for each of these procedures, for example, for the issuance of a DZI and or DRFI, a zoosanitary export certificate or a plant export certificate. Through SISPAP users can trace the status of their import and export applications and modify them, as well as pay for these formalities online.

119. To export livestock products to Colombia, the countries of origin of the products to be imported can register their products or establishment in SISPAP. If the product or establishment is not registered, the importer must make a written request for an opinion on the feasibility of the import operation to the ICA's Technical Directorate for Risk Assessment. If there are no restrictions on the entry of the product and it is wished to register the establishment as an exporter to Colombia, then an application endorsed by the veterinary services of the country of origin must be submitted. Depending on the result of the analysis of the information provided, if deemed necessary, a pre-authorization inspection of the establishment of origin may be ordered. Once a favourable opinion has been given, the establishment will be entered in the database and will be able to export to Colombia, subject to application for a DZI. Authorization to export is granted for one year for businesses that produce animals for animal improvement, slaughter animals or process meat; for

[108] ICA online information: "*Evaluación de Riesgo*". Viewed at: http://www.ica.gov.co/getdoc/fb18dace-21dc-41d1-9733-80057e0f95e6/Evaluacion-del-Riesgo.aspx.

three years for those that produce animal breeding stock, produce biologicals for veterinary use, process raw materials of animal origin for manufacturing animal feed, produce animal feed, process milk and milk by-products and produce fish, crustaceans, molluscs and other aquatic invertebrates; and for one to three years, depending on the riskiness of the product, for those that produce other goods considered dangerous for the animal population.

120. In accordance with Decree No. 1.840 of 1994, the ICA is responsible for the Epidemiological Information and Phytosanitary Surveillance System (SisFito), whose objective is to determine the presence or absence of pests within the national territory. SisFito interacts with entities and associations such as Corporación Colombia Internacional (CCI), Corpoica, Cenicafé, Cenipalma, Fedearroz and Augura in officially certifying the phytosanitary condition of the country's various agricultural species. SisFito monitors exotic pests with a high risk of introduction and a severe potential impact on production, endemic pests, including those that are regulated since they affect international trade, and pests of economic importance for the various cultivated species. SisFito has developed an IT platform which enables the ICA to consolidate information on the phytosanitary status of the country and the surveillance of high-risk exotic pests.

121. Where the safety of processed foods is concerned, INVIMA requires sanitary marketing registration valid for ten years. Every batch of product arriving at a Colombian port during the period of validity of the sanitary registration is physically examined by the health authority; laboratory analysis is compulsory for foods identified as posing a greater degree of risk to public health.

122. The authorities have noted that since 2007 INVIMA has had a Sanitary Surveillance Control System (SIVICOS) through which users can make online applications and payments and officials can issue certificates. Moreover, SIVICOS allows INVIMA inspectors to log in and view information concerning imports and exports.

123. Under Resolution No. 00148 of 2005, importing or marketing seed for sowing requires certification and registration with the National Register of Cultivars. Imports of seeds for sale must comply with the quality standards established for each seed species and with the packaging and labelling regulations, which require imported seeds to be sold in the original packages with the original labels.

124. The ICA is authorized to prohibit the production or importation of a cultivar for phytosanitary or biosecurity reasons. Seeds must comply with the information requirements relating to genetically modified organisms (GMOs). Decision 00013 of 1998 created the National Technical Council to assist the ICA in dealing with GMOs for agricultural use. Resolution No. 946 of 2006 establishes the procedure used by the ICA for handling living modified organism (LMO) applications. Regulatory Decree No. 4.525 of 2005 establishes the conditions for the transboundary movement, transit, handling and use of LMOs and creates national technical biosecurity committees responsible for assessing the risks posed by GMOs. There are procedures for marketing livestock products containing GMOs. Marketing is not authorized until the biosecurity assessment has been approved (Resolution No. 02.935 of 2001).

125. Resolution No. 00329 of 2001 states that laboratories which analyse agricultural inputs and pesticide residues must be registered with the ICA. Foreign laboratories can register on presentation of certificates issued by a recognized international body. The national registration of a pesticide requires a risk and environmental management assessment and laboratory analysis certificates. Resolution No. 0150 of 2003 establishes the arrangements for the registration of imports of finished fertilizer products or raw materials for manufacturing them. There are also approval and registration

requirements that must be satisfied in order to import fertilizers for experimentation and certification is required to be an importer, exporter or seller of fertilizers.

126. Before sanitary registration can be granted a documentary, technical and legal assessment must be made. A positive assessment is followed by the immediate granting of registration. There is also a post-marketing check which can result in the suspension of the registration.

127. During the review period, the Ministry of Agriculture and Rural Development, in accordance with the provisions of Law No. 101 of 1993, Resolution No. 169 of 2007 and other regulations, was authorized to grant certain agricultural producers a sanitary incentive in order to support the control and sanitary management of pests and diseases (see section (4)(iv)).

128. Colombia applies the Andean regional sanitary and phytosanitary regulations and has participated with the other CAN countries in efforts to harmonize phytosanitary regulations and SPS procedures in Andean intraregional and third-country trade. At Andean regional level, common procedures for issuing phyto- and zoosanitary permits and certificates have been adopted, together with rules for the registration, control, marketing and use of veterinary products. During the review period, the Andean Community amended its sanitary regulations on animals, products of animal origin and by-products in relation to bovine cattle, horses, swine and poultry. Changes were also made in the basic catalogue of exotic animal pests and diseases of the subregion. Colombia and the other member countries of the Andean Community maintain common SPS requirements with respect to 31 agricultural products and most animals and their products. There are harmonized requirements and procedures for the registration and control of chemical pesticides for agricultural use.

129. The authorities have noted that they are implementing a sanitary upgrade programme. Disbursements under this programme totalled Col$26,670 million (some US$13.5 million) over the two-year period 2010-2011. The main measures include a sanitary upgrade for pig production, the implementation of a cattle identification system, improved phytosanitary standards for horticultural production, sanitary and phytosanitary status building, and the safety and admissibility of agricultural products.

(3) MEASURES AFFECTING EXPORTS

(i) Registration, documentation and export licences

130. The Directorate of Taxes and National Customs (DIAN) is the authority in charge of processing exports (including the sale of goods from the national territory to a free zone), through the customs IT system known as the Single Model of Revenue and Automated Control Services (MUISCA). The prior requirements, for example, of a sanitary or environmental nature, which must sometimes be met in order to export, can be processed on-line through the Single Window for Foreign Trade (VUCE). The natural or legal person intending to export must be enrolled in the Single Tax Register (RUT) as an international exporter or trader. Coffee exporters must also make an annual application for enrolment in the Register of Coffee Exporters.[109] This is a means of monitoring the minimum requirements laid down by the National Committee of Coffee Growers with which coffee bean exporters must comply.[110]

---

[109] MINCOMEX Resolutions No. 0355 and No. 0518 of 2002 and External Circular No. 32 of 2002.

[110] The requirements laid down by the National Coffee Growers' Committee for exporters to be included in the register are set out in Resolution No. 1 of July 2009.

131. If the f.o.b. value of the goods exported exceeds US$10,000, the formalities must be handled by a customs clearing agent, except in the case of users of a special export programme (PEX) (Article 11 of Decree No. 2.685 of 1999) and exporters considered to be "high export users", who are not obliged to use the services of a clearing agent.

132. Decree No. 2.685 of 1999 established the category of high export users (ALTEX) (Articles 35-40), which enables DIAN to recognize and register legal persons that satisfy the following conditions: have, in the course of the 12 months prior to submission of the application, exported goods with an f.o.b. value of at least US$2 million, and this value exported, directly or through an international trading company, represents at least 30 per cent of the value of their total sales in the same period; or the value exported, directly or through an international trading company, represents an f.o.b. value of at least US$21 million.

133. The shipper's export declaration (DEX) must be accompanied by the international sales contract, commercial invoice, packing list, and transport or shipping document. Before shipment is authorized, through the IT services, the declarant (exporter or customs clearing agency) must, if the product to be exported so requires, provide, as appropriate: previous registrations (emeralds[111], medicines, panela[112]), marketing permit (fish and molluscs)[113], previous authorizations (primary forest products)[114], releases (arms, ammunition, explosives), phytozoosanitary[115] or sanitary inspection certificates (food)[116], certificates of origin (preferential agreements), and tax payment certificate (coal, coffee, panela).[117] Up to the end of 2011, the MCIT, through the Group on the Qualification of Origin and Domestic Production, granted certificates of origin. Since 1 January 2012, DIAN has issued certificates of origin needed by the exporter. Once clearance has been authorized, the exporter may ask for the VAT to be refunded.

134. The customs authority applies technical risk analysis criteria, which determine whether an examination of the documents or physical inspection is necessary or shipment can be authorized automatically. Documentary checks are carried out solely on the basis of the information contained in the declaration and its accompanying documents. If it is decided that the goods must be physically inspected, the inspection is carried out by the customs authority, for the purpose of verifying their nature, origin, state, quantity, value and tariff classification. In general, goods exported by high export users are not subject to physical customs inspection. Once the inspection is complete, shipment is authorized through the IT services and the definitive export declaration is lodged and signed by the declarant.

135. To prevent environmental degradation or for public health reasons, Colombia regulates the ports through which certain products, such as primary forest and fishery products, are exported.

136. Like its import regime, apart from ordinary exportation Colombia's export regime covers a range of other procedures (Table III.19).

---

[111] Compendium of Foreign Trade Legislation, Decree No. 2.477 of 1984.

[112] Compendium of Foreign Trade Legislation, Law No. 40 of 1990.

[113] Compendium of Foreign Trade Legislation, Law No. 13 of 1990.

[114] Compendium of Foreign Trade Legislation, Decree No. 2.811 of 1974.

[115] ICA online information: "*Normas del ICA*". Viewed at: http://www.ica.gov.co/Normatividad/Normas-Ica.aspx?page=1.

[116] Compendium of Foreign Trade Legislation, Decree No. 3.075 of 1997.

[117] Compendium of Foreign Trade Legislation, Decrees No. 2.656 of 1988 and No. 1.999 of 1991.

Table III.19
Export procedures

Export procedure	Description
Temporary exportation for outward processing	Regulates the temporary exportation of goods in free circulation in the national customs territory for manufacturing, processing or repair abroad or in a free zone. The goods must then be re-imported within the period indicated in the corresponding export declaration, with the possibility of a one-year extension.
Temporary exportation for reimportation in the same state	Allows the temporary exportation of goods in free circulation in the Colombian customs territory to a foreign destination (including a free zone) for a specific use within a given time-limit of not more than one year, specified by the declarant. The goods must be reimported before the authorized time-limit expires, without having undergone any changes abroad, apart from normal wear and tear.
Re-exportation	Regulates the outright exportation from the national customs territory of goods that were under a temporary admission procedure or the processing or assembly procedure.
Reshipment	Regulates the exportation from the national customs territory of goods from abroad that are in storage and have not been legally abandoned or subjected to any import procedure.
Special export programmes (PEX)	The operation by means of which, under a commercial agreement, a foreign resident purchases raw materials, inputs, intermediate goods, packaging or containers from a producer resident in Colombia and arranges for their delivery to another producer also resident in the national customs territory who undertakes to produce and export the goods manufactured from these raw materials, inputs or intermediate goods or using the packaging material or containers, in accordance with instructions received from the foreign buyer.
Exportation of household goods	The household goods of Colombian residents who leave the national customs territory to take up residence abroad. Under this procedure an export authorization application and the corresponding declaration must be lodged as if it were a case of outright exportation.
Temporary exportation	The procedure under which goods are imported for processing or assembly, by industries recognized as such and authorized for the purpose by DIAN. Its availability remains restricted.
Exportation via postal traffic and urgent consignments	This procedure can be used for exporting mail consignments, consignments that leave the national territory via the official postal network and urgent consignments, provided that their value does not exceed US$5,000 and they require quick delivery.
Exportation of samples of no commercial value	Samples of no commercial value are goods declared as such whose total f.o.b. value does not exceed US$10,000, with the exception of samples of no commercial value exported directly by the National Federation of Coffee Growers or by Proexport, which are not subject to this ceiling. The goods which may not be exported under the samples of no commercial value procedure include: coffee (except when exported by the National Federation of Coffee Growers), emeralds, articles manufactured from precious metals; gold and its alloys; platinum and metals of the platinum group; goldsmith's or silversmith's ash, gold waste or scrap; and mineral products with auriferous concentrates, silver and platinum.

Source: Decree No. 2.685 of 26 December 1999 (and its amendments).

(ii) Other charges and minimum prices

137. Colombia imposes export charges for the purpose of promoting the development of certain sectors. At present, charges are levied on exports of mild coffee, unset emeralds and coal.[118] During the review period, the rates at which the parafiscal contribution taxes on emeralds and coal are applied remained unchanged and they continue to be used to finance the National Emeralds Fund and the Coal Promotion Fund.[119]

138. As for the coffee contribution, which is used to finance the National Coffee Fund, in 2007, it went from being an *ad valorem* charge to being a specific charge of US$0.06 per pound of coffee exported, provided the international price of Colombian coffee exceeds a certain price per pound. The contribution per producer may not be less than US$0.02 per pound of coffee exported. The tax base for levying the "coffee contribution" is the "representative price" established by the national government. This price is calculated daily on the basis of the price of "C" contracts on the New York Stock Exchange, plus the premium awarded to Colombian coffee on the international market.[120]

---

[118] Decrees No. 2.407 of 2000 and No. 2.656 of 1988 and Law No. 788 of 2002, Article 63.

[119] Decree No. 2.407 of 2000.

[120] Decree No. 3.263 of 2002.

139. The parafiscal contribution applied to unset emerald exports is 1 per cent of the value of the exports in foreign currency. This contribution is paid by the exporter and used to finance the National Emeralds Fund.[121]

140. Coal exporters must provide the customs office of exportation with proof of payment of the royalties on coal production assessed on the reference price fixed by the Ministry of Mining and Energy (Chapter IV).

141. Colombia uses minimum prices for coal exports. The price for the coal exported is fixed on the basis of technical and "relevant commercial" criteria, such as the weighted-average f.o.b. price in Colombian ports over the six months prior to the date of determination, after allowing for transport and port costs, the quality of the coal and the characteristics of the coalfield. If there were no exports during the preceding six months, the international price for coal of a similar quality is used as the base price.[122]

(iii) Export restrictions

142. In Colombia, exportation is generally free, except for the limitations and prohibitions established by the laws and international conventions in force. Moreover, both the Higher Council for Foreign Trade and the Committee on Customs, Tariff and Foreign Trade Affairs are authorized to recommend the adoption of measures to control exports, including by prohibiting them in order, for example, to ensure export quality or keep the domestic market supplied, as well as to determine packaging standards and other requirements.[123]

143. In order to satisfy domestic demand, Colombia sets quotas for the domestic sale and exportation of fishery resources. These quotas are determined by the Board of Directors of the National Institute for Fishing (INP). The export quota may be exceeded if it can be shown that the product could not be sold on the domestic market.[124]

144. The National Government is empowered to regulate trade by adopting mechanisms that enable the Colombian economy to overcome external or internal market conditions that are adversely affecting the country's commercial interests.[125] In 2011 (June), Colombia adopted, for one year, quotas for exports of live bovine animals (cows) (HS subheadings 0102.90.00.90 and 0102.10.00.10)

[121] Decree No. 2.407 of 2000, Articles 1 and 4.

[122] Compendium of Foreign Trade Legislation, Decree No. 2.656 of 1988.

[123] Decree No. 2.553 of 1999. In accordance with Decree Law No. 444 of 1967, the State powers for regulating exports are: to issue regulations for channelling exports of certain products through specialized entities, for the purpose of protecting foreign markets by guaranteeing quality and timely delivery and harmonizing export volume with domestic production capacity; to set standards relating to quality, packaging, marks and other requirements that ensure optimum conditions for the marketing of national products in foreign markets; to determine the degree of manufacturing or processing that certain products must have in order to be exported; to establish temporary limitations on exports of staple commodities whose production has been adversely affected by poor harvests or the like and which cannot be economically replaced by other commodities produced locally or abroad; to limit or prohibit the exportation of commodities needed to supply the domestic market when there is a shortage of them on the world market and while the circumstances responsible for the shortage persist; and to establish restrictions to protect flora and fauna and non-renewable natural resources.

[124] Compendium of Foreign Trade Legislation, Decree No. 2.256 of 1991.

[125] Law No. 7 of 1991.

for the purpose of maintaining the flow of trade in these goods and ensuring the rebuilding of the national herd to improve the supply of meat and meat products for export.[126]

145. There is a ban on exporting articles that form part of the national artistic, historical and archaeological heritage. These articles may leave the country only temporarily, under the temporary exportation for reimportation in the same state procedure, for a period of not more than three years, to be used in exhibitions.[127] It is prohibited to export individual specimens of live species of wild fauna, unless they are intended for scientific research or their exportation has been expressly authorized by the State.[128] Colombia applies restrictions on exports of certain products in accordance with commitments undertaken as a signatory to international agreements.[129]

(iv) Support for exports

146. In 2011, Colombia notified the WTO that, since 31 December 2006 it had not granted any subsidies within the framework of the special import-export programme for capital goods and spare parts (SIEX) or under the free zone regime or other subsidy programmes.[130] Colombia notified the WTO Committee on Agriculture that there had been no subsidization of agricultural exports between 2006 and 2010.[131]

147. In connection with the notification required under paragraph 1 of Article XVI of the GATT 1994 and Article 25 of the Agreement on Subsidies and Countervailing Measures, Colombia notified the WTO that during the periods 2007-2009 and 2009-2011 it did not grant any subsidies and that, consequently, within its territory there were no national measures that needed to be notified under the above-mentioned provisions.[132]

(a) Free zones

148. Law No. 1.004 of 2005 revised the free zone regime to ensure that it was not inconsistent with the provisions of the Agreement on Subsidies and Countervailing Measures (ASCM). The free zone regime established in 2005 is a means of creating jobs and attracting new capital investment for the purpose of promoting competitiveness in the production of goods and the provision of services mainly, but not exclusively or necessarily, for foreign markets.[133] During the review period, Decree No. 383 of 2007 (and its amendments) governed the new regime and introduced the conditions and requirements for establishing free zones and for registering users (or assessing them to determine whether they meet the requirements to operate in a free zone).[134] Moreover, special conditions were

---

[126] Decrees No. 2.000, No. 3.046 and No. 4.025 of 2011.

[127] Decree Law No. 444 of 1967 and Decree No. 2.685 of 1999.

[128] Compendium of Foreign Trade Legislation, Decree No. 2.811 of 1974.

[129] Colombia is a signatory to: the Convention on International Trade in Endangered Species of Wild Fauna and Flora; the Basel Convention on the Control of Transboundary Movements of Hazardous Wastes and their Disposal; and the Montreal Protocol on Substances that Deplete the Ozone Layer.

[130] WTO documents G/SCM/N/186/COL-G/SCM/N/220/COL of 30 May 2011 and G/SCM/N/160/COL of 31 May 2011.

[131] WTO documents G/AG/N/COL/39 of 11 February 2010, G/AG/N/COL/39/Corr.1 of 9 March 2010, G/AG/N/COL/44 of 13 January 2011 and G/AG/N/COL/45 of 25 November 2011.

[132] WTO document G/SCM/N/186/COL and G/SCM/N/220/COL of 30 May 2011.

[133] WTO document G/SCM/N/146/COL of 5 September 2006.

[134] Decree No. 383 of 2007 amended the provisions on free zones contained in Decree No. 2.685 of 1999 on customs legislation (Articles 392-429) and this in its turn was amended by Decrees No. 4.051 of 2007, No. 780 of 2008, Nos. 4.285, 4.085 and 4.584 of 2009, Nos. 1.769, 4.809 and 4.801 of 2010, and No. 711 of 2011.

established for the departments of Cauca, Caquetá, Huila, Nariño and Putumayo, as well as for 37 municipalities bordering on the Bolivarian Republic of Venezuela.[135] At regional level, Decision No. 671 (2007) of the Andean Community on the harmonization of customs procedures stipulates that "free zones are governed by the provisions of the national legislation of each member country" (Article 57). Legal persons domiciled in the country or branches of foreign companies, recognized technology parks, port companies, and institutions that provide health services are eligible for the free zone regime.

149. Two types of free zones may be established in Colombia: permanent zones, which may consist of multiple users or a single enterprise (uni-enterprise or special), and temporary zones.[136]

Permanent free zones (multi-enterprise) and special permanent free zones (uni-enterprise)

150. In a permanent free zone (ZFP), that is, a delimited area of the national territory, multiple industrial users of goods or services[137] and commercial users[138] may set up businesses. The special permanent free zone (ZFPE) is a regime that applies to a single industrial user whose business project is considered likely to have a significant impact on Colombia's economic and social development.[139] The ZFPE regime is available to new industrial, agro-industrial[140], and services (including health) enterprises, port companies, and already established enterprises, provided they generate new investment.[141] ZFPEs may be located in any part of the national territory. In 2011, 59.7 per cent of ZFPEs were engaged in the production of goods and services.[142] DIAN is the institution responsible for approving the establishment of a ZFP/ZFPE.[143] The operator user responsible for managing and developing the zone must be domiciled and legally represented in Colombia or, if a foreign company, must have established a branch in Colombia.[144] The operator user of a ZFPE must be a legal person other than the industrial user.[145] The operator user of a ZFP is authorized to manage one or more zones.[146]

---

[135] Decrees No. 1.197 of 2009, No. 1.142, No. 2.595 and No. 2.695 of 2010, and No. 2.129 of 2011.

[136] Law No. 1.004 of 2005, Article 4.

[137] Logistics and transport, telecommunications, research, medical care, tourism, technical support, and auditing and consultancy (Decree No. 383 of 2007, Article 393-20).

[138] Commercial users engage in marketing or storage activities (Decree No. 383 of 2007, Article 393-21). Taken together, they may not occupy an area greater than 5 per cent of the permanent free zone (Decree No. 4.051 of 2007, Article 16).

[139] Decree No. 4.051 of 2007, Article 2.

[140] Biofuel, meat and fish, oils and fats (animal and vegetable), dairy products, food products not previously classified (prepared or preserved vegetables and fruit, tea, soups, wines, vinegar, sauces and yeasts) and coffee and coffee-milling products (Decree No. 4.285 of 2009, Article 2 and Mondragón, 2010).

[141] Decree No. 4.051 of 2007, Articles 6 and 7.

[142] Decree No. 4.051 of 2007, Articles 6 and 7 and information provided by the authorities.

[143] DIAN declares the existence of free zones for a maximum of 30 years (with the possibility of extension) (Decree No. 383 of 2007, Article 392-2). A port company ZFPE will continue to exist until the port concession expires (Decree No. 4.584 of 2009, Article 1). The declaration is subject to the approval, by the Intersectoral Free Zone Commission, of the Free Zone General Development Master Plan submitted by the operator user (Decree No. 4.051 of 2007, Article 3). The Commission is composed of seven members, including the Ministries of Commerce, Industry and Tourism and Finance and Credit and the Minister responsible for the activity it is intended to promote (Decree No. 711 of 2011, Article 1).

[144] Decree No. 4.051 of 2007, Articles 5 and 6. The operator user of the ZFP/ZFPE is authorized to act as such by DIAN (Decree No. 383 of 2007, Article 393-14).

[145] Decree No. 4.051 of 2007, Article 3.

[146] Decree No. 383 of 2007, Article 393-14.

151. Colombia prohibits the pursuit of certain activities in free zones, namely: (i) the exploration, exploitation or extraction of non-renewable natural resources specified in the Mining and Petroleum Code; (ii) the provision of financial services; (iii) the provision of residential public utility services, except for energy generators or providers of national long-distance public telephony services; and (iv) any activity performed within the framework of a State concession contract.[147]

152. In order to operate a ZFP/ZFPE users must meet minimum investment, equity and job creation requirements within an agreed time-limit (Table III.20). These requirements may vary with the department in which the free zone is located and, in the case of the ZFPE, with the activity also (Table III.20). During the review period there were two special temporary regimes for ZFPEs with time-limits for taking advantage of them. The latest date for taking advantage of the ZFPE regime in Caquetá, Cauca, Huila, Nariño and Putumayo was 31 December 2010[148] and in the 37 municipalities bordering on the Bolivarian Republic of Venezuela 31 December 2011.[149] Applications for a new free zone made in these departments after the above-mentioned dates were authorized on the terms and conditions laid down in the general regulations for establishing free zones.

153. In addition to the above-mentioned requirements for ZFP/ZFPE operators, industrial users in ZFPs, depending on their total assets, must meet investment and job creation requirements which may also vary with the location of the ZFP (Table III.21).[150] The various requirements are intended to facilitate the operation of small enterprises by subjecting them to different investment and employment commitments which increase as the enterprise grows.[151]

Table III.20
Requirements applicable to free zone users

Category	Decree No.	Equity (SMMLV[a])	Investment (SMMLV[a])	Directly employed[c]	Other requirement	Term
Permanent free zone	4.051 of 2007, Article 5	23,000	46,000	-	Five registered users	5 years
Permanent free zone in 47 municipalities in Cauca and Huila[b]	780 of 2008, Article 1	-	92,000	-	Ten registered users	5 years
Special or "uni-enterprise" permanent free zone						
Goods	4.051 of 2007, Article 6	-	150,000	150[c]	-	3 years
Services	4.051 of 2007, Article 6	-	10,000-46,000 46,000-92,000 > 92,000	500 350 150	-	3 years
Health services	4.051 of 2007, Article 6	-	10,000-46,000 46,000-92,000 > 92,000	250 175 75	Indirect jobs: 250 Indirect jobs: 175 Indirect jobs: 75	3 years
Agro-industrial projects	4.051 of 2007, Article 6	-	75,000	500	-	3 years
Port companies	4.051 of 2007, Article 6	-	150,000	20	Indirect jobs: 50	3 years

[147] Decree No. 4.051 of 2007, Article 2.
[148] Decree No. 2.595 of 2010, Article 1.
[149] Decree No. 2.695 of 2010, Article 1.
[150] The operator user of a ZFP authorizes the users of goods and services and commercial users operating in the zone (Decree No. 383 of 2007, Article 393-14). DIAN authorizes the sole industrial user of a ZFPE (Decree No. 4.051 of 2007, Article 9).
[151] Information provided by the authorities.

Category	Decree No.	Equity (SMMLV[a])	Investment (SMMLV[a])	Directly employed[c]	Other requirement	Term
Already active enterprises	4.051 of 2007, Article 7	150,000	692,000	-	Double the taxable net income	3 years
Already active enterprises in 47 municipalities in Cauca and Huila[b]	780 of 2008, Article 3	75,000	75,000	-	-	2 years
Departments of Caquetá, Cauca, Huila, Nariño and Putumayo; 37 municipalities bordering on the Bolivarian Republic of Venezuela	1.197 of 2009, Article 4 2.129 of 2011, Article 4 2.695 of 2010, Article 1	-	5,000	50	-	2 years

a On 1 January 2012, the minimum monthly wage in force (SMMLV) was Col$566,700. The SMMLV is adjusted annually.
b See Law No. 383 of 1997, Article 42.
c For every 23,000 SMMLV of additional investment the number of jobs required is reduced by 15, provided the total is never less than 50.

Source: WTO Secretariat.

Table III.21
Main requirements applicable to industrial users of permanent free zones

Total assets (SMMLV[a])	Investment (SMMLV[a])		Directly employed	
	Rest of Colombia	Cauca and Huila[b]	Rest of Colombia	Cauca and Huila[b]
< 500	-	-	-	20
500-5,000	-	2,000	20	20
5,000-30,000	5,000	7,500	30	30
> 30,000	11,500	15,000	50	50

a On 1 January 2012, the minimum monthly wage in force (SMMLV) was Col$566,700. The SMMLV is adjusted annually.
b 47 municipalities (see Law No. 383 of 1997, Article 42).

Source: Decree No. 4.051 of 2007, Article 19 and Decree No. 780 of 2008, Article 4.

154. ZFP/ZPFE users benefit from tax concessions and simplified customs and foreign trade formalities. The rate of income tax for industrial users of ZFP/ZPFEs is 15 per cent, whereas the general rate is 33 per cent.[152] Likewise, imports into ZFP/ZPFEs are exempt from customs taxes (Table III.22). Industrial users can sell 100 per cent of their output in the national customs territory (NCT), paying customs taxes only on inputs imported from third countries.[153] Exports from ZFP/ZPFEs to foreign markets also benefit from the tax incentives accorded to exports from the NCT, such as the Tax Reimbursement Certificate (CERT) and exemption from or refund of VAT.[154] However, since the last review in 2006, some benefits have been withdrawn: the right to deduct the VAT paid on the purchase or importation of industrial machinery, which was abolished on

[152] Law No. 1.004 of 2005, Article 5 and Tax Statute, Article 240-1.
[153] Proexport *et al.* (2010) and Comptroller-General of the Republic (2009).
[154] The CERT would be applied only to the value added in the free zone, without the inclusion of the value of the raw materials used in the production, processing or working of the goods exported from the national customs territory (NCT). At present, the CERT is 0 per cent (information provided by the authorities).

30 April 2007[155]; and the income tax deduction for investment in fixed assets[156], abolished in 2010 for industrial users and from 2011 for commercial users and other taxpayers.[157]

155. The revision of the ZFP/ZPFE regime led to a significant increase in the number of ZFP/ZFPEs, which rose from 11 in 2006 to 88 at the end of 2011.[158] By the end of 2011, the ZFP/ZFPEs had generated Col$9.8 trillion of investment and 12,454 direct jobs.[159] In 2011, 752 enterprises were operating under the ZFP/ZFPE regime. Although the number of enterprises producing goods and services increased, the number of commercial enterprises decreased, since the latter do not benefit from the reduction in income tax.[160]

Table III.22
Specific benefits for free zone users

Description	Legal basis
Tax concession	
Single income tax rate of 15 per cent for industrial users and operator	Law No. 1.004 of 2005, Article 5; Tax Statute, Article 240-1
The sale of raw materials, parts, inputs and finished goods between users is exempt from VAT (with right to refund)	Law No. 1.004 of 2005, Article 7; Decree No. 4.051 of 2007, Article 23; and Tax Statute, Articles 481 and 850
Customs concession	
Exemption from payment of customs taxes (duty and VAT) on the introduction of goods from abroad while they remain within the free zone	Tax Statute, Articles 481 and 850
Foreign trade benefits	
Goods from abroad can be imported into a free zone provided that the transport document shows that they are for the account of a user. Export operations are authorized by the operator user; no shipping authorization or export declaration is required	Decrees No. 2.685 of 1999 and No. 4.051 of 2007, Articles 21 and 22
The goods are not subject to any time-limit on their stay in storage	Decree No. 2.685 of 1999
Possibility of temporarily removing the raw materials for partial processing outside the free zone for up to nine months	Decree No. 2.685 of 1999
Ease of managing inventories and logistical operations between port, border and inland free zones	Decree No. 2.685 of 1999
Exports to third countries benefit from the international trade agreements negotiated by Colombia	Decree No. 2.685 of 1999
Goods considered originating within the framework of the trade agreements signed by Colombia[a]	

a Peru does not recognize the Colombian origin of goods manufactured in Colombian free zones (CAN Decision No. 414 of 1997).

Source: Law No. 1.004 of 2005, Decree No. 4.051 of 2007, Tax Statute and Ministry of Commerce, Industry and Tourism (2010), *Handbook on the Submission of Applications for the Declaration of Free Zones*, June. Viewed at: http://www.dnp.gov.co/PortalWeb/Portals/0/archivos/documentos/DDE/Manual-ZF.pdf.

[155] Law No. 1.004 of 2005, Article 11 and Tax Statute, Article 485-2.

[156] Law No. 863 of 2003, Article 68. This concession was granted on 40 per cent of the value of the investment between 2007 and 2010 (Tax Statute, Article 158-3) and on 30 per cent as from 2010 (Law No. 1.370 of 2009, Article 10 and Tax Statute, Article 158-3).

[157] Law No. 1.370 of 2009, Article 11, Tax Statute, Article 240-1, Law No. 1.430 of 2010, Article 1 and Tax Statute, Article 158-3.

[158] Information provided by the authorities.

[159] Ramos and Rodríguez (2011).

[160] Ramos and Rodríguez (2011).

Temporary free zones

156. Decree 2685 of 1999 and its amendments regulate the temporary free zones established provisionally where international fairs and exhibitions of importance for the Colombian economy and trade are being held. Temporary free zones are set up for the duration of the event, but can begin operating three months before the event and remain in operation for up to six months afterwards (with the possibility of an extension). There are two kinds of users: the manager user and the exhibitor user. Imports of goods into temporary free zones benefit from the same facilities with respect to customs formalities as imports into ZFP/ZFPEs (Table III.22). Upon the expiration of the period of establishment of the temporary zone, if the goods used in the exhibition are not exported or transported to another free zone, they are deemed to have been legally abandoned.[161] A temporary free zone that has operated continuously for more than 15 years may apply to be declared a ZFPE, provided that it generates 150,000 SMMLV (US$38.6 million) in new investment and creates a minimum of 20 direct and formal jobs, within a period of three years.[162]

Special economic export zones

157. Since 2006, the special economic export zones regime, implemented by Law No. 677 of 2001, has not been used.[163] DIAN is responsible for administering and supervising these zones.[164]

(b) Tax Reimbursement Certificate (CERT)

158. Exporters (of goods and services) continue to have the right to claim total or partial reimbursement of indirect taxes, charges and contributions by applying to the MCIT for a tax reimbursement certificate (CERT)[165], which is regulated by Decree No. 636 of 1984. The CERT is used when justified by the prevailing economic conditions. Since 2006 it has been used only in 2007, 2008 and 2011 for final exports of certain products; the exceptions include exports of coffee, petroleum (and petroleum products), precious stones and bananas.[166] The products that can benefit from the CERT vary with the conditions.[167] For example, recently (in 2011) Colombia used the CERT to soften the negative impact of the revaluation of the peso.[168] Only outright exports of products manufactured or produced in Colombia are entitled to the CERT. Thus, it cannot be used for goods that are re-exported, temporary exports and exports of samples or products in non-commercial quantities.[169] The CERT is calculated on the basis of a formula.[170] Where exports from the national

[161] Decree No. 383 of 2007.
[162] Ministry of Commerce, Industry and Tourism (2010).
[163] For further information, see WTO (2006).
[164] Decree No. 4.048 of 2008.
[165] Laws No. 48 of 1983, Articles 2 and 4 and No. 7 of 1991, Article 7. The application is processed online through the portal of the Ministry of Commerce, Industry and Tourism (Ministry of Commerce, Industry and Tourism online information: "*Certificado de Reembolso Tributario*". Viewed at: https://www.mincomercio.gov.co/publicaciones.php?id=10115).
[166] There are also exceptions for Chapters 1 to 16: live animals and animal products and vegetable products; Chapters 25, 26 and 27: mineral products; Chapter 36: powders, explosives and other subheadings contained in the chapter; Chapter 81: other base metals and articles thereof, including waste and scrap; Chapter 93: arms, ammunition and parts and accessories thereof; Chapter 97: works of art, collectors' pieces and antiques; and Chapter 98.
[167] Decrees No. 2.327 and No. 2.678 of 2007, No. 1.499, No. 1.514, No. 1.532, No. 2.882, No. 2.924 and No. 2.986 of 2008 and No. 3.045 and No. 3.180 of 2011.
[168] Information provided by the authorities.
[169] International trading companies and those that sell them goods on condition that they are exported are also deemed to be exporters (Decree No. 636 of 1984).

customs territory are concerned, the value of the CERT (the amount reimbursed) is calculated by multiplying the f.o.b. value of the exports (in US dollars) by the exchange rate representative of the market (at the time of exportation) and by a refund percentage fixed by the Government.[171] The refund percentage fell from 4 per cent in 2007 and 2008 to 1.5 per cent in 2011.[172] Where exports from a ZFP/ZPFE and exports that benefit from incentive programmes under the Vallejo Plan (see below) are concerned, the formula employs the national value added (in US dollars), in place of the f.o.b. value. CERTs are paid out in Colombian pesos.

159. The MCIT establishes the percentage refunds which vary according to the product and the destination of the exports.[173] In 2007 and 2008, exports to Aruba, Bolivia, Bonaire, Curacao, Ecuador, Peru, Panama and Venezuela and in 2011, those destined for Bolivia, Ecuador, Peru and Venezuela were unable to benefit from the CERT.[174] These percentages are fixed for a minimum of three months and can be changed, if necessary, by decree. For exports shipped between 1 January and 31 July 2007 and between 1 February and 30 June 2008, the refund percentage was 4 per cent.[175] This level was reduced to 1.5 per cent from 1 January to 30 April 2011.[176] During July 2008 and December of 2010 the CERT was not used.

160. Exporters are not authorized to apply for a CERT if the destination of the exports is Bolivia, Ecuador, Peru or Venezuela. Up to 2008, exports for Aruba, Bonaire, Curacao and Panama were also ineligible for the CERT.

161. During the review period, the products/sectors that benefited the most from the use of the CERT were as follows: products of the chemical or allied industries; products of the food industries; beverages; plastics; textiles, hides and skins; and rubber and rubber products. Exporters can use the refund to pay income and supplementary taxes, customs duties, VAT or any other tax, with the approval of the collecting entity.

(c) Other tax exemptions

162. Goods that are exported do not incur VAT or municipal or departmental taxes.[177]

163. Sales of raw materials, parts, inputs and finished goods from the national customs territory to industrial users in free zones are exempt from VAT, with the right to a refund.[178] Goods sold in Colombia to international trading companies also give entitlement to the refund of VAT provided that they are exported, directly or processed.

164. Exporters of certain services may apply for the VAT to be refunded. These services are: (i) services provided in Colombia to be used or consumed exclusively abroad by enterprises or

[170] MCIT, Resolution No. 478 of 25 August 2011.

[171] MCIT, Resolution No. 478 of 25 August 2011 (Article 3); and External Circular No. 028 of 2008.

[172] Decrees No. 2.327 and No. 2.678 of 2007, No. 1.499, No. 1.514, No. 1.532, No. 2.882, No. 2.924 and No. 2.986 of 2008, and No. 3.045 and No. 3.180 of 2011

[173] Laws No. 48 of 1983, Article 3 and No. 7 of 1991, Article 7.

[174] Information provided by the authorities.

[175] Decrees No. 2.327 and No. 2.678 of 2007 and No. 1.499, No. 1.514, No. 1.532, No. 2.882, No. 2.924 and No. 2.986 of 2008.

[176] Decrees No. 2.045 and No. 3.180 of 2011.

[177] Corporación Colombia Internacional online information: "*Incentivos gubernamentales para la exportación*". Viewed at: http://www.cci.org.co/cci/cci_x/Sim/Manuales/Logistica%20exportadora/incentivos_servicios/Nincentivos04a.htm.

[178] Decree No. 4.051 of 2007, Article 23 and Tax Statute, Articles 481 and 850.

persons that do not have a place of business or activities in Colombia, so long as the supplier or provider of the service does not have to travel (for example, call centre, architectural, engineering, accountancy, design and translation services); and (ii) tourism services provided to persons resident abroad for use in Colombia.[179] Entities that provide an international trading company with intermediary production services may also apply for the VAT to be refunded on condition that the end product for which the service was provided is exported.

165. Export contracts are exempt from stamp duty.[180]

166. Although Decree Law No. 688 of 1967 permits the establishment of a customs drawback system for exporters of manufactured goods, in actual fact Colombia does not operate a system of this kind.

(d) Special import-export programmes (or Plan Vallejo)

167. Under the special import-export programmes (or Plan Vallejo) total exemption from customs duties and VAT is granted on the temporary importation of inputs, raw materials and intermediate products, provided that they are used for producing goods for export or for providing services directly linked with the production or export of such goods.[181] The payment of VAT may also be deferred for a period of five years. Imports of raw materials/inputs eligible for the Plan Vallejo are also exempt from import licensing requirements (section (2)(vii)).[182]

168. The Plan Vallejo includes several incentive programmes, with export requirements, from which natural and legal persons, who may be businessmen, producers, exporters or traders enrolled in the Single Tax Register, may benefit.[183] Access to the Plan Vallejo is available to importers of raw materials or intermediate products who produce and export the end product; importers and producers of intermediate products that are sold to an exporter; and those who provide services linked with the production of goods for export.[184]

169. To qualify for the Plan Vallejo for raw materials/inputs, 60 or 100 per cent of whatever is produced from the imported raw material/input must be exported.[185] In the case of the Plan Vallejo for services, it is necessary to export services for a minimum value equivalent to 150 per cent of the f.o.b. value of the capital goods and spare parts imported. To benefit from the Plan Vallejo for spare parts intended to be incorporated in capital goods, 70 per cent of the increase in production generated by the incorporation of the parts must be exported. On the other hand, the Plan Vallejo Junior entitles the exporter to import again, free of tax, the raw materials or inputs used in the production of goods for export, if he has paid all the import taxes on the inputs already used; the exporter has a year from the date of exportation to apply.[186]

---

[179] Tax Statute, Articles 481 and 850 and Decree No. 1.805 of 2010.
[180] Tax Statute, Article 530.
[181] WTO (2006) and Chamber of Commerce of Bogota (undated).
[182] Proexport (2010a).
[183] Chamber of Commerce of Bogota (undated).
[184] Proexport *et al.* (2010).
[185] Proexport online information: "*Preguntas frecuentes: Otras preguntas de interés (exportaciones): artículos 172D y 173B del Plan Vallejo*". Viewed at: http://www.proexport.com.co/servicios-al-ciudadano/preguntas-frecuentes.
[186] Proexport (2010a).

170. Under the Special Import-Export Systems programme described in Decree Law No. 444 of 1967 and its amendments, producers and exporters may sign contracts with the Government to import, with exemption from advance deposit, licensing, and consular fees and customs duties, raw materials and other inputs for use in the production of articles exclusively intended to be sold abroad. These firms are obliged, among other things, to use (absorb) in the process of manufacturing the products for export those inputs of domestic origin which it is technically and economically feasible for them to use. Producers of articles which are not directly intended for export, but are going to be used in their entirety by third-party enterprises for producing exports can also qualify for the programme. In this case, the contracts must be signed jointly by the firm planning to import and by the third party or parties that will manufacture the articles for export. If for good reason the raw materials imported under this regime or the products manufactured using them are not eventually exported and the importer wants to have them taken into free circulation, he must obtain the appropriate import licences and pay the corresponding customs duties with a surcharge of 100 per cent.[187]

(e) International trading companies

171. The international trading companies (C.I.) created by Law No. 67 of 1979, which enjoy tax concessions such as exemption from VAT and export tax[188], are Colombian or joint venture companies that market and sell abroad Colombian products purchased on the domestic market or manufactured by their associated producers, and/or that import goods or inputs to supply the domestic market or for manufacturing exportables. These companies are also eligible for the CERT.[189]

172. In 2011, the total value of goods exported through international trading companies amounted to US$186.4 million, equivalent to 0.36 per cent of total exports.[190]

(f) Other export promotion programmes

Special export programmes (PEX)

173. Colombia continues to implement the special export programmes (PEX) regulated by Decree No. 2.685 of 1999 (Articles 329-334), which established them, and by Decree No. 1.530 of 2008, which amended them. PEX users are also eligible for CERTs, as well as for other tax incentives granted to exporters.

174. Under the PEX regime, a foreign buyer purchases raw materials from a producer resident in Colombia, who undertakes to deliver them to a contractor, also resident in Colombia, who exports the end product manufactured from the raw materials obtained from the initial buyer. The producer and the contractor must agree the quantity, the date and the conditions of delivery of the raw materials and the end product. Up to 2008, the contractor had a maximum period of three months from receiving the raw materials to export the end product, but DIAN could grant a three-month extension. The domestic contractor was also required to obtain a bank guarantee for 30 per cent of the value of the raw materials. Decree No. 1.530 of 2008 abolished this period and the end product is now exported in accordance with the single shipping procedure applicable to outright exports. According to the information provided by the authorities, very little use has been made of this instrument. Since

[187] Decree Law No. 444 of 1967, Article 177.
[188] Gómez *et al.* (2010).
[189] Decree No. 0380 of 16 February 2012.
[190] Information provided by the authorities.

the mechanism was introduced very few programmes have been approved and of these only two are still in effect.

175. Decree No. 2.685 of 1999 established the category of high export users (ALTEX) described above. In general, ALTEX users are exempt from the payment of VAT on imports of industrial machinery intended for processing raw materials.[191] Likewise, the exports of ALTEX users are not subject to physical inspection.[192] Moreover, they can benefit from the PEX regime and are offered the opportunity of obtaining an industrial processing warehouse that enables them to import inputs and raw materials with relief from customs duties and charges and VAT, provided that the goods are used in manufacturing export products.[193]

Other programmes

176. In 2008, the National Agricultural Credit Commission created a special credit facility at subsidized rates for the purpose of financing projects to meet the capitalization requirements for agricultural products destined wholly or partially for the external market.[194] This credit facility was used only in 2008 and part of 2009.[195] In addition, through the Agricultural Guarantee Fund (FAG), a Special Exporters Guarantee Fund was set up to guarantee loans granted using this special facility.

177. In order to support aquaculture and promote exports of shrimp, tilapia and trout, in 2010 an incentive was introduced for the supply of these products.[196] In addition, in 2008 and 2009 a sanitary incentive for export aquaculture was implemented.[197]

(v) Financing, insurance and guarantees

178. The Foreign Trade Bank of Colombia (Bancoldex) was established in 1991 as a financial institution responsible for providing export financing.[198] Bancoldex is a semi-public company whose main shareholder is the Ministry of Commerce, Industry and Tourism.[199] Bancoldex is currently a development bank supervised by the Financial Supervisory Authority of Colombia, which functions as a second-tier bank to meet the credit needs of any enterprise, whether it exports or not. Abroad, Bancoldex offers financing to buyers of Colombian goods and services, through pre-authorized intermediaries.[200] The interest rate on loans provided by Bancoldex corresponds to the rediscount rate granted to the intermediary plus the additional points (spread) agreed between the intermediary and the enterprise that receives the funds.

---

[191] To qualify for this concession, the ALTEX user must annually provide evidence of compliance with the requirement to export at least 30 per cent of his sales. The machinery may not be assigned to third parties, other than to a leasing company to obtain financing. Non-compliance means that the ALTEX user must refund the unpaid VAT (plus interest) and pay a fine of 5 per cent of the f.o.b. value of the machinery (Tax Statute, Article 428).

[192] Chamber of Commerce of Bogota (undated).

[193] Proexport *et al.* (2010).

[194] Resolution No. 32 of 2008.

[195] Information provided by the authorities.

[196] Resolution No. 157 of 2010.

[197] Resolution No. 116 of 2008.

[198] Decree No. 2.505 of 1991.

[199] The MCIT owns 91.9 per cent of the capital. The other main shareholder is the Ministry of Finance and Credit (7.9 per cent) (Bancoldex online information: "*Accionistas*". Viewed at: http://www.bancoldex.com/contenido/contenido.aspx?catID=92&conID=509).

[200] Bancoldex online information: "*Banco de segundo piso*". Viewed at: http://www.bancoldex.com/contenido/contenido.aspx?catID=92&conID=148.

179. Bancoldex acts as a second-tier bank, which means that rather than lending to exporters directly it lends through authorized financial intermediaries. Bancoldex offers financing to both direct and indirect exporters.[201] There are various arrangements for providing exporters with financing (Table III.23). Bancoldex currently holds 4.1 per cent of the total credit portfolio. In 2011, Bancoldex granted loans worth Col$4.2 trillion as compared with Col$2.25 trillion in 2006.

Table III.23
Export financing arrangements

Description	Amount financeable	Term	Beneficiaries
Financing for the buyer of goods and services			
Buyer credit facility			
Bancoldex finances or refinances the advances and other payments made by the foreign buyer of Colombian goods and/or services, through financial intermediaries domiciled inside or outside the country of the importer, using bank payment instruments[a]	In US dollars or in euros. Up to 100% of the value of the goods or services imported or to be imported	Consumer goods: up to 1 year. Intermediate goods: up to 18 months. Capital goods: up to 5 years	Foreign buyers of Colombian goods and/or services; Colombian exporters; foreign financial intermediaries
Financing for engineering and construction projects and other services			
The development of engineering and/or construction projects abroad carried out by Colombian enterprises can also be financed in the same way as under the buyer credit facility	Up to 100% of the Colombian component of goods, services and inputs linked with the project. Up to 50% of the component imported from third countries that form part of the project. Up to 85% of the local costs and expenses necessary for implementation of the project. The amount will depend on the Colombian component's share of the total cost of the of the project	n.a.	Importer of engineering and/or construction projects carried out by Colombian enterprises; Colombian exporters of goods and/or services; foreign financial intermediaries
Purchase of securities			
Securities generated in the international banking operation			
Purchase of securities[b] generated in a forward trading operation and guaranteed by an eligible financial intermediary, domiciled inside or outside the country of the foreign buyer	n.a.	n.a.	Colombian exporters; foreign buyers of Colombian goods and/or services
Purchase of securities covered by a credit insurance policy - Liquidex in US$			
Purchase at a discount of negotiable invoices (*facturas cambiarias de compraventa*) or bills of exchange	n.a.	n.a.	n.a.
Currency hedges			
By means of this instrument, the exporter negotiates a fixed exchange rate when he receives payment of his foreign currency	n.a.	n.a.	Exporters who have a direct relationship with Bancoldex. The export payment instrument must have been received by Bancoldex

n.a. Not applicable.

a Among other things, letters of credit (L/C), guaranteed bills of exchange, promissory notes and commitments to pay.
b Among other things, banker's acceptances or deferred payments derived from forward L/C, guaranteed bills of exchange and promissory notes.

Source: Bancoldex online information, "*Comercio exterior: Para exportadores: Productos y servicios*". Viewed at: http://www.bancoldex.com/contenido/categoria.aspx?catID=45.

---

[201] Dueñas (2008).

180. Bancoldex offers a special ATPDEA credit facility for SMEs exporting to the United States.[202] Due to the suspension of United States tariff preferences (ATPDEA) for Colombian products between February and October 2011 (Chapter II)[203], Bancoldex found itself obliged to make special credit lines available to the exporters affected by the suspension. In February 2011, Bancoldex made available a US$150 million credit line to enable exporters (direct and indirect) to finance their working capital, up to a maximum of US$5 million per enterprise. The loan was granted for one year.[204] In March 2011, a second US$30 million credit line was granted to those enterprises that export directly or through international trading companies to enable them to pay the duties on their products. The loan covered up to a maximum of 100 per cent of the duties and was granted for six months.[205]

181. Colombia has no official export insurance or guarantee programmes. This type of insurance is provided by private insurers, including Segurexpo, a subsidiary of Bancoldex.[206] Segurexpo insures against commercial, country and extraordinary risks. In August 2011, Segurexpo had 43.8 per cent of the export insurance market, followed by Crediseguro with 41.2 per cent.[207]

(vi) Export promotion and marketing assistance

182. Since 1992, Proexport, through its eight national offices and its 22 representative offices abroad, has been the body entrusted with the promotion of non-traditional exports.[208] Proexport advises exporters on how to gain access to the international market. Through the Expopyme programme, Proexport also helps Colombian small and medium-sized businesses to enter the international market.[209] Moreover, it offers specialized services to foreigners interested in purchasing goods and services in Colombia. In 2011, Proexport invested Col$100,000 million in the promotion of exports, foreign investment and tourism.[210]

(4) MEASURES AFFECTING PRODUCTION AND TRADE

(i) Competition policy

183. Since its last review in 2006, Colombia has amended its competition legislation by adopting a new law in 2009 for the purpose of "updating the regulations on the protection of competition to adapt

---

[202] WTO (2006).

[203] ABC Economía online information. Viewed at: http://abc-economia.com/tema/atpdea/; and Proexport online information: "*Congreso de Estados Unidos renovó el ATPDEA para empresarios colombianos hasta julio del 2013*". Viewed at: http://www.proexport.com.co/noticias/congreso-de-estados-unidos-renov%C3%B3-el-atpdea-para-empresarios-colombianos-hasta-julio-del-20.

[204] Bancoldex, External Circular No. 004 of 2011. Viewed at: http://www.bancoldex.com/contenido/contenido.aspx?catID=339&conID=2749.

[205] Bancoldex, External Circular No. 008 of 2011 and Circular Letter of 30 March 2011. Viewed at: http://www.bancoldex.com/contenido/contenido.aspx?catID=339&conID=2905.

[206] Segurexpo online information: "*La empresa*". Viewed at: http://www.segurexpo.com/web/sp/Nuestra-Empresa/Quienes-Somos/index.aspx.

[207] Information provided by the authorities.

[208] Tourism and foreign investment are also promoted (Proexport online information: "*Nuestra historia*". Viewed at: http://www.proexport.com.co/conozca-proexport/nuestra-historia; and "*Red de oficinas*". Viewed at: http://www.proexport.com.co/proexport/red-de-oficinas).

[209] Proexport online information: "*Programa adecuación de ofertas empresariales*". Viewed at: http://www.proexport.com.co/noticias/historial/programa-adecuacion-de-ofertas-empresariales.

[210] Proexport online information: "*Presupuesto*". Viewed at: http://www.proexport.com.co/proexport/transparencia/presupuestos.

them to current market conditions, make it easier for users to keep track of these regulations and to optimize the tools available to the national authorities for the purpose of fulfilling their constitutional duty to protect free economic competition within the national territory". The main provisions on restrictive business practices are contained in the Constitution, in Law No. 1.340 of 24 July 2009 (establishing rules for the protection of competition), in Law No. 155 of 1959, and in Decrees No. 2.153 of 1992 and No. 19 of 2012. The Ministry of Commerce, Industry and Tourism is responsible for formulating competition policy.[211]

184. Under Article 6 of Law No. 1.340 of 2009, the Supervisory Authority for Industry and Trade (SIC) is the national authority for the protection of competition. In 2011, the SIC was restructured and converted into the single competition protection authority.[212] Thus, the SIC has exclusive powers to conduct investigations, impose fines and adopt other decisions relating to infringements of the provisions on the protection of competition. The SIC is also responsible for overseeing compliance with the provisions on unfair competition. The Special Administrative Division for Civil Aviation (air transport) and the Financial Supervisory Authority deal with business integration operations in their respective sectors.[213]

185. There is a special regime for the agricultural sector, explained in Article 5 of Law No. 1.340 of 2009 (Application of the General Competition Regime in the Agricultural Sector). The law stipulates that, for the purposes of the additional clause of Article 1 of Law No. 155 of 1959, the agricultural sector is deemed to be a basic sector of interest for the general economy and that therefore anti-competitive agreements may be authorized for the purpose of stabilizing this sector of the economy. Thus, the Ministry of Agriculture and Rural Development must give a prior binding and reasoned opinion in relation to the authorization of agreements and understandings whose purpose is to stabilize this sector of the economy. Similarly, the following are exempt from the application of the Law on Competition: price stabilization funds, parafiscal funds for the promotion of agriculture, the establishment of minimum support prices, the regulation of domestic markets for agricultural products, chain agreements in the agricultural sector and the Safeguards Regime, and the other mechanisms envisaged in Laws No. 101 of 1993 and No. 81 of 1988.[214]

186. Article 333 of Colombia's National Constitution establishes the principles of free enterprise, free competition and economic freedom as rights of all, within the limits laid down by law. The Constitution makes the State responsible for preventing economic freedom from being obstructed or restricted and for preventing any abuse by individuals or enterprises of their dominant position in the domestic market.

187. The general regime for the protection of competition has four main pillars: (a) anti-competitive practices; (b) integration operations; (c) administrative unfair competition; and (d) competition law.

188. With regard to anti-competitive practices, the general rules are defined in Article 1 of Law No. 155 of 1959 and Articles 47, 48 and 50 of Decree No. 2.153 of 1992. In addition, some sectors have special rules which, in accordance with Article 2 of Law No. 1.340 of 2009, are given precedence over the general rules. Agreements prohibited under the competition regulations include those having the following purposes or effects: direct or indirect price-fixing; determination of

[211] Decree No. 210 of 2003.

[212] Decree No. 4.886 of 2011.

[213] Laws No. 142 of 1994 and No. 182 of 1995 and Decree No. 663 of 1993.

[214] Article No. 31 of the Law No. 1.340 of 2009, Decree No. 2.478 of 1999 and Law No. 101 of 1993 (General Law on Agricultural and Fishery Development).

discriminatory sales or marketing conditions for third parties; distribution of market shares between producers or distributors; allocation of production or supply quotas; allocation, distribution or limitation of sources of supply of production inputs; limitation of technical developments; tied sales; refraining from producing a good or service or affecting its levels of production; collusion in bidding or tendering, distribution of awards, distribution of tenders or fixing the terms of bids; and preventing third parties from obtaining access to markets or marketing channels.

189. The abuse of dominant position includes predatory pricing; the application of discriminatory conditions for equivalent operations; tied sales; selling to one buyer on terms different from those offered to another where the intention is to reduce or eliminate competition in the market; price discrimination; and obstructing or preventing third parties from obtaining access to markets or marketing channels.

190. This list of practices susceptible of distorting competition is not exhaustive; the Colombian legislation provides only a list of examples of practices of this kind. In addition to the above-mentioned practices, business integration operations that materially restrain competition while failing to compensate with efficiencies are also prohibited. Moreover, acts of unfair competition specified in Law No. 256 of 1996 which impair or have an impact on the market are liable to investigation under the competition regime.

191. With respect to the public utilities regulated by Law No. 142 of 11 July 1994 (residential water supply, sanitation, refuse collection, electricity, gas distribution, switched basic public telephony and local mobile telephony in the rural sector), Article 98 of the Law (Competition-restricting tariff practices) prohibits public utility providers from: (a) charging customers of a competitive market, or one whose tariffs are not subject to regulation, tariffs lower than operating costs, especially if the same enterprise provides services in other markets in which it has a dominant position or in which its tariffs are subject to regulation; (b) offering tariffs lower than its average operating costs with the intention of driving out competitors, preventing the entry of new bidders or gaining a dominant position *vis-à-vis* the market or potential customers; and (c) discriminating against some customers with the same commercial characteristics as others, by charging the former higher tariffs than the latter, even if the discrimination takes place within a competitive market or one whose tariffs are not regulated. Violation of these prohibitions may result in the authorities regulating the unregulated tariffs.

192. In the financial sector, in accordance with the Organizational Statute of the Financial System[215], all agreements or understandings between businessmen, decisions of business partnerships and concerted practices which, directly or indirectly, have as their purpose or effect the prevention, restriction or distortion of the play of free competition within the financial and insurance system are prohibited.

193. Decree No. 1.663 of 1994 stipulates that the State guarantees free and fair competition within the health services market, including inputs and equipment used for the provision of those services. Consequently, all agreements, acts and understandings, and concerted practices and decisions which, directly or indirectly, have as their purpose or effect the prevention, restriction or distortion of the play of free competition within the health services market or the prevention, restriction or interruption of the provision of health services are prohibited.

194. Under the procedure governed by Decree No. 2.153 of 1992, Law No. 1.340 of 2009 and Decree No. 19 of 2012, upon initiating an investigation, whether at the request of an applicant or

[215] Decree No. 663 of 1993.

ex officio, the SIC studies the information contained in the complaint lodged by a third party or which has come into its possession in some other way with a view to deciding on its admissibility and determining whether the case should be filed or has sufficient merit to justify proceeding to a preliminary inquiry. For the aforementioned analysis, the SIC can make use of its powers to gather more information. For example, to establish the existence of an infringement of the legal provisions and adopt the appropriate measures, the SIC is empowered to request documentary evidence from natural and legal persons and carry out inspections. It may also question under oath, in accordance with the formalities laid down in the Code of Civil Procedure, anyone with knowledge that might help it to establish the facts or gather the necessary information.[216]

195. The outcome of the preliminary inquiry will determine whether or not there is a need for a formal investigation. If there is, then those investigated are personally notified in order that they may seek or furnish the evidence they intend to present. During the investigation, opportunities are provided for the SIC to seek evidence and to make an offer of guarantees.[217] Third parties may intervene in the proceedings.[218] The SIC may impose interim measures provided that it is considered that not to adopt them would jeopardize the effectiveness of a possible decision to impose sanctions. The SIC could, for example, request the immediate suspension of any behaviour that could prove contrary to the provisions of the regulations on the protection of competition. Once the investigation has been instituted, the Deputy Superintendent of the SIC calls a hearing at which the parties present the evidence submitted in the course of the proceedings and the arguments they intend to make in the light of that evidence, after which he submits to the Superintendent a reasoned report indicating whether, in his opinion, there has or has not been an infringement. This reasoned report is not binding on the Superintendent. The report is communicated to the party investigated and to interested third parties for comment. Finally, the Superintendent issues the resolution that brings the proceedings to a conclusion. The investigated party may apply for reconsideration.

196. Law No. 1.340 of 2009 increased the fines applicable to natural and legal persons. The SIC is authorized to impose, for each violation and on each infringer, fines of up to of 100,000 current legal minimum monthly wages (SMMLV) or up to 150 per cent of the profits derived from the behaviour of the infringer, whichever is the greater. The SIC is also empowered to impose on any person that assists, facilitates, authorizes, executes or tolerates conduct in breach of the rules on the protection of competition fines up to the equivalent of 2,000 SMMLV at the time of imposition of the penalty. The SIC is authorized by Law No. 1.340 of 2009 to grant leniency, for example, exemption from the application of fines, to natural or legal persons that have participated in conduct that breaches the rules on the protection of competition but collaborate with the authorities. This concession may be granted even if the competition authority has already instituted the corresponding proceedings.

---

[216] For further online information, see SIC: "*Definición sobre competencia*". Viewed at: http://www.sic.gov.co/es/web/guest/libre-competencia.

[217] An investigation for breach of the rules on restrictive trade practices may be terminated prematurely by the furnishing of guarantees. This requires the investigated party to submit an offer before the expiration of the time allowed by the SIC for seeking or furnishing evidence. If the guarantees are accepted, then in the administrative instrument ordering the closure of the investigation, the SIC must specify the conditions under which the continuity of compliance with the obligations assumed by the investigated party will be verified. Non-compliance with the obligations stemming from acceptance of the guarantees will be deemed to be a breach of the rules on the protection of competition and give rise to the sanctions for which the law provides, following a request for the explanations required by the SIC.

[218] Third parties may intervene within 15 working days of publication of the initiation of the investigation, by informing the SIC of the grounds and evidence they intend to submit. Competitors, consumers, accredited consumer leagues and associations and, in general, anyone with a direct interest in the investigation may intervene as a third party.

197. Business concentrations are regulated by the Colombian legislation. They must be notified in advance if: (a) jointly or individually, during the tax year preceding the planned operation the enterprises wishing to merge have operating income or total assets of more than 100,000 SMMLV (some US$30.6 million)[219]; or (b) jointly hold a 20 per cent or greater share of the relevant market.[220] Enterprises participating in operations subject to the notification requirement must provide the SIC with the information specified in the Single Circular.[221]

198. The SIC has 30 days from the time it receives the information to rule on the operation, by approving, imposing conditions or rejecting the concentration. If it fails to make a ruling within this 30-day time-frame, the operation will be deemed to have been approved. In some cases the SIC may refrain from objecting to an integration operation provided that the enterprises concerned give certain undertakings to identify and isolate or eliminate the anti-competitive effect of the integration operation and implement the structural or behavioural remedies or solutions imposed by the SIC with respect to the operation in question.

199. If an integration operation is not notified, or if the operation is carried out before the end of the period within which the SIC is allowed to rule, apart from the appropriate sanctions for violation of the rules on the protection of competition, the SIC is authorized, subject to investigation, to order the roll-back of the integration operation. However, to be able to do this, the SIC must determine that the operation involves an undue restraint on free competition. The SIC may also order the roll-back of the concentration operation if the conditions under which it was authorized are not fulfilled.

200. Under Article 12 of Law No. 1.340, the SIC is authorized to recognized the plea of efficiency. That is to say, even if the operation has effects on competition, the SIC may refrain from objecting to it if the interested parties can show, in studies based on methodologies of recognized technical merit, that the beneficial effects of the operation for consumers exceed the possible negative impact on competition and that these effects cannot be achieved by other means.

201. During the period 2006-June 2011, a total of 517 concentration operations were notified and 507 decisions were taken. In 95 per cent of cases, the decisions were to grant unconditional approval of the integration operation. Conditions were imposed on the integration operation in nine cases and in only two was the application rejected (Table III.24).

Table III.24
Business integration operations notified to the SIC, 2006-2011

Year	Applications	Integration decisions	Approved	Conditions set	Objections raised
2006	105	102	98	4	0
2007	80	75	73	2	0
2008	81	81	78	1	1
2009	78	77	63	0	0
2010	125	123	124	1	0
2011 (June)	48	49	47	1	1
Total	**517**	**507**	**483**	**9**	**2**

Source: WTO Secretariat, based on information provided by the SIC.

[219] Resolution No. 75.837 of 2011.
[220] If subparagraph (a) is satisfied but if, collectively, the enterprises planning to merge account for less than 20 per cent of the relevant market, the operation will be deemed to have been automatically authorized. In this case, the sole obligation is to notify the SIC of the concentration operation.
[221] Title VII, Chapter 2, Single Circular of the Supervisory Authority for Industry and Trade.

202. During the period 2006-June 2011, the SIC initiated 101 investigations, arriving at a decision in 56 cases and terminating seven cases by accepting guarantees. The other cases ended with the complaint being withdrawn or being found to be inadmissible, or are still in progress.[222] Sanctions were imposed in one third of cases. During the period analysed, the SIC made notable progress with regard to the average duration of an investigation, reducing it from 1,515 days in 2006 to 375 in 2011 (Table III.25).

Table III.25
Activities of the SIC, 2006-2011

Year	Total number of investigations	Total decisions	Sanctions imposed	Guarantees accepted	Average time (from initiation to decision) (days)
2006	11	10	3	1	1,515
2007	15	14	8	3	954
2008	8	8	7	0	527
2009	8	3	2	1	505
2010	26	9	4	2	468
2011 (June)	33	12	9	0	375
Total	**101**	**56**	**33**	**7**	**724**

Source: WTO Secretariat, based on information provided by the SIC.

203. Within the context of this review, the authorities have pointed out that, despite the reforms and improvements implemented and the reduction in the length of investigations, there are still shortcomings in the functioning of the competition authority. In this respect, a series of points have been identified in a National Development Plan for making good these deficiencies. The measures proposed include: easing the shortage of human resources; establishing a sectoral economic studies group to promote competition; creating/proposing alternative sources of financing for the authority; making a compilation of all the laws and regulations on competition; giving greater visibility to decisions not subject to confidentiality; regulating the exceptions to the competition regime; broadening the scope of competition law; amending the procedures for the notification and pre-assessment of concentrations and the preparation of handbooks/guidelines; assessing the advantages of establishing a system under which such functions could be assigned to a collegiate body.

204. In order to improve the operational and institutional structure of the SIC, in the Plan of Action 2011 it is suggested that bilateral contacts with the competition authorities of Latin America, the United States and the European Union be further developed; and that Colombia should participate actively in the working groups of the OECD's International Network of Competition Authorities and the International Competition Network (ICN).[223]

(ii) Price controls

205. Decree No. 2.876 of 1984, Law No. 81 of 1988 and Law No. 142 of 1994 authorize various ministries, depending on the good or the product, to establish and implement pricing policy by means of a resolution.[224] Where there is doubt as to the entity responsible for establishing and implementing

[222] Information provided by the authorities.

[223] Colombia has been admitted to the OECD as an observer in matters relating to the protection of competition.

[224] The establishment of a pricing policy, its application, and the setting of prices for goods and services subject to control are the responsibility of: the Ministry of Agriculture, for products of the agricultural

pricing policy, the National Economic and Social Policy Council (CONPES) will decide. Likewise, if there were a high degree of vertical integration between the raw material and the industrial process, CONPES would determine whether the prices would be regulated by the Ministry of Economic Development or the department responsible for controlling the raw material. Price and margin controls can be applied at any stage in the production or distribution of a product or service.[225]

206. Pricing policy can be applied ex officio or at the request of manufacturers, producers, distributors, importers and consumer associations. The entities entrusted with the implementation of pricing policy must determine the goods and services whose prices are to be controlled in the sectors within their competence and decide between the three ways in which price controls can be applied in Colombia: the direct control regime; the regulated freedom regime; and the monitored freedom regime.[226] Under the direct control regime, the entity fixes, by resolution, the maximum price for the producer and/or distributor. If the price of the goods or services comes under the regulated freedom regime, the competent entity will define the criteria and methodology necessary for the producers and distributors to be able to determine or modify the maximum prices. The producers and distributors may freely determine the price of the goods and services that fall under the monitored freedom regime, with the obligation to inform in writing the respective regulatory body of any change in price. Enterprises whose goods or services are subjected to any form of price control have the right to ask for the price to be changed or for changes in the price to be permitted.

207. Law No. 142 of 1994, which applies to residential public utilities, specifically water supply, sanitation, refuse collection, electricity, gas distribution, switched basic public telephony and local mobile telephony in the rural sector, stipulates that the tariffs for these services may come under the regulated or monitored freedom regime.

208. In those sectors in which restraints on competition exist, the SIC, after carrying out an investigation, can recommend to the various entities responsible for price controls the imposition of price controls and the type of controls that should be imposed.

209. At present, the few products whose prices are controlled include petrol[227], some medicaments, natural gas and LPG, drinking water, basic sanitation and electricity.

(iii) State trading, State-owned enterprises and privatization

(a) State trading

210. Under Article 336 of the Political Constitution, Article 61 of Law No. 14 of 1983, Decree No. 1.222 of 1986 and Law No. 788 of 2002, the Departments, that is, the territorial divisions of the country, are independent administrators of the liquor monopoly as a means of raising revenue,

---

sector; the Ministry of Mining and Energy, for petroleum and petroleum products, coal, gas for distributors, and other mineral products; the Ministry of Public Works and Transport, for urban and suburban passenger and mixed land transport fares, and when subsidized by the State, intermunicipal and interdepartmental land transport fares and those for river transport; the Administrative Department of Civil Aviation, for national air fares; the National Tourism Corporation, for hotel, restaurant, bar and similar business services; and the Ministry of Economic Development, for public spectacles, the products of the manufacturing industry and services of a commercial nature not covered by other entities (Law No. 81 of 23 December 1988).

[225] Law No. 81 of 23 December 1988 and Decree No. 2.876 of 27 November 1984, establishing rules on price controls and other arrangements.

[226] Law No. 81 of 23 December 1988.

[227] Laws No. 488 of 1998 and No. 681 of 2001.

preferably for the education and health services.[228] The departmental distilleries produce, export and import alcoholic beverages. However, individual traders may export and import them, subject to the conclusion of a contract with the Department concerned. This agreement contains, among other clauses, provisions specifying the term of the contract and the quantity of spirits that can be distributed, together with the Department's percentage share of the sale price of the products under the monopoly.[229] This mechanism is applied to various spirits, including rum, gin, vodka and brandy, and is exclusively reserved for the State.[230]

211. The State, through the defence company INDUMIL, has the exclusive right to import, export, manufacture and market arms, raw materials for producing explosives, and machinery and devices for manufacturing them.[231]

(b) State-owned enterprises and privatization

212. In Colombia there are two categories of State-owned enterprises: State industrial and commercial enterprises (EICE) and semi-public companies (SEM). Both types of enterprise engage in industrial, commercial and foreign trade activities and operate in conformity with the rules of private law, with the exceptions stipulated in the specific law that establishes them. The State holding in an EICE is equal to at least 90 per cent, but these enterprises enjoy administrative and financial autonomy.[232] EICEs can also be set up as "partnership enterprises" if the State shares partnership status with other public entities.[233] SEMs are formed under the commercial company regime with public and private participation. The State holding in a SEM may not be less than 50 per cent.[234]

213. State-owned enterprises are regulated and overseen by various commissions and supervisory authorities, depending on the sector in which they are active (Table AIII.3). At the end of 2011, there were 61 State-owned enterprises, the majority of which were EICEs. They were operating in ten sectors, in particular, in the energy sector (Table AIII.3). Since 2006, the State has wound up 11 State-owned enterprises. The authorities note that State-owned enterprises do not enjoy exclusive privileges. The State-owned enterprises existing in 2011 accounted for 13.6 (0.6) per cent of total exports (imports) of goods in 2006 and around 29.5 (0.24) per cent in 2011. The increase in exports is almost entirely attributable to exports by Colombiana de Petróleos S.A. - Ecopetrol.[235]

(iv) Incentives

214. Colombia continues to use tax incentives as a means of promoting domestic and foreign investment (Chapter II) and other support programmes for developing specific sectors and achieving social and regional equality. Some of these programmes which relate to agriculture were notified to the WTO in 2010.[236]

---

[228] WTO document G/STR/N/13/ COL of 1 July 2010.

[229] WTO document G/STR/N/12/COL of 6 July 2009.

[230] WTO documents G/STR/N/13/COL of 1 July 2010, G/STR/N/12/COL of 6 July 2009 and G/STR/N/10/COL and G/STR/N/11/COL of 8 June 2007.

[231] Law No. 525 of 1999 and Decrees No. 2.535 of 1993, No. 1.809 of 1994 and No. 334 and No. 1.419 of 2002.

[232] Law No. 489 of 1998, Articles 85 and 86.

[233] National Planning Department (2010a).

[234] If the public capital in a SEM reaches 90 per cent or more, it is converted into an EICE (Law No. 489 of 1998, Article 97).

[235] Information provided by the authorities.

[236] WTO document G/AG/N/COL/48 of 25 November 2011.

(a) Credit programmes

215. Bancoldex, a second-tier bank, provides loans for users through authorized financial intermediaries. There are two categories of loans: credit modalities and special lines of credit. Credit modalities include various lines of credit for meeting the financing needs of micro, small, medium and large enterprises in any sector of the economy, without establishing special access conditions. Under this scheme they are granted credit for fixed investment, business capitalization, debt consolidation and working capital. Bancoldex offers credit in both pesos and US dollars, for a maximum term of ten years and with a grace period that depends on the line of credit and the currency and can vary from one year for dollar loans to three years for loans in pesos.

216. Special lines of credit include lines of credit with preferential financial conditions that are subject to financing limits and compliance with special conditions. This type of loan is reserved for specific enterprises, depending on their geographical location and size and the use to be made of the credit requested. At present, there are 23 special lines of credit, of which 16 are intended to finance micro, small and medium-sized businesses. In 2011, Bancoldex granted loans totalling Col$4.1 million (Table III.26).

Table III.26
Loans granted by Bancoldex, by sector, 2006 and 2011
(Col$)

	2006	2011
Total	**2,250,899.37**	**4,105,787.64**
Sectors		
Agricultural and agro-industrial	224,886.77	423,751.63
Trade	243,886.78	306,801.20
Metallurgy, mechanical engineering and electrical equipment	157,761.14	192,329.50
Minerals	24,809.69	40,746.82
Other manufactures	93,105.59	93,798.46
Paper, paperboard, publishing and printing	92,955.10	78,304.77
Chemicals, plastics and petroleum	141,212.21	557,153.03
Services	666,866.65	1,119,693.18
Financial services	471,837.92	1,128,405.02
Unclassified	3,847.24	40,237.39
Textiles, made-up goods and leather	129,730.27	124,566.64

Source: Information provided by the Colombian authorities.

217. Colombia has a Fund for Financing the Agricultural Sector (FINAGRO), set up under Law No. 16 of 1990 to provide the agricultural and rural sector with a national agricultural credit system and an autonomous entity specialized in the management of agricultural credit. FINAGRO supplies the working and investment capital required for production, marketing and primary processing. As well as production, marketing and processing, financing is available for support services for farming, livestock, fishing, aquaculture and forest production and for rural activities such as: crafts, rural tourism, metal and gemstone working, and mining. Rediscount rates and the interest rates at which loans are granted depend on the type of producer requesting the loan, in accordance with the classification established by FINAGRO, and are based on the FTD rate (Table III.27).[237] The

[237] The FTD or Fixed Term Deposit rate is the principal measure of interest rates in Colombia. It represents the average interest rate on 90-day certificates of deposit held by Colombian banks.

repayment and grace periods for FINAGRO loans depend on the crop or production cycle of the activity to be financed.[238] FINAGRO also offers emergency funding for farmers in the event of loss of crops or livestock, for example, for the "winter wave" (rainy season).[239] Thus, in 2011, it was decided that small producers severely affected by the "winter wave", whose loans were with the Banco Agrario de Colombia S.A., would be granted relief of up to 95 per cent on the balance of the principal.

218. In addition, there are loan guarantee funds in Colombia financed from public resources, such as: the National Guarantee Fund (FNG), the Financial Institutions Guarantee Fund (FOGAFIN) and the Agricultural Guarantee Fund (FAG). The FNG is the entity through which the Government facilitates access to credit for micro, small and medium-sized enterprises (MSMEs) by offering guarantees. To obtain a FNG guarantee, the enterprise or interested party must apply to the financial intermediary from which it intends to seek a loan.[240] FOGAFIN was established by Law No. 117 of 1985 for the purpose of supporting registered financial institutions. FOGAFIN is overseen by the Financial Supervisory Authority of Colombia and its functions include: participating temporarily in the capital structure of registered institutions; ensuring that registered institutions have the means to provide financial asset liquidity; and developing the deposit insurance system.[241] The FAG guarantees loans granted on FINAGRO terms for use in new agricultural projects. When a FINAGRO agricultural loan is sought, the bank asks for guarantees to back the loan; if these are lacking, insufficient or unsuitable, the FAG will guarantee the obligations to the bank.

Table III.27
FINAGRO terms of credit

Beneficiary	Assets	Maximum amount of loan	Rediscount rate	Interest rate
Small producer[a]	Up to Col$77,662,000	Up to Col$54,363,400	FTD – 3.5% (EA)	Up to FTD + 6% (EA)
Rural woman, low income	Up to Col$77,662,000	Up to Col$54,363,400	FTD – 3.5% (EA)	Up to FTD + 4 % (EA)
Medium producer	Up to Col$2,678 million	According to project	FTD + 1% (EA)[b]	Up to FTD + 10% (EA)
Large producer	More than Col$2,678 million	According to project	FTD + 1% (EA)[b]	Up to FTD + 10% (EA)

a In addition to assets, must satisfy one or other of the following two conditions: (a) at least 75 per cent of assets invested in the agricultural sector; or (b) at least two thirds of income coming from an agricultural activity.
b For working capital loans and for marketing and support services the rediscount rate will be FTD + 2 (EA).

Note: E.A: effective annual rate.

Source: Ministry of Agriculture and Development Rural and FINAGRO (2011), *Portafolio de Servicios*. Viewed at: http://www.finagro.com.co/html/cache/Portafolio_Servicios_2011_2.pdf.

(b) Micro, small and medium-sized enterprises (MiSME)

219. The MiSME sector has been of major importance for the Colombian economy and continues to be a priority for the national development strategy; therefore the State is trying to foster and promote it by means of various support programmes. Law No. 590 of 2000, or MiSME Law, and its amendments (Laws No. 905 of 2004 and No. 1.450 of 2011) provide a set of tools and instruments for supporting the sector. The aim of the law is to promote the creation of new enterprises and to

---

[238] For further details, see: Ministry of Agriculture and Rural Development and FINAGRO (2011b).
[239] For further details, see: Ministry of Agriculture and Rural Development and FINAGRO (2011a).
[240] FNG online information: "*Fondo Nacional de Garantías*". Viewed at: http://www.fng.gov.co/fng/portal/apps/php/index.get.
[241] FOGAFIN online information. Viewed at: https://www.fogafin.gov.co/Web/Formularios/Public/Content/frmContent.aspx?id=119&padre=90.

strengthen existing ones, among other things by means of a special nationwide tax regime. Up until 2011, the parameter for defining the micro, small and medium-sized enterprise was the SMMLV (Table III.28). Since June 2011 it has been possible to use other criteria, namely, the number of employees, the value of gross annual sales and the value of total assets; however, the ranges that will apply for these three criteria and, where necessary, the distinctions between sectors have not yet been regulated.[242] For the purposes of the concessions granted to micro, small and medium-sized enterprises, the determining factor will be the value of the gross annual sales.[243]

Table III.28
Definition of MiSMEs

Category	Value of assets	Employees
Micro	Up to 500 SMMLV	Up to 10
Small	Between 501 and 5,000 SMMLV	Between 11 and 50
Medium-sized	Between 5,001 and 30,000 SMMLV	Between 51 and 200

Source: Law No. 905 of 2004.

220. The Law on MiSMEs established fiscal incentives to promote the development of these business units, authorizing regional entities to introduce special regimes for their creation and support. These special regimes involve lower tax rates, exclusion periods for the payment of taxes and contributions, and a range of fiscal stimuli aimed at fostering development. In addition, to encourage incorporation into the formal sector and the survival of the enterprises set up following the enactment of the Law in 2000, contributions to the National Apprenticeship Service (SENA), the Colombian Family Welfare Institute (ICBF) and the benefit agencies were reduced by 75 per cent during the first year, 50 per cent during the second year and 25 per cent during the third year. These concessions were extended for small enterprises set up between 2010 and 2014 by introducing progressive payment for the parafiscal contributions of their employees, as well as progressive payment of income tax for enterprises located in the departments of Amazones, Guainía and Vaupés.[244] These incentives were offered with a view to encouraging incorporation into the formal sector and generating employment, as well as facilitating the creation of new enterprises.

221. Law No. 590 of 2000 and its implementing decrees also created the category of microcredit, which can only be granted to microenterprises[245] and must not exceed 120 SMMLV. Moreover, if it is found that there are shortages in the credit market that are affecting MiSMEs, then, in coordination with the Board of Directors of the Bank of the Republic, an amount or minimum proportion of resources or credit lines that must be set aside for institutions that lend to MiSMEs will be temporarily determined.

222. Support for MiSMEs is based on a National System for the Support and Promotion of MiSMEs. Within this system, financial support is regarded as one of the most important components and efforts are directed towards improving the supply of credit for MiSMEs, increasing their capitalization and applying non-financial instruments aimed at supporting and promoting them. To this end, the Colombian Fund for the Modernization and Technological Development of MiSMEs (FOMIPYME) was set up, as an account assigned to the MCIT and administered by a trust, for the purpose of financing projects, programmes and activities for the technological development of

[242] Article 43 of Law No. 1.450 of 16 June 2011.
[243] Article 43 of Law No. 1.450 of 16 June 2011.
[244] Law No. 1.429 of 29 of December 2010.
[245] These are enterprises with not more than ten employees whose total assets, housing excluded, are less than 500 SMMLV.

MiSMEs. The State gives SMEs access to various sources of low-cost financing backed by the FNG (Table III.29).

223. In 2000, the Colombian Fund for the Technological Modernization of MiSMEs (FOMIPYME) was set up, as an account assigned to the MCIT, to support the technological development and promotion of MiSMEs. Resources made available through FOMIPYME are non-reimbursable if used for projects to develop, among other things, technological capacity, information systems and information technologies. The Fund cofinances up to 65 per cent of the total value of the programme, project or activity approved, with a maximum of 2,100 SMMLV.[246] In 2011, FOMIPYME was replaced by the Modernization and Innovation Fund for Micro, Small and Medium-Sized Enterprises, as a separate account management system of the Foreign Trade Bank of Colombia S.A. - Bancoldex.[247]

Table III.29
Sources of government financing for MiSMEs

Objective	Services
Colombian Fund for the Modernization and Technological Development of Micro, Small and Medium-Sized Enterprises (FOMIPYME)	
Modernization and technological development of SMEs through the cofinancing of programmes, projects and activities for their technological development	Enterprise creation; support for mini-production chains; technological and production-oriented development; market access and marketing; innovation in SMEs
Development Project Finance Fund (FONADE)	
Promote the integral development of SMEs for the purposes of job creation, regional development, intersectoral integration and the production-oriented supply of small-scale capital	Business analysis for innovation and reorganization; implementation of retrofitting projects; implementation of new technologies; comprehensive technical assistance with retrofitting processes; business modernization projects targeting international markets
National Guarantee Fund (FNG)	
To meet the needs of the financial system by guaranteeing loans granted to finance projects led by natural or legal persons, up to a certain percentage	The lines of business and amounts that can be financed vary with the entity from which the loan is being sought and the credit line itself
Bancoldex	
To make it easier for MiSMEs to access credit by offering them an automatic guarantee, through the FNG or its regional funds. This guarantee reduces the credit risk for the financial intermediary by a percentage of the loan requested using Bancoldex resources	Credit for MiSMEs that make loan applications under the special line of credit "Support for Productivity and Competitiveness" - Programme "*aProgresar*"
Modernization and Innovation Fund for Micro, Small and Medium-Sized Enterprises	
Non-reimbursable cofinancing of programmes, projects and activities aimed at promoting MiSME innovation and competitiveness	Business innovation, production linkups; development of suppliers, distributors and clusters or cross linkages

Source: Directorate for Micro, Small and Medium-Sized Enterprises, Ministry of Commerce, Industry and Tourism.

(c) Assistance for research and development and improved competitiveness

224. In order to support the development of science and technology in the primary, industrial, services and other sectors, Colombia created the Administrative Department of Science, Technology and Innovation (COLCIENCIAS) under Law No. 1.286 of 2009. This public agency runs the National System of Science, Technology and Innovation (SNCTI), which is charged with: formulating, coordinating and implementing State science and technology policy; financing research,

[246] Administrative Sciences Faculty online information: "*Fondo Colombiano de Modernización y Desarrollo technológico de la Micro, Pequeña y Mediana Empresa - FOMIPYME*". Viewed at: http://www.ulibertadores.edu.co:8089/index.php?idcategoria=1543.

[247] Article 44 of Law No. 1.450 of 2011 amending Law No. 590 of 2000.

innovation and technological development projects; and providing financial support for the establishment and consolidation of technological development centres. Colciencias has joined the National Competitiveness System (SNC), which helps to reinforce the results of government support for innovation, science and technology.[248]

225. The promotion of technological development is also the aim of the Francisco José de Caldas National Fund for Science, Technology and Innovation, a financial mechanism that enables COLCIENCIAS to combine public, private and international resources and donations to finance the development of scientific, technological and innovative programmes, activities and entities. The resources of the Fund are administered through an asset pool managed by a trust company.

226. One of the objectives of the National Productivity and Competitiveness Programme (PNPC), implemented since 1999, is to provide soft financing and incentives for projects aimed at improving the productivity and competitiveness of directly or indirectly exporting or potentially exporting enterprises.[249]

227. Persons that invest, directly or through research centres or technological development centres recognized by COLCIENCIAS, in projects designated scientific, technological or innovative by the National Science and Technology Council may deduct from their taxable income 125 per cent of the value invested in the tax period in which the investment was made. The investment projects must relate to areas of strategic importance for the country such as basic sciences, social sciences and the humanities, industrial development, agricultural sciences, the environment, housing, education, health, electronics, telecommunications, information technology, biotechnology, mining and energy. This deduction may not exceed 20 per cent of the taxable income determined before subtracting the value of the investment. The same concessions are also available to taxpayers who make donations and investments for the purpose of promoting agro-industrial investment projects approved by the competent government entity, provided they are developed by non-profit entities recognized as such by the Ministry of Agriculture.[250]

(d) Other support schemes

228. Given the importance of the agricultural sector in Colombia, in addition to the credit programmes implemented by FINAGRO and the backing provided by the FAG, there are other programmes for supporting the sector in general, as well as specific programmes. Under the Agricultural Debt Relief Programme, small and medium-sized producers are offered assistance, for up to two years, with their interest payments, and the debt can also be restructured.[251] The aid is granted by MADR and provided by FINAGRO for each debt to be restructured, through the financial intermediary with which the producer contracted the debt. Likewise, to protect the income of producers in the export sector from exchange rate fluctuations, the Government offers assistance with foreign exchange hedging that covers between 60 and 80 per cent of the cost of the premium. To protect crops against adverse weather conditions, the Government provides support for agricultural insurance that covers between 30 and 60 per cent of the value of the policy. At present, only one insurer offers this type of product.

---

[248] Information provided by the authorities.

[249] National Economic and Social Policy Council (2004 and 2008c).

[250] Law No. 633 of 2000.

[251] At present, for small producers in the first year the support corresponds to 100 per cent of the interest payment and in the second year to 60 per cent. For medium-sized producers the support corresponds to 100 per cent of the interest payment in the first year and 40 per cent in the second (information provided by the authorities).

229. Among the specific programmes two stand out, namely, those for cotton and rice. The aim of the cotton price compensation programme or Guaranteed Minimum Price for Cotton (PMG) is to protect the incomes of domestic farmers from international price fluctuations by making up the difference between the market price (New York Stock Exchange) and a guaranteed minimum price per tonne of fibre. The PMG of the Interinstitutional Committee for Cotton Crop Competitiveness (CICA) is established by taking into account the production costs per hectare for the previous five years and updating them using the producer price index. The MADR announces the PMG before planting begins, and this support is paid during the marketing period. The support granted through the PMG increased from US$18,091,000 in 2006 toUS$25,592,000 in 2010.[252] To prevent the fall in producer prices due to the surpluses that normally occur in the second half of each year, the Government offers an incentive to store rice.

230. Colombia uses stabilizing mechanisms to deal with the variability of the world prices of certain products such as coffee and petroleum. As a stabilizing mechanism for the coffee sector, Colombia has the National Coffee Fund. The Savings and Petroleum Stabilization Fund (FAEP) established in 1995 continues in force; the Fund is a foreign account management system for the temporary transfer of royalties and payments for tax saving and petroleum stabilization purposes, administered by the Bank of the Republic. The Fuel Price Stabilization Fund was set up in 2007.[253] The Fund makes it possible to keep domestic petrol prices stable in the event of fluctuations on the external market.

(v) Government procurement

(a) Overview

231. Since its last review in 2006, Colombia has carried out a major reform of its government procurement system. This was partly in response to the reviews conducted by the World Bank in 2001 and 2005, which stressed the lack of an entity in charge of government procurement, responsible for purchasing policy and for promoting uniformity among contracting authorities.[254] Moreover, CONPES 3.186 of 2002 "*A State Policy for the Transparency and Efficiency of Government Procurement*" and CONPES 3.249 of 2003 "*Government Procurement Policy for a Managerial State*" pointed out the need for a policy-making body in the area of government procurement.[255]

232. In response to these concerns, by means of Decree No. 3.620 of 2004 the Colombia Government Procurement Intersectoral Commission (CINCO) was established.[256] Its primary government procurement functions include: (i) ensuring the cohesion and coordination of the activities of the competent public entities; (ii) proposing the adoption of public policies aimed at reducing costs; (iii) proposing measures for improving transparency; and (iv) formulating parameters for the proper public management of pre-contract and contract procedures, together with other functions determined by law.[257] CINCO served as a forum for discussion of the draft reforms of the

[252] Information provided by the authorities.

[253] Law No. 1.151 of 2007.

[254] World Bank (2005).

[255] National Economic and Social Policy Council (2002 and 2003).

[256] CINCO is permanently composed of: the Minister for Finance and Public Credit, a representative of the Office of the President of the Republic, and the Director of the National Planning Department, who takes the chair. In addition, the Director of the Connectivity Agenda and a representative of the Office of the Vice-President of the Republic participate in the Commission without the right to vote.

[257] Electronic System for Government Procurement online information:, "*Sobre la Comisión Intersectorial de Contratación Pública*". Viewed at: https://www.contratos.gov.co/puc/infoCINCO.html.

government procurement system.[258] As from March 2012, CINCO will be replaced by the National Government Procurement Agency - *Colombia Compra Eficiente.*[259]

233. As well as institutional reforms, since its last review Colombia has undertaken important regulatory reforms, especially the enactment of Law No. 1.150 of 2007, which introduced measures to improve the efficiency and transparency of government procurement procedures. Among other things, this Law establishes the principles of consideration in turn, objective selection and non-payment for tender documentation; sets a time-limit for the settlement of contracts; and introduces changes in selection procedures. It should be noted that the new legislation extended disqualification from contracting with the State to natural persons who have been found guilty of peculation, extortion, bribery and perversion of the course of justice in all its forms or transnational bribery (including companies in which they are partners, with the exception of public limited companies).[260]

(b) Legislative framework

234. The main legal basis for government procurement is the General Law on Government Procurement, Law No. 80 of 1993 and Law No. 1.150 of 2007, implemented by Decrees No. 855 of 1994, No. 2.170 of 2002, No. 4.375 and No. 2.434 of 2006, No. 4.533 of 2008, No. 2.473 of 2009 and No. 4.266 of 2010 (Table III.30). The purpose of this legislation is to establish the rules and principles that govern the contracts awarded by all State entities. Nevertheless, there are exceptions: some procurement procedures and some State entities are governed by special provisions; for example, the procurement regime for residential public utility services is governed by civil law.[261] There are also special laws on government purchasing in such cases as contracts for the exploration and exploitation of natural resources; public services; State welfare enterprises; personal communications, mobile telephony, long-distance telephony and television services; postal services; radio broadcasting; purchases by the Bank of the Republic; and purchases by the National Television Commission.

235. The conduct of State entities is governed by the following principles: transparency, objective selection, economy and responsibility. In accordance with the principle of transparency, all State contracts must be awarded by open tender or competition and the end result must be published.[262] The principle of objective selection means that the public entity chooses the bid most favourable for that entity.[263] In accordance with the principle of economy, the selection procedures should impose only those requirements that are strictly necessary to ensure that the process is effective and free of unjustified delays.[264] Finally, the principle of responsibility ensures that public servants seek to

---

258 Electronic System for Government Procurement online information: "*Sobre la Comisión Intersectorial de Contratación Pública*". Viewed at: https://www.contratos.gov.co/puc/infoCINCO.html.

259 Decree Law No. 4.170 of 2011.

260 Law No. 1.150 of 2007. Viewed at: https://www.contratos.gov.co/Archivos/normas/Ley_1150_2007.pdf.

261 Proexport *et al.* (2010), page 132.

262 Article 24 of Law No. 80 of 1993. Viewed at: https://www.contratos.gov.co/puc/normas.html.

263 Article 5 of Law No. 1.157 of 2007. Viewed at: https://www.contratos.gov.co/puc/normas.html.

264 Article 25 of Law No. 80 of 1993.

achieve the purposes of the procurement, see to it that the contract is correctly performed and protect the rights of those involved.[265]

236. Since 2007, natural or legal persons, whether Colombian or foreign, domiciled or with a branch in Colombia, that wish to conclude contracts with the State must be enrolled in the Single Bidders Register (RUP), implemented by Decree No. 1.464 of 2010. The registration must be handled by the Chamber of Commerce of the principal domicile of the interested party, which will be responsible for making the relevant checks before issuing a certificate determining the qualifications of the bidder to participate in a selection process with State entities.[266] Registration in the RUP may be waived in the following cases: (i) single tendering; (ii) procurements that do not exceed 10 per cent of the low-value amount; (iii) provision of health services; (iv) concession contracts; (v) disposal of State property; (vi) in relation to State-owned enterprises, their own commercial and industrial activities; (vii) purchase of products of agricultural origin; and (viii) if the contractor is a foreign natural or legal person without domicile or a branch in Colombia. In this latter case, the conditions of legal and financial standing, organization and experience will be verified directly by the contracting entity and the RUP will not be required as certification. Moreover, the conditions must be equivalent and may not be stricter than those required by the RUP.

Table III.30
Legislative framework for government procurement

Legislation	Description
Law No. 80 of 1993 implemented by Decrees No. 679 of 1994, No. 287 of 1996, No. 1.896 and No. 2.166 of 2004, No. 4.375 of 2006, No. 4.533 of 2008 and No. 2.473 and No. 4.266 of 2010	General Law on Government Procurement
Law No. 527 of 1999	Access and use of data messages, electronic commerce and digital signatures and establishing certification bodies
Law No. 816 of 2003	Support for the domestic industry through government procurement
Law No. 962 of 2005	Provisions concerning rationalization of formalities and administrative procedures of State agencies and entities and of individuals who perform public functions or provide public services
Law No. 1.150 of 2007 implemented by Decrees No. 1.170 and No. 4.444 of 2008, No. 1.430, No. 1.464 and No. 2.473 of 2010	Measures for the efficiency and transparency of Law No. 80 of 1993 and other general provisions concerning procurement with public resources. Single Bidders Window (RUP)
Law No. 1.474 of 2011	Rules on strengthening the mechanisms for prevention, investigation and sanctioning of acts of corruption and the effective monitoring of the administrative process
Decree Law No. 4.170 of 2011	Creation of the National Government Procurement Agency (*Colombia Compra Eficiente*)
Decree No. 3.512 of 2003	Organization, functioning and operation of the Information System for Monitoring Government Procurement (SICE)
Decree No. 3.620 of 2004	Creation of the Colombia Government Procurement Intersectoral Commission (CINCO)
Decree No. 2.178 of 2006	Creation of the Electronic System for Government Procurement (SECOP)
Decree No. 2.474 of 2008 amended by Decrees No. 127, No. 2.025 and No. 3.576 of 2009 and No. 1.039, No. 3.844 and No. 4.266 of 2010	Partially implements Laws No. 80 of 1993 and No. 1.150 of 2007 concerning selection procedures, publicization and objective selection and promulgates other provisions
Decree No. 3.460 of 2008	Parameters for the granting of a favourable prior opinion of the National Economic and Social Policy Council (CONPES) for extending or adding to national public works concession contracts

[265] Article 26 of Law No. 80 of 1993.

[266] The bidder qualification requirements are those that determine whether or not a person is qualified to proceed to the bid investigation phase (Law No. 1.150 of 2007).

Legislation	Description
Decrees No. 4.828 of 2008 and No. 490, No. 931 and No. 2.493 of 2009	Guarantee regime in government procurement
Decree No. 2.516 of 2011	Minimum amount selection procedure
Decree No. 3.485 of 2011	Implements SECOP

Source: WTO Secretariat, based on information provided by the Colombian authorities and online information from the Single Procurement Portal: "*Normatividad relationada con la contratación pública y el SECOP*". Viewed at: https://www.contratos.gov.co/puc/reglamentacion.html.

237. With regard to the evaluation of the bid, there are three technical criteria depending on the selection procedure: price, quality and the weighing of price against quality. The price is a determining factor if the goods and services have uniform technical characteristics and are commonly used, while quality takes precedence where consultancy services are concerned. If the subject of the bid is complex, then the two factors, quality and price, should be weighed against each other.

(c) Procurement procedures

238. In accordance with Law No. 1.150 of 2007, the procurement procedures seek to guarantee the principles of transparency and objective selection. The selection procedures are mainly regulated by Decree No. 2.474 of 2008 and are as follows: open tendering, abridged selection, call for prices and description of experience, and single tendering (Table III.31). As a general rule, contractors must be selected by open tender, except in those cases expressly stipulated by law in which the contractor is chosen using some other selection procedure.[267] All tender proceedings are published in the Electronic System for Government Procurement (SECOP).

Table III.31
Contractor selection procedures, 2011

Procedure	Description
Open tendering	Open invitation by a public entity for interested contractors to submit bids, the most favourable of which will be chosen, subject to certain terms and conditions laid down by the public entity inviting the tenders
Abridged selection	Objective selection procedure for cases in which because of the characteristics of the subject matter of the contract, the circumstances of procurement or the quantity or end use of the goods, works or services it is possible to employ simplified processes to ensure efficient contract management. Appropriate for: the purchase of commonly used goods and services with uniform technical characteristics; low-value contracts; contracts for the provision of health services; procurement where the open tendering procedure has been declared void; the disposal of State property; the purchase of products of agricultural origin or use; transactions and contracts having as their direct object the own activities of State-owned industrial and commercial enterprises or semi-public companies; the contracts of entities responsible for the implementation of programmes for the protection of persons under threat, demobilization and reintegration, displaced people, protection of human rights and people with some degree of exclusion; and the procurement of goods and services for national defence and security
Call for prices and description of experience	Procedure for the selection of consultants or projects in which open competition or prequalification systems can be used. Technical requirements and professional qualifications are given precedence, while the economic requirement is secondary
Single tendering	Exceptional selection mechanism enabling public entities to conclude contracts without the need for a prior competitive selection process. Appropriate only in cases of: manifest urgency; loan procurement; inter-administration contracts; procurement of goods and services for national defence and security where their purchase must remain confidential; contracts for the development of scientific and technological activities; contracts for fiduciary services; where there is only one bidder in the market; provision of professional and management support services; and the rental or purchase of real estate

[267] Proexport *et al*. (2010).

Procedure	Description
Minimum amount	10% of the low-value amount

Source: Law No. 1.150 of 2007 and Proexport, Brigard & Urrutia Abogados and Brigard & Castro S.A. (2010), *Guía Legal para hacer Negocios en Colombia*, June. Viewed at: http://www.inviertaencolombia.com.co/Adjuntos/064_Guia_legal_para_hacer_negocios_en_colombia.pdf.

239. The law regards recourse to single tendering as an exception to the general rule of open tendering, to be employed in special situations where there is no viable competitive bidding procedure. Single tendering is justified in the following circumstances: manifest urgency; procurement of loans; inter-administration contracts (the obligations derived from the contract must be directly related with the purpose of the implementing entity); procurement of goods and services in the defence sector and the Department for the Administration of Security (DAS) where their purchase must remain confidential; contracts for the development of scientific and technological activities; contracts for fiduciary services; where there is only one bidder; the rental or purchase of real estate; and the provision of professional and management support services.[268] Where single tendering is employed, it is not necessary to receive several bids, provided that the principle of objective selection is applied. In this case, the single bid received is compared with previous studies carried out by the entity, with market conditions and prices and, where appropriate, with the prices recorded in the SICE. In January 2012, the SICE was abolished, so that at present the most favourable bid may be the winner.

240. In cases of single tendering only the justification is published in the SECOP, together with information concerning the contract, additions, amendments or suspensions and information concerning enforceable sanctions that may be imposed during or after the performance of the contract, the instrument of termination by mutual agreement, or the administrative act of unilateral termination.

241. If the government procurement regime of the implementing entity is not that of the General Law on Government Procurement (Law No. 80 of 1993), the performance of the contract will be subject to the principles contained in Article 209 of the Constitution, which relates to the duty of objective selection and the disqualification and conflict regime.

(d) Preferences at General Government level

242. Under the CAN, Colombia is obliged to grant other member countries national treatment in connection with the purchase of services by government agencies and public entities. Where procurement outside the CAN is concerned, the principle of reciprocity applies. In State procurement proceedings suppliers of goods or services of foreign origin are granted the same treatment and are subject to the same conditions, requirements, procedures and award criteria as Colombians, in accordance with the principle of reciprocity governed by Article 20 of Law No. 80 of 1993.[269] Nevertheless, Colombian State entities must guarantee the participation of Colombian suppliers of goods and services on competitive conditions with respect to quality, delivery and price, in accordance with Article 21 of Law No. 80 of 1993. The Law states that, other things being equal, preference will be given to offers of goods and services of domestic origin. Moreover, where foreign bids are otherwise on equal terms, preference will be given to that which incorporates the most Colombian human resources, the greatest local content or the best technology transfer conditions.

[268] Article 2 of Law No. 1.150 of 2007.

[269] Article 20 of Law No. 80 of 1993.

243. However, in 2003, Colombia introduced preference margins for domestic suppliers and foreign suppliers that use Colombian goods, materials or personnel. Law No. 816 of 8 July 2003, which aims to provide support for domestic industry, allows the granting of a preference margin of between 10 and 20 percentage points for offers of Colombian goods or services and between 5 and 15 percentage points for offers of foreign goods and services that incorporate Colombian components or professional, technical and operating services. If, after qualification, the offer of a foreign bidder is on equal terms with that of a domestic bidder, the contract is awarded to the domestic bidder or to the foreign supplier that uses domestic components.[270]

(e) Electronic government procurement

244. The legislation on electronic government procurement consists of Law No. 1.150 of 2007, Law No. 527 of 1999 and Law No. 962 of 2005. Under these laws, electronic carriers, media and applications can be used for the corresponding formalities, notifications and publications. The aim is to make members of the public aware of the information required by law for each selection process and to enable them, where appropriate, to make comments or submit bids. It is therefore mandatory for all State entities to publish their contract information on the Single Procurement Portal, in accordance with Decree No. 2.474 of 2008. This portal constitutes the information phase of the SECOP, in accordance with the provisions of Article 3 of Law No. 1.150 of 2007. The Single Procurement Portal is the tool used by State entities to publish their procurement proceedings, from the pre-contractual stage up to finalization of the contractual phase.[271] State entities subject to the procurement regime established by the General Law on Government Procurement (Law No. 80 of 1993) are obliged to use the Portal; for other public entities its use is voluntary.

245. In recent years, the proceedings published electronically have increased at a rapid rate. In 2008 and 2009, 68,524 and 98,531 procurement proceedings were published, respectively. In 2010, according to the National Planning Department, 115,329 proceedings, representing contracts with a value of Col$41.7 trillion, were published.

(f) Monitoring of procurement

246. The management of government procurement is subject to three types of controls: disciplinary (exercised by the Office of the Attorney General of the Nation), fiscal (exercised by the Office of the Comptroller General of the Republic) and criminal (exercised by the Office of the Prosecutor General of the Nation).

247. To have administrative decisions reviewed it is possible to make applications for reconsideration or appeal. As far as the pre-contractual phase is concerned, it is possible to bring actions against the decision awarding the contract and individual procedural decisions, while as regards the performance of the contract the appropriate course is to bring a trade dispute action. Likewise, it is possible to employ direct dispute settlement mechanisms such as conciliation and technical expertise, together with which provisional measures may be ordered and the case judged in accordance with the Code of Civil Procedure and the Commercial Code and with the provisions of CAN Decision No. 486.

248. To strengthen the transparency and integrity of government procurement proceedings, Law No. 598 of 18 July 2000 created the Information System for Monitoring Government

[270] Viewed at: http://www.secretariasenado.gov.co/senado/basedoc/ley/2003/ley_0816_2003.html.

[271] Online information from the Electronic System for Government Procurement, "Frequently Asked Questions". Viewed at: https://www.contracts.gov.co/puc/faq.html.

Procurement (SICE), the Single Catalogue of Goods and Services (CUBS) and the Single Reference Prices Register (RUPR), granting the Office of the Comptroller General of the Republic authority to set up its organization and operations.[272] Apart from the objective of monitoring the financial management of the authorities and individuals or entities that manage public resources, the three institutions were established for the purpose of, *inter alia*: reducing the current costs of government procurement; designing, implementing and consolidating an information system for improving the current conditions of procurement; and guaranteeing the constitutional and legal principles of equality, integrity, efficacy, economy, celerity, impartiality, publicity, efficiency, fairness, transparency, responsibility and social control.[273] The SICE was suspended in January 2012.

(vi) Intellectual property rights

(a) Overview

249. Colombia is party to the Convention establishing the World Intellectual Property Organization (WIPO), ratified by Law No. 456 of 1979, and is a signatory to various international intellectual property agreements (Table III.32).

Table III.32
Participation in intellectual property treaties

Convention/treaty	Date of accession
Rome Convention for the Protection of Performers, Producers of Phonograms and Broadcasting Organizations	17 September 1976 (Law No. 48 of 1975)
Berne Convention for the Protection of Literary and Artistic Works (Colombia is party to the Paris Act)	7 March 1998 (Law No. 33 of 1987)
International Convention for the Protection of New Varieties of Plants	13 September 1996 (Law No. 243 of 1995)
Paris Convention for the Protection of Industrial Property (Colombia is party to the Stockholm Act)	3 September 1996 (Law No. 178 of 1994)
Geneva Convention for the Protection of Producers of Phonograms against Unauthorized Duplication of their Phonograms	16 May 1994 (Law No. 23 of 1992)
Patent Cooperation Treaty	28 February 2001 (Law No. 463 of 1998)
WIPO Copyright Treaty	6 March 2002 (Law No. 565 of 2000)
WIPO Performance and Phonograms Treaty	20 May 2002 (Law No. 545 of 1999)
Treaty on the Law of Trademarks and its Regulation	31 July 2009 (Law No. 1.343 of 2009)
Protocol concerning the Madrid System for the International Registration of Marks	29 June 2011 (Law No. 1.455 of 2011)

Source: WTO Secretariat, based on WIPO information. Viewed at: http://www.wipo.int/wipolex/es/profile.jsp?code=CO.

250. At supranational level, Colombia, as a Member of the Andean Community (CAN), applies directly to its internal legal system the decisions on intellectual property adopted by the Commission of the Cartagena Agreement. These decisions deal with the following topics: industrial property[274],

[272] SICE online information: "*Normatividad: Leyes*". Viewed at: http://www.sice-cgr.gov.co/leyes.html.

[273] Transparencia por Colombia online information: "*Transparencia en la Contratación*". Viewed at: http://www.transparenciacolombia.org.co/transparencia//tabid/68/Default.aspx. Transparencia por Colombia is a non-profit organization set up in 1998 to promote the anti-corruption campaign and transparency, in the public and private sectors, and to build institutional capacity. It is the National Chapter of Transparency International (TI), an anti-corruption international NGO that operates in more than 90 countries.

[274] The common industrial property regime was adopted by means of Decision No. 486 (in force since 1 December 2000), as amended by Decision No. 689.

copyright and related rights[275], access to genetic resources[276], and the protection of new plant varieties.[277]

251. As far as the regime for the protection of intellectual property rights is concerned, the national legal framework has not changed significantly since the last review in 2006 (Table III.33). However, where administrative procedures are concerned, instructions issued by the Supervisory Authority for Industry and Trade have led to the automation of applications for the registration of trademarks and other related formalities, which can now be completed online.

Table III.33
Legislation on intellectual property

Subject	Legislation
Copyright	Law on Copyright, Law No. 23 of 1982
	Regulation of Law No. 23, Decree No. 3.942 of 2010
	Law amending Law No. 23, Law No. 44 of 1993
	Law adding to Law No. 23, Law No. 232 of 2010
	Regulation of Andean Decision No. 351, Decree No. 162 of 1996
	Regulation of the National Copyright Register, Decree No. 60 of 1995
Industrial property	Decision No. 486 of 2000
	Decision No. 689 of 2008
	Commercial Code, Decree Law No. 410 of 1971
	Partial regulation of Decision No. 486, Decree No. 2.591 of 2000
	Partial regulation of Decision No. 486, Decree No. 3.081 of 2005
	Procedure for the declaration of the existence of reasons of public interest in accordance with the provisions of Article 65 of Decision No. 486, Decree No. 4.302 of 2008
	Partial amendment of Decree No. 4.302, Decree No. 4.966 of 2009
	Single Circular of the Supervisory Authority for Industry and Trade
	Resolution No. 33.190 of 2007 establishing the procedure for delegating the power to authorize the use of an appellation of origin
New plant varieties	Common regime for the protection of the rights of breeders of new plant varieties, Decree No. 533 of 1994
	Amendment of Article 13 of Decree No. 533, Decree No. 2.468 of 1994
	Amendment of Article 7 of Decree No. 533, Decree No. 2.687 of 2002
	Regulation of Andean Decision No. 436 of 1998 on the registration and control of chemical pesticides for agricultural use, Decree No. 502 of 5 March 2003
Test data	Regulation on aspects related with the information supplied to obtain sanitary registration with respect to new chemical entities in the area of medicaments, Decree No. 2.085 of 2002
	Protection of undisclosed information on test data concerning chemical pesticides for agricultural use, Decree No. 502 of 2003

Source: WTO Secretariat.

252. With respect to the institutional framework, Decree No. 1.162 of 2010 established the Intersectoral Intellectual Property Commission (CIPI), with responsibility for coordinating and directing the National Intellectual Property Administrative System, which consists of a set of policies, approaches, regulations, activities, resources, programmes and institutions, public and private, related

[275] The common regime on copyright and related rights was adopted by means of Decision No. 351 of 17 December 1993.

[276] The common regime on access to genetic resources was adopted by means of Decision No. 391 of 2 July 1996.

[277] The regime on the protection of the rights of breeders of new plant varieties was adopted by means of Decision No. 345 of 31 of October 1993.

with intellectual property.[278] The CIPI also coordinates the various government positions on intellectual property issues and assesses the impact of intellectual property policies on national competitiveness and productivity.[279]

253. The National Copyright Directorate (DNDA), attached to the Ministry of the Interior, designs, directs, administers and implements government policies on copyright and related rights. Moreover, the DNDA administers the National Copyright Register and is responsible for inspecting and monitoring the collective management societies.[280] At the same time, the Supervisory Authority for Industry and Trade (SIC), attached to the Ministry of Commerce, Industry and Tourism, administers the National Industrial Property System. Thus, the SIC decides whether a patent or utility model should be granted, as well as dealing with applications relating to distinctive signs (trademarks, slogans, trade names and logos) and their registration. The SIC also rules on applications for compulsory licences and the registration of industrial designs and layout-designs of integrated circuits. In addition, the SIC decides on applications for declarations of protection of appellations of origin.[281]

254. The Colombian Agricultural Institute (ICA) applies the protection regime to new plant varieties, grants breeder's certificates and administers the National Register of Protected Plant Varieties.[282] The ICA is also responsible for protecting undisclosed information concerning test data on chemical pesticides for agricultural use.[283] Finally, the National Institute for the Surveillance of Food and Drugs (INVIMA), attached to the Ministry of Social Welfare, protects undisclosed information concerning test data submitted to obtain the sanitary registration of pharmaceutical products containing new chemical entities (Decree No. 2.085 of 2002).[284]

[278] The CIPI is composed of the following officials with the right to vote: the Minister for the Interior and Justice or his representative; the Minister for Foreign Relations or his representative; Minister for Finance and Public Credit or his representative; the Minister for Agriculture and Rural Development or his representative; the Minister for Social Welfare or his representative; the Minister for Commerce, Industry and Tourism or his representative; the Minister for National Education or his representative; the Minister for the Environment, Housing and Regional Development or his representative; the Minister for Information Technology and Communications or his representative; the Minister for Culture or his representative; the Director of the National Planning Department or his representative; and the Director of the Administrative Department for Science, Technology and Innovation or his representative.

[279] Decree organizing the National Administrative Intellectual Property System and establishing the Intersectoral Intellectual Property Commission, Decree No. 1.162 of 13 April 2010. Viewed at: http://www.derechodeautor.gov.co/htm/legal/legislacion/decretos_arch/Decreto%201162%20de%20Abril%2013%20de%202010.pdf.

[280] Decree No. 2.041 of 29 August 1991 creating the National Copyright Directorate as a special administrative unit, establishing its organizational structure and determining its functions. Viewed at: http://www.derechodeautor.gov.co/htm/legal/legislacion/decretos_arch/DECRETO%20%202041%20DE%201991.pdf.

[281] Decree No. 3.523 of 15 September 2009 modifying the structure of the Supervisory Authority for Industry and Trade and determining the functions of its sections. Viewed at: http://www.sic.gov.co/es/web/guest/delegatura-para-la-propiedad-industrial.

[282] Decree No. 533 of 1994, Common regime for the protection of the rights of breeders of new plant varieties. Viewed at: http://www.upov.int/members/en/npvlaws/colombia/colombia.pdf.

[283] National Economic and Social Policy Council (2008a).

[284] Decree No. 2.085 of 2002, Regulations on aspects related with information supplied to obtain sanitary registration with respect to new chemical entities in the area of medicaments. Viewed at: http://web.invima.gov.co/portal/documents/portal/documents/root//decreto_2085_2002.pdf.

(b) Copyright and related rights

255. Colombia's copyright regime is governed by Decision No. 351 of the Commission of the Cartagena Agreement recognizing appropriate and effective protection for authors and other right holders, including related rights[285], in works of the mind in the fields of literature, art or science, whatever the genre or form of expression and regardless of their literary or artistic merit or intended use.[286]

256. At national level, the regime is governed by the Copyright Law, Law No. 23 of 1982, as amended by Law No. 44 of 1993, and Decree No. 2.150 of 1995. Copyright covers scientific, literary and artistic works (including books, speeches, lectures and cinematographic works, among others). The holders have exclusive enjoyment of the following rights: (i) to dispose of their work free of charge or against payment; (ii) to exploit it, for commercial or non-commercial purposes, by means of printing, engraving, copying, moulding, phonographic recording, photography or any other means; and (iii) to receive remuneration for its public performance or dissemination.[287]

257. Under Law No. 23 of 28 January 1982, the economic rights belong to the holder of the copyright and related rights during his lifetime, and after his death are to be enjoyed by those who have lawfully acquired them, for a period of 80 years. If the holder is a legal person or an official entity or some institution of public law, the term of protection will be 30 years from publication or, in the case of related rights, from the date of performance.

258. Decree No. 3.942 of 2010 governs the establishment, operation and inspection of societies for the collective management of copyright and related rights. Collective management societies have been developed only to exercise the right of public reproduction in the music sector, reprographic reproduction in the book sector, the right of communication of the performers in an audiovisual work and the right of public communication and reproduction in multimedia format in the audiovisual sector.

259. The limitations on, and exceptions to, copyright include those specified in legal provisions, judicial decisions, orders and other regulations, together with quotations and reproductions for educational purposes. Where related rights are concerned, the following are permitted: private use, for teaching purposes, right to quote, ephemeral recordings and use in current affairs broadcasts.

260. Colombia's copyright legislation provides for civil and criminal remedies to enable holders to assert their rights. Copyright holders and the holders of related rights are entitled to apply to the civil courts for judgments on matters they may raise for the purpose of exercising their prerogatives.[288] Moreover, holders may institute proceedings for offences defined in Articles 270 to 271 of the

---

[285] Consequently, the protection covers: performers (speakers, singers, announcers, actors, dancers, musicians, narrators); phonogram producers (a natural person who fixes a performance of exclusively aural sounds); and broadcasting organizations (radio or television companies that transmit programmes for public reception).

[286] Article 1 of Decision No. 351, Common Regime on Copyright and Related Rights. Viewed at: http://www.comunidadandina.org/normativa/dec/D351.htm.

[287] Law No. 23 of 28 January 1982, Copyright Law. Viewed at: http://www.derechodeautor.gov.co/htm/legal/legislacion/leyes_arch/23.pdf.

[288] Chapter XVIII of Law No. 23 of 28 January 1982.

Penal Code. Infringement of copyright can lead to a term of imprisonment of between 32 and 90 months for violations of moral rights or between 4 and 8 years for violations of economic rights.[289]

(c) Patents

261. The patent system is governed by CAN Decision No. 486, by means of which protection is granted to invention patents for both products and processes, in all branches of technology, provided that they are new, involve an inventive step and are susceptible of industrial application. In Colombia this Decision is implemented by Decree No. 2.591 of 2000 and by the Single Circular of the Supervisory Authority for Industry and Trade.

262. The patent application procedure begins with the filing of the necessary documentation with the SIC, which first carries out a formal examination to verify compliance with the requirements of the legislation, especially those laid down in Articles 26 and 27 of Decision No. 486 with respect to the information contained in the application.[290] The SIC's next step is to publish the application to acquaint the public with its contents; any interested party may oppose the application to prevent it from becoming a patent. Within six months of the date of publication, the applicant must request an examination to determine whether the invention is patentable. The SIC will examine whether the invention satisfies the requirements of patentability in order to either grant or refuse a patent. If a patent is refused, the applicant may apply for reconsideration.[291]

263. As the patent right is territorial in nature, for the protection to be effective outside Colombia, the applicant must file a corresponding application in each of the countries in which he wishes to obtain this type of protection. An alternative is to file a patent application under the Patent Cooperation Treaty (PCT), in which case by means of a single patent application the procedure can be commenced in any of the countries party to the Treaty.[292]

264. The term of protection for a patent is 20 years from the date on which the application is filed. During this period the holder may exploit the patent, which includes the exclusive and direct marketing of the product patented, or marketing through third parties under licence, or transferring the rights obtained by selling them to a third party which exploits the invention.[293] The following are not patentable: discoveries; living organisms, or whatever exists as found in nature; scientific theories; mathematical methods; therapeutic and surgical methods; financial or business methods; the use of already existing products, whether or not patented; works of an artistic, literary or scientific nature; or computer programs as such.

265. Decision No. 486 states that on the expiration of a period of three years following the granting of the patent or four years following the application, whichever is the longer, a compulsory licence may be granted for the industrial manufacture of the product covered by the patent, but only if the patent has not been worked on a scale sufficient to satisfy the demands of the market or the

[289] Law No. 599 of 24 July 2000, Penal Code. Viewed at: http://www.derechodeautor.gov.co/htm/legal/legislacion/leyes_arch/599.pdf.

[290] The documents required for a patent application are: a form identifying the applicant; abstract; specifications; claims; drawings or samples; evidence of payment of the specified fee (changes annually); a copy of the power if filing through an attorney; if the application is being made by a company, a certificate of existence and legal representation; and a document confirming the assignment by the inventor to the applicant company or natural person, if other than the inventor.

[291] SIC online information: "*Patentes*". Viewed at: http://www.sic.gov.co/es/web/guest/patentes.

[292] SIC online information: "*Patentes*". Viewed at: http://www.sic.gov.co/es/web/guest/patentes.

[293] SIC online information: "*Patentes*". Viewed at: http://www.sic.gov.co/es/web/guest/patentes.

exploitation of the invention has been suspended for more than one year, and provided that the applicant has previously made efforts to obtain a contractual licence from the patent holder. In the case of semiconductor technology, a compulsory licence will be authorized only for public non-commercial use or to remedy a practice declared to be anti-competitive.[294]

266. A compulsory licence may also be granted for reasons of public interest, emergency or national security at any time, subject to these situations being declared to exist and only for as long as they continue. The procedure is governed by Decree No. 4.302 of 2008, as amended by Decree No. 4.966 of 2009 and by the Single Circular of the Supervisory Authority for Industry and Trade. At the same time, compulsory licences may also be granted, either ex officio or at the request of a party, in the event of practices detrimental to the exercise of free competition, especially where they constitute an abuse of a dominant position. Compulsory licences are subject to adequate remuneration and must be used predominantly for the supply of the domestic market.

267. CAN Decision No. 689 of 2008 amended Decision No. 486 to permit the development and expansion of industrial property rights through the domestic legislation of the member countries. Thus, Colombia can develop and expand its domestic legislation in relation to: the conditions of disclosure of the invention; the correction of omissions; and the compensation of the patent owner for unreasonable delay in issuing the patent on the part of the National Office.[295]

(d) Trademarks

268. CAN Decision No. 486 also protects trademarks, which include any sign capable of distinguishing products or services in the market. At national level, trademark law is based on Decree No. 2.591 of 2000.

269. Moreover, Colombia accepts the registration of collective marks and certification marks. The former is a type of mark used by associations of producers, manufacturers, service providers, organizations or any group of persons to indicate the common characteristics of the products or services produced by the collective. The mark may be used by those who make the product or provide the service under the conditions laid down in the regulations on use. The certification mark is intended to guarantee the quality or standard of a product or service.[296] The following are not considered to be marks: generic or technical names of products or services which could mislead trade circles or the public as to the nature, provenance, mode of manufacture or characteristics of the products concerned; consist of the name of a protected new plant variety; or are contrary to morality or public order or violate third-party rights.

270. Once granted, a trademark remains protected for a term of ten years from the date on which it was awarded, renewable for further periods of ten years. It should be noted that the protection of the mark is restricted to Colombian territory. Therefore marks registered abroad are not considered to be registered in Colombian territory. However, there are international agreements or treaties which stipulate that the registration of a mark in a territory may be prevented if it resembles or is identical to another registered in another territory.[297]

[294] Decision No. 486, Article 61. Viewed at: http://www.comunidadandina.org/normativa/dec/D486.htm.

[295] Article 1 of Decision No. 689. Viewed at: http://www.comunidadandina.org/normativa/dec/D689.htm.

[296] SIC online information: "*Marcas*". Viewed at: http://www.sic.gov.co/es/web/guest/marcas.

[297] SIC online information: "*Marcas*". Viewed at: http://www.sic.gov.co/es/web/guest/marcas.

(e) Appellations of origin

271. In Colombia, the appellation of origin regime is regulated by CAN Decision No. 486, Decree No. 3.081 of 2005, Resolution No. 33.190 of 2007 and the Single Circular containing the set of guidelines to help users complete industrial property formalities. Under this regime, an appellation of origin is considered to be the name of a country, region or specific locality, or a name which relates to a specific geographical area, used to designate a product originating therein and whose quality, reputation or other characteristics are exclusively or essentially attributable to the geographical environment in which it is produced, including natural and human factors.[298] The following are not considered to be appellations of origin: those that do not satisfy the definition; are common or generic indications; are contrary to morality or public order; or capable of misleading the public as to the geographical provenance, nature, mode of manufacture, or quality, reputation or other characteristics of the products in question.

272. Applications for an appellation of origin to be declared protected may be filed by natural or legal persons directly engaged in the extraction, production or manufacture of the product or products it is intended to protect with an appellation of origin. However, where a collective right is concerned, the owner is the Colombian State represented by the SIC. Nevertheless, the SIC may delegate the administration of the appellation of origin to public or private entities that represent the persons engaged in the extraction, production or manufacture of the products identified with the appellation of origin.[299]

273. The period of validity of the declaration of protection of an appellation of origin is determined by the continued existence of the conditions that give the product its recognized qualities. Nevertheless, the SIC may declare the protection cancelled if the conditions which justified the declaration of protection, for example, quality, reputation, and natural and human factors deriving from the geographical environment of origin, are not maintained. The protection afforded to an appellation of origin is restricted to the country in which it was granted. Therefore appellations of origin protected abroad are not considered to be protected in Colombian territory, while Colombian appellations are not considered to be protected abroad.[300]

(f) Industrial designs

274. In Colombia, industrial designs are protected by CAN Decision No. 486 and Decree No. 2.591 of 2000. An industrial design comprises any new special appearance of a product that results from some pattern of lines or combination of colours or some two-dimensional or three-dimensional external shape, contour, configuration, texture or material that does not change the intended use or purpose of the product.[301]

275. The application procedure for protecting an industrial design is very similar to that for obtaining a patent and involves the following steps: (i) filing of the documents with the SIC; (ii) formal examination of the documents and drawings filed, during the first 15 days; (iii) publication of the application in the Industrial Property Gazette for 30 working days to enable interested third parties to oppose the registration of the design; and (iv) an in-depth examination to enable the SIC to

[298] Article 201 of Decision No. 486.

[299] SIC online information: "*Denominación de origen*". Viewed at: http://www.sic.gov.co/es/web/guest/denominacion-de-origin.

[300] SIC online information, "*Denominación de origen*". Viewed at: http://www.sic.gov.co/es/web/guest/denominacion-de-origen.

[301] Article 113 of Decision No. 486.

decide whether to grant or refuse registration. If the application is accepted, the protection will run for ten years (non-renewable) from the filing date. If it is rejected, the applicant is entitled to apply for reconsideration and to appeal.[302]

276. It is not possible to apply to register industrial designs, the commercial exploitation of which must be prevented to protect morality or public order; whose appearance is dictated entirely by considerations of a technical nature; or which consist solely of a shape necessary to enable the product that incorporates the design to be mechanically assembled or connected with another product of which it forms part.[303]

(g) Protection of new plant varieties

277. The common regime for the protection of the rights of breeders of new plant varieties is governed by Decision No. 345 of 1993, which was implemented by Decree No. 533 of 1994, as amended by Decree No. 2.468 of 1994 and Decree No. 2.687 of 2002. This legislation seeks to protect all cultivated varieties of botanical genera and species provided that their cultivation, possession or use are not prohibited for reasons of human, animal or plant health and they are new, homogeneous, distinguishable and stable and have been assigned a name that constitutes their generic designation.[304]

278. The term of the breeder's certificate (varietal protection) is 25 years in the case of vines, forest trees and fruit trees, including their rootstocks, and 20 years for other species, reckoned from the date on which the certificate was granted. Protection is territorial, so that the interested party will have to complete the protection formalities for a variety in Colombia even if it is already protected in one or more other countries.[305] No protection is provided for plant varieties bred privately for non-commercial purposes; for experimental purposes; or to obtain and exploit a new variety, unless it is one essentially derived from a protected variety.

(h) Protection of test data with exclusivity

279. The Colombian legislation on the protection of test data with exclusivity consists of Decree No. 2.085 of 2002 for medicaments and Decree No. 502 of 2003 for chemical pesticides for use in agriculture. These decrees protect the undisclosed information contained in the test reports on a new chemical entity, if the authorities require these data to be submitted as a condition of approving the marketing of a particular product, provided that their origination involved a considerable effort. Colombia protects test data for a period of five years from the date on which marketing is approved (Table III.34).[306]

[302] SIC online information. Viewed at: http://www.sic.gov.co/es/web/guest/disenos-industriales.
[303] Article 116 of Decision No. 486.
[304] Article 4 of Decision No. 345. Viewed at: http://www.comunidadandina.org/normativa/dec/D345.htm.
[305] ICA online information: "*Derechos de Obtentor*". Viewed at: http://www.ica.gov.co/getdoc/faa710d6-9a5f-4f5e-91bf-f0d685e28054/Derechos-de-Obtentor.aspx.
[306] Decree No. 2.085 of 2002 (viewed at: http://www.presidencia.gov.co/prensa_new/decretoslinea/2002/septiembre/19/dec2085190902.pdf) and Decree No. 0502 of 2003 (viewed at: http://www.bvsde.paho.org/bvsacd/cd38/Colombia/D502-03.pdf).

Table III.34
Overview of intellectual property rights, 2011

Field	Term of protection	Exceptions
Copyright and related rights		
Literary and artistic works	80 years (natural person) 50 years (legal person)	Legal provisions, judicial decisions, orders and other regulations; right of quotation and reproduction for educational purposes
Artistic performances, phonographic productions and radio broadcasts	80 years (natural person) 50 years (legal person)	Private use, current affairs, use for teaching purposes, right to quote and make ephemeral recordings
Patents		
Any invention, whether of products or of processes, in all areas of technology, provided that it is new, involves an inventive step and is susceptible of industrial application	20 years from date of filing of the application	Discoveries; living organisms, biological processes or biological material as found in nature; literary, artistic works; plans, rules and methods; games; computer programs; ways of presenting information; inventions whose exploitation must be prevented to protect public order or morality; health or life of persons or animals or to preserve plants or the environment; plants, animals; therapeutic or surgical methods
Trademarks		
A trademark is any sign capable of distinguishing products or services in the market. Signs susceptible of graphic representation can be registered as a trademark	10 years from the date on which it was granted, renewable for periods of 10 years	Generic or technical name of the product or service; that could mislead commercial circles or the public as to the nature, provenance, mode of manufacture or characteristics of the products in question; that consist of a geographical indication; that consist of the name of a protected plant variety; that are contrary to morality or public order or violate third-party rights
Appellation of origin		
Name of a country, region or specific locality, or name related with a specific geographical area, used to designate a product originating therein and whose quality, reputation or other characteristics are exclusively or essentially due to the geographical environment in which it is produced, including natural and human factors	Determined by the continued existence of the conditions that justified protection	Do not satisfy the definition; are common or generic indications; are contrary to morality or public order; or could mislead the public as to the geographical provenance, nature, mode of manufacture, or the quality, reputation or other characteristics of the products in question
Design		
Any new special appearance of a product that results from some pattern of lines or combination of colours, or any two-dimensional or three-dimensional external shape, contour, configuration, texture or material that does not change the end use or purpose of the product	10 years from the filing date; non-renewable	Industrial designs whose commercial exploitation must be prevented to protect morality or public order; whose appearance is entirely dictated by considerations of a technical nature; and those which consist solely of a shape necessary to enable the product incorporating the design to be mechanically assembled or connected with another product of which it forms part
New plant varieties		
All cultivated varieties of botanical genera and species provided that their cultivation, possession or use are not prohibited for reasons of human, animal or plant health, and they are new, homogeneous, distinguishable and stable and have been assigned a name that constitutes their generic designation	From the date of granting of the breeder's right, 25 years in the case of vines and forest and fruit trees; 20 years for other species	When done privately for non-commercial purposes; for experimental purposes; or to obtain and exploit a new variety, unless it is one essentially derived from a protected variety. Whoever keeps and plants for his own use, or sells as raw material or food, the product obtained from the cultivation of the protected variety
Protection of test data with exclusivity		
Pharmaceuticals: undisclosed information concerning the safety and effectiveness of an active principle which has not been included in pharmacological standards in Colombia and which has involved a considerable effort	5 years from approval for marketing	When: the holder has authorized the use of the information; it is similar to another that has been authorized in Colombia and the term of protection has expired; it is necessary to protect the public interest; the new chemical entity has not been marketed in the country one year after the marketing permit was issued

Field	Term of protection	Exceptions
Agricultural chemicals: undisclosed information contained in the test reports on a new chemical entity and which has involved a considerable effort	5 years from approval for marketing	When: the holder has authorized the use of the information; it is necessary to protect the public interest; the new chemical entity registered has not been marketed in the country one year after registration was granted

Source: Information provided by the Colombian authorities.

(i) Enforcement

280. By establishing the CIPI in 2009[307] Colombia made a notable effort to improve coordination between the entities responsible for the enforcement of intellectual property rights. However, where protection is concerned there are still shortcomings due to the lack of resources and training for the entities entrusted with administering and managing intellectual property rights.[308] Accordingly, there is a need to build up the capacity of the competent authorities.

281. In relation to genetic resources, for example, according to WIPO, there are weaknesses in connection with the following: the shortage of personnel specialized in the legal, scientific and economic aspects; the availability of services and information for evaluation purposes; and the capacity to promote projects and proposals for improving the ability to tap genetic resources.[309] Moreover, according to a CONPES study, the Office of the Prosecutor General of the Nation and the criminal investigation department do not have the resources necessary to carry out criminal investigations.[310] According to the same study, with regard to criminal procedure, it is important to note that greater precision is required in connection with the handling of physical evidence in order to simplify the procedures for obtaining evidence that leads to trial, for example, with respect to the number or percentage of samples that must be analysed and preserved to establish the illegality of certain goods.[311]

282. Moreover, with regard to the protection of distinctive signs, CONPES mentions that in Colombia there are domestic enterprises dedicated to trademark infringement, as well as many counterfeit imports. The main sectors affected by the illegal use of trademarks are: footwear, clothing, home electrical appliances, spare parts and tobacco. It is also pointed out that where administrative formalities are concerned, despite the efforts made by the SIC, there are still problems, especially in connection with registration and more particularly in dealing with applications for distinctive signs and new creations.[312]

---

[307] Decree No. 1.162 of 13 April 2010 organizing the National Intellectual Property Administrative System and establishing the Intersectoral Intellectual Property Commission. Viewed at: http://www.derechodeautor.gov.co/htm/legal/legislacion/Decrees_arch/Decreto%201162%20de%20Abril%2013%20de%202010.pdf.

[308] National Economic and Social Policy Council (2008a), page 28.

[309] WIPO (2010).

[310] National Economic and Social Policy Council (2008a), page 29.

[311] National Economic and Social Policy Council (2008a), page 29.

[312] National Economic and Social Policy Council (2008a), page 34.

IV. TRADE POLICIES BY SECTOR

(1) OVERVIEW

1. Because of its contribution to employment and the generation of foreign currency, Colombia's agricultural sector is of key importance for the country's economic development. Agricultural policy currently focuses on boosting development in rural areas, making agriculture more competitive and diversifying markets. Colombia is accordingly striving to make further progress in negotiating and implementing trade agreements. Although this is not declared explicitly, Colombia's agricultural policy also seeks to contribute towards food security. The agricultural sector benefits from domestic support programmes, access to loans on preferential terms and debt refinancing programmes, subsidies for agricultural insurance and mitigation of exchange rate risks. In addition, Colombia uses other mechanisms to enable producers to withstand fluctuations in global prices, for example, price stabilization funds.

2. The aim of Colombia's mining policy is to reorganize the institutional structure of the mining and energy sector, ensure adequate supplies of hydrocarbons and electricity, and generate the resources needed to boost Colombia's development. It gives national treatment for foreign investment in the mining and hydrocarbons sectors. To obtain a contract for an exploration concession, foreign companies must set up a subsidiary domiciled in Colombia. The hydrocarbons sector is a leading generator of foreign currency and is open to private investment, although the State-owned company ECOPETROL S.A. continues to play a key role in extraction, refining, import, distribution and transport of petroleum and its by-products. Colombia still subsidizes the sale of fuel on the domestic market. Although it has been revised, this subsidy still represents a heavy fiscal burden.

3. The electricity sector is also open to private participation, which accounts for 45 per cent of total generation. During the period under review, Colombia introduced the wholesale electricity market, adopting measures to deal with potential shortages.

4. The manufacturing sector can also benefit from a number of export support programmes. For certain manufactured goods, Colombia still uses reference prices as parameters to verify their declared value during customs inspection.

5. In the financial sector, there are no legal limitations on foreign capital holdings in commercial banks or insurance companies. A special authorization is required before insurance can be taken out with companies domiciled abroad. The financial institutions have maintained sound prudential indicators following the reforms introduced into the regulatory framework and the system of (prudential) supervision. Colombia emerged successfully from the 2008-2009 international financial crisis by taking measures such as postponement of the distribution of profits and building up reserves to deal with any deterioration in companies' financial situations, together with closer supervision. It also made use of the countercyclical component provided in its regulations to respond to changes in the risk level. Interest rates are generally determined by the market, but are based on directives from the Financial Supervisory Authority (SFC).

6. There are no restrictions on Colombian or foreign private capital holdings in the supply of telecommunications services. Nevertheless, foreign firms must set up a subsidiary in Colombia in order to operate on the domestic market. In 2009, Colombia introduced a new law to unify the legal framework for fixed and mobile telephony. This new law is intended to promote investment in the sector and established a general authorization regime (and not authorization by service), together with a transitional period for phasing out the subsidies regime for the low-income population. Suppliers of

telecommunications services are free to fix their rates, but the Communications Regulatory Commission (CRC) has the right to intervene if there is insufficient competition or the quality or supply of services is not acceptable. Some rates are monitored, however, and there is currently a ceiling for calls from fixed to mobile telephones.

7. The goal of the policy on (scheduled) domestic transport of passengers is to make market access easier and so promote competition. Colombia does, however, impose a maximum number of operators on each route, which depends on the number of passengers carried annually. Airports are managed under a concession regime or by the departments/municipalities where they are located. Cabotage air services are restricted to Colombian aircraft. There is also a nationality requirement: 90 per cent of the personnel employed by Colombian airlines and agencies/branch offices of foreign airlines established in Colombia must be Colombian nationals. This restriction applies under conditions of reciprocity.

8. Access to the maritime transport market is based on the principle of reciprocity. Nationality requirements exist for the crews of Colombian-registered vessels. The captain, officers and 80 per cent of the crew on Colombian-registered vessels must be Colombian nationals. Cabotage maritime transport is restricted to Colombian-registered vessels, although an authorization may be given to charter/lease a foreign-registered ship if no Colombian ships are available or suitable. International and cabotage shipping companies set their rates and freight charges, but these must be communicated to the authorities, which may revise or reject them. The construction, maintenance and management of public and private ports are the responsibility of port management companies under a 20-year concession regime.

9. There are registration requirements for the supply of certain types of tourism services. Suppliers of specified tourism services must pay a parafiscal contribution to promote tourism, and this has applied to shopping centres as well since 2011. Colombian or foreign investors are eligible for a series of incentives, mainly for the rehabilitation or building of hotels and the supply of ecotourism services.

(2) AGRICULTURE

10. Colombia's agricultural sector is of prime importance for the country's economic development and is deemed to be a strategic sector, both because of its contribution to GDP and because it generates jobs and foreign currency. Moreover, it has enormous growth potential, as a large area of agricultural land is not yet farmed.

11. In the late 1990s, the agricultural, forestry and fisheries sector suffered a profound crisis, following which its growth fell back compared to the rest of the economy. Over the past decade, the sector grew by an average of 2 per cent annually compared to 4 per cent for the economy as a whole. After recovering during the period 2006-2007, from 2008 onwards it again stagnated, because of the international crisis according to the authorities, before rebounding from 2010 onwards. Despite this erratic growth, the agricultural sector accounted for 6.5 per cent of GDP in 2011 and is the third largest source of jobs in the economy: some 18 per cent of the labour force works in agriculture, coming after trade (25.9 per cent) and local services (19.6 per cent). Agricultural exports accounted for 12.4 per cent of total exports (Table IV.1).

Table IV.1
Principal indicators for agriculture, 2005-2011

	2005	2006	2007	2008	2009[a]	2010[a]	2011[a]
Contribution to current GDP (%)	7.7	7.4	7.1	6.9	6.9	6.5	6.4
Real growth rate (%)	2.8	2.4	3.9	-0.4	-0.7	1.0	2.2
Employment (percentage of total employment)[b]	21.0	19.0	18.3	18.1	18.7	18.6	18.1
Share of agricultural value added (%)							
Coffee products	11.4	11.4	10.9	10.1	9.2	11.7	11.6
Other agricultural products	45.3	46.3	46.6	47.5	49.4	48.7	49.9
Live animals and animal products	37.7	36.6	36.9	37.1	35.9	34.4	33.5
Forestry, logging and related activities	5.6	5.7	5.6	5.4	5.4	5.2	5.0
Exports[c]							
Agricultural products (US$ millions)	4,599	4,922	5,858	6,693	5,971	5,757	7,059
Agricultural products (percentage of exports)	21.7	20.2	19.5	17.8	18.2	14.5	12.4
Agricultural products (rate of growth, %)	28.8	7.0	19.0	14.3	-10.8	-3.6	22.6
Most important products (percentage of exports)[c]							
Coffee, not roasted, whether or not decaffeinated; coffee husks and skins; coffee extract, essences and concentrates and preparations based on such products or coffee-based	7.7	6.7	6.3	5.6	5.4	5.4	5.1
Cut flowers and foliage	4.3	4.0	3.7	2.9	3.2	3.1	2.2
Bananas (including plantains), fresh or dried	2.4	2.2	1.9	1.7	2.5	1.9	1.4
Beet or cane sugar, not refined, in solid form	1.3	1.5	0.9	0.4	1.2	1.1	1.1
Palm oil or fractions thereof	0.4	0.4	0.7	0.9	0.4	0.2	0.3
Food products, n.e.s.	0.4	0.3	0.3	0.3	0.3	0.2	0.1
Fish, frozen (excluding fillets and minced fish)	0.3	0.2	0.2	0.3	0.3	0.2	0.1
Imports							
Agricultural products (US$ millions)	2,199	2,704	3,470	4,542	3,774	4,486	5,718
Agricultural products (percentage of total imports)	10.4	10.3	10.5	11.5	11.5	11.0	10.5
Agricultural products (rate of growth, %)	2.3	23.0	28.4	30.9	-16.9	18.9	27.5
Agricultural trade balance (US$ millions)	2,400	2,218	2,388	2,151	2,197	1,271	1,341

a Provisional data.
b Population employed.
c Includes re-exports for 2009 and 2010.

Source: National Administrative Department of Statistics (DANE), Comtrade database (SITC, Rev.3) and information provided by the Colombian authorities.

12. The recovery in the agricultural sector mainly took the form of an increase in the area under cultivation and in the production of non-traditional products, which have become very important commercially, for example, fruit, special coffees, biofuels (palm oil) and vegetables. Sustainable growth will only be possible, however, if the bottlenecks in this sector can be overcome. These include the following: the low level of competitiveness and output in some branches, the poor state of the rural infrastructure, inefficient use of land and water, the absence of mechanisms to market agricultural products, and lack of markets.[1]

13. The reason for the high cost of agricultural production is the lack of flexibility in the cost structure, making it more vulnerable to the prices of inputs and products and fluctuations in exchange rates. The rise in the peso in recent years has, however, lowered the cost of importing some inputs - agricultural chemicals, seeds and machinery - but has not been translated directly into producer prices, while at the same time the higher cost of labour has mainly affected export crops such as coffee, flowers, sugar cane and palm oil, which are labour-intensive.

14. The low level of competitiveness and output can mainly be attributed to inefficient use of production factors, notably land and water, the low level of innovation in production systems and lack of investment in Colombian agriculture. There are a number of factors which discourage investment,

[1] National Department of Planning (2010b).

for example: the absence of any tradition of managing the specific climate and market risks associated with agricultural activities; limited access to and use of information; and problems in obtaining loans, particularly for small-scale producers. Financial deepening in agriculture, 10.2 per cent in 2008, continues to be much lower than that for the economy as a whole, which was 32.2 per cent that year.[2]

15. A salient feature of Colombia's agricultural markets is the lack of diversification and of competitiveness, both domestically and abroad. Around 90 per cent of agricultural exports are made up of just seven products (coffee, flowers, fruit, bovine meat, sugar, processed foods, oils and fats). Although Colombia does not have any problems regarding the availability of food as a whole, inasmuch as 90 per cent of domestic demand is met by domestic production, there are problems in terms of access to food for the low-income population, a situation that is to a large extent related to problems of regional distribution, transport and marketing.[3]

16. The objective of the current national policy, set out in the 2010-2014 National Development Plan, is to make the economy more competitive. The agricultural sector is viewed as one of the five sectors with high growth potential that will catalyze the country's economic development. Agricultural policy, drawn up and implemented by the Ministry of Agriculture and Rural Development (MADR)[4], currently focuses on developing mechanisms to generate jobs and income in rural areas, making agricultural production more competitive, equitable regional development, agricultural risk management, and the expansion and diversification of domestic and foreign markets.[5] To achieve this, Colombia is seeking to make further progress in negotiating and implementing trade agreements. As an essential adjunct to the policy to expand and diversify domestic and foreign markets, Colombia plans to continue with the process of consolidating the agricultural health and food safety policy implemented by the Colombian Agricultural Institute (ICA).

17. Many of the trade measures and support programmes for the agricultural sector are also intended to contribute towards food security, although this is not an explicit objective of Colombia's agricultural policy. These measures and programmes include export quotas and price controls; likewise, special programmes such as the 2008-2011 Coffee Policy Agreement, which has a component with programmes for sowing yellow maize and beans in coffee-growing areas, seek to improve food security in these areas and in the country as a whole.[6]

(i) Measures at the border

18. Tariff protection in the agricultural sector (WTO definition) is much higher than in other sectors. The gap in comparison with the industrial sector has widened following the temporary reduction of tariffs on a wide range of manufactures. In 2010, the average tariff on agricultural products (WTO definition) was 18.3 per cent (16.5 per cent in 2006), higher than the protection given to non-agricultural products. Although tariff protection for agricultural products fell to 14.5 per cent in August 2011, the decrease is much less than in the case of non-agricultural products, on which the

[2] National Department of Planning (2010b).

[3] National Department of Planning (2010b).

[4] The primary responsibility of MADR, created by Law No. 25 of 1913, is to draw up agricultural, fisheries and rural development policies, plans and programmes, in accordance with Articles 64, 65 and 66 of Colombia's Political Constitution (Decree No. 967 of 2001).

[5] MADR (2010a).

[6] Online information from MADR, "*Políticas y Programas Misionales: Apoyos Económicos y Financiamiento: Caficultores*". Viewed at: http://www. minagricultura.gov.co/07presupuesto/07a_ ein_caficul.aspx.

average rate of applied MFN duties fell from 11.3 per cent in 2006 to 7.2 per cent in April 2011 and 4.9 per cent in August of the same year. On average, the highest rates by WTO category applied to agricultural products, specifically animals and products of animal origin and dairy produce, at rates of 25.2 and 55.5 per cent, respectively, in 2011 (from August onwards), and 32.4 and 58.9 per cent in 2010, an increase in comparison with the rates applied in 2006, which were 23.6 and 21.3 per cent, respectively. The maximum tariff in 2010 was 119.1 per cent, which applied to seven lines in HS 02.07 (poultry meat and edible offal), while the maximum rate in 2011 (from August onwards) was 98 per cent and applied to 14 lines in HS 04.02 (milk and cream, concentrated).

19. Colombia still applies the Andean Price Band System (SAFP) to agricultural products. In 2010, it applied to 163 tariff lines (0.9 per cent of all tariff headings). In general, the products subject to the price band are: rice, barley, yellow maize, white maize, yellow soya beans, wheat, unrefined soya bean oil, unrefined palm oil, white sugar, raw sugar, whole milk, chicken cuts and pig meat (Box IV.1). In 2011, the SAFP applied to 141 tariff lines, but was suspended for rice, white maize and whole milk.

Box IV.1: Andean Price Band System (SAFP) for agricultural products

By Decision No. 371 of November 1994, the Andean Community (CAN) established the SAFP for agricultural products with the aim of stabilizing import costs for a specific group of agricultural products characterized by highly unstable international prices.

The purpose of the SAFP is to exert a stabilizing effect by curbing the volatility of international prices for imported products, mitigating fluctuations in international prices. The system operates by establishing a floor price (or lower band) and a ceiling price (or higher band). When the international price is below the floor price, a special import duty is imposed, but when total import costs exceed the higher limit, a tariff reduction is granted.

The price band system covers a total of 154 products: 13 "marker" products and 141 related products. The marker products are those "whose international prices are used to calculate the bands" (Decision No. 371, Article 4). Related products are those related to the production chain or substitute products similar to the marker product.

The average c.i.f. prices recorded over the previous two weeks on the international market are used to calculate the reference price that will determine the band. Reference prices remain in effect for a fortnight and "constitute the taxable base for the application of import duties" (Decision No. 371, Article 9). They are published by the CAN Secretariat. The fortnightly report may be viewed on the following websites: www.dian.gov.co, www.agronet.gov.co or www.comunidadandina.org.

The rules for calculating the reductions or additional duties are linked to the Common External Tariff (CET) and to changes in international prices in comparison with the floor and ceiling prices. As provided by Article 11 of Decision No. 371, if the reference price is lower than the c.i.f. floor price, an additional variable duty is imposed corresponding to the difference between the two, multiplied by one plus the CET for the marker product. Similar treatment applies when the international price is above the ceiling price, but in that case, the tariff is reduced. If the international price falls between the two limits (floor and ceiling prices), only the corresponding CET applies.

Source: Directorate of Taxes and National Customs (DIAN) and CAN.

20. During the period under review, Colombia notified the products subject to tariff quotas during the period 2006-2010 to the WTO. These included: meat, dairy produce, grains and cereals, soya

beans, oils and fats, and cotton.[7] Colombia does not make use of these quotas as the applied tariff is below the in-quota tariff. The system for allocating quotas has not changed since 2006, with the exception of quotas for whey (HS subheading 0404101000) (Table IV.2).

Table IV.2
Agricultural tariff quotas

Product	HS heading	Description of import arrangement applicable
Yellow maize White maize Other rice in the husk Husked rice Other semi-milled or wholly milled rice Broken rice Other sorghum Other soya beans Cotton	1005.90.11.00 1005.90.12.00 1006.10.90.00 1006.20.00.00 1006.30.00.90 1006.40.00.00 1007.00.90.00 1201.00.90.00 5201	The import quota is allocated on a competitive basis amongst participants registered with MADR. Quota allocation is by means of public auctions in which importers take part through the bid registration system.
Meat of bovine animals, fresh Meat of bovine animals, frozen Meat and edible meat offal	0201 0202 0210	The import quota is allocated amongst importers who participated in previous auctions, with a share reserved for new importers determined in accordance with the market situation.
Cuts and offal, fresh or chilled Cuts of fowls of the species *Gallus domesticus*, frozen Cuts and offal, fresh or chilled Cuts of turkeys, frozen Cuts of ducks, geese or guinea fowl, fresh or chilled Cuts of ducks, geese or guinea fowl, frozen	0207.13 0207.14 0207.26 0207.27 0207.35 0207.36	An import licence is required from the Import Committee of the Ministry of Trade, Industry and Tourism (MCIT), the criterion for approval being protection of the domestic industry.
Whey, partially or fully demineralized	0404.10.10.00	The import quota is allocated to applicants on a *pro-rata* basis in accordance with their share of the total requests submitted to MADR.

Source: WTO documents G/AG/N/COL/35 of 9 June 2006 and G/AG/N/COL/35/Add.1 of 13 January 2011.

21. In 2010-2011, Colombia only opened quotas for five products (0.1 per cent of all tariff headings), of which four were included in the government mechanism for administering agricultural quotas (MAC), which was set up in 2004 for imports from countries not members of CAN and applies to the following products: rice, yellow maize, white maize, soya beans, sorghum and cotton.[8] During the period under review, Colombia imposed quotas under the MAC for yellow maize, white maize, soya beans and cotton lint. Each year, MADR issues a decree listing the products subject to quotas, the volume and the in-quota tariff.[9] The quotas opened under the MAC are allocated through a public auction and using the MAC minimizes government intervention in the allocation of quotas. Colombia uses the MAC to guarantee domestic supplies of certain products.[10] If the importers taking part in the auctions also buy up a percentage of domestic production, they are eligible for a reduction in the in-quota tariff.

22. The majority of products subject to tariff quotas are also subject to the SAFP; of the 163 tariff lines subject to the price band, 157 were also subject to tariff quotas. Likewise, of the four products for which Colombia opened a tariff quota under the MAC in 2010 and 2011, three (yellow hard maize, white hard maize and soya beans) were also subject to the SAFP.

[7] WTO documents G/AG/N/COL/37 of 9 October 2009, G/AG/N/COL/41 of 13 January 2011 and G/AG/N/COL/47 of 25 November 2011.

[8] Decree No. 430 of 2004.

[9] Decrees No. 2.333 of 2008, No. 4.676, No. 760 and No. 4.551 of 2009, No. 140, No. 2.770 and No. 4.662 of 2010 and No. 4.900 of 2011.

[10] Decrees No. 430 of 2004 and No. 4.900 of 2011.

23. Colombia has reserved the right to apply the special safeguard clause in the WTO Agreement on Agriculture to 57 four-digit tariff headings, but has not yet used it.

24. Some non-tariff measures also apply to the import of agricultural products, for example, a series of import requirements, including licensing, authorization, import registration, and plant and animal health permits (Chapter III).

25. In 2011, Colombia temporarily restricted the export of certain types of live cattle in order to restock herds and so increase the exportable supply of meat and meat products.[11]

(ii) Domestic support and subsidies

26. Colombia notified the WTO Committee on Agriculture that it did not grant any subsidies for agricultural exports between 2006 and 2010.[12] In 2010, it notified some agricultural support programmes aimed at boosting the sector's development, as well as access to loans, agricultural insurance and control and sanitary management of pests and diseases. These measures are covered by Law No. 101 of 1993, which allows the Government, when circumstances so warrant, to grant incentives directly related to production and the volumes produced to agricultural producers and fishermen, on a temporary and selective basis.

27. Until 2010, when the measure was suspended[13], some agricultural products exported (for example, flowers, foliage, plantains, bananas, palm oil), and fisheries and aquaculture products (for example, shrimp, tilapia and trout) benefited from a sanitary incentive intended to support the control and sanitary management of pests and diseases.[14] The support consisted of a payment per hectare, provided that the ICA received proof of proper phytosanitary management and the maintenance of jobs in the beneficiary sectors and that a specified volume was exported, which varied according to the product. Each year, MADR issued a resolution showing the total amount of the subsidy for each heading and the requirements, whether jobs or foreign currency to be generated, in order to receive the subsidy.[15] For example, for flowers and foliage, in 2010 MADR set aside Col$50 billion (around US$26.3 million) for this incentive, for which producers exporting US$1,000 or more of flowers in 2009 and managing to maintain at least 80 per cent of the certified jobs over the period January to June 2009 were eligible. Enterprises whose personnel decreased by over 20 per cent lost the whole amount of the incentive.[16] According to the authorities, this line was never used.

28. Colombia makes use of price stabilization mechanisms in order to deal with fluctuations in world prices for certain agricultural products. The Price Stabilization Funds (FEPs), created by Law No. 101 of 1993, are intended to guarantee producers' incomes, regulate domestic production, and prevent price speculation, in addition to promoting agricultural exports. Currently, there are FEPs for five products: cotton; sugar; cocoa; meat, milk and their by-products; and palm oil.[17] The

[11] Decrees No. 2.000, No. 3.046 and No. 4.025 of 2011.

[12] WTO documents G/AG/N/COL/39 of 11 February 2010, G/AG/N/COL/39/Corr.1 of 9 March 2010, G/AG/N/COL/44 of 13 January 2011 and G/AG/N/COL/45 of 25 November 2011.

[13] Information provided by the authorities.

[14] Resolutions No. 116 of 2008 and No. 254 of 2009, Law No. 101 of 1993, Resolution No. 169 of 2007 and other rules.

[15] Law No. 101 of 1993, resolutions and other rules.

[16] MADR (2010b).

[17] The FEP for cotton, which is managed by the Colombian Cotton Confederation (CONALGODON); the FEP for centrifugal sugars, molasses obtained by extracting or refining sugar, and sugar syrups, managed by the Colombian Sugar Cane Growers' Association (ASOCAÑA); the FEP for cocoa, managed by the National Federation of Cocoa Growers (FEDECACAO); the FEP for promoting the export of meat, milk and their

Funds operate by estimating a price for each product based, *inter alia,* on international prices in the relevant markets. Depending on the estimated price, producers or exporters make "transfers" to the Fund or are compensated by the Fund, according to the price difference. The Funds act as a savings and insurance scheme.

29. Colombia has a National Coffee Fund which acts as a purchasing guarantee mechanism for coffee producers to ensure that they receive the best possible price and can sell their whole crop. Moreover, in 2008, a programme was implemented to protect coffee growers' incomes and guarantee them adequate remuneration. Producers sign a price protection contract (CPP), which guarantees a minimum price of Col$600,000 (US$32) per 125 kg.[18]

30. In addition to the foregoing, there are three specific price stabilization programmes: support for cotton, rice and milk. The equalization programme for cotton prices, or the minimum guaranteed price for cotton, is a policy introduced in 2001 and implemented during the period 2003/2004 to protect Colombian farmers' incomes from fluctuations in international prices by offering compensation for the price differential between market prices (New York Exchange) and a minimum guaranteed price per tonne of lint. The Government gives an incentive for storing rice so as to prevent prices falling as a result of the surpluses that normally occur during the second half of each year. The price of milk is regulated by means of a reference price, on which producers receive an increase or a reduction depending on the hygiene quality and the composition of the milk.[19]

31. In 2011, MADR decided that the price of agricultural inputs, specifically fertilizers and pesticides for agricultural use, should be made subject to the "monitored freedom regime" for prices. This regime allows prices to be freely determined throughout the distribution chain, although they must be communicated to MADR. MADR can thus determine whether it should intervene in any inputs market and make the product subject to the "regulated freedom regime", under which maximum selling prices are fixed for inputs. If the maximum selling price is not observed, MADR may make the product subject to the "direct price control regime", setting the price for all levels in the marketing chain by means of a resolution. The Ministry may, however, only impose direct price control after having gone through the previous two stages and if the conditions that led to its original intervention persist. MADR stops intervening once it has been determined that the conditions that led to its intervention have ceased to exist.[20]

32. MADR also implements other support programmes to enable the agricultural and fisheries sector to contend with climate problems or to renew plantations, *inter alia,* so as to encourage investment in higher value crops and exports, as well as other programmes specifically for small and medium-sized producers (Table IV.3).

---

by-products, managed by the Colombian Cattle Breeders' Federation (FEDEGAN); and the FEP for palm kernel oil, palm oil and fractions thereof, managed by the National Federation of Palm Oil Producers (FEDEPALMA).

[18] Online information from MADR, "*Políticas y Programas Misionales: Apoyos Económicos y Financiamiento: Caficultores*". Viewed at: http://www.minagricultura.gov.co/07presupuesto/07a_ein_caficul.aspx.

[19] MADR, Resolutions No. 051 of 2003 and No. 012 of 2007. National Dairy Council, Agreement No. 007 of 2002.

[20] Resolutions No. 387 of 22 December 2011 "establishing the pricing policy for agricultural inputs", No. 389 of 26 December 2011 "making some fertilizers and pesticides for agricultural use subject to the monitored freedom regime", and No. 390 of 26 December 2011 "making veterinary medicines and biological products for livestock use subject to the monitored freedom regime".

33. The Agriculture, Secure Income (AIS) Programme was implemented by MADR until 2010, when it was replaced by the Rural Development with Equity Programme (DRE). Its objective was to make the national agricultural sector more competitive, protect the incomes of producers affected by the distortions caused by foreign markets, and lessen rural inequalities. The Programme made use of a number of tools such as the Special Line of Credit (LEC)[21], the Rural Capitalization Incentive (ICR), the Technical Assistance Incentive (IAT) and the Public Irrigation and Drainage Assembly.

34. The purpose of the DRE, implemented from 2010 onwards, is to provide small and medium-sized producers[22] with support to improve their competitiveness, help lessen inequalities in the field and reinforce national food security. Its main components are: the LEC; the ICR; the IAT; rural micro-credit; support for irrigation and drainage projects; and cofinancing of research and technological development.[23]

Table IV.3
Incentives granted by MADR

General programme	Specific programme	Description/objective
Beneficiaries of support because of the effect of frost	Incentives for flower-growers affected by frost	The objective is to compensate for the losses suffered by growers of flowers for export as a result of frost in Colombia.
Beneficiaries of the Forestry Incentive Certificate (CIF)	CIF	Support granted to cover part of the cost of planting and upkeep for producers who plant new commercial forests on land suitable for forestry. The CIF's support concerns: plantation of indigenous species: 75% of the cost; plantation of exogenous species: 50% of the cost; upkeep from the second to the 5th year after plantation: 50% of the cost; upkeep of areas of natural woodland located within the plantation and forestry management, for 5 years: 75%.
Coffee Policy Agreement	Competitiveness programme	The objective was to renew coffee bushes. Support of Col$240 for fertilizer for each coffee bush replanted. Granted up to 2011.
	Conversion of land	Incentive of Col$1 million/hectare for growers who desist from planting coffee bushes in less than optimal areas and take up other agricultural activities, preferably producing food.
	ICR for coffee	The objective is to promote the production of higher value coffee. The ICR consists of payment of up to 40% of loans to be used for investment in the infrastructure required to obtain quality certificates for coffee and to produce special coffees of higher value.
	Fertifuturo programme	The aim is to encourage proper fertilization of coffee bushes and increase their productivity. MADR gave discounts for cash purchase of fertilizer or paid the interest for purchases on credit terms. Granted up to 2011.
	Additional climate insurance subsidy for coffee-growers	Coffee growers who take out insurance for their crops receive a subsidy for 60% of the cost of the premium and also reduced interest rates for their loans in order to maintain and renew coffee bushes, as part of the LEC "Risk-free Coffee", offered by the Agrarian Bank.
	Continuity, sustainability and future programme	The aim is to raise output by replacing old coffee bushes and planting new ones. For this purpose, an ICR amounting to 40% is given to small-scale producers who replace up to 20% of their plantations, and 20% to medium-sized producers.

[21] The terms for the LEC in the AIS include a subsidized interest rate (Fixed Term Deposit (DTF) rate - 2 percentage points), and a term of up to 15 years, including grace periods of up to three years. The DTF rate represents the average interest rate on 90-day deposit certificates owned by Colombian banks. The term and the grace period are determined by the income and expenditure flows in the production activity that is the subject of the investment financed.

[22] Small producers are those whose assets were equivalent to 145 times the current monthly legal wage (SMMLV) corresponding to Col$77,662,000 (US$40,800) in 2011, and medium-sized producers are those whose assets amounted to 5,000 SMMLV i.e. Col$2,678,000,000) (US$1.4 million) in 2011.

[23] MADR (2010a).

General programme	Specific programme	Description/objective
Fishing and aquaculture	Fuel subsidy	Fuel price subsidy for industrial fishing vessels and aquaculture.
	Incentive programme for the supply of aquaculture products for export	To provide support to producers of shrimps, tilapia and trout intended for export, Colombia implements the Incentive programme for the supply of aquaculture export products.

Source: Online information from MADR "*Políticas y Programas Misionales: Apoyos Económicos y Financiamiento: Incentivos de Flores por heladas*". Viewed at: http://www.minagricultura.gov.co/07presupuesto/07a_inflor_hela.aspx; "*Políticas y Programas Misionales: Apoyos Económicos y Financiamiento: Listados de Beneficios Agro Ingreso Seguro*". Viewed at: http://www.minagricultura.gov.co/05recomendados/03_recomendado.aspx; "*Políticas y Programas Misionales: Apoyos Económicos y Financiamiento: Listados de Beneficio Agro Ingreso Seguro:* MADR and Corporación Colombia Internacional (2009), *Pesca y Acuicultura: Colombia 2009*. Viewed at: http://www.cci.org.co/cci/cci_x/datos/BoletinesIncoder/Publicaciones/Informecompleto2009.pdf and MADR Resolution No. 157 of 2010.

35. The LEC can be used to finance the sowing of crops with a short life cycle, for example: rice, white and yellow maize, sorghum, barley, oats, beans, vetch, vegetables, fruit (except those benefiting from the ICR), soya beans, plantains, yucca, potatoes, sesame, cotton, tobacco, groundnuts and achira. These lines of credit are at subsidized rates of interest: the subsidy given by the Fund for Financing the Agricultural Sector (FINAGRO) varies depending on the producer's volume and ranges from 5 to 7.5 per cent.[24]

36. The ICR is a payment towards the balance of the principal of the loan taken out by the producer in order to carry out new investment projects intended to upgrade infrastructure for production, agricultural and fisheries marketing, and to finance the sowing of medium-yield crops.[25] The ICR is also granted according to the type of producer through a financial intermediary.[26] Under the IAT, the Government subsidizes up to 80 per cent of the value of agricultural technical assistance services for small and medium-sized individual producers.[27]

(iii) Financing and insurance

37. FINAGRO, created by Law No. 16 of 1990, is an autonomous entity specializing in managing agricultural and rural loans. It finances the working capital and investment required for production,

[24] Small-scale individual producers: DTF rate + 1 per cent; small associate producer: DTF rate; medium-sized individual producer: DTF rate + 2 per cent; medium-sized associate producer: DTF rate + 1 per cent; medium-sized or large producer incorporating small producers: DTF rate + 1 per cent. The DTF rate represents the average interest rate on 90-day deposit certificates owned by Colombian banks. See FINAGRO (2012), Chapter V: *Líneas especiales de crédito*.

[25] The ICR may only be used for the following activities: planting and cultivation of late yield crops; preparing land and managing hydraulic resources; purchasing production machinery and equipment; agriculture and aquaculture; production infrastructure; primary processing and marketing of goods; development of biotechnology and its incorporation into production processes; and forestry and pastoral production systems.

[26] Small producers: 40 per cent; medium-sized producers: 20 per cent; and medium-sized or large producers incorporating small producers (provided that they invest with a small producer and that the latter is responsible for 60 per cent of the project): 40 per cent.

[27] Online information from MADR, "*Asistencia Técnica*". Viewed at: http://www.minagricultura.gov.co/11contacto/preg_asistencia.aspx; and information provided by the authorities.

marketing and primary processing.[28] The interest and discount rates on the loans depend on the type of producer requesting the loan, in accordance with the classification defined by FINAGRO (Table III.27). The terms and grace periods for FINAGRO loans depend on the crop or production cycle of the activity to be financed.[29] FINAGRO also gives farmers emergency resources in case they lose their crops or livestock, for example, because of harsh winter weather.[30] To combat the harsh winter in 2011, small producers severely affected were given relief amounting to up to 95 per cent of the capital balance.

38. During the period 2008-2009, FINAGRO gave a special line of working capital loans at subsidized interest rates for some agricultural products wholly or partly intended for foreign markets.[31] This line, which according to the authorities is no longer available, could be used to finance working capital, or for investment and payment of the financial liabilities of producers of bananas, plantains, flowers, foliage, aromatic herbs, shrimps, and of fish-farmers. The production could be totally or partly intended for foreign markets.[32] The financing could cover up to 100 per cent of the capitalization requirements, the project's direct costs, or the payment of liabilities *vis-à-vis* the financial sector, including capital plus the interest payable. The amount of the loan per beneficiary was determined by the beneficiary and the financial intermediary.

39. The Agricultural Guarantee Fund (FAG) guarantees credits granted on FINAGRO terms for use in new agricultural projects. When an application for a FINAGRO agricultural loan is made, the banking institution requires security to underwrite the commitment; if no security is available or it is not sufficient or appropriate, FAG guarantees these commitments with the bank. Since 2008, FAG has had a special account called the Special Exporters' Guarantee Fund to provide security for FINAGRO loans through the LEC for exporters.[33]

40. In view of the importance of the agricultural sector in Colombia, besides the loan programmes implemented by FINAGRO and the support given by FAG, there are other programmes to support the sector in general, in addition to special programmes. The programme for agricultural debt relief for producers affected by the 2010-2011 Niña phenomenon (or PADA OLA INVERNAL Programme) allows some small and medium-sized agricultural producers affected to renegotiate the loans taken out after 1 June 2010.[34] The standardization of working capital and/or investment loans means consolidating debt and includes extending the original term for repayment by at least one year, with a maximum of five years, including a one-year grace period. The interest rate may not exceed the ceiling set in the indicative loan plan for each type of producer; in the case of medium-sized

[28] Production, marketing, processing and support services for agricultural, livestock, fisheries, fish-farming and forestry and rural activities can be financed through FINAGRO, for example: handicrafts, rural tourism, processing of precious metals and stones and mining.

[29] For further details, see MADR and FINAGRO (2011b).

[30] For further details, see MADR and FINAGRO (2011a).

[31] The interest rate on loans granted under this scheme was the annual effective DFT rate, irrespective of the type of producer. For loans granted using the financial intermediary's own resources, for each transaction disbursed and registered with the Fund, FINAGRO gave 3.3 effective annual percentage points of subsidy on capital balances, irrespective of the type of producer. This allowance was paid in line with the time-frame for the payment of interest agreed for each transaction. For loans discounted with FINAGRO, the discount rate was the DTF rate, and for each discounted transaction, while it was in effect, FINAGRO gave financial intermediaries 2.3 effective annual percentage points on capital balances and FINAGRO received 1 per cent while the loans and the relevant discounts were in effect. See FINAGRO (2012), Chapter V: Special lines of credit.

[32] National Agricultural Credit Commission, Resolution No. 32 of 2008.

[33] *Ibid.*

[34] Resolutions Nos. 1, 3 and 15 of 2011 of the National Agricultural Credit Commission.

producers, however, standardization will make the maximum rate of the annual effective DTF plus eight points the standard. Relief, in the form of lower interest rates, may be for up to 100 per cent of the amount of the interest during the first year, up to 60 per cent in the second year for small producers, and up to 40 per cent for medium-sized producers. For small producers, the reduction must not exceed a 9.5 per cent annual effective rate on the interest payable over the first year, or 5.7 per cent for the second year. Likewise, for medium-sized producers, the reduction must not exceed 11.5 per cent annual effective rate for the first year or 4.6 per cent for the second year. FAG guarantees operations under this Programme.

41. In addition to the National Agricultural Credit Commission, FINAGRO may renegotiate loans to small and medium-sized producers that have been disbursed as an LEC under the AIS Programme, provided that the subsidy rate determined for the original loan and the schedule of interest payments originally agreed, both for the principal and the interest, remain in effect.[35] The restructuring applies to current loans that have not been repaid; the term and grace period may be extended, but may not exceed three years.

42. Agricultural producers have to face a number of risk factors and uncertainties that can affect the stability of their incomes, for example, fluctuations in prices for their products and inputs and the exchange rate trend, as well as the climate. In order to deal with these situations, in addition to the DRE Programme and the other programmes mentioned above, there are various mechanisms intended to improve risk management and help to attract and retain private investment.[36] In 2010, to protect the incomes of producers in the export sector confronted by exchange rate fluctuations, MADR implemented a programme to protect the incomes of producers of exportable agricultural goods. In 2010-2011, MADR set aside Col$49 billion for an incentive to cover 60 to 80 per cent of the cost of insurance premiums for exchange rate fluctuations so that producers growing flowers, bananas and plantains, as well as other exporters, could purchase instruments to enable them to offset exchange rate losses.[37]

43. Agricultural insurance is a risk-mitigation mechanism by which agricultural producers may protect their investments, taking out insurance policies, either individually or collectively, through insurers, to protect themselves against climatic risks.[38] In a resolution of the National Agricultural Credit Commission, the agricultural insurance programme and the subsidy for agricultural insurance premiums are determined annually, to be financed through the National Agricultural Risk Fund.[39] In 2011, the Government subsidized agricultural insurance, covering 30 to 60 per cent of the amount of the policy, but with a ceiling depending on the product (Table IV.4).[40]

[35] Resolution No. 19 of 2009 of the National Agricultural Credit Commission.

[36] MADR (2010a).

[37] Some 75 per cent of the resources were allocated to these three products. Online information from MADR, "*Políticas y Programas Misionales: Apoyos Económicos y Financiamiento: Programa de Coberturas 2010-2011: Instructivo Técnico del Programa de Protección de Ingresos para Productores de Bienes Agrícolas Exportables*". Viewed at: http://www.minagricultura.gov.co/07presupuesto/07a_din_cobertu.aspx.

[38] Agricultural insurance was introduced by Law No. 69 in 1993, and is managed by the National Agricultural Credit Commission.

[39] MADR, Resolution No. 000020 of 25 January 2011.

[40] National Agricultural Credit Commission, Resolution No. 1 of 2010.

Table IV.4
Agricultural sector

Product	Maximum area insured (hectares)	Maximum value to be insured per hectare (Col$ millions)
Crops with a short life cycle	40,500	16.0
Medium-yield crops and late crops	20,000	18.6
Forestry products	15,000	6.0
Other crops with per hectare costs exceeding Col$40 million	200	100.0
Disasters/micro-insurance	98,500	0.9

Source: MADR, Resolution No. 20 of 2011.

(3) MINING (INCLUDING HYDROCARBONS)

(i) Mining

44. In 2011, the mining sector (including hydrocarbons) accounted for 10.3 per cent of GDP. The mining sector is also an important generator of export revenue (see Chapter I). Colombia is Latin America's leading producer and exporter of coal and one of the world's major exporters of emeralds. It also produces gold, ferro-nickel, cement, steel and platinum. The non-petroleum mining sector is almost entirely in the hands of the private sector, although the State still has control over petroleum.

45. In 2010, Colombia produced 74.4 million tonnes of coal, and it is estimated that production in 2011 rose to 84.8 million tonnes, the highest level ever recorded. Coal is mainly mined by Carbones del Cerrejón, Drummond and La Loma, which account for over 90 per cent of Colombia's production. As to nickel, 49.4 million tonnes were produced in 2010, while 53.6 tonnes of gold were also produced.

46. The Ministry of Mining and Energy (MME) is responsible for formulating, implementing and regulating domestic policy on exploration, exploitation, and processing of minerals. Previously, up to November 2011, the Colombian Geological and Mining Institute (Ingeominas) was responsible for issuing mining permits and ensuring that permit holders complied with the requirements, collecting royalties and undertaking basic exploration in order to assess the potential resources of the subsoil. These tasks are currently carried out by the National Mining Agency (ANM), recently created by Decree No. 4.134 of 3 November 2011, as a decentralized special government agency, with its own legal status, assets and administrative, technical and financial autonomy, attached to the MME. The ANM is now the new mining authority and is responsible for contracts and for control of minerals, as well as for the Colombian Geological Service, more specifically activities related to assessment of the subsoil. The ANM is responsible for managing the State's mineral resources and for granting rights for their exploration and exploitation, as well as for concluding, administering and monitoring concession contracts and other mining rights covering the exploration and exploitation of State-owned minerals. Another of its functions is to prepare, implement and disseminate strategies to promote mineral exploration and exploitation and to make proposals and support the MME in formulating government policy and in drawing up sectoral plans for mining.[41]

47. Non-renewable natural resources are the inalienable and permanent property of the State, pursuant to Article 332 of the Constitution. The State may authorize Colombian or foreign natural or legal persons to engage in mining.

[41] Decree No. 4.134 of 3 November 2011.

48. Colombia's current mining and energy policy is built around three central elements: to reorganize and reinforce the institutional structure for mining and energy; to guarantee supplies of hydrocarbons and electricity; and to generate resources to boost Colombia's development.

49. Law No. 685 of 2001, or Mining Code, which is the main legislation in this sector, guarantees foreign investors the principle of national treatment.[42] Foreign companies wishing to obtain a mining concession must establish a subsidiary domiciled in Colombia before they can conclude an agreement on an exploration and/or exploitation mining concession. The Mining Code introduced far-reaching reforms into the regulatory framework, defining the economic offsets and determining the legal stability of contracts, which may not be amended in any way by subsequent legislation. The Code also introduced streamlined procedures and technical and operating reports, and established the National Royalties Fund.

50. Law No. 1.382 of 2010 amended various provisions of the Mining Code. For example, Article 18 of the Law added a paragraph to the Mining Code on the contractor's economic capacity, according to which, for projects covering over 150 hectares, before the mining project can move ahead, the interested party must prove its economic capacity in accordance with the parameters determined by the MME, which must be proportional to the area requested. A Mining Control Fund was also set up with resources derived from payment of the control and monitoring of mining rights. The payment includes the amount of the professional fees payable for carrying out the task proposed, and the total travel and accommodation expenses for the professionals needed to monitor mining rights. Other legal amendments introduced during the period under review include Decree No. 2.715 of 2010 (regulation of the legalization of traditional mining) and Decrees No. 3.083 of 2007, No. 4.289 of 2009 and No. 700 of 2010, as well as Article 113 of Law No. 1.450 of 2011 (regulations on the direct loading of coal).

51. Mining activities are subject to general taxes and to two special taxes, surface taxes and royalties. Concessionaires must pay an annual surface tax corresponding to the whole area of the concession. Its amount ranges from one to three minimum daily wages per hectare depending on the size of the concession. The Mining Code also imposes payment of a royalty for exploiting the minerals. This consists of a fixed percentage of the gross product exploited that is the subject of the mining right, calculated at the mine face.

52. The MME's Mining and Energy Planning Division (UPME) issues resolutions every quarter determining the basic rates for payment of royalties. During the period under review, a new internal procedure was set up for the payment, collection, distribution and drawing of royalties and compensation. In addition, Resolution No. 180.507 of 1 April 2009 amended some of the criteria for determining the basic rate for payment of royalties on coal for export, which is weighted by volume, with the corresponding quality indicators for each coal mining area in Colombia.

53. Pursuant to Decree No. 2.407 of 2000, a 1 per cent tax is levied on the value of emeralds exported in order to finance programmes to develop the industry and for social and economic development in production zones. The National Emeralds Fund is responsible for collecting the tax and administering this programme.

54. With its 2010-2014 Multi-Year Investment Plan, the MME hopes to raise the level of royalties collected from US$7 billion in 2010 to US$14 billion in 2020. It is hoped to use these resources to upgrade the country's infrastructure, protect the environment and boost social

[42] Articles 18 and 19 of Law No. 685 of 2001 and Decree No. 2.080 of 2000.

development. Efforts are also being made to increase direct investment in the mining sector and finance a mechanism for buying up surplus production.

(ii) Hydrocarbons (including petroleum products)

55. In 2011, average crude petroleum production was 915,263 barrels/day, and 968,000 barrels/day in December 2011.[43] The authorities expect production to continue rising, up to 1.25 million barrels/day in 2014. In 2011, production of gas was 1,032 million m^3/day and is expected to rise to 1.35 million in 2014. The growth in crude petroleum production is to be achieved by means of a 100 per cent increase in the transport capacity of pipelines as a result of a US$6.5 billion investment plan to be carried out between 2011 and the end of 2013. As regards gas, US$1 billion is being invested to increase transport capacity.

56. In Colombia, the company ECOPETROL S.A. is mainly responsible for producing crude petroleum either directly or through production-sharing agreements with private oil companies. ECOPETROL S.A. is a semi-public company of a commercial nature, organized in the form of a Colombian public limited company, linked to the MME, in accordance with Law No. 1.118 of 2006.[44] In 2011, ECOPETROL S.A. produced 87 per cent of Colombia's crude petroleum. It has a share in the production of petroleum and natural gas by-products. In 2011, its exports amounted to US$17.5 billion, 73 per cent more than in 2010, while sales to free zones amounted to US$3.1 billion, a 52 per cent increase in comparison with the previous year.

57. ECOPETROL S.A. acts as producer, administrator and regulator of the petroleum industry, although Decree No. 1.760 of 2003 modified the company's basic structure and made it into a public limited company with shares, responsible only for exploration and the production of petroleum and its by-products. ECOPETROL S.A. is currently organized as a public limited company linked to the MME, in accordance with Law No. 1.118 of 2006. Its corporate purpose is "the development, in Colombia or abroad, of commercial or industrial activities that are relevant or related to the exploration, exploitation, refining, transport, storage, distribution and marketing of hydrocarbons, their by-products and products".[45]

58. Pursuant to Decree No. 4.299 of 2005, petroleum may be freely refined in Colombia. Nevertheless, the majority of the refining, transport, import and storage infrastructure is owned and operated by ECOPETROL S.A. Colombia has a 5,099 km long pipeline network and a 3,078 km multi-product pipeline network, both belonging to ECOPETROL S.A. and its associates. It has three oil refineries, all owned by ECOPETROL S.A. Their capacity will be increased in the near future. In early 2012, two projects in this respect were under way: one to expand refining capacity at the Cartagena refinery to 165,000 barrels/daily, with investment of US$3.891 billion, which it was hoped would be ready in June 2013, and another to modernize the Barrancabermeja refinery, with investment of US$3.386 billion, and commencement of operations in August 2015. In the natural gas market, ECOPETROL S.A. and its subsidiaries account for over 60 per cent of production, while Chevron-Texaco has 20 per cent and other producers 20 per cent.

---

[43] Online information from UPME, "*Principales indicadores*". Viewed at: http://www1.upme.gov.co/index.php/zona-de-informacion/principales-indicadores.html.

[44] Online information from ECOPETROL S.A. Viewed at: http://www.ecopetrol.com.co/contenido.aspx?catID=30&conID=38178.

[45] Online information from ECOPETROL S.A., "*Objetivos*". Viewed at: http://www.ecopetrol.com/.co/contenido.aspx?catID=30&conID=44712.

59. The Constitution provides that hydrocarbons deposits are the inalienable and permanent property of the State. The MME, through its Hydrocarbons Directorate, is responsible for adopting and regulating domestic policy on hydrocarbons.[46] It is also responsible for supervising operators and determining prices in the sector, with the exception of residential gas services, which are the responsibility of the Energy and Gas Regulatory Commission (CREG). The National Hydrocarbons Agency (ANH), a body attached to the MME, was created by Decree No. 1.760 of 2003 to be responsible for: administering areas with hydrocarbons deposits; drawing up, negotiating and concluding new exploration and exploitation contracts for State-owned hydrocarbons; collecting royalties and monetary offsets under the said contracts; and determining the volumes and prices of crude petroleum to be refined domestically. The ANH allocates new exploration and production areas to any company that meets the specified requirements. According to its statutes, the ANH is the authority responsible for promoting the optimum and sustainable use of Colombia's hydrocarbons resources, managing them as a whole and reconciling the interests of society, the State and companies in the sector.[47]

60. The various activities in the petroleum chain (refining, import, storage, wholesale distribution, transport and retail distribution) are open without restriction to companies with Colombian or foreign capital. The Law guarantees third parties access to the transport of crude petroleum through ECOPETROL S.A.'s system of pipelines and for products through its multi-product pipelines, as well as the right to build new connections to existing multi-product pipelines.[48]

61. Since 1998, Colombia's policy has been gradual liberalization of the price of regular petrol.[49] The selling price of petroleum products to final consumers conforms to two possible regimes: monitored freedom to set prices or regulated freedom. The basic price is set by the MME using a methodology that takes into account the margins for each participant in the petroleum chain, international price trends for fuel, and variations in the exchange rate.[50] One other important factor when calculating the basic price is the global fuel tax, which is a standing charge that is adjusted annually according to the inflation target defined by the Bank of the Republic. For petrol for motor vehicles and fuel oil for engines (diesel fuel), the surcharges of 25 per cent and 6 per cent, respectively, on these products also affect the basic price.[51] In principle, the dismantling of specific subsidies should have come to an end in June 2010. The authorities have indicated that this was not possible because of the sharp rise in international fuel prices that year and the dismantling continued

[46] Online information from MME. Viewed at: http://www.minminas.gov.co.

[47] Online information from the National Hydrocarbons Agency, "*Misión y Visión*". Viewed at: http://www.anh.gov.co/es/index.php?id=12.

[48] Law No. 681 of 9 August 2001.

[49] In 1999, the MME adopted a methodology for determining the price of petrol based on the parity of import prices at the port of Barrancabermeja, with monthly adjustments according to the variation in the f.o.b. Gulf of Mexico coast price and the trend in the exchange rate. Nevertheless, between 1999 and 2002, the Government did not reflect the variation in international fuel prices in the domestic prices, thereby giving ECOPETROL S.A. an economic subsidy. Between 2002 and 2006, to avoid price fluctuations, a methodology was adopted based on the expected forward price of West Texas Intermediate (WTI) Gulf of Mexico coast oil, plus a refining margin of US$2.5 per barrel, which widened still further the gap between the international price and that on the Colombian domestic market. In 2006, the Government therefore decided to adopt as a reference the Gulf of Mexico coast market price for products of Colombian quality and the cost of transport between the Colombian coast and the Gulf coast, with discounts depending on each product. This was intended to speed up the process of dismantling implicit subsidies for liquid fuels.

[50] The costs which compose part of producers' incomes were the f.o.b. Gulf coast price, international freight, insurance, tariffs, inspection costs, stamp duty and the fee for the Pozos Colorados Galán multi-product pipeline (which transports petrol from Santa Marta to Barrancabermeja). See MME (2011).

[51] Laws No. 681 of 9 August 2001 and No. 488 of 24 December 1998.

in 2011. By December 2011, 95.5 per cent of the subsidy for petrol for motor vehicles had been dismantled, while for diesel fuel the figure was 88 per cent. The amount of the subsidies for petrol for motor vehicles fell from Col$5.1 trillion in 2008 (around US$2.7 billion) to some US$1.1 billion in 2011.

62. The MME has an information system for liquid fuels (SICOM), created by Law No. 1.151 of 2007, which brings participants in the domestic chain together in one information system and through which the marketing, distribution, transport and storage of liquid petroleum-based fuels, fuel alcohol and biodiesel fuel are organized, controlled and harmonized. SICOM keeps lists of major consumers and authorized agents in the chain.[52]

63. The Petroleum Savings and Stabilization Fund remains in effect as a regional and sectoral development fund for production zones. The National Royalties Fund, created in 1991, collected the income from royalties not directly allocated to departments or municipalities, but was replaced in 2011 by the General Royalties Scheme. This Scheme was created by Decree No. 4.923 of 2011 and finances projects with a regional impact, including those for fuel gas, using the income from the royalties assigned to it. The Special Development Fee Fund, created by Law No. 401 of 1997, amended by Law No. 887 of 2004, Law No. 1.151 of 2007 and Law No. 1.450 of 2011, and managed by the MME, is financed by resources from the so-called Development Fee, which is the 3 per cent on the value of the tariff paid on gas that is actually transported and is levied on all transporters in the Natural Gas Transport Scheme. Its purpose is to promote and co-finance projects to develop the infrastructure for using natural gas in municipalities and in the rural sector.[53]

64. Companies producing, transporting, distributing or marketing fuel gas using the pipeline must contribute to the Solidarity Fund for Subsidies and Income Redistribution.[54] Under Resolution No. 015 of 1997, CREG determined that the figure for the solidarity contribution for users in the industrial and commercial sectors was 8.9 per cent, and 0 per cent for fuel gas used to generate gas-based electricity, for the petrochemical industry and for gas for vehicles. Decree No. 4.596 of 2011 provided that the industrial sector was exempt from the solidarity contribution.

65. The main changes introduced into the legislation on hydrocarbons and gas are shown in Table IV.5.

Table IV.5
New legislation on hydrocarbons and gas, 2006-2011

Legislation	Content
Decree No. 2.400 of 2006	Regulating the construction of international interconnections for natural gas
Resolution No. 180.196 of 2006	Issuing the technical regulations on stationary cylinders and tanks used for the public residential supply of liquefied petroleum gas (LPG) and the procedures for their maintenance
Resolution No. 180.928 of 2006	Issuing the technical regulations applicable to service stations supplying compressed natural gas for use in vehicles

[52] Online information from SICOM. Viewed at: http://www.sicom.gov.co/index.shtml.

[53] Online information from MME, "*Fondo Cuota de Fomento*". Viewed at: http://www.minminas.gov.co/minminas/gas.jsp?cargaHome=3&id_categoria=124&id_subcategoria=265.

[54] In order to calculate the subsidies given to users through this Fund's resources, public-service suppliers of fuel gas supplied through the physical network must estimate annually the subsidies to be granted and the contributions to be invoiced (and received from other marketing entities) in the subsequent year and send in this estimate by the last week of April at the latest, pursuant to Decree No. 847 of 2001. Law No. 1.428 of 2010 modified the percentages of the subsidy for residential categories 1 and 2 of the household public service for fuel gas supplied by pipeline.

Legislation	Content
Decree No. 2.629 of 2007 and Decree No. 4.892 of 2011	Establishing provisions to promote the use of biofuels in Colombia, and measures applicable to motor vehicles and other engine-powered machinery and equipment which are fuel-operated
Resolution No. 182.142 of 2007	Issuing the rules for the registration of producers and/or importers of biofuels for use in diesel engines and establishing other provisions concerning their mixture with diesel fuel of fossil origin
Resolution No. 182.087 of 2007	Establishing the technical and environmental requirements for bio-diesel fuels and their mixture with diesel fuel
Law No. 1.151 of 2007, amended by Law No. 1.450 of 2011	Creating the current SICOM of the MME
Resolution No. 180.581 of 2008	Issuing the technical regulations for plants bottling LPG
Law No. 1.274 of 2009	Law on the procedure for appraisal of petroleum concessions
Decree No. 4.500 of 2009	Amending Article 5 of Decree No. 880 of 2007, dealing with the programmed rationing of natural gas or electricity
Resolution No. 180.134 of 2009	Modifying the price structure for diesel fuel mixed with biofuel for use in diesel engines
Resolution No. 181.495 of 2009	Regulating and controlling activities concerning the exploration and exploitation of hydrocarbons, maximizing their final recovery and avoiding wastage
Law No. 1.428 of 2010	Amending the percentage of the subsidy for household categories 1 and 2 of the public service for fuel gas supplied by pipeline
Decree No. 2.100 of 2011	Establishing mechanisms to promote guaranteed supplies of natural gas nation-wide and determining other provisions. Provides incentives for exploration and exploitation of hydrocarbons. Promotes exports of natural gas
Decree No. 4.915 of 2011	Amending Decree No. 4.299 of 2005. The purpose of Decree No. 4.299 of 2005, amended by Decrees No. 1.333 of 2007 and No. 1.717 of 2008, is to define the requirements, obligations and penalty system applicable to entities in the distribution chain for petroleum-based liquid fuels
Decree No. 4.596 of 2011	Implementing Article 102 of Law No. 1450 of 2011, establishing exemption from the solidarity contribution for the industrial sector
Resolution No. 122-01 of 2011	Publishing the declaration of production of natural gas by producers and producer/suppliers
Resolution No. 180.693 of 2011	Technical regulations for the storage of LPG in San Andrés Islands
Resolution No. 180.780 of 2011	Technical regulations on stationary tanks, depots, outlets and points of sale
Resolution No. 181.704 of 2011	Establishing the calculation methodology for determining the supply of natural gas index

Source: WTO Secretariat, based on information provided by the authorities.

66. Colombia's legislation regulates the export of natural gas in order to ensure that domestic demand is satisfied. Decree No. 2.100 of 15 June 2011 is particularly important, as it contains provisions on the priority to be given to domestic consumption: producers, producers/suppliers, traders and transporters must give priority to demand for gas for domestic consumption. Decree No. 2.100 also provides that exporters must give priority to the demand for natural gas for domestic consumption when there are "unavoidable restrictions on supplies of natural gas or serious emergencies or programmed rationing of natural gas", making it necessary to suspend export commitments. The Decree also provides that producers of gas from non-traditional sources may directly generate thermo-electricity that uses the gas they produce as a primary source and that MME, ANH and CREG may provide additional incentives to promote the exploitation and marketing of gas from non-traditional sources.

67. Through its producers of natural gas, Colombia signed an agreement with the Bolivarian Republic of Venezuela to market natural gas.

(4) ELECTRICITY

68. In December 2011, Colombia had 14,408 MW of installed electricity generating capacity.[55] In 2011, the total volume of electricity generated was 58,620 GWh, of which 77.5 per cent was

[55] Online information from UPME, "*Principales indicadores*". Viewed at: http://www.upme.gov.co/index.php/zona-de-informacion/principales-indicadores.html. In 2011, 63.7 per cent

generated in hydroelectric power stations, 15.9 per cent in thermal stations, and 6.3 per cent in smaller or co-generating stations.[56] Domestic demand for electricity was 57,157 GWh, producing a surplus that was exported, 1,294 GWh to Ecuador and 249 GWh to the Bolivarian Republic of Venezuela.[57] The authorities have indicated that in the future Colombia will also export electricity to Panama through an international interconnection with the capacity to transport 300 MW, which is expected to be completed in 2015.

69. In 2011, 487 registered companies were generating electricity in Colombia, with private enterprises generating around 45 per cent of installed capacity and government participation of 55 per cent.[58] As far as marketing is concerned, there were 85 registered companies. Regarding transmission, 110 companies with a grid covering 14,300 km and voltage of 220 KV or more were operating; 90 per cent of the grids belong to semi-public companies. There are 30 companies distributing electricity of less than 220 KV through a grid covering 10,100 km.

70. Law No. 143 of 1994 or the Electricity Law provides for the separation of activities into four groups (generation, transmission, distribution and marketing), prohibits vertical integration (with the exception of those companies set up prior to the enactment of the Law) and guarantees free access to transmission and distribution grids to any supplier, generator or user that so requests. Law No. 142 of 1994 or Law on Household Public Services is intended to create a market-oriented and competitive environment and to regulate the participants' business practices. The sector's legal framework contains a number of provisions that seek to encourage competition and limit any dominant position, requiring that no company may provide more than one quarter of the installed generating and/or marketing capacity.[59]

71. State participation based on the public service model has a threefold role: definition of energy policy, regulation, and monitoring and control. It leaves the development of activities under the free entry and free competition regime in private hands. MME is responsible for defining policy. UPME is in charge of developing strategic plans and energy expansion, including the National Energy Plan and the Expansion Plan for electricity generation and transmission, which is indicative as far as generation is concerned and mandatory in the case of transmission. Regulation and definition of the methodology used to calculate rates and promote free competition are CREG's responsibility.[60] The Supervisory Authority for Household Public Services monitors and controls the supply of household public services. The Administrator of the Commercial Interchange System (ASIC) is responsible for managing the wholesale energy market and the National Dispatching Centre (CND) is responsible for planning, supervision and control of the integrated operation of the generating and transmission resources of the National Interconnected System (SIN).[61] The National Operations Council (CNO),

---

of electricity came from hydraulic resources; 31.5 per cent from thermal sources; and 4.8 per cent from smaller or co-generating stations.

[56] Information provided by the authorities. See also online information from X.M. S.A., "*Descripción del sistema eléctrico colombiano*". Viewed at: http://www.xm.co/Pages/DescripciondelSistemaElectricoColombiano.aspx.

[57] Further details on this sector may be viewed in the online information from UPME. Viewed at: http://www.upme.gov.co/Index2.htm.

[58] Online information from CREG, "*Colombia y el sector eléctrico in cifras*". Viewed at: http://www.creg.gov.co/cxc/secciones/colombia_cifras/colombia_cifras.htm.

[59] CREG, Resolution No. 001 of 2006.

[60] CREG is composed of eight members: the Minister for Mining and Energy, who acts as chair; the Minister for Finance and Public Credit; the Director of the National Planning Department; and five experts in energy matters, exclusively, appointed by the President of the Republic for four-year terms.

[61] CND, together with ASIC, belong to the XM public limited company and public services company, regulated by CREG.

composed of representatives of companies in the sector, deals with the technical aspects in the sector, while the Marketing Advisory Committee (CAC), composed of companies supplying electricity (as well as generating and/or distributing electricity and independent), assists CREG in monitoring and reviewing the commercial aspects of the wholesale electricity market (MEM). The SIC is responsible for competition policy matters.

72. MME is responsible for granting concessions for generation, interconnection and transmission grids among regions. Under Law No. 143 of 1994, regional authorities give concessions for regional transmission and municipalities grant concessions for distribution, provided that there is no entity prepared to provide such services on the same terms. The term of a concession contract is determined by the entity granting it in each case and may not exceed 30 years, renewable for a maximum of 20 years. Concessions for the public electricity service have only been granted in the non-interconnected zones of San Andrés and Amazonas (not connected to the national grid (SIN)).

73. Pursuant to Law No. 143 of 1994, users are divided into regulated users and non-regulated users. Electricity provided by suppliers to final users whose rates are regulated (regulated users) must be purchased by these companies on the MEM, either under long-term bilateral agreements (financial coverage contracts) or on the spot market (see below). Electricity rates for regulated users are determined according to a regulated freedom regime under which CREG establishes the methodology for calculating the rates used by companies to determine the maximum price for their services. This price must reflect the costs of the production chain.

74. Law No. 142 of 1994, or Law on Household Public Services, provides for subsidies for the basic or subsistence consumption of residential users belonging to the most vulnerable sectors of the population. These users are subsidized through the contributions of users in the higher-income sectors, and by commercial users and some industrial users (regulated or non-regulated), who pay 20 per cent over the cost of supplying the service for which they are billed. In 2011, the electricity sector received subsidies amounting to Col$1.48 trillion (around (US$800 million)). The authorities have indicated that, in addition to the contributions made by higher-income household users and by business users and some industrial users, beneficiary household users will receive around Col$1.26 trillion in State contributions to cover the total subsidies to be granted in 2012.

75. Electricity is sold on the MEM. This is composed of a series of systems for exchanging information among generators and suppliers operating in the SIN, which enables them to conduct both short- and long-term buying and selling of electricity. All the energy required to meet the demand of users connected to the SIN, represented by the suppliers, goes through this market, and is provided by generators which connect their power plants or generating facilities to the SIN. Both generators and suppliers are MEM agents. Generators must include in the MEM all their power plants or generating facilities of 20 MW or over connected to the SIN and the electricity must be centrally dispatched by the CND. All suppliers serving final users connected to the SIN are obliged to conduct their energy transactions through the MEM. Final users (regulated or non-regulated) may not participate directly in the MEM.

76. Energy transactions in the MEM take the following forms: hourly transactions on the spot market; bilateral financial contracts on energy; and auctions for the purpose of allocating Reliability Charge Firm Energy Commitments (OEFs).[62] Generators may participate in one or all of these

[62] Reliable Charge is a mechanism intended to ensure the reliability of supplies of electricity in the long term at efficient prices. In the course of auctions, generators are allocated OEFs, giving them the right to an established and stable amount for a fixed term in exchange for the commitment to supply a defined volume of energy when spot prices exceed a threshold established by CREG in advance, called the scarcity price.

transactions. This scheme of operations, as well as the rules for its functioning and participation, have remained the same since the MEM started to operate.

77. With regard to transactions on the energy market, generators make a price offer each day and declare their availability for generation hourly, without taking into account the state of the transmission grid in a single nodal exchange. The lowest offers are selected to supply demand hour by hour in an "ideal" dispatching system that does not incorporate any restrictions that may be present in the transmission grid. The price offers made by generators taking part in the MEM must reflect the variable costs of generation and opportunity costs. The latest price used to meet total demand for energy hourly is the price to be paid for all infra-marginal resources in the same hour and is called the spot price. The demand for energy from suppliers not covered by bilateral contracts must be paid at this spot price. The ASIC is responsible for paying commitments and financial liabilities of participants in the market.

78. The second method used for buying and selling energy is that of bilateral contracts, which are commitments undertaken by generators and suppliers to sell or buy energy at freely regulated prices and quantities and under contractual terms negotiated freely between the parties. The purpose of these contracts is to lessen exposure of both the supplier and the end-user to price volatility on the spot market. The physical delivery of the energy committed in the contracts occurs via the spot market, so such contracts contain no dispatching commitment between the parties but only cover the price. There are no restrictions on the amount of energy to which a generator or supplier may commit itself in bilateral contracts or on the time-frame to be covered by such contracts. The only requirement is that the contract should specify the volume to be used hourly by the ASIC for purposes of payment. Energy bought by suppliers under bilateral contracts and intended for regulated users is governed by rules determined in such a way as to ensure competition among generators in this type of transaction, whereas the energy bought by suppliers for non-regulated users is negotiated at prices and on terms freely agreed between the parties.[63]

79. Lastly, the purpose of auctions is to allocate OEFs between generators and investors in order to guarantee the reliability of supplies of firm energy over the long term at "efficient" prices, even when there is a critical hydrological situation. In ideal dispatching, an agent with an OEF undertakes to generate a volume of energy daily whose maximum amount is the energy determined in the OEF. OEFs are acquired by demand through transactions centralized by the ASIC. They are allocated to various generators and investors through auctions. They are only allocated to agents who possess or plan to possess generating facilities as of a fixed date and who are selected at the auction, as well as existing generators. Auctions are held four years before the firm energy is required.[64] The period during which the OEF remains in effect is decided by the owner or the commercial representative of the generating facility concerned, but it must be within certain predetermined parameters. If at the time of the auction: (i) the generating facility has not yet started to be built, the minimum term of the relevant OEF may be one to 20 years; (ii) if the generating plant or facility is in the process of being

---

[63] Online information from CREG, "*Características generales del Mercado Mayorista: Transacciones en el MEM: Contratos bilaterales*". Viewed at: http://www.creg.gov.co/cxc/secciones/mercado_mayorista/contratos.htm.

[64] The time that elapses between announcement of the date of the auction for allocating OEFs and expiry of the term of the OEFs is classified into three periods: (i) preselection; (ii) planning; and (iii) period of the commitment. The preselection period ends on the day on which the auction is held and the planning period lasts for three years. For projects whose construction exceeds the three years of the planning period, CREG allows investors to sell some of their future firm energy at auctions held seven, six or five years before the firm energy under the project becomes available.

built or equipped, the OEF may have a term of one to ten years; and (iii) if it is operating commercially at the time of the auction, the OEF remains in effect for one year.

80. The OEF is enforceable when the spot price exceeds the scarcity price[65], reflecting a critical situation for electricity supplies. In such cases, an agent with an OEF must supply the energy to which it is committed through its own generation and, if this is insufficient, must buy energy from the so-called "safety rings"[66] or buy it on the electricity market. If an agent has tried the safety rings mechanisms and the electricity market but is still unable to comply with its OEF, it has to compensate for the rationing introduced. When the spot price does not exceed the scarcity price, the generator is paid with the reliability charge and the amount of this remuneration per known and stable unit of energy over a determined period results from the auction at which the OEF was allocated.[67] This payment is assessed and collected by the ASIC and paid by users of the SIN through the rates paid to suppliers.

81. At the subregional level, the exchange of electricity is regulated by CAN Decision No. 536, which prohibits the application of tariffs or other restrictions on imports or exports of electricity among CAN members.[68] Imports and exports must be through a generating and/or marketing company set up in Colombia and through the wholesale market.[69] Colombia has electricity interconnections with Ecuador and the Bolivarian Republic of Venezuela, and will have an interconnection with Panama as of 2015. The exchange of electricity with non-members of CAN is regulated by CREG.

(5) MANUFACTURES

82. Since the previous review, the manufacturing sector's share of GDP has fallen slightly, from 14.6 per cent in 2006 to 13.4 per cent during the third quarter of 2011. The principal manufacturing industries are chemicals, petroleum refining, beverages, non-metallic products and textiles.

83. MCIT's Directorate of Productivity and Competition is responsible for coordinating the National Productivity and Competition Policy for the manufacturing sector, by developing joint action by the public, private and academic sectors. MCIT coordinates supply chain competition agreements for motor vehicle parts/motor vehicles; leather, footwear and manufactures thereof; household appliances; professional electronics; mechanical engineering; petrochemicals; cosmetic and hygiene products; pulp, paper and the graphic industry, *inter alia*. Under the current Business Development Programme (PDE), the authorities are implementing a production transformation programme, identifying and developing emerging sectors and introducing a new targeted industrial strategy organized around sectoral committees which act as channels to facilitate communication among the parties.

[65] This price is determined by CREG and updated monthly on the basis of variations in the price index for fuel, and indicates the moment at which the OEFs are enforceable. It is also the price at which the energy supplied will be paid when the OEFs are enforced. See online information from CREG, "*Obligación de Energía Firme: Verificación del cumplimiento*". Viewed at: http://www.creg.gov.co/cxc/secciones/obligacion_energia_firme/verificacion.htm.

[66] The safety rings are a series of instruments whose purpose is to facilitate supplies to meet demand in critical situations and compliance with the OEFs of generators.

[67] Since its original regulation in 1996, for the former capacity charge a term of ten years was defined, which ended on 30 November 2006. After expiry of this term and following approximately two years of studies, proposals and discussion with industry and other interested parties, this charge was replaced by the current reliability charge, applicable since 1 December 2006.

[68] CAN Decision No. 536 of 19 December 2002.

[69] CREG Resolution No. 057 of 19 May 1998.

84. The PDE seeks to meet its objectives by means of four main elements: (i) development of human capital; (ii) adapting legislation and regulations to industry's needs; (iii) boosting industry by attracting foreign investment to and developing the sector, its trade associations and its management and promotion capacity; and (iv) upgrading infrastructure. The authorities have indicated that it is not intended to grant subsidies in order to achieve these objectives. A strategy has also been implemented to bring the informal sector's activities into the formal sector so as to increase the overall productivity of the manufacturing sector. Another strategy is to promote the domestic market through the "Buy Colombian" initiative. As part of the strategy, business round tables have been organized with broad participation at the national level, which include meetings to foster commercial dealings between entrepreneurs from MSMEs and strategic buyers.

85. In addition, the National Planning Department coordinates the National Innovation Strategy, intended to bolster the country's innovative capacity, in particular that of its production sector. The aim of this Strategy is to appropriate and adapt technology, generate value in organizations and research and development relevant to Colombia's specific needs. With this in view, several lines of action have been defined, including the creation of an innovation and development unit (INNpulsa Colombia) to provide better tools for promoting innovation.

86. According to the ISIC definition[70], the average MFN tariff applied by Colombia to manufactures fell sharply during the period under review, from 12.3 per cent in 2006 to 8.2 per cent in April 2011 and 6.2 per cent in August of the same year.

87. Colombia still applies a number of trade protection measures (see Chapter III(2)(viii)) on manufacturing sector imports. Between 2006 and 2011, Colombia initiated 23 anti-dumping investigations and applied 11 new definitive measures; at 30 June 2011, Colombia had 12 measures in force, all applying to imports from China. Colombia also uses non-automatic licensing (see Chapter III(2)(vii)). Licensing applies irrespective of the origin of the product.

88. Under the automotive agreement with Ecuador, the automotive industry has continued to benefit from certain measures such as the 0 per cent tariff on vehicles for assembly. Furthermore, under this agreement, the tariffs on automobiles, minibuses carrying fewer than 16 passengers and small trucks (with a total load of less than 4.537 tonnes) are 35 per cent less than the MFN tariff, the tariffs on assembled vehicles are up to 35 per cent, the import of second-hand vehicles is banned, and VAT rates for certain imported vehicles are higher.

89. Even though Colombia has not used minimum prices since 2003, it still uses reference prices as a control measure to verify the prices declared for imported goods. Currently, there are reference prices for 51 sectors in the economy, many of them in manufacturing, for example, footwear, textiles, made-up articles, vehicles, iron and steel, and plastics. Since 2004, Colombia has used indicative prices as a sub-category of reference prices. The use of these indicative prices is mandatory for certain imports of textiles, made-up articles and footwear originating from all countries other than those with which Colombia has signed free trade agreements (Chapter III(2)(ii)).

90. The manufacturing sector is eligible for various export support programmes, under which users are given tax concessions and benefit from streamlined customs procedures. One such is the free zone programme. Three types of free zone can be established in Colombia: permanent zones, special permanent zones and transit zones. There are minimum requirements on investment, assets and employment (see Chapter III(4)(iv)). Exporters of manufactured goods also have the right to total or partial refund of indirect taxes, charges and contributions subject to an application to the Bank of

[70] ISIC, Revision 3, groups 15 to 37.

the Republic for a tax reimbursement certificate (CERT), and may also take advantage of the Vallejo Plan, which gives full exemption from tariffs and VAT for temporary import of inputs, raw materials, intermediate goods, capital goods and spare parts, provided that they are used to produce goods for export or to provide services directly related to the production or export of such goods.

(6) SERVICES

91. In 2011, services accounted for around two thirds (54 per cent) of Colombia's GDP. Colombia has a deficit in trade in services. In 2010, imports of business services amounted to US$7.981 billion and exports to US$4.446 billion. Both imports and exports grew at an average rate of 10.8 per cent between 2005 and 2010.

92. Colombia adopted specific commitments in five of the 12 GATS sectors: business services; telecommunications services; construction and related engineering services; financial services; and tourism and travel-related services. It took part in the negotiations on telecommunications and financial services after the Uruguay Round and its commitments in both these areas appear in the Fourth and Fifth Protocols to the GATS. Colombia established exemptions to the principle of MFN treatment as regards telecommunications, audiovisual services, financial services and land transport.[71]

93. As part of its horizontal commitments under the GATS, Colombia reserved the right to maintain restrictions on ownership of real estate by foreigners in border regions, along the Colombian coastline and in the islands of the San Andrés and Providencia archipelago. It undertook to allow up to 10 per cent of unskilled workers and 20 per cent of skilled employees or specialists, administrative staff or persons in posts of responsibility in companies employing more than ten persons to be foreigners.

94. During the services negotiations in the Doha Round, Colombia submitted an initial offer in September 2003 and a revised offer in July 2005.[72]

95. Since 1998, Colombia and the other CAN members have had a general framework of principles and rules for liberalization of trade in services in the Andean region, contained in Decision No. 439.[73] The liberalization process is based on a negative list approach under which measures contrary to the market access and national treatment provisions in Decision No. 439 are listed in an inventory. The inventories of measures maintained by each country were adopted in October 2001.[74] Colombia's inventory comprises 75 measures, nine of which apply to all sectors. The remaining measures apply to business services, financial services, teaching services, environmental services, transport services and communications services.

(i) Financial services

(a) Market features

96. In December 2011, Colombia's financial sector comprised 69 credit institutions, including 23 banks. There were also 61 insurance companies and 51 insurance brokers, 159 other financial institutions such as trusts and stock-brokers. Despite the large number of institutions, the trend

[71] WTO documents GATS/EL/20 of 15 April 1994 and GATS/EL/20/Suppl.1 of 28 July 1995.

[72] The initial offer is contained in WTO document TN/S/O/COL of 18 September 2003.

[73] CAN Decision No. 439 of 11 June 1998.

[74] *Idem.*, Decision No. 510 of 30 October 2001.

towards concentration of financial institutions has continued, particularly in the case of banks, as already indicated during the previous review. Colombia's largest bank, the Bank of Colombia, holds 21.7 per cent of the assets in the banking sector, and the second bank, the Bank of Bogotá, 14 per cent. Together, the five largest banks hold 63 per cent of assets. Similarly, in the insurance sector, two insurance companies hold around 40 per cent of the assets in the life insurance branch and four have around one half of the assets in the general insurance branch.

97. In November 2011, the financial system's assets, including funds managed by entities overseen by the SFC amounted to Col$724.57 trillion (US$372 billion), 15 per cent above the level a year earlier, corresponding to annual real growth of 10.64 per cent.[75] Of these funds, Col$405.44 trillion were assets belonging to entities overseen by the SFC and Col$319.13 trillion were funds managed by monitored entities (for example, mutual funds). The assets of loan institutions amounted to Col$322.5 trillion (Col$359.7 trillion if the specialized official institutions are included) (Table IV.6). Assets and funds managed by trust companies and pension funds amounted to Col$102.5 and Col$102.9 trillion, respectively.

Table IV.6
Structure of the financial sector, December 2011

Establishment	Number of establishments	Assets
Loan establishments	**69**	**Col$359.686 billion**
		(% of total assets)
Banks	23	76.8
Colombian private capital	13	55.4
Foreign private capital	9	16.3
Public capital	1	5.1
Financial corporations	4	1.3
Colombian capital	2	1.2
Foreign capital	2	0.1
Commercial financing companies	24	8.6
Cooperatives	7	1.2
Specialized official institutions[a]	11	12.0
Insurance companies	**115**	**Col$35.541 billion**
		(% of total assets)
Life insurance companies	19	30.6
General insurance companies	23	62.5
Capitalization companies	5	4.3
Insurance and reinsurance brokers	54	0.9
Insurance cooperatives	2	1.3
Agencies of foreign reinsurers in Colombia	12	..
Other financial institutions	**159**	**Col$10.208 billion**
		(% of total assets)
General deposit warehouses	4	5.3
Managers of pension and retirement funds	12[b]	27.5
Managers of low value payment systems	6	3.6
Specialized foreign exchange intermediation and financial services companies	2	0.3
Trust companies	27	18.7
Investment management companies	10	0.7
Stockbrokers	55	41.7
Mutual funds	43	0.8
Other (suppliers of infrastructure)	13	1.4

[75] SFC (2011).

Establishment	Number of establishments	Assets
Total	356	Col$405.435 billion

.. Not available.

a Second tier institutions, including Bancóldex and FOGAFIN, FINDETER, FEN, FINAGRO, ICETEX, FONADE, the National Savings Fund, FOGACOOP, FNG and the Military Housing Fund.

b Six private institutions and six public institutions (entities managing the joint average-premium plan with defined benefit).

Source: SFC.

98. In response to the international financial crisis, in late 2008 and early 2009 financial institutions were requested to defer the distribution of profits and to build up reserves to deal with any deterioration in their financial situation. The countercyclical component provided for in Colombia's regulations was used to address changes to the risk situation (see below). Moreover, risk methodologies were revised, and in some instances updated in the light of recent international experience, together with some elements of the Credit Risk Management Scheme (SARC), security valuation and losses caused by unsecured consumer credit default.

(b) Legal framework, sectoral policies and WTO commitments

99. Article 335 of Colombia's Constitution provides that financial, stock market and insurance activities, to the extent that they involve handling, utilizing or investing deposits, are activities of public interest, and therefore require State authorization, as prescribed by law. The Constitution also states that, when intervening in such activities, the Government must foster democratization of loans.

100. The Constitution also specifies how responsibilities are shared among the various authorities which issue regulations on the conduct of financial activities. The Congress of the Republic is empowered to enact framework laws to regulate financial, stock market and insurance activities, as well as the handling, utilization and investment of resources deposited by the public. On the basis of these framework laws, the Executive may issue decrees to regulate financial activities: these decrees have wider scope than ordinary decrees and are in the form of decrees having force of law, in other words, legal rules with force of law issued by the Executive in exercise of its general regulatory powers without the need for prior authorization from the Legislature.

101. The Constitution also provides that the Executive is responsible, in accordance with the law, for the inspection, oversight and control of persons engaged in financial, stock market or insurance activities or any other activity involving the handling, utilization or investment of resources deposited by the public. This function is exercised through Colombia's SFC, a technical body with financial and administrative autonomy, which issues general regulations contained in resolutions and circulars in order to inform the institutions concerned how they should conduct their activities.

102. The Bank of the Republic acts as the central bank. It is organized in the form of a legal person under public law, with administrative, financial and technical autonomy, and is subject to a legal regime specific to it. The following are the basic functions of the Bank of the Republic: to regulate the supply of money, international exchange and credit; issue the legal currency; manage international reserves; act as lender of last resort and banker for loan establishments; and serve as the Government's fiscal agent. The Bank of the Republic's Board of Directors is the highest monetary, exchange and credit authority which, subject to the framework laws enacted by Congress, issues resolutions and circular letters in this respect. These regulations are also of a special nature and their status is similar to that of a law.

103. To summarize, the regulations applicable to the financial sector are organized according to a line of authority, i.e.: at the top, Colombia's Political Constitution; next, the framework laws enacted by the Congress of the Republic, ordinary legislation, resolutions and circular letters issued by the Bank of the Republic in exercise of its functions, and decrees having force of law issued by the Government in exercise of its special powers, such as the Basic Statute of the Financial System. At the next level down are the regulatory decrees issued by the Government to implement framework laws and, finally, circulars and resolutions issued by the SFC in exercise of its inspection and oversight responsibilities.

104. Pursuant to Article 2 of Decree No. 4.712 of 2008, the Ministry of Finance and Public Credit is in charge of defining, formulating and implementing the country's economic policy, including financial, exchange, monetary and credit policy, without prejudice to the role given to the Board of Directors of the Bank of the Republic or the responsibilities it exercises through designated or related bodies in order to conduct activities requiring State intervention in financial, stock market or insurance activities or any other activities concerning the handling, utilization or investment of resources derived from public savings and the national treasury. The Ministry of Finance and Public Credit coordinates financial, monetary, credit, exchange and fiscal policies with the Board of Directors of the Bank of the Republic.

105. The Ministry of Finance and Public Credit is also responsible for preparing draft decrees and issuing resolutions, circulars and other administrative acts of a general or specific nature required to carry out its functions; for helping to control and detect money-laundering operations; regulating the public securities market through the SFC; participating in drawing up regulations for financial, stock market, insurance and cooperative activities and any other activities concerning the handling, utilization or investment of resources derived from public savings, in coordination with the SFC or the Supervisory Authority for Economic Solidarity, and also in drawing up social security regulations; and managing the resources of the Regional Authorities' National Pension Fund (FONPE). The SFC and the Supervisory Authority for Economic Solidarity are attached to the Ministry of Finance and Public Credit.

106. The minimum capital requirements for the various types of financial institution are determined by law, in accordance with Article 80 of the Basic Statute of the Financial System. They are updated annually to reflect inflation, measured by the increase in the CPI, furnished by DANE (Table IV.7), and calculated by the corresponding multiplication in millions of pesos.

Table IV.7
Minimum capital requirements for entities subject to SFC control and oversight[a], 2006-2011
(Col$ millions, unless otherwise indicated)

Type of establishment	2006	2007	2008	2009	2010	2011 (Nov)
Banking establishments	56,823	59,369	62,748	67,561	68,913	71,098
Financial corporations	20,665	21,591	22,820	24,571	25,063	25,858
Commercial financing companies	14,638	15,294	16,165	17,405	17,754	18,317
Trust companies	4,309	4,503	4,760	5,126	5,229	5,395
Pension fund management companies	8,612	8,998	9,510	10,240	10,445	10,777
Retirement fund management companies	4,309	4,503	4,760	5,126	5,229	5,395
Pension and retirement management fund companies	12,918	13,497	14,265	15,360	15,668	16,165
Other financial establishments	3,447	3,602	3,807	4,099	4,181	4,314
Foreign exchange dealers[b]	5,168	5,400	5,708	6,145	6,269	6,468
Inflation at December[c] (%)	4.48	5.69	7.67	2.00	3.17	

a As provided by Article 80 of Law No. 795 of 2003.
b External Resolution No. 8 of 2000 of the Governing Board of the Bank of the Republic.
c Annual variation in the total national weighted average CPI at December, calculated by DANE.

Source: SFC.

107. Savings and loan cooperatives, which are authorized to provide financial services only to their members and are supervised by the Supervisory Authority for Economic Solidarity, must have minimum amounts of capital, known as "minimum social contributions in the solidarity sector", pursuant to Article 42 of Law No. 454 of 1998. As is the case for financial institutions, these amounts are updated annually according to Article 80 of the Basic Statute of the Financial System.

108. Savings deposits are guaranteed by the Financial Institutions Guarantee Fund (Fogafin), created by Law No. 117 of 1985, which is an autonomous legal person under public law of a unique nature, subject to monitoring by the SFC. Fogafin's overall objective is to preserve the trust shown by depositors and creditors in registered financial institutions, maintaining balance and economic equity and preventing unjustified economic or other benefits accruing to shareholders and managers that are harmful to the financial institutions. Fogafin is empowered to act to strengthen the registered institutions financially and to participate temporarily in their capital.

109. Fogafin is also in charge of organizing and implementing the Deposit Insurance Scheme and, consequently, for buying up the obligations of institutions being liquidated or providing finance for those with savings in such institutions.[76] The Deposit Insurance Scheme is a mechanism which, before any financial institution registered with Fogafin is liquidated, guarantees depositors the recovery of all of part of their deposits. If a registered financial institution is liquidated and taken over by the SFC, the deposit insurance is paid out by Fogafin. The institutions registered with Fogafin and covered by the insurance consist of banks, financial corporations, finance companies and other institutions whose establishment has been authorized by the SFC.

110. In January 2012, the maximum insurance cover was Col$20 million per depositor, applicable independently for each financial institution registered. The deposit insurance is financed through the premiums paid by the institutions registered. The premiums correspond to 0.3 per cent annually of the amount of their liabilities to the public and are paid quarterly; in some situations, there may be additional charges or refunds.[77] The following products are covered by the insurance: current account deposits, simple deposits, fixed-term deposit certificates (CDT), savings deposits, special savings accounts, mortgage bonds, special deposits, collection banking services, and unemployment funds managed by the National Savings Fund.

111. The SFC requires that supervised institutions should formulate and implement a Market Risk Management System (SARM) to enable them to identify, assess, control and monitor such risks effectively. Such a system should enable the institutions monitored to adopt timely decisions for appropriate risk mitigation and, where applicable, to determine the appropriate amount of capital to be maintained in relation to the risk level of each institution. The SARM implemented by loan institutions, special official institutions and higher-level cooperative bodies and that relating to own account operations and own resources of stockbrokers must enable them to manage their market risk satisfactorily and calculate the amount of capital they need to maintain to cover it.

[76] For further details, see online information from Fogafin. Viewed at: https://www.fogafin.gov.co/Web/Formularios/Public/Content/frmContent.aspx?id=119&padre=90.

[77] Pursuant to the current legal requirements, Fogafin gives a refund or makes an additional charge for premiums based on the annual CAMEL status of each entity, calculated according to a system of weights and ratings. Each indicator has a range of one to five, in which one is the minimum number of points and five the maximum. In order to receive a refund, the institution's average CAMEL classification must exceed three points. The refund corresponds to a percentage ranging from 0.01 to 50 per cent of the amount paid during the year immediately preceding as a deposit insurance premium. If the institution's classification is less than three, it has to pay an additional amount corresponding to a percentage ranging from 0.01 to 50 per cent of the amount paid during the previous year as a deposit insurance premium.

The SARM implemented by trust companies, pension and retirement fund management companies, investment management companies, average premium plan management institutions, insurance companies and capitalization companies must permit them to manage the market risk independently, both as regards the company's cash flow and the joint funds or portfolios they manage. In general, the SARM must take into account the following market risks: interest rate in legal currency; interest rates; exchange rates; share prices; and investment in joint portfolios.

112. In order to deal with any external shocks, among Colombia's individual provisions[78], besides a pro-cyclical component corresponding to the share of the individual provision in the loan portfolio that reflects the credit risk of each debtor therein, there is an individual countercyclical component corresponding to the share of the individual provision that reflects possible changes in the credit risk of debtors when these shares fall still further. This provision is constituted in order to lessen the impact of unforeseen circumstances.

113. Government policy on the financial system is based on three elements: financial inclusion, development of the capital market, and prudential policy. As far as financial inclusion is concerned, the Ministry of Finance and Public Credit, together with the Ministry of Information and Communications Technology (MINTIC) and the various industries concerned, have embarked upon the task of raising the level of formalization and facilitation for mass access to financial services, by using new technology and lowering the costs of transaction services. In order to boost the level of formalization, the Government has promoted the introduction of credit records for clients in order to facilitate access to loans, together with revision of the existing guarantee scheme. The capital market development policy has focused on building a long-term vision in order to develop the capital market as an efficient source of financing for the production sector, raising the level of financial intermediation and promoting its role as a supplier of risk transfer mechanisms. Another objective is to make the capital market into an investment alternative for savings in the economy. The 2010-2014 National Development Plan pinpoints the need for progress in defining the vision and overall policy for developing the capital market in support of the production sector. For this purpose, a policy document (CONPES) will be implemented, defining strategies that cover aspects such as the regime to protect investors, the operation of the fixed and variable income market, the development of investment vehicles, risk transfer mechanisms and the securities market infrastructure. It is also planned to consolidate the process of convergence with international accounting standards. The authorities have indicated that, in December 2012, the International Financial Reporting Standards (IFRS) and the International Accounting Standards (IAS) will come into effect for issuers of securities and bodies of public interest.[79] In December 2011, the Government issued the regulations that enable voluntary convergence with the IFRS.[80]

114. As regards prudential measures, the Ministry of Finance and Public Credit has drawn up a programme of regulatory reforms whose priority is to revise the capital quality and solvency requirements for all financial industries. It is expected that these reforms will come into effect gradually by type of industry. This process, as well as the impact of the possible reforms on the financial system's stability, is discussed in the Technical Subcommittee of the Financial Monitoring Committee, composed of the Ministry of Finance, the SFC, the Bank of the Republic and Fogafin.

[78] Defined in paragraph 1.3.4.1.1. of the SFC's Basic Accounting and Financial Circular - Calculation of individual provisions under reference models.

[79] Public interest bodies are those which receive, handle or manage resources from the public, for example, banking institutions, financial corporations, commercial financing companies, financial cooperatives, capitalization companies, insurance companies or pension fund management companies.

[80] Decree No. 4.946 of 2011 issuing provisions on the exercise of voluntary application of international accounting and financial reporting standards.

The authorities have indicated that, through this programme, it is sought to achieve a proper balance between an ambitious policy for inclusion and access to financial services (including the capital market), its sustainability and the stability of the financial system.

115. In its WTO commitments, Colombia included an exemption from the principle of MFN treatment for financial services by making access to the financial services market by foreign suppliers subject to the existence of "satisfactory possibilities of access" for Colombian suppliers in the country of origin of the foreign suppliers. Colombia's specific commitments indicate that authorization for financial establishments is subject to an economic needs test. The establishment of branches is not allowed, and the supply of financial services requires prior government approval.[81] Colombia undertook not to impose limitations on cross-border supply or consumption abroad for reinsurance and retrocession services. The commitments on the presence of natural persons do not go beyond those in the horizontal commitments.

(c) Banking services

116. The Ministry of Finance and Public Credit is involved in regulating banking activities in coordination with the SFC or the Supervisory Authority for Economic Solidarity. According to the Basic Statute of the Financial System, the SFC's main task is to inspect, supervise and control the institutions composing the financial system. The SFC may issue resolutions, external circulars and circular letters to the institutions subject to its supervision. The Bank of the Republic is the highest exchange, monetary and credit authority, as provided by Law No. 31 of 1992 (see Chapter I(2)(iii)).

117. Colombia has made a number of reforms to the legal framework for its banking sector since the previous Review in 2006 (Table IV.8). The most important laws remain Law No. 45 of 1990 and Law No. 35 of 1993, which establish the legal basis for the functioning of the financial sector. During the period under review, Law No. 1.328 of 2009 was introduced, *inter alia,* to deal with the 2008-2009 global financial crisis by reinforcing the SFC's activities and supervisory responsibilities (see below).

Table IV.8
Principal legislation governing banking and securities activities

Legislation	Content
Law No. 45 of 1990 issuing rules on financial intermediation, regulating insurance activities, giving certain powers, and issuing other provisions	Structural reform of Colombia's financial system. Liberalization of markets and internationalization of the economy, introduction of the multi-bank model. Authorizes loan establishments to participate in ownership of institutions managing portfolios, engaged in trust fund activities, managing pensions and retirement funds, selling insurance and broking. Also contains provisions on insurance activities: general; criteria for access to insurance activities; requirements for engaging in insurance activities; annulment or suspension of authorization permits; dissolution and official insurance.
Law No. 35 of 1993 establishing general rules and indicating therein the objectives and criteria to be observed by the National Government in regulating financial, stock market and insurance activities and any other activity concerning the handling, utilization or investment of resources deposited by the public, and issuing other provisions on financial and insurance matters	Regulates intervention, inspection, supervision and control by the National Government over financial, stock market and insurance activities. Defines procedures for selling government shares in financial institutions and insurance establishments.

[81] WTO document GATS/SC/20/Suppl.3 of 26 February 1998.

Legislation	Content
Law No. 510 of 1999 issuing provisions concerning the financial and insurance system, the public securities market, the Supervisory Authorities for Banking and Securities, and granting certain powers	Reform of the financial system, including changes to the takeover regime and requirements for establishing financial institutions. It also creates a new long-term mechanism for housing loans. This Law was amended and partly repealed by Laws No. 676 of 2001 and No. 964 of 2005, and by Article 54 of Decree No. 775 of 2005.
Law No. 546 of 1999 issuing rules on housing, indicating the overall objectives and criteria to be observed by the National Government in regulating a special mechanism for its financing, creating tools for savings to be used for such financing, determining measures relating to taxes and other costs for building and buying and selling of housing, and issuing other provisions	Amends the structure for financing housing by introducing a so-called constant real value unit (UVR), which is used to adjust the value of loans over time in accordance with living costs (CPI). The Law authorizes CONPES to determine the methodology for calculating the value of the UVR. Currently, this value is calculated by the Bank of the Republic for each day of the year. Develops models and structures for mortgages and encourages the development of government guarantees for loans for social housing.
Law No. 795 of 2003 modifying certain rules in the Basic Statute of the Financial System, and issuing other provisions	Introduces changes to institutions that preserve and protect public trust, the exclusion of assets and liabilities and gradual dismantling of operations. It also reforms the sanctions regime. Includes rules on the following issues: conflict of interest regime, rules of conduct for managers, users' rights to information, and authorizes loan establishments to carry out two new operations: non-trust management of portfolios and residential leasing operations.
Law No. 964 of 2005 issuing general rules and indicating therein the objectives and criteria to be observed by the National Government in regulating the handling, utilization or investment of resources deposited by the public in the form of securities, and issuing other provisions (Securities Market Law)	Issues provisions on: objectives and criteria for intervention by the National Government involving the handling or investment of resources deposited by the public in the form of securities, activities in the securities market and the concept of value, supervision of the overall securities market information system, compensation schemes and fulfilment of obligations, accounts records and securities transactions, central counterparty risk houses, self-regulation of the securities market, protection of investors, violations, administrative penalties and sanctions procedure.
Law No. 1.328 of 2009 issuing rules relating to financial, insurance and securities market matters, and other provisions	Introduces a regime to protect financial consumers including, *inter alia*, the following topics: rights and obligations, Financial Consumers Service Scheme (SAC), provision of information to consumers and clauses on abusive practices. It also makes changes to the Colombian pension scheme by creating a multi-fund system, which must take into account the risk profile of those affiliated. The Law authorizes loan institutions to carry out two new operations (granting loans in order to take over control of other companies or associations and conducting leasing and rental operations without purchase options) and classifies the former exchange houses as financial services companies, changing their legal title to "exchange intermediation and special financial services companies" and authorizing them to conduct new operations, making them non-banking agents. The Law also introduces changes to ensure compliance with Colombia's commitments under trade integration agreements with other countries with a view to liberalizing trade in financial services. The Law gives the SFC the authority to carry out comprehensive and consolidated supervision.
Decree No. 663 of 1993 updating the Basic Statute of the Financial System, amending its headings and numbering	Regulatory text incorporating all the legislation applicable to the financial sector and, as a compilation of laws, has force of law. The Statute has been updated over time by incorporating laws enacted subsequent to its adoption.
Decree No. 2.555 of 15 July 2010 compiling and reissuing rules on the financial, insurance and securities market sector, and issuing other provisions	New updated compilation of the main rules governing the financial and insurance sector.

Source: SFC.

118. As the financial sector is deemed to be of public interest according to the Constitution, an authorization permit must be obtained from the SFC in order to set up and operate a bank in Colombia, including the subsidiary of a foreign bank. The requirements for the permit are set out in the Basic Statute of the Financial System and include, in addition to the criteria for establishment and minimum capital requirements, a study proving satisfactorily that the company is viable. The requirements do not differ according to the origin of the capital, except in the case of applications to set up a subsidiary of a foreign bank, in which case the SFC is empowered to seek information in order to be sure that the subsidiary will be the subject of supervision on the part of the competent foreign authority jointly with the parent company, in accordance with generally accepted international principles.

119. Before giving a new financial institution a permit to operate, the SFC must publish a notification of the intention to set up the institution in a national newspaper, giving as a minimum the names of the persons it is proposed to associate in the business, the name of the planned institution, the amount of its capital and the place in which it will operate; this notification must be published twice, at a seven-day interval. The SFC has six months in which to take a decision and issue the permit.[82] The SFC may refuse a permit when an application does not meet the requirements laid down in the law or when, in its view, the applicants have not provided satisfactory proof of the character, responsibility, suitability and financial solvency of the persons taking part in the operation. An authorization permit issued to a bank by the SFC is for an indefinite period and may not be assigned. In 2011, the minimum capital required to set up a bank in Colombia was Col$71,098 million (around US$37.4 million).

120. There are no legal limitations on private capital holdings in commercial banks, including foreign capital.[83] Foreign investors may hold capital in institutions subject to control and supervision by the SFC, taking up or buying shares, bonds convertible into shares or cooperative contributions in any amount. With the exception of matters relating to the transfer of resources abroad, foreign investment in Colombia shall, for all purposes, be treated in the same way as investment by Colombian citizens. Foreign banks may set up a subsidiary or open a representative office in Colombia, but not a branch. All banks domiciled in Colombia, including subsidiaries of foreign banks, must be set up in the form of commercial public limited companies or cooperative associations.[84]

121. In order to promote their products in Colombia, banks with foreign capital must be established in Colombia. Establishment in Colombia gives the right to supply the same services as banks with Colombian capital, as the services which banks may offer do not differ according to the origin of their capital. Colombian residents may make deposits with foreign banks without an official authorization, but they must register with the Bank of the Republic in order to obtain a loan from a foreign bank.[85] Pursuant to Decree No. 2.951 of 2004, there are no restrictions on the amount of transactions with foreign establishments.

122. There are no legal limitations on the number of banks that may operate in Colombia, nor on the number of agencies which banks may open once established in Colombia. An authorization from the SFC must be obtained in order to open or close an agency. The services which banks may offer are set out in the Basic Statute of the Financial System. SFC authorization must also be obtained in order to open a representative office of a foreign bank. The requirements for such a permit are set out in Decree No. 2.951 of 2004. Representative offices must have a representative for Colombia, and are not subject to minimum capital requirements.

123. Any transaction by national or foreign investors intended to acquire 10 per cent or more of the paid-up shares of any body subject to SFC supervision, whether carried out in one or more operations, requires approval from the SFC, which must ensure that the transfer of the shares will be to the public's advantage. SFC approval is not necessary when the persons seeking to buy shares or bonds to be converted into shares in the same institution have obtained such approval within the three years preceding the date of the transaction in question.

[82] Basic Statute of the Financial System, Article 53.
[83] Basic Statute of the Financial System, Article 91.
[84] Basic Statute of the Financial System, Article 53.
[85] Articles 24 and 55 of Resolution No. 8 of the Bank of the Republic of 2000.

124. The SFC must be notified of any mergers of financial institutions. After receiving notification of the merger, it may object within two months thereafter, but may only do so in the following cases: if the takeover company or the new company does not comply with the minimum capital requirements laid down in the law; if the takeover company or the new company does not comply with the appropriate levels of assets or solvency rules in force; if, as a result of the merger, the takeover company or the new company is able to maintain or fix unfair prices, limit services or prevent, restrict or distort free competition in the markets in which it participates, either as a parent company or through one of its subsidiaries (provided that the takeover company or the new company covers at least 25 per cent of the corresponding market); or if the merger might be contrary to the public interest or the stability of the financial system.

125. Financial institutions, with the exception of financial corporations, may have a holding in the capital of: trust companies, stock-brokers, general deposit warehouses and companies managing pension and retirement funds; and in companies providing technical or administrative services, including security, management of custodial accounts and related services, collection services and companies providing computer systems and services.[86] Their holdings in such financial services companies may not be less than 51 per cent, except in the case of deposit warehouses. Total investment by a bank in other companies may not exceed 100 per cent of its capital, capital reserves and capital revaluation account.

126. The banking intermediation margin fell from 9 per cent in 1995 to around 7 per cent in 2005. This partly reflects resurgent competition and the marked improvement in the quality of portfolios in recent years. The lower loan risk of companies and consumers as a result of growing macroeconomic stability has also helped to narrow the margin. Nevertheless, measures such as the tax on financial transactions and mandatory investment by loan establishments, for example, in agricultural development instruments, has meant that the intermediation margin has not narrowed still further and that the cost of credit has remained at a relatively high level (see also Chapters I and IV(2)).

127. Interest rates in general are determined by the market, except for those covered by legal provisions. Nevertheless, the SFC approves a current bank interest rate each month on the basis of the information supplied by financial establishments for the previous month. Pursuant to Article 884 of the Commercial Code and Decree No. 2.555 of 2010, the interest rates that banks charge on loans and loan arrears may not exceed one and a half times the current bank interest rate, which serves as a benchmark, i.e. an annual effective rate of 50.18 per cent for microcredit and 29.88 per cent for consumer and ordinary loans. These figures result from SFC approval of the annual effective current bank rate of interest of 33.45 per cent for microcredit and 19.29 per cent for consumer and ordinary loans for the period from 1 October 2011 to 30 September 2012 and from 1 January to 31 March 2012, respectively. Interest on housing loans is also subject to ceilings determined by the Bank of the Republic.[87]

128. The prudential indicators for banking have remained sound throughout the period under review. Average solvency (risk-weighted capital adequacy ratio) rose to 14.6 per cent in November 2011, above the average for the previous decade (14.12 per cent) and notably in excess of the regulatory minimum, which is 9 per cent. Non-performing loans represented 2.8 per cent in November 2011. The level of coverage of non-performing loans was 163.5 per cent in

[86] External Circular No. 007 of 1996, Title I, Chapter VII, paragraph 2.2.
[87] Law No. 546 of 1999.

November 2011.[88] The improvements in the prudential indicators are to a large extent the result of the reforms to the regulatory and supervisory framework.

129. In 2011, regulated financial institutions continued to record relatively high profits, even though these were less than for 2010. The profits from managed funds, on the other hand, plummeted in 2011 compared to the previous year (Table IV.9).

Table IV.9
Return on assets and return on equity of supervised institutions and managed funds, 2010, 2011
(Percentage)

Type of intermediary	November 2010		November 2011	
	Return on assets	Return on equity	Return on assets	Return on equity
Loan establishments	2.2	15.9	2.1	15.4
Insurance industry	4.6	17.9	1.6	6.7
Pension and retirement fund management companies	19.1	24.6	11.9	15.1
Trust companies	17.7	23.4	16.1	21.9
Stock market companies	2.3	12.5	2.0	8.9
Brokers on the Colombian Securities Market (BVC)	2.4	13.4	2.0	9.2
Brokers on the Colombian Commodities Exchange (BMC)	-4.1	-6.2	1.1	1.7
Investment fund management companies	13.1	15.5	13.7	20.4
Suppliers of infrastructure	6.6	8.4	5.2	7.0
Special official establishments	1.3	7.9	1.0	6.3
Profitability (companies)	2.6	2.1	15.61	13.3
Pension and retirement funds	14.8	15.0	-1.1	-1.1
Mandatory pension funds	15.8	15.9	-0.8	-0.8
Voluntary pension funds	7.4	7.8	-2.7	-2.8
Retirement funds	11.6	11.7	-2.6	-2.6
Mutual investment funds	12.6	13.2	-2.3	-2.4
Funds managed by trust companies	3.8	3.9	3.5	3.6
Profitability (funds)	10.1	10.4	1.0	1.0

Source: SFC.

130. The authorities have indicated that the broad lines of the supervisory process implemented in Colombia comply with the standards proposed in Pillar 2 (supervisory process) of the Basel II document.[89] As far as capital requirements are concerned, in Colombia, the minimum capital to assets weighted by credit risk is 9 per cent, compared to the 8 per cent proposed in Basel II. In order to calculate the denominator (weighted assets by credit risk), Colombia has adopted a standard method using the scheme proposed in Basel II, but has refrained from differentiating between establishments that have different external classification levels, as Basel II suggests. The authorities have indicated that a working group composed of members of the financial security network is working on bringing Colombia's standard model closer to that proposed by the Basel Committee in the Basel II document.

131. The authorities have also indicated that Colombia has not adopted an internal model method to calculate exposure of banks to credit risk for the purposes of the minimum capital requirements, other than the suggestions in Basel II. Colombia uses a VaR methodology to calculate the capital/market risk ratio but has not adopted a capital/operating risk system.

[88] SFC (2011).

[89] The Basel II document proposes a banking regulation scheme consisting of three pillars: minimum capital requirements, supervisory process, and market discipline.

132. The Basic Statute of the Financial System obliges banks to adopt control mechanisms in order to ensure that their transactions are not used to launder money.[90] Such mechanisms must meet the minimum requirements set out in the SFC's External Circular No. 040 of 2004.[91] The Financial Information and Analysis Division, under the Ministry of Finance and Public Credit, draws up and implements policies to detect, prevent and combat money laundering.

133. Since 1998, Colombia has imposed a tax on the majority of financial transactions.[92] The tax on financial movements (GMF) was designed to be a temporary mechanism to finance the emergency measures adopted during the financial crisis. The rate is 0.4 per cent and applies to banking operations such as withdrawing cash or transferring resources between financial products, and to joint portfolios. The current Government planned to scale down the tax until it is totally abolished in 2018.

134. As to loans granted by banks, in 2011, around 30.2 per cent were for consumption, 23 per cent for industry, 12 per cent for trade and 8.6 per cent for the purchase of real estate. Agricultural credit accounted for only 2.1 per cent of commercial banks' portfolios (Table IV.10).

Table IV.10
Trend in the net loans portfolio and receipt of deposits in the commercial banking sector, 2006-2011
(Col$ millions and percentage)

	2006	2007	2008	2009	2010	2011
Assets	158,399,694	188,256,597	219,376,834	239,021,692	274,852,167	309,644,395
Total loans	100,067,986	126,945,637	149,424,717	152,980,095	178,707,292	203,629,327
US$ equivalent	44,697	63,008	66,601	74,835	93,396	114,164
Loans by economic sector			(% of total loans)			
Agriculture	1.91	1.87	1.86	2.25	2.22	2.1
Industry	22.91	22.76	25.72	24.26	23	23.04
Services	22.13	21.36	19.88	19.88	22.47	21.5
Real estate	9.2	8.63	8.22	8.9	7.86	8.62
Trade	13.72	13.37	12.97	12.91	12.61	12
Consumption	28.5	30.27	29.37	29.6	29.37	30.21
Other	1.65	1.75	1.98	2.26	2.47	2.5
Total deposits in Colombian and foreign currency	106,384,507	125,461,052	147,694,464	157,474,234	172,313,435	190,899,721
US$ equivalent	47,519	62,271	65,830	77,034	90,029	107,027
Maximum interest rates (% annual)	32.08	33.93	33.93	36.89	44.00	32.08
Loans (%)	13.04	16.61	17.72	9.92	8.23	10.96
Deposits (%)	6.75	8.82	10.25	4.22	3.47	4.00

Source: SFC.

(d) Insurance services

135. The SFC is also responsible for supervising Colombia's insurance sector. During the period under review, some reforms to the sector's legal framework were introduced, the main ones being Law No. 1.328 of 2009 or Financial Reform Law (Table IV.11).

[90] Articles 102-107.
[91] Chapter XI, Title I.
[92] Article 29 of Decree No. 2.331 of 1998 and Laws No. 633 of 2000 and No. 863 of 2003.

Table IV.11
Principal laws regulating insurance activities

Legislation	Description
Law No. 45 of 1990	Issues rules on financial intermediation, regulates insurance activities, giving certain powers, and determines other provisions
Law No. 35 of 1993	Establishes general rules and indicates therein the objectives and criteria to be observed by the National Government in regulating financial, stock market and insurance activities and any other activity concerning the handling, utilization or investment of resources deposited by the public, and issues other provisions on financial and insurance matters
Law No. 795 of 2003	Adapts certain rules in the Basic Statute of the Financial Sector, and determines other provisions
Law No. 964 of 2004	Determines general regulations and indicates therein the objectives and criteria to be observed by the National Government in regulating activities relating to the handling, utilization or investment of resources deposited by the public in the form of securities, and issues other provisions
Law No. 389 of 1997	Amends Articles 1.036 and 1.046 of the Commercial Code
Law No. 1.328 of 2009	Issues rules on financial, insurance and securities market matters, and other provisions
Decree No. 2.555 of 15 July 2010	Compiles and reissues rules on the financial, insurance and securities market sector, and determines other provisions

Source: SFC.

136. In order to be able to provide insurance services in Colombia, insurance companies must be legally established in the country. SFC authorization must be obtained to set up and operate an insurance company in Colombia. The requirements for the permit and the procedures followed by the SFC when granting it are the same as those for banks. Permits are granted to provide specified types of insurance. Companies authorized to provide personal life insurance or reinsurance may not offer other types of insurance.

137. In 2011, the minimum capital required to set up an insurance company was Col$6,480 million (around US$2.8 million), except for companies which only provide export credit insurance, for which the minimum capital was Col$5,775 million.[93] The minimum capital required to set up a reinsurance company was Col$25,916 million (approximately US$11.3 million). To these amounts must be added the technical capital required to operate in each type of insurance, which ranges from Col$708 million for transport insurance to Col$2,122 million for automobile insurance.[94]

138. The requirements relating to solvency margins and technical reserves laid down in the legislation apply equally to companies with Colombian or foreign capital.

139. In general, pursuant to Article 61 of Law No. 1.328 of 2009, Colombian residents may not conduct insurance operations in Colombia with foreign companies not authorized to engage in insurance activities in Colombia. Foreign insurance companies may solely and exclusively provide in Colombian territory or to Colombian residents insurance relating to international maritime shipping, international commercial aviation and space launching and freight (including satellites), to cover risks relating to the goods being transported, the vehicle transporting the goods and any liability arising therefrom, as well as insurance covering goods in international transit. The SFC may impose mandatory registration on foreign insurance companies wishing to offer such insurance in Colombia or to Colombian residents. Except for the aforementioned cases, foreign insurance companies may not offer, promote or advertise their services in Colombia or to Colombian residents. Pursuant to Article 188 of the Basic Statute of the Financial System, the SFC may grant exceptions and, for reasons of general interest, to authorize a company to conduct insurance activities in Colombia

[93] Article 80 of the Basic Statute of the Financial System and Law No. 795 of 2003.
[94] Decree No. 1.222 of 2003.

without necessarily being established there. This clause will be repealed as of 15 July 2013 when Article 101 of Law No. 1.328 of 2009 comes into force.

140. Natural or legal persons resident in Colombia may take out any type of insurance abroad, with the exception of social-security-related insurance; mandatory insurance; insurance for which the party insured must, prior to taking out the insurance, prove that he already has mandatory insurance; and insurance in which the party insured is a State body. Nevertheless, the Government is empowered to determine the conditions under which government bodies may take out insurance with foreign insurance companies.

141. Likewise, foreign insurance brokers may engage in intermediation in Colombian territory or for Colombian residents solely in respect of the aforementioned insurance.

142. There are no legal limitations on private capital holdings, including capital from abroad, in insurance companies. Foreign insurance companies may set up a subsidiary or open a representative office in Colombia, but not a branch. All insurance companies domiciled in Colombia, including subsidiaries of foreign companies, must be set up in the form of commercial public limited companies or cooperative associations.

143. There are no legal limitations on the number of insurance companies that may operate in Colombia, nor on the number of agencies which insurance companies established in Colombia may open. An authorization from the SFC must be obtained in order to open or close an agency. There are no differences between the types of service that insurance companies with Colombian or foreign capital may supply.

144. For reinsurance, reinsurers registered in the Register of Foreign Reinsurers and Reinsurance Brokers kept by the SFC may provide services to Colombian clients. Such companies may operate from abroad provided that they comply with the aforementioned registration requirements; they may also choose to open a representative office in Colombia. The criterion taken into account by the SFC when examining an application for inclusion in the Register is the status given to the company by an eligible international agency. The Legal Basic Circular lists the eligible agencies and the criteria to be met by agencies that are not listed. At December 2011, 260 companies were listed in the Register of Foreign Reinsurers and Reinsurance Brokers; 15 of these had a representative office in Colombia.

145. An authorization permit from the SFC must also be obtained in order to open a representative office of an insurance or reinsurance company. The requirements for such a permit are the same as those for banks. Such offices must have a representative for Colombia and are not subject to minimum capital requirements.

146. There is no official control of the policies and premiums of insurance companies, but they must comply with the principles laid down in the Basic Statute of the Financial System. Insurance companies must send models of their policies to the SFC.

147. The nominal value of premiums in the insurance industry, including insurance cooperatives, amounted to Col$11.85 trillion in 2010 (some US$6,223 million). Just over 60 per cent was in the general insurance branch, while the remainder related to life insurance (Table IV.12).

Table IV.12
Total premiums per branch, 2006-2011
(Col$ millions)

Branch	2006	2007	2008	2009	2010	2011
Life	**3,094,136**	**3,426,359**	**4,658,624**	**5,283,690**	**5,138,138**	**2,943,447**
Personal life	312,723	340,780	366,979	387,909	430,362	210,831
Joint life	641,309	767,716	850,980	936,597	1,016,264	585,695
Other life insurance	1,682,744	1,740,810	2,777,179	3,215,291	2,889,697	1,657,133
Accident and sickness	**498,377**	**576,470**	**679,569**	**776,152**	**861,696**	**468,020**
Damages	**4,165,448**	**4,740,282**	**5,166,927**	**5,617,478**	**6,116,814**	**3,355,974**
Fire and allied insurance	638,562	660,965	725,846	852,085	952,356	495,619
Vehicles and automobiles	1,444,923	1,667,827	1,727,906	1,740,031	1,892,732	976,451
Other general insurance	2,477,391	2,813,500	3,169,016	3,565,932	3,875,385	2,189,014
Bonds	**295,455**	**359,615**	**350,872**	**537,031**	**595,758**	**309,381**
Total	**7,555,038**	**8,526,257**	**10,176,423**	**11,438,199**	**11,850,709**	**6,608,802**

Source: Information provided by the Colombian authorities.

(ii) Telecommunications

148. During the period under review, Colombia made important changes to its telecommunications legislation. In late July 2009, it enacted Law No. 1.341 of 2009 (Information and Communications Technology Law, or ICT Law), which consolidated the legal framework for the sector.[95] The ICT Law repealed the legislation previously in force.[96] It also recognizes that "the supply of telecommunications networks and services is a public service under State ownership".[97] This Law replaced the previous system which differentiated between services and included three regimes depending on the type of service (tariff freedom, monitored freedom and regulated tariffs) by a general tariff freedom regime. Law No. 1.341 of 2009, together with Decree No. 4.948 of 2009, constitutes the legal framework for Internet services. The authorities have indicated that the Law also focuses on promoting investment in the information and telecommunications technology sector. Over the period 2005-2011 there was large-scale investment in the sector, amounting to around Col$26.5 trillion (US$14,700 million), three quarters of which was private investment (Table IV.13).

Table IV.13
Investment in the telecommunications sector, 2005-2011
(Col$ billions)

Investment	2005	2006	2007	2008	2009	2010	2011
Private	2,495	3,083	2,394	3,330	2,810	3,189	3,626
Public	809	809	809	809	809	809	758
Total	**3,304**	**3,892**	**3,203**	**4,139**	**3,619**	**3,998**	**4,384**

Source: Information provided by the Colombian authorities.

149. MINTIC (formerly the Ministry of Communications) is responsible for formulating telecommunications policy. Market regulation is the responsibility of the CRC (formerly the

[95] Guerra (2009).

[96] Namely, Decree No. 2.870 of 2007 implementing the convergence of telecommunications services and networks, Decree No. 2.926 of 2005 (amending Decree No. 2.542 of 1997) implementing switched long-distance basic public telephony services (national and international), Decree No. 575 of 2002 implementing the supply of personal communications services, PCS, Law No. 555 of 2000 regulating the supply of personal communications services, PCS, Law No. 422 of 1998 (amending Law No. 37 of 1993) regulating the supply of mobile telephony services, Decree No. 1.900 of 1990 implementing the supply of telecommunications services and Law No. 72 of 1989 defining the regime for telecommunications services concessions.

[97] Law No. 1.341 of 2009.

Telecommunications Regulatory Commission), which is attached to the Ministry. All telephony operators pay 0.1 per cent of their gross income to CRC for the regulatory services provided. The National Spectrum Agency (ANE), under MINTIC and created by the ICT Law, carries out technical control of the radio spectrum, but it is MINTIC's responsibility to allocate frequency bands.[98]

150. There are no limitations on Colombian or foreign private capital holdings in the supply of telecommunications services. In order to operate on the domestic market, however, foreign companies must set up a branch office in Colombia.[99]

151. Under the legislation in force up to 2009, a supplier had to request a concession, licence or other authorization depending on the telecommunications service it wished to supply. These were granted for up to ten years (renewable) through a selection process, mainly in the form of an auction in the case of mobile telephony and at the request of the party for other telecommunications services, depending on availability in the spectrum. The permits granted were renewed for the same term originally granted provided that the supplier met the requirements laid down in the legislation. The 2009 ICT Law has provided a general authorization regime for the supply of telecommunications networks and services subject to payment of offsets.[100] Consequently, since 2009, new suppliers or those opting for the new regime in Law No. 1.341 have been generally authorized provided that they are registered in the Register of Suppliers of Telecommunications Networks and Services (ICT Register) kept by MINTIC.[101] Registration can be done online[102] and applies to each supplier of networks or services, but not to each of the services to be supplied, and the information contained therein is available to the public.[103] Once MINTIC has checked the veracity of the documents provided by the supplier when registering, it is listed in the ICT Register and may then start operating.[104] All legal persons providing or intending to provide telecommunications networks and/or services, as well as natural or legal persons holding permits for the use of scarce resources, as defined in Article 5 of Decree No. 4.948/09, including Internet service providers (ISP), must be listed in the ICT Register.

152. Suppliers who were granted a concession prior to the ICT Law have been able to keep it until its expiry or to opt for the new authorization regime.[105] The authorities have pointed out that the advantage of opting for the authorization regime is that the supplier may provide telecommunications networks and services without the need for authorization permits for each of them as the radio spectrum is not linked to the service to be supplied; moreover, the payment of offsets for telecommunications services has been modified, changing from the previous figure of 3.3 per cent of net income to 2.2 per cent of gross income under the new regime. The authorities have indicated that, of the 4,736 telecommunications concession holders existing at the end of January 2010, by February 2012, 876 suppliers of telecommunications networks and services had been given a general authorization and 395 were listed in the ICT Register.

---

[98] Law No. 1.341 of 2009.

[99] Article 469 of the Commercial Code, Decree No. 410 of 1971 and Law No. 671 of 2001.

[100] Law No. 1.341 of 2009 and Lizcano Ortiz (2010).

[101] Law No. 1.341 of 2009, and Guerra (2009).

[102] Decree No. 4.948 of 2009, Article 8.

[103] Decree No. 4.948 of 2009, Article 7 and online information from MINCIT, "*Respuesta a inquietudes sectoriales, radicación 351273 del 11 de mayo 2010*". Viewed at: http://www.andesco.org.co/site/assets/media/camara/financiera/Doctrina/ConceptoContraprestaciones.pdf.

[104] Decree No. 4.948 of 2009, Article 10.

[105] Law No. 1.341 of 2009, Article 68.

153. Permits to use the radio spectrum are issued by MINTIC for a period of up to ten years, through an objective selection procedure.[106] At least three months before the permit to use the spectrum expires, the supplier may request its renewal for the same period as that originally granted; renewal is neither automatic nor free of charge. Permits may be transferred subject to authorization by the Ministry.[107]

154. Authorized suppliers and those holding concessions pay an offset for providing telecommunications networks and services and for using the radio spectrum.[108] MINTIC determines the amount for each offset in a resolution. The offset for providing telecommunications networks and services is 2.2 per cent of the quarterly gross income of authorized suppliers and 3.3 per cent of the net income of those maintaining their concessions.[109] A formula is used to calculate the offset for use of the radio spectrum.[110] The offsets go towards the Information and Communications Technology Fund (formerly the Communications Fund), which mainly finances universal access to telecommunications services, particularly for low-income sectors of the population. Some of the Fund's resources help to finance the activities of the ANE.[111] At the end of 2011, the Fund's budgetary resources amounted to Col$1.04 trillion (US$58 million).

155. Until the enactment of the ICT Law in late July 2009, Colombia had a subsidies regime intended to facilitate access by low-income sectors of the population to switched basic public (fixed) telephony services (TPBC), and to mobile local telephony services in the rural sector.[112] The regime consisted of making medium-high/high-income users, as well as commercial and industrial users, subsidize low-low/low-income users.[113] Even though the 2009 ICT Law repealed the subsidies regime, there is a five-year transitional period which began at the end of December 2009.[114] During this period, suppliers of local switched basic public telephony services (TPBCLE) do not pay the offset to the Information and Communications Technology Fund, but, to replace the subsidy, it goes to facilitate access by low-income users to TPBC services, mobile local telephony services and Internet and broadband services.[115] During the transitional period, if the amount of the offset turns out to be insufficient to replace the subsidy, the resources of the Information and Communications

[106] Although Law No. 1.341 of 2009 allows the direct allocation of the radio spectrum when "the general interest" or "extension of coverage" are paramount, in 2010 the Constitutional Court declared these expressions to be unenforceable, thus limiting MINTIC's power directly to grant permits to use the spectrum solely to that of ensuring continuity of service and for the time strictly necessary to enable the authorities to follow an objective selection procedure.

[107] Decree No. 1.341 of 2009, Articles 11 and 12.

[108] Decree No. 1.341 of 2009, Articles 10 and 13.

[109] MINTIC, Resolution No. 290 of 2010, Article 2, and Decree No. 1.972 of 2003.

[110] For further details, see MINTIC, Resolution No. 290 of 2010, Article 5, and Decree No. 1.972 of 2003.

[111] Law No. 1.341 of 2009.

[112] Law No. 142 of 1994, Article 1.

[113] Law No. 142 of 1994, Article 87.3, and WTO (2006). The subsidies regime classifies users into six categories depending on their level of income: category 1: low-low; category 2: low; category 3: medium-low; category 4: medium; category 5: medium-high; and category 6: high (Law No. 142 of 1994, Article 102).

[114] Law No. 1.341 of 2009, Articles 69 and 73, and Decree No. 5.052 of 2009.

[115] Law No. 1.341 of 2009, Article 69, Decree No. 5.052 of 2009 and Law No. 1.450 of 2011, Article 58.

Technology Fund are used to cover the deficit.[116] If, on the contrary, there is a surplus, this goes to the Fund.[117]

156. The subsidy only covers basic subsistence consumption.[118] This is expressed in minutes and is determined by the CRC in a resolution (Table IV.14).[119] Suppliers offering price plans that offer minutes over and above the basic subsistence consumption only receive subsidies for the minutes which fall within the basic subsistence consumption. For suppliers offering unlimited calls plans, the subsidy is: (i) the result of the supplier's average revenue per minute during the preceding year compared to the number of minutes corresponding to basic subsistence consumption; or (ii) the amount of the domestic single subsidy per line (Table IV.14).[120] As an example of the amount of the subsidy, the authorities indicated that between the end of January and the end of October 2010, a total of Col$54,761 million (around US$30.5 million) was paid out to suppliers pursuant to Law No. 1.341 of 2009 and Law No. 1.450 of 2011. In connection with this review, the authorities indicated that MINTIC's policy is to transfer the current subsidies for telephony to Internet access. It is proposed that the subsidies remain in effect under a transitional regime for a period of five years.

Table IV.14
Subsidies in the telecommunications sector since 2006

User	Period	Basic consumption (minute)	Domestic single subsidy per line (Col$)
Category 1 (low-low income)	01.01.2006-30.09.2011	200	n.a.[a]
	01.10.2011-30.10.2012	100	3,692.9
	31.01.2012-30.01.2013	75	2,.769.7
	31.01.2013-30.04.2014	50	1,846.4
	31.01.2014-30.01.2015	25	923.2
	As of 2015	0	0.0
Category 2 (low income)	01.01.2006-30.09.2011	200	n.a.[a]
	01.10.2011-30.10.2012	100	2,954.3
	31.01.2012-30.01.2013	75	2,215.7
	31.01.2013-30.04.2014	50	1,477.1
	31.01.2014-30.01.2015	25	738.6
	As of 2015	0	0.0

n.a. Not applicable.

a The domestic single subsidy per line started to come into effect in October 2011 and only applies to unlimited calls plans (CRC, Resolution No. 3.140 of 2011).

Source: CRC Resolutions No. 3.052 and No. 3.140 of 2011.

157. Suppliers are free to fix their rates, but the CRC may regulate prices when there is not sufficient competition, when there is a breakdown in the market or when the quality of the services offered does not correspond to the levels required, but it must do so in accordance with the procedures stipulated in the aforementioned Law.[121] From 2006 (Resolution CRC No. 1.250 of 2005) up to the end of July 2009 (Resolution CRC No. 2.063 of 2009), there was a regime of monitored rates for

[116] Law No. 1.341 of 2009, Article 69, and Law No. 1.450 of 2011, Article 58.

[117] Law No. 1.341 of 2009, Article 69.

[118] CRC Resolution No. 87 of 1997, Article 5.3.1. Basic subsistence consumption is defined as consumption intended to meet the basic needs of low-income users.

[119] Law No. 142 of 1994, Article 99.6, and CRC, Resolution No. 3.052 of 2011.

[120] CRC Resolution No. 3.140 of 2011. The national single subsidy per line started to come into effect as of October 2011 and only applies to the so-called "unlimited plans", prepayment services which include unlimited communication throughout Colombia.

[121] Law No. 1.341 of 2009, Article 23.

fixed telephony in Colombia; this regime only applied in certain municipalities.[122] All suppliers had to register their rates. Suppliers providing switched basic public telephony services and having a market share exceeding 60 per cent were subject to a regulated rates regime. This regime even applied when there was not sufficient competition.[123] Since 2009, rates for fixed telephony services have been freely determined. Colombia has a monitored rates regime under which the CRC imposes a ceiling rate (excluding VAT and the additional transport charge) on calls from fixed to mobile telephones.[124] Since 2005, a gradual decrease in the ceiling rate per minute has been noted (Col$392 in 2005 and Col$153.97 in 2012).[125]

158. When a supplier interconnects to the fixed or mobile network of another supplier, he has to pay an access charge. Since 2007, the CRC has fixed the maximum amount of this charge. The supplier is also obliged to inform its clients of the charges paid.[126] The CRC is planning to lower access charges to mobile networks in stages from 2012 up to 2015.[127] The authorities have indicated that this measure has led to a decrease in mobile rates paid by users to make calls to a network other than that of their supplier.

159. Since 2008, suppliers have been obliged to allow the physical infrastructure such as telephone poles and lines to be shared under leasing contracts. The monthly leasing charge, published in a CRC resolution, is adjusted annually on the basis of the producer price index (PPI) determined by DANE. A supplier which lends its physical facilities to another supplier may also require that the arrangement remain in place for a minimum period of up to one year and an offset of a reasonable amount to be agreed between the parties.[128] The authorities have pointed out that sharing infrastructure helps to eliminate the fiscal and regulatory problems of installing new telecommunications network infrastructure.

160. Digital portability has existed in Colombia since 2002 when a decree provided that suppliers of fixed and mobile telephony services were obliged to provide clients with this service.[129] In 2008, however, the Government issued a law under which the implementation of digital portability became mandatory.[130] Mobile digital portability has been implemented since 29 July 2011; the legal deadline expires on 31 December 2012, but the CRC has drawn up a timetable to speed up its implementation.[131] For fixed telephony services, digital portability has not been introduced because the studies conducted by the CRC determined that it was neither technically nor economically viable.

161. In Colombia, there are 26 fixed telephony operators and seven mobile telephony operators (Table IV.15). The market is led by two groups: América Móvil through Telmex (fixed services) and

[122] CRC Resolution No. 1.296 of 2005.
[123] CRC Resolution No. 1.250 of 2005, Article 5.2.2.
[124] CRC Resolutions No. 3.497 of 2011, Article 1, and No. 87 of 1997, Article 5.8.2.
[125] CRC Resolutions No. 1.296 of 2005, No. 2.156 of 2009, Article 1, and No. 3.497 of 2011, Article 1.
[126] CRC Resolutions No. 1.763 of 2007 and No. 2.585 of 2010.
[127] CRC Resolution No. 3.136 of 2011, Article 1.
[128] CRC Resolution No. 2.014 of 2008.
[129] Decree No. 25 of 2002, Article 40.
[130] Law No. 1.245 of 2008. The authorities have indicated in this regard that, although Decree No. 25 of 2002 already provided that digital portability was an obligation on telecommunications operators even if one changed from one operator to another which provided the same telecommunications service as far as the numbering of universal personal telecommunications (UPT) and services was concerned, this Decree did not include rules on digital portability for fixed or mobile telephony, as Law No. 1.245 of 2008 has done.
[131] Online information from CRC, "*Respuestas a preguntas frecuentes sobre portabilidad numérica*". Viewed at: http://www.portabilidad.gov.co/index.php?option=com_content&view=category& layout=blog& id=6&Itemid=5.

Comcel (mobile services); and Grupo Telefónica through Colombia Telecomunicaciones (fixed services) and Movistar (mobile services).[132] Comcel and Movistar have been providing 3G services since 2008.[133] Comcel's share of the mobile telephony market remained stable (65 per cent market share) during the period under review. The majority of Colombian users have fixed telephony services contracts with Colombia Telecomunicaciones or ETB.[134] Broadband services are mainly available in the larger cities and there is growing interest in mobile Internet on the part of users. In January 2011, the Government announced that the spectrum frequency would be increased so as to foster new technology. Five operators share 90 per cent of the Internet market (Comcel-Telmex, ETB, Movistar-Colombia Telecomunicaciones, Tigo and UNE).[135]

Table IV.15
Telecommunications indicators, 2006-2011

Service	2006	2007	2008	2009	2010	2011[a]
Operators of public telecommunications services						
Local fixed telephony	31	31	31	27	26	26
Mobile telephony	3	3	3	3	4	4
National long-distance telephony	8	7	7	7	8	8
International long-distance telephony	10	9	9	12	10	11
Internet service providers	47	47	42	42	42	45[b]
Fixed telephony						
Number of fixed lines in service	7,861,857	7,984,290	8,053,796	7,473,867	7,186,165	7,157,756
Density of fixed lines in service (telephones/100 inh.)	18.11	18.18	18.12	16.62	15.79	15.55
Fixed telephony rates (US$)						
Local household installation costs	28.59	38.64	..	43.12	..	..
Local business installation costs	40.69	43.84	88.12	..	..	..
Monthly rate for household lines	4.91	5.44	8.51	6.83	11.32	11.17
Monthly rate for business lines	5.85	7.67	15.38	22.89	17.75	34.98
Cost of a national long-distance call per minute	0.12	0.10	0.07	0.08	0.11	0.08
Cost of an outgoing international long-distance call per minute	0.31	0.31	..	0.34	0.38	0.36
Mobile telephony						
Number of cellular subscribers (millions)	29,762,715	33,941,118	41,364,753	41,154,631	44,477,653	46,200,421[b]
Teledensity (telephones/100/inh.)	68.57	77.20	93.06	91.50	97.4	100.3[b]

.. Not available.

a Figures for the first three quarters.
b Whole of 2011.

Source: Information provided by the Colombian authorities.

162. In February 2009, the CRC decided that Comcel was occupying a dominant position in the market for outgoing mobile calls, based on the fact that it had a high and persistent share of the

[132] CRC (2010).

[133] Online information from the United States International Trade Administration, "Telecommunications Market Snapshot: Colombia". Viewed at: http://web.ita.doc.gov/ITI/itiHome.nsf/9b2cb14bda00318585256cc40068ca69/33e888803bbeec978525788c0047fbe1/$FILE/telecom%20market%20snapshot-colombia.pdf.

[134] CRC (2010).

[135] Online information from the United States International Trade Administration, "Telecommunications Market Snapshot: Colombia". Viewed at: http://web.ita.doc.gov/ITI/itiHome.nsf/9b2cb14bda00318585256cc40068ca69/33e888803bbeec978525788c0047fbe1/$FILE/telecom%20market%20snapshot-colombia.pdf; and CRC (2010).

market that allowed it to act independently of the relevant market signals. The CRC decided to take a regulatory measure under which the mobile rate plans offered by Comcel to its clients would be determined according to a tariff schedule that would be reviewed by the Commission.[136] It also obliged Comcel to make a wholesale offer available to suppliers of content and applications.[137] The authorities have indicated that it is considered that the situation in the outgoing mobile calls market has not changed compared to that identified in 2009 and therefore the CRC is currently reviewing the situation to impose new measures on Comcel.

163. Five submarine cables give Colombia international connections.[138] Since April 2009, operators of submarine cable heads have been obliged to give other operators commercial access opportunities. Operators of submarine cable heads may freely determine the charges for access.[139]

164. The following are exempt from payment of VAT: monthly local basic subsistence consumption telephony invoiced to low-low/low-income users, services from public telephones and Internet connection and access services for low-low/low/medium-low-income users.[140]

(iii) Air transport and airports

(a) Air transport

165. In Colombia, air transport is the responsibility of the Ministry of Transport and the Special Administrative Division for Civil Aviation (Aerocivil). The Ministry of Transport formulates policies for the transport sector.[141] Aerocivil comes under the Ministry of Transport and is the authority in the area of aeronautics which promotes and regulates the development, coverage and growth of civil aviation, the industry and aeronautical research, in order to guarantee national and international geographical connectivity. Aerocivil coordinates air transport policy with the Ministry. It also authorizes the building of airports and provides navigation and aeronautical telecommunications services.[142]

166. Air transport in Colombia is governed by the Commercial Code (Book V)[143], Colombia's Aviation Regulations (RAC) and international agreements. The RAC are issued by Aerocivil and bring together all the provisions on aeronautical activities and on Colombian and foreign entities engaged in aeronautics.[144] Since the previous Review of Colombia in 2006, the RAC have frequently

[136] CRC Resolutions No. 2.062 of 2009 and No. 2.066 of 2009.

[137] CRC Resolution No. 2.067 of 2009 and Decree No. 2.870 of 2007, Article 10. A wholesale offer is a business plan which an operator makes generally available and which sets out the reasonable and non-discriminatory commercial, economic and technical conditions under which it offers the necessary elements such as minutes, bandwidth or similar elements wholesale to third parties so that they can provide services to the public (Decree No. 2.870 of 2007).

[138] CRC (2010).

[139] CRC Resolution No. 2.065 of 2009.

[140] Tax Statute, Article 476, and Law No. 142 of 1994, Article 102.

[141] Decree No. 2.053 of 2003, Article 1.

[142] Decree No. 260 of 2004, Articles 1, 2 and 5.

[143] Decree No. 410 of 1971.

[144] Colombian Aviation Regulations, Part I.

been modified in order to implement the provisions of the International Civil Aviation Organization (ICAO).[145]

167. The aim of government policy on domestic (scheduled) passenger transport is to liberalize and streamline market access in order to promote competition. Since 2003, Colombia has, however, imposed a maximum number of operators per route that depends on the number of passengers carried annually.[146] Since 2006, a maximum of three operators have been authorized to provide services on routes carrying less than 100,000 passengers, five on routes that carry from 100,000 to 400,000 passengers, and six on routes carrying over 400,000 passengers.[147] The authorities have indicated that the policy on access to the (scheduled) domestic market for freight is free access throughout Colombia, with freedom to decide on frequencies and no limit on the number of companies.

168. Colombia has so far signed 34 bilateral air transport agreements and one multilateral agreement (CAN). It has signed 12 new agreements since 2006 and has revised some others (Table AIV.1).[148] The authorities draw attention in particular to the implementation of the new open skies agreement negotiated with the United States, which will come into effect in 2013 after a transitional period that began in 2011. The terms for the agreements concluded and revised by Colombia implement new guidelines issued by the Ministry of Transport in 2009.[149] In the area of passenger transport, the guidelines are the following: application of the multiple designation principle allowing the operation of routes by several airlines; the granting of fifth freedom rights; the determination of rates according to the "country of origin" clause, which allows a party to reject the rates when the flight starts in its territory, unlike the dual approval clause, which requires that parties agree on rates; and implementation of corporate arrangements which allow airlines to share aircraft under a code share regime (Table AIV.1). As to the carriage of freight, the new guidelines in the agreements focus on the multiple designation principle, the granting of fifth freedom rights and free scheduling, as well as charter flights.[150] Colombia emphasizes that the agreements negotiated have resulted in an unlimited number of freight flights and at least seven weekly passenger flights in order to promote tourism in particular. In this respect, Colombia gives free access to airports in tourist destinations (Armenia, Barranquilla, Cartagena, San Andrés and Santa Marta).[151]

169. In 2004, CAN members mutually undertook to grant fifth freedom rights for scheduled and non-scheduled cargo flights within the Andean subregion. CAN members grant the free exercise of fifth freedom traffic rights for non-scheduled freight flights outside the subregion and for scheduled passenger, freight and mail flights, separately or combined, with the granting of rights being subject to bilateral or multilateral negotiations.[152] In this connection, in January 2012 negotiations were held between Colombia and Ecuador and resulted in the expansion of mixed passenger, mail and freight

[145] Article 37 of the 1944 Chicago Convention and Decree No. 260 of 2004. See also online information from Aerocivil, "*Normatividad: Reglamentos Aeronáuticos de Colombia (RAC)*". Viewed at: http://portal.aerocivil.gov.co/portal/page/portal/Aerocivil_Portal_Internet/normatividad/rac/indice_general.

[146] Online information from Aerocivil, "*Política Aerocomercial: Revisión de la Política Aerocomercial*". Viewed at: http://portal.aerocivil.gov.co/portal/page/portal/Aerocivil_Portal_Internet/normatividad/politica_aerocomercial.

[147] Aerocivil, Group for the Assessment of Aerocommercial Projects, Record of meeting 33, 13 and 15 March 2006.

[148] Olivera *et al.* (2011).

[149] For further details, see Ministry of Transport (2009).

[150] Ministry of Transport (2009).

[151] Ministry of Transport (2009) and Olivera *et al.* (2011), "Annex 4".

[152] CAN Decision No. 582 of 2004, Articles 2 and 7.

services; it was agreed that, outside the CAN, both Colombia and Ecuador will exercise fifth freedom rights throughout America, except for the United States and Canada.

170. Air traffic in Colombia is governed by the principle of reciprocity where there is no relevant international agreement. In such cases, Aerocivil authorizes foreign airlines to operate provided that the country of origin gives Colombian airlines reciprocal treatment.[153] The principle of reciprocity governs scheduled passenger flights between Colombia and Canada, and Guatemala.[154]

171. Domestic passenger traffic is provided by six airlines: Aerolínea Antioquia, Aires, Avianca, Copa Airlines Colombia (AeroRepública operating under the name Copa Airlines), Easy Fly and Satena. International routes are operated by 26 airlines. In all, 11 Colombian companies and 15 international companies currently provide freight services; passenger airlines carry 45 per cent of domestic freight and 14 per cent of international freight. Avianca is still the largest company in terms of domestic and international transport of passengers and freight. In 2010, it carried 54.4 per cent of the passengers on domestic flights and 34.6 per cent of passengers on international flights. Coming much further down the scale as regards international transport is Copa Airlines Colombia, which came in second place with 9.75 per cent of passengers carried.[155] Through its subsidiary Tampa, Avianca has 32 per cent of the international freight market, way above LANCO, a Colombian freight airline owned by LAN Chile, which has 8 per cent of the market.[156]

172. Any domestic or foreign airline wishing to provide scheduled or non-scheduled commercial transport services must obtain an operating permit from Aerocivil. These permits are for an indefinite term and may be cancelled if they are revoked by Aerocivil or the airline withdraws. Only Colombian legal persons may apply for operating permits.[157] Likewise, any aircraft operating in Colombian airspace must be registered in the National Aviation Register in order to obtain a registration certificate from Aerocivil's National Aviation Registration Office.[158] Only Colombian natural or legal persons owning and/or operating aircraft may undertake registration formalities. Colombia recognizes the registration certificates issued by ICAO member States if a Colombian airline operates foreign aircraft within Colombia or abroad. Aircraft registered in Colombia or abroad but operating within Colombia acquire Colombian nationality. Permission from Aerocivil is required to import aircraft.[159]

173. Cabotage air transport is restricted to Colombian aircraft.[160] There are also nationality requirements. Ninety per cent of the personnel of Colombian airlines and agencies/branches of foreign airlines established in Colombia must be Colombian nationals. This restriction is subject to

[153] Commercial Code (Decree No. 410 of 1971), Article 1870, and Colombian Aviation Regulations, Part II, paragraph 3.6.3.3.2.2.

[154] Olivera *et al.* (2011).

[155] OECD (2011).

[156] Online information from Aviacol.com, "*Entrevista al Presidente de Avianca Fabio Villegas*", 22 September 2009. Viewed at: http://www.aviacol.net/articulos-de-aviacion/articulos-de-opinion/entrevista-entrevista-presidente-de-avianca-fabio-villegas.html.

[157] In order to obtain an operating permit, the company must prove its administrative, technical and financial capacity in relation to the activities it intends to conduct and such conditions must be maintained as long as it holds an operating permit. Technical capacity is determined by the operating permit and the operating specifications issued by Aerocivil's Air Safety Secretariat in the Ministry of Transport. Operating permits are issued for five years, and are automatically renewed for the same period. Operating permits for air carriers issued by Aerocivil are for an indefinite term until they are revoked or voluntarily annulled.

[158] Colombian Aviation Regulations, Part XX.

[159] Colombian Aviation Regulations, Part XX.

[160] Commercial Code (Decree No. 410 of 1971), Article 1.785.

reciprocity, in other words, it does not apply if the country of origin of the foreign airline does not impose similar restrictions on Colombian airlines. Aerocivil may also decide not to apply this restriction if it can "duly" justify its decision.[161] The captain of a Colombian-registered aircraft must be a Colombian citizen. Colombia has not imposed restrictions on foreign capital holdings in national airlines since 1991.

174. Aerocivil is the body responsible for authorizing domestic and international charter flights for passengers and freight, provided that there is no "undue competition" with scheduled services. The operator of a charter flight must obtain an operating permit from Aerocivil and inform the latter of the number of passengers or the volume and nature of the freight.[162]

175. Even though a new general law on competition was introduced in 2009, the Constitutional Court's interpretation of Law No. 1.340 of 2009 maintained Aerocivil's exclusive competence to authorize certain commercial operations by airlines, including code-sharing contracts, joint operation or the use of chartered aircraft.[163] Since 2006, Avianca has entered into a number of mergers to enable it to consolidate its operations in the regional aviation market (Table IV.16). Its merger with TACA in particular created the third largest airline in Latin America.[164] There has been no case of anti-competitive trade practices since 2006.[165]

Table IV.16
Mergers and acquisitions in the air transport market, 2009-2010

Year	Parties	Description	Objective
2009	Avianca and TACA (El Salvador)	Consolidation. Authorization was given through the business operation called a contribution contract	Strategic alliance to position the companies at the global level
2010	Avianca and SAM (Colombia)[a]	Merger by absorption	To improve competitiveness and lower costs
2010	Avianca and TACA, and AeroGal (Ecuador)	Acquisition	To consolidate Avianca-TACA's operations in Latin America
2010	LAN (Chile) and Aires	Acquisition	To participate in the Colombian passenger market

a SAM was an Avianca subsidiary.

Source: WTO Secretariat and information provided by the Colombian authorities.

176. Aerocivil determines tariff policy for national and international air transport.[166] Until 2007, there was a floor-rates scheme for airlines providing scheduled national and international passenger transport. In 2007, Aerocivil liberalized the minimum rates in support of the government policy to promote tourism. The authorities have indicated that liberalization of the floor led to a 27.7 per cent decrease in the cost of domestic air tickets and 17 per cent for international routes. Although Aerocivil allows airlines freely to determine the minimum ticket price, it still controls their maximum

[161] Commercial Code (Decree No. 410 of 1971), Article 1.803. According to the authorities, this has only happened occasionally in order to meet temporary shortages of pilots or technicians available to fly certain types of aircraft.

[162] Colombian Aviation Regulations, Part III.

[163] Law No. 1.340 of 2009, Articles 6 and 8. In April 2011, the Constitutional Court declared admissible the paragraph in Article 8 of Law No. 1.340, stating that the general rule on SIC's exclusive competence did not apply to aviation-related competition, but was an exception to it so that Aerocivil would retain its rights in respect of free competition among airlines.

[164] Online information from IATA, "Remarks of Giovanni Bisignani at ATAC Breakfast Bogota", 17 March 2011. Viewed at: http://www.iata.org/pressroom/speeches/pages/2011-03-17-01.aspx.

[165] OECD (2011).

[166] Ministry of Transport, Decree No. 260 of 2004, Article 5.

level.[167] If an airline wants to apply a rate above the maximum, it must justify this to Aerocivil, explaining the grounds for its request.[168]

177. Domestic freight rates can be determined freely and are generally fixed on the basis of the flying time for the aircraft providing the service.[169] International freight rates are subject to ceilings per kilo, per route and per product.

178. The legislation allows the State to grant subsidies to the aviation industry, but solely to State-owned enterprises.[170] The authorities have indicated that during the period under review the Government did not grant any subsidies to the aviation industry.

(b) Airports

179. Colombia has 581 airports, of which 70 belong to Aerocivil, 344 are private and 167 are the responsibility of departments/municipalities. There are 11 international airports. The airport at Bogotá handles the majority of domestic and international passenger and freight traffic.[171] The building of the "coffee airport", commenced in 2004 and financed by the Government, Aerocivil and the competent regional entities, has not yet finished. The airport, which will handle international medium-haul flights, will give the departments/municipalities in the "coffee zone" a centre for transporting freight, as well as an opportunity to develop the region's tourism potential.[172] The "coffee airport" is expected to start operating in 2014.

180. Companies holding concessions must be Colombian firms specializing in the activity concerned.[173] Government holdings in such companies must not exceed 50 per cent[174]; the legislation does not impose any limit on foreign investment. Concession contracts are awarded for 15 to 25 years[175] and their extension must be approved by CONPES.[176] The concession holder pays Aerocivil for use of the airport infrastructure, either a fixed amount, a percentage of gross income or a combination of the two, depending on the contract negotiated.[177] The income generated by concessions enables Aerocivil to finance investment and operating costs for loss-making airports, invest in air safety and control and help to maintain regional airports.[178] The Delegated Supervisory

[167] Aerocivil, Resolution No. 3.299 of 2007. The authorities have indicated that, as far as maximum rates are concerned, variations in domestic air ticket prices are authorized subject to a request from the airline; the parameter to be taken into account is the CPI over one year, and the surcharges for certain inputs such as fuel and factors that affect costs such as devaluation are also taken into account.

[168] OECD (2011).

[169] Online information from Aerocivil, "*Normatividad: política aerocomercial: documentos: Política tarifaría nacional/internacional*". Viewed at: http://portal.aerocivil.gov.co/portal/page/portal/Aerocivil_Portal_Internet/normatividad/politica_aerocomercial/Documentos. Aerocivil Resolution No. 00994 of 28 February 2012 provided that rates and fuel charges could be freely determined.

[170] Commercial Code (Decree 410 of 1971), Article 1863, and WTO (2006).

[171] Colombian Chamber of Infrastructure (2009) and Ríos Plata (2011).

[172] CONPES (2009a).

[173] Decree No. 1.647 of 1994, Article 3.

[174] *Ibid.*

[175] Olivera *et al.* (2011).

[176] Law No. 1.150 of 2007, Article 28. The provisions on granting extensions can be found in Decree No. 3.460 of 2008.

[177] Olivera *et al.* (2011).

[178] CONPES (1994).

Authority for Concessions, part of the Ports and Transport Supervisory Authority, oversees compliance with the obligations on the infrastructure and services by concession holders.[179]

181. Although the purpose of the concession regime is to modernize and upgrade infrastructure, the costs incurred through cancellation or delays remain high. In this connection, the additional charges on airlines for cancellation or delays amounted to Col$474 billion in 2010.[180] In a survey carried out by Bogotá's Chamber of Commerce, users of passenger and freight terminals at Bogota airport drew attention to certain shortcomings in the baggage handling and ground services.[181]

182. In the airports it owns, Aerocivil fixes and collects the fees for airport services, i.e. airfield rights and flight protection services.[182] It updates the fees annually by means of a resolution.[183] The fees are determined according to the gross volume of the operation and, for domestic flights only, according to the volume of the goods and the number of passengers using the airport annually.[184] Aerocivil imposes a surcharge on the fees when flights (both domestic and international) operate between 6 p.m. and 6 a.m. (5 per cent surcharge) or outside the times indicated in the Aeronautical Information Publication (surcharge corresponding to 40 times the current legal minimum wage or the equivalent in United States dollars).[185] Flights coming from certain Ecuadorian, Peruvian and Venezuelan airports going to certain Colombian airports are subject to domestic fees.[186]

183. Aerocivil also determines the airport taxes in the airports it owns, but does not collect them. The airlines are responsible for collecting this tax.[187] Between 2007 and 2011, airport taxes gradually rose from Col$3,700-10,000 to Col$4,500-12,000 for domestic routes and US$33 to US$35 for international routes.[188] Passengers boarding at certain Colombian airports going to certain Ecuadorian, Peruvian and, up to 2010, Venezuelan airports pay a preferential international airport tax.[189] Airlines receive a commission for collecting the airport tax provided that they transfer the amounts collected within the time-limits determined by Aerocivil.[190] The commission for collecting the airport tax is 6 per cent for international tax not included in the ticket price, and 3 per cent when it is included; and 5 per cent for domestic flights.

---

[179] Decree No. 1.016 of 2000, Article 13, and online information from the Ports and Transport Supervisory Authority. "Our Institution: *Superintendencia Delegada de Concesiones.*" Viewed at: http://www.supertransport.gov.co/super/index.php?option=com_content&view=article&id=181&Itemid=193&lang=en.

[180] Olivera *et al.* (2011).

[181] Online information from the Bogotá Chamber of Commerce, "*Resultados de la encuesta de servicios del Aeropuerto El Dorado realizada por la CCB*", 29 January 2010. Viewed at: http://www.ccb.org.co/contenido/sala_prensa.aspx?catID=569.

[182] Ministry of Transport, Decree No. 260 of 2004, Article 5, and Aerocivil, Resolution No. 318 of 2011.

[183] Online information from Aerocivil, "*Normatividad: Resolución*". Viewed at: http://portal.aerocivil.gov.co/portal/page/portal/Aerocivil_Portal_Internet/normatividad.

[184] Category A: international airports (over 300,000 passengers); category B: 50,000-300,000 passengers; and category C: fewer than 50,000 passengers (Decree No. 1.647 of 1994, Article 1). See also Aerocivil, Resolution No. 318 of 2011, Article 1.

[185] Aerocivil, Resolution No. 318 of 2011, Articles 6 and 8.

[186] Aerocivil, Article 7.

[187] Aerocivil, Resolution No. 6.251 of 2008, Article 3.

[188] Aerocivil, Resolutions No. 317 of 2007, Articles 10 and 11, and No. 318 of 2011, Articles 10 and 11.

[189] Aerocivil, Resolutions No. 228 of 2010, Article 10, and No. 318 of 2011, Articles 10 and 11.

[190] Aerocivil, Resolution No. 6.251 of 2008, Article 12.

184. In private airports or those under a concession, Aerocivil only collects the flight protection service fee. The airfield rights and the airport taxes are paid directly to the owner or holder of the concession provided that Aerocivil has previously approved the rates.[191]

185. Aerocivil allocates slots. An airline which has used at least 85 per cent of its slots may opt for renewal. If two airlines are competing for the same slot, preference will be given to the airline already operating this slot on other days of the week or to the airline that has complied most faithfully with its slots. Aerocivil's air transport office may authorize airlines to exchange slots.[192] Pursuant to Resolution No. 07466 of 22 December 2011, priority when allocating slots will be given to scheduled flights that have to operate in accordance with a particular itinerary, and 80 per cent of the slots will be reserved for these.

186. When buying an air ticket, the passenger pays a series of taxes and charges which include the airport tax, VAT, the fuel surcharge and the administrative fee. Some passengers, however, are exempt from payment of airport taxes (for example, passengers in transit, diplomats, crew members).

187. Since 2003, Aerocivil has regulated the collection of the fuel surcharge, which accrues to the airline providing the service.[193] This is mandatory for passenger transport but optional for freight, and for the latter is payable per kilo carried. For passengers, it depends on the type of aircraft used on domestic routes and the distance covered on international routes.[194] Aerocivil determines the surcharge each month and publishes it on its website, in accordance with Resolution No. 3.672 of 8 July 2011.[195] When determining the surcharge, a reference price and the distance covered is taken into account for international routes and, until 2008, this also applied to domestic routes.[196] Since 2008, the technical specifications of the aircraft (turboprop or jet) providing the service have been taken into account for domestic routes rather than the distance covered. Travel agencies collect the fuel surcharge on behalf of airlines through the sale of air tickets.[197] Travel agencies have been compensated by the airlines for the additional costs incurred in collecting the surcharge since 2008. As of July 2009, this compensation amounted to 1 per cent of the amount collected; in August 2008 and July 2009, agencies received 2 per cent.[198]

188. Since 2006, an administrative fee for issuing air tickets has been imposed; this is paid to travel agencies or to the airlines themselves when they sell tickets directly. For international routes, the administrative fee depends on the price of the ticket; in 2006, it was between US$5 and US$27, rising to US$15-US$95 from 2009 onwards. For domestic routes, the rate was Col$40,037 until 31 March 2012, irrespective of the cost of the ticket.[199] This amount is adjusted annually according to the variation in the CPI.

189. Passengers taking international flights from Colombian airports must also pay national stamp duty and an exit tax in addition to the fuel surcharge and the administrative fee, with some

---

[191] Aerocivil, Resolution No. 318 of 2011, Article 17.

[192] Colombian Aviation Regulations, Part III.

[193] Aerocivil, Resolution No. 839 of 2003. This is currently governed by Resolution No. 3.897 of 31 August 2005 for international freight and by Resolution No. 2.941 of 27 June 2008 for passengers.

[194] OECD (2011).

[195] Online information from Aerocivil, "*Normatividad: Resoluciones*". Viewed at: http://portal.aerocivil.gov.co/portal/page/portal/Aerocivil_Portal_Internet/normatividad.

[196] Aerocivil, Resolutions No. 2.941 of 2008, Articles 2-4, and No. 897 of 2005, Article 1.

[197] Aerocivil, Resolution No. 3.422 of 2008.

[198] Aerocivil, Article 1.

[199] Aerocivil, Resolution No. 3.596 of 2006, Article 3.

exceptions.[200] The national stamp duty is paid by Colombians and foreigners resident in Colombia leaving Colombian territory. The Government determines the amount annually by decree and it is collected by the airlines.[201] The national stamp duty is currently US$34.[202] The exit tax is paid at the airport by all passengers leaving Colombia (US$33 for stays of less than two months and double for longer visits). Some airlines, however, include it in the cost of the air ticket.[203]

190. Since 2006, with some exceptions, foreign passengers arriving in Colombia have had to pay a tourism tax. During the period under review, this tax rose from US$5 to US$10 from 2009 onwards. It will be US$15 from 2012 onwards. The airlines collect this tax and pay it to the Ministry of Finance and Public Credit each quarter.[204]

191. Any Colombian or foreign legal person planning to provide airport ground handling services for arrivals, parking and departures of aircraft, persons, goods or baggage, as well as for their handling or dispatching or transit maintenance and other facilities required at airports by operators of Colombian or foreign aircraft flying to or from Colombia, must apply for and obtain the corresponding operating permit from Aerocivil in the Ministry of Transport. There are minimum capital requirements for obtaining the permit, which vary according to the service to be provided.[205] Colombian or foreign commercial air services companies may receive, dispatch and maintain their own aircraft without obtaining a special permit from Aerocivil when this is covered by their operating specifications. The supply of such services to other companies or aircraft requires compliance with the criteria laid down. Since 2009, Aerocivil has issued permits for five years, with automatic renewal.[206] Prior to this, renewal was not permitted and the period for providing the service was three years.[207] Where the supply of ground services includes the dispatch of aircraft, dispatchers must be Colombian nationals unless a special exemption is given.[208] These authorizations are contained in the operating specifications and/or general operating manual for the respective airline.

(iv) Maritime transport and ports

(a) Maritime transport

192. In Colombia, three ministries are responsible for maritime transport: the Ministry of Defence, the Ministry of Transport and MCIT. The Ministry of Transport is in charge of formulating and adopting policies, plans, programmes, projects and economic regulation relating to transport, transit and infrastructure for modes of transport, and technical regulations on transport and transit in Colombia.[209] The General Maritime Directorate (DIMAR) under the Ministry of Defence is responsible for implementing maritime transport policy and for overseeing and controlling such

[200] OECD (2011).

[201] Aerocivil, Resolution No. 6.251 of 2008, Articles 2 and 3.

[202] Online information from the Colombian Association of International Airlines, "*Guía al pasajero: Impuestos*". Viewed at: http://alaico.org/2010/www/interna.php?id=102. Resolution No. 11.963 of 17 November 2011 and Law No. 1.111 of 27 December 2006.

[203] Online information from Experiencia Colombia, "*Impuestos turísticos*". Viewed at: http://www.experienciacolombia.com/impuestos-turisticos.php?Colombia.

[204] Law No. 1.101 of 2006, Article 4.

[205] Colombian Aviation Regulations, Part III, paragraphs 3.7.2 and 3.7.3. Viewed at: http://portal.aerocivil.gov.co/portal/pls/portal/!PORTAL.wwpob_page.show?_docname=29219721.PDF.

[206] Colombian Aviation Regulations, Part III, paragraphs 3.7.2 and 3.7.3.

[207] WTO (2006).

[208] Colombian Aviation Regulations, Part III, paragraph 3.7.3.1.1.

[209] Decree No. 087 of 17 January 2011, and online information from MCIT, "*Normatividad Servicios de transporte*". Viewed at: https://www.mincomercio.gov.co/publicaciones.php?id=14803.

activities.[210] The Ports and Transport Supervisory Authority, a body attached to the Ministry of Transport, has the task of inspecting, supervising and controlling the supply of the public transport service, its infrastructure and services.[211] MCIT's main task in relation to maritime transport is to provide leadership, coordinate with the other competent authorities and participate in the relevant international negotiations as maritime transport services are included in the WTO services sectoral classification list.

193. Colombia's current legislation has been in force since 2001 and provides that access to the maritime transport market is subject to the principle of reciprocity.[212] If there is no reciprocity, the Ministry of Transport, in cooperation with DIMAR and MCIT, is empowered to restrict in full or in part access to Colombia's maritime transport market.[213] When assessing the need to impose measures, the Ministry of Transport must take into account "Colombia's international trade interests".[214] The authorities have indicated that Colombia did not restrict access to its international maritime transport market during the period under review.

194. At the regional level, if third countries impose restrictions or discriminate against maritime transport companies belonging to CAN members, they in turn may, jointly, restrict access to international maritime traffic for companies established in the countries imposing the restrictions.[215] The authorities have indicated that there was no such occurrence during the period under review.

195. Cabotage maritime transport is restricted to Colombian-registered vessels. Nevertheless, if no vessel is available or suitable, DIMAR may authorize the chartering or leasing of a foreign-registered vessel for certain services.[216] The authorities have indicated that no preference is given to a particular registration. The concept of national registration extends to CAN countries on the basis of reciprocity. Currently, foreign-registered vessels account for 10 per cent of total cabotage traffic, given that such services are infrequent. For the purposes of this Review, the authorities have indicated that there has been an increase in the number of exceptions to the cabotage restrictions.

196. There has been no change to the procedure for registering a vessel in Colombia since 2001, when the current legislation came into force. Only the owners of vessels are authorized to register them and must be natural or legal persons established in Colombia.[217] Registration may be either permanent or temporary. Temporary registration is for a maximum of six months and is granted while the permanent registration procedure is being completed.[218] After six months have elapsed following temporary registration, the documentation required for definitive registration must be completed; if this is not the case, registration is rejected. There is no fee for temporary registration, but the fee for permanent registration depends on the vessel's tonnage, pursuant to Resolution No. 0129 DIMAR-DIGEN of 6 May 2008. Registration applications are made to the port authorities where the register is kept. In the case of temporary registration alone, applications may be made

[210] Decree-Law No. 2.324 of 1984, Articles 4 and 5.

[211] Online information from the Ports and Transport Supervisory Authority. Viewed at: http://www.supertransporte.gov.co/super/index.php?option=com_content&view=article&id=180&Itemid=192&lang=en.

[212] Decree No. 804 of 2001, Article 46.

[213] Decree No. 804 of 2001, Article 49.

[214] WTO (2006).

[215] CAN, Decision No. 390 of 1996, Article 4.

[216] Decree No. 3.887 of 2008, Article 1.

[217] Commercial Code (Decree No. 410 of 1971), Article 1.458, and Law No. 730 of 2001, Article 2.

[218] Law No. 730 of 2001, Articles 17 and 20, and information provided by the Colombian authorities.

to DIMAR.[219] Registration is issued by DIMAR. Both Colombian and foreign vessels may be registered; once the latter have been registered, they become Colombian vessels.[220] The following must also be registered: the purchase, sale and building of vessels; mortgage deeds, encumbrances and impoundment; financial leasing; and charter of a vessel.[221]

197. Colombian and foreign international maritime transport companies, as well as Colombian cabotage companies, must have authorization and an operating permit issued by DIMAR; for non-scheduled transport of passengers or cargo, a special operating permit is given. Authorization and operating permits, as well as special operating permits, are given for all types of transport: international or cabotage; passenger; or combined cargo and passenger transport. The authorization and operating permit are for an indefinite term, provided that the company respects the conditions originally required for their granting; permits, including special permits, may not be transferred. In order to obtain any type of permit to operate in Colombia, foreign shipping companies must have a shipping agent in Colombia, as required by the Commercial Code.[222] Colombia currently has 215 international maritime transport shipping companies (including operators and non-operators), of which 98 are Colombian and carry only 2 per cent of Colombia's international maritime traffic. The total number of maritime transport companies (national and international) is over 600.

198. DIMAR applies a controlled freedom regime for international maritime transport rates, but neither regulates nor fixes them. International maritime transport and cabotage companies determine their own rates and freight charges, but must inform DIMAR of these, which registers them and may, either ex officio or at the request of parties, revise them or object to them.[223] Domestic maritime transport rates are controlled by the Ministry of Transport and the Ports and Transport Supervisory Authority (see below). Cabotage freight rates are set by the shipping companies themselves by tonne (or kilo), by port and by product.[224]

199. Colombian international maritime transport companies are authorized to join liner conferences. Liner conferences which include Colombian ports are open and also allow the parties to adjust their rates independently.[225] These must be registered with DIMAR and the rates communicated to it.[226] The conferences must appoint a representative domiciled in Colombia and accredited by DIMAR. The latter may reject a liner conference registration if its provisions involve practices that are contrary to Colombia's competition policy; if there is no reciprocity for Colombian enterprises from the other signatory countries; or if the supply of services to or from Colombian ports is prohibited.[227] Five liner conferences are currently registered[228], four fewer than in 2007, and they carry 80 per cent of Colombia's international maritime traffic.

200. Charter, association or tie-in contracts for Colombian-registered vessels signed by companies domiciled in Colombia, as well as contracts for vessel repair or maintenance services, are exempt

[219] Decree No. 730 of 2001, Article 17.

[220] Commercial Code (Decree No. 410 of 1971), Articles 1.437 and 1.439.

[221] Law No. 730 of 2001, Article 13.

[222] WTO (2006).

[223] Decree No. 804 of 2001, Articles 11, 41 and 42.

[224] Decree No. 804 of 2001, Article 43.

[225] Allowing the free entry or withdrawal of Colombian companies (Decree No. 804 of 2001, Articles 36 and 39).

[226] Decree No. 804 of 2001, Articles 36, 38 and 42.

[227] Online information from MCIT, "*Normatividad: Servicios de transporte*". Viewed at: https://www.mincomercio.gov.co/publicaciones.php?id=14803.

[228] Online information from DIMAR, "*Zona de Consultas y Descargas: Conferencias marítimas*". Viewed at: http://www.dimar.mil.co/VBeContent/newsdetailmore.asp?id=1288&idcompany=146.

from the fiscal stamp duty.[229] There is no VAT on registration or payment of flag registration of vessels.[230]

201. There are nationality requirements for the crews of Colombian-registered vessels. The captain, officers and 80 per cent of the rest of the crew of Colombian-registered vessels must be of Colombian nationality.[231] Nationals of CAN member countries are exempt from this requirement and are regarded as Colombians.

202. Any foreign-registered vessel arriving in a Colombian port must have a shipping agent accredited by DIMAR, who represents the shipowner in Colombia.[232] There are no nationality restrictions for shipping agents, although there is an establishment requirement for the company representing them in Colombia, which has to have a commercial operating licence from DIMAR. In Colombia, foreign-registered vessels are not authorized to provide port services in Colombian waters. DIMAR may, however, authorize them to supply such services for a renewable period of six months, but it may not exceed one year, if there are no suitable Colombian vessels.[233]

(b) Ports

203. The Comprehensive Plan for the Physical, Port and Environmental Infrastructure of Coastal Zones lists eight main port areas: Barranquilla, Buenaventura, Cartagena, Santa Marta, Morrosquillo Gulf, La Guajira, San Andrés Island and Tumaco.[234] The Plan has also identified the potential of Urabá Gulf as a major port.[235]

204. The State owns five major ports (Barranquilla, Buenaventura, Cartagena, Santa Marta and Tumaco). Law No. 1 of 1991 determined the legal framework for private sector participation in the management, development and construction of maritime ports. In implementation of this Law, in 1993 the ports belonging to the State and operated by the Colombian ports company (Colpuertos) were handed over to regional port companies (SPR) under a concession for a period of 20 years. Consequently, the construction, maintenance and management of both public and private ports is currently the responsibility of port companies under a 20-year concession regime. Nevertheless, if a port company requires more than 20 years to recover the value of its initial investment or if it makes new investments, a concession for a longer period may be granted, but may not exceed 30 years.

205. The Ministry of Transport is responsible for Colombia's port infrastructure, but any plan for port expansion must be approved by CONPES. In the case of port concessions, the latter is the highest body if there is opposition. CONPES may reject a plan for reasons of national interest, because of the impact on port costs or on the competitiveness of exports, for geographical or strategic reasons, or because of its potential impact on prices for Colombian consumers. Once CONPES has approved a plan, it is adopted by regulatory decree. Through these plans, the Ministry defines the port

[229] Law No. 730 of 2001, Article 30.

[230] *Idem.*, Article 32.

[231] Decree-Law No. 2.321 of 1984, Article 99.

[232] Commercial Code (Decree No. 410 of 1971), Articles 1.455 and 1.489-1.494.

[233] Decree No. 1.423 of 1989, Article 38. DIMAR, press release of 31 August 2011. Viewed at: http://www.dimar.mil.co/VBeContent/library/documents/DocNewsNo5512DocumentNo9233.PDF.

[234] The major port areas are geographical areas in the coastal zone where there is the highest density of port structure existing or being developed, or where future ports are planned. The major port areas are: Barranquilla, Buenaventura, Cartagena, Morrosquillo Gulf, Guajira, San Andrés Island, Santa Marta, Tumaco and Urabá Gulf.

[235] CONPES (2009b).

investment required to facilitate trade and lower port costs which affect the competitiveness of Colombian products.[236] In 2009, CONPES approved a 2009-2011 port expansion plan providing for investment of Col$551,105 million to upgrade access routes to ports.[237] This was the only port expansion plan approved during the period under review. In 2007, however, other CONPES policies were implemented to make Colombia's ports more efficient; this is part of the initiative to facilitate trade and improve the Colombian economy's competitiveness.[238] In view of the importance of coal as an export, in 2008 a strategy was implemented to increase capacity at certain maritime ports for the transport of coal.[239]

206. Port companies operating in private ports are free to determine their rates, but must communicate them to the Delegated Supervisory Authority for Ports.[240] In order to be granted a concession, the applicant must set up a port public limited company, with the building, operation and management of ports, *inter alia*, as its corporate purpose. Capital may be private, public or mixed.

207. In the case of Government-owned ports operated under a concession, port companies' rates are determined according to the requirements adopted by the Ministry of Transport in 1993 under a regime of controlled freedom to determine rates. Rates must be competitive, cover the costs of the port company and allow it to be profitable, and must be registered with the Ports and Transport Supervisory Authority. The same rates are charged for import, export or cabotage. They are registered with the Delegated Supervisory Authority for Ports, published twice yearly in two national newspapers and adjusted every two years.[241] The Supervisory Authority may reject the rates and request that they be modified if they do not comply with the requirements laid down or are 25 per cent higher than the "competitive rate" it has determined for each port company.[242] Nevertheless, if it is decided that the number of port companies is sufficient and the infrastructure so permits, freedom to set rates may be authorized.[243]

208. The concession regime requires all port companies to pay an offset to the State (80 per cent) and to the municipality where the port is located (20 per cent) for the use and exploitation of public areas.[244] An additional offset is paid to the State if the port for which the concession is granted already has infrastructure.[245] The offsets are calculated according to a formula defined in the port expansion plans.[246] During the period under review, the calculation methodology established in 1993 did not change.[247] In 2008 and 2010, however, two new methodologies were introduced to calculate the value of the offsets for those regional port companies which renegotiated their concession contracts (Barranquilla, Buenaventura and Santa Marta) or for companies managing coal ports.[248] These offsets are fixed in United States dollars. The offsets accruing to the State, which amounted to

[236] Law No. 1 of 1991, Article 2.
[237] CONPES (2009b).
[238] CONPES (2007, 2008c and 2008d).
[239] CONPES (2008b).
[240] Law No. 1 of 1991, Article 19.
[241] Ministry of Transport, Resolution No. 723 of 1993, Articles 10, 13 and 14.
[242] For further details on calculation of the rates, see Ministry of Transport, Resolution No. 723 of 1993, Article 14.
[243] Law No. 1 of 1991, Article 20.
[244] Decree No. 856 of 2003, Article 1. In the case of the port at San Andrés, 20 per cent is paid to the department as there is no municipality on the island.
[245] CONPES (2009b).
[246] Decree No. 856 of 2003, Article 1.
[247] For further details, see CONPES (1993), "Annex C".
[248] For further details, see Decree No. 1.873 of 2008 and CONPES (2010b).

US$17 million in 2009, are paid to the National Highways Institute (INVIAS), which is responsible for maintaining land and river access routes to ports.[249]

209. There has been a steady increase in port traffic since 2007. Almost 500 million tonnes of goods were handled between 2007 and 2010, of which 94 per cent were for foreign trade (Table IV.17). Bulk cargo accounted for 80 per cent of general cargo traffic; over half of this was coal and one quarter petroleum and petroleum products.[250]

Table IV.17
Port traffic, 2007-2010
(Tonnes)

	2007	2008	2009	2010
Foreign trade	106,958,203	115,587,558	111,303,950	131,884,906
Imports	19,695,101	21,309,615	19,478,862	21,938,929
Exports	87,263,102	94,277,943	91,825,088	109,945,977
Cabotage	466,101	393,111	404,540	353,009
International transit	3,734,238	5,606,582	7,480,327	10,659,811
Total	**111,158,542**	**121,587,251**	**118,824,731**	**142,897,726**

Source: Ports and Transport Supervisory Authority (2010), *Movimiento de carga por los puertos de Colombia: Informe Consolidado Año 2009*, April. Viewed at: http://www.supertransport.gov.co/super/index.php?option=com_phocadownload&view=category&id=177&Itemid=375&lang=en; Ports and Transport Supervisory Authority (2011), *Movimiento de carga en los puertos marítimos colombianos: Informe Consolidado Año 2010*, January. Viewed at: http://www.supertransport.gov.co/super/phocadownload/Estadisticas/Puertos/Informe Consolidado%202010%20Definitivo_1.pdf; and information provided by the Colombian authorities.

(v) Tourism

210. In 2010, hotel and restaurant services accounted for 2.7 per cent of GDP, and in December 2011 the number of persons employed in the trade, hotels and restaurants sector (12-month average) was 5.5 million. There were almost 2.5 million visitors to Colombia in 2010 (2 million in 2006), who generated US$2.7 billion in revenue (US$2 million in 2006).[251]

211. Law No. 300 of 1996 or the General Tourism Law regulates Colombia's tourism sector. It underscores the importance of tourism for Colombia's economic and social development.[252]

212. MCIT has formulated tourism policies, advised by the National Tourism Committee since 2011.[253] It also coordinates the preparation of the Sectoral Tourism Plan (PST) with the National Planning Department and regional authorities. Subject to acceptance by CONPES, the PST is incorporated into the National Development Plan, which sets out the guidelines for government policy.[254] Since 2006, MCIT has submitted a PST for the period 2008-2010 and has proposed another covering the period 2011-2014 called "Tourism: factor of prosperity for Colombia". The 2008-2010 PST proposes strategies to make Colombia's tourism products more competitive, focusing, *inter alia*,

[249] CONPES (2009b). Since 2009, INVIAS has not been responsible for access channels to the port of Barranquilla, which are now the responsibility of the Regional Autonomous Corporation of Río Grande de la Magdalena (Cormagdalena) and it therefore received 60 per cent of the offsets; the remaining 40 per cent went to municipalities for reforestation and maintenance of aqueducts and sewage systems (Law 1242 of 2008, Article 64).

[250] Ports and Transport Supervisory Authority (2011) and CONPES (2009b).

[251] Information provided by the authorities and MCIT (2011b).

[252] Law No. 300 of 1996, Article 1.

[253] Decree No. 210 of 2003, Article 1, and MCIT, Resolution No. 557 of 2011.

[254] Law No. 300 of 1996, Article 16.

on improving the quality of tourism services and infrastructure, developing specialized products to be offered, encouraging investment and promoting skills training.[255] The 2011-2014 Plan continues to build on the strategy to improve competitiveness in areas such as reinforcing the national and regional institutional structure, improving the quality of tourism services and destinations, developing human talent in light of tourism demand and generating jobs, upgrading the infrastructure and connectivity, attracting investment, and developing and promoting specialized products, all this within the context of sustainable development of tourism. MCIT has also implemented a tourism quality programme under which it certified 423 providers of tourism services in 2010.

213. Before starting up, suppliers of 13 categories of tourism services must register, on line, in the National Tourism Register kept by the Chambers of Commerce.[256] Only suppliers with establishment certificates and legal representation, as well as a business registration number issued by a Chamber of Commerce, may seek registration in the National Tourism Register. After the application has been received, there are 30 days in which to issue the registration certificate.[257] The information in the Register is available to the public and service providers must update it annually; failure to do so leads to sanctions such as an order to close the establishment, issued by MCIT to the local or municipal magistrate.[258] Both listing in the Register and updating entries are free of charge.[259] By December 2011, the National Tourism Register had 14,727 registrations, most of them tourist accommodation (47 per cent) and travel agencies (28.3 per cent).[260]

214. As of 2013, tourist guides will have to take part in professional training courses in order to update their registration.[261] In addition to being listed in the National Tourism Register, in order to provide services a tourist guide must be in possession of a professional tourist guide permit, which is issued by the Professional Council of Tourist Guides.[262] The formalities for obtaining the permit require the applicant to deposit with the Colombian Agrarian Bank, in the name of the Council, an amount equivalent to 15 current legal daily minimum wages.[263] If an applicant resides outside Bogota, he must also pay a further Col$264,450 for administrative formalities. A professional permit is indefinite.[264] Foreign tourist guides may exercise in Colombia provided that they observe the requirements in Colombian legislation. They must obtain a professional tourist guide permit and be listed in the National Tourism Register. Guides may exercise throughout Colombia; the cost of their services is fixed freely and is not regulated. Foreign travel agencies may establish an agency or subsidiary in Colombia; they must be registered with the Chamber of Commerce and in the Single Tax Register (RUT) and meet the other municipal or local requirements.

---

[255] MCIT and the National Planning Department (2011) and MCIT (2008b).

[256] Law No. 1.101 of 2006, Article 12; and online information from MCIT, "*Registro Nacional de Turismo*". Viewed at: https://www.mincomercio.gov.co/minturismo/publicaciones.php?id=12184.

[257] Decree No. 2.074 of 2003, Articles 4 and 6.

[258] Decree No. 2.074 of 2003, Articles 1 and 11. If the owner changes or the establishment is sold, the Register is updated immediately.

[259] MCIT, Resolution No. 236 of 2005.

[260] Online information from MCIT, "*Estadísticas de turismo*". Viewed at: https://www.mincomercio.gov.co/publicaciones.php?id=16590.

[261] MCIT, Resolution No. 4.896 of 2011.

[262] Decree No. 503 of 2007, Articles 3 and 4.

[263] Online information from MCIT, "*Registro Nacional de Turismo*". Viewed at: https://www.mincomercio.gov.co/minturismo/publicaciones.php?id=12184.

[264] Decree No. 503 of 2007, Article 7.

215. Colombia has 6,928 accommodation facilities listed in the National Tourism Register, of which almost 90 per cent are independent facilities. The major chains present in Colombia are Estelar, Decamerón, Dann, GHL and Royal, which each have 15 facilities.[265]

216. Several incentives are available to investors, as well as to Colombian and foreign tourists in Colombia. Suppliers of ecotourism services (which have been practising since 2003) are exempt from payment of income tax for a period of 20 years, as are the suppliers of hotel services. The latter may remain exempt for 30 years if they provide services solely in hotels built or rehabilitated between 2003 and 2007.[266] Investors may also be eligible for the Vallejo Plan for services and for deductions from payment of taxes and parafiscal contributions granted by the Government in order to encourage business development and job creation.[267] Foreign tourists are also eligible for VAT refunds when buying certain goods[268] and they pay a rate of 10 per cent (instead of 16 per cent) for hotel services.[269] There are also 15 per cent discounts on hotel rates and at least 50 per cent on the cost of entry to Government-owned tourism sites for Colombian and foreign tourists over 62 years of age.[270]

217. Suppliers of 21 categories of tourism services must pay a parafiscal contribution to promote tourism.[271] This contribution has also applied to shopping centres since 2011.[272] It is equivalent to 2.5 per mille of the income of the service provider, with the exception of bars and restaurants for tourists[273], which pay 1.5 per mille, and airlines, which pay US$1 per passenger on international flights going to or coming from Colombia.[274] This contribution is used to finance the Tourism Promotion Fund.[275] In 2010, the total amount of the contribution was Col$23,500 million.[276] The promotion of tourism is also financed by collecting a tourism tax that has been paid by foreign passengers travelling to Colombia on international flights, with some exceptions, since the end of 2006. This revenue goes to programmes to promote tourism implemented through Proexport or the Tourism Promotion Fund, depending whether they are of international or national scope.[277] In 2010, revenue from the tourism tax amounted to Col$16 billion (Col$7 billion in 2008).[278]

218. Municipalities with fewer than 100,000 inhabitants and of considerable cultural value may introduce a "tourism toll" on access routes to tourism sites. This must not exceed the current legal daily minimum wage for public or commercial vehicles and half the current legal daily minimum wage for private vehicles. The funds collected are intended for the conservation of tourism sites.[279] The authorities have indicated that, so far, no tourism tolls have been introduced in Colombia.

---

[265] World Tourism Organization and Iberoamerican General Secretariat (2009).

[266] Proexport (2010b).

[267] Law No. 1.429 of 2010.

[268] Made-up articles and footwear, perfume, leather goods, compact discs, handicrafts, liquor and food, toys, emeralds and hand-made jewellery.

[269] Proexport (2010b).

[270] Law No. 1.171 of 2007 and MCIT, Resolution No. 4.322 of 2011.

[271] Law No. 1.101 of 2006, Article 3, and Decree No. 1.036 of 2007, Article 1.

[272] MCIT, Resolution No. 4.895 of 2011.

[273] Those bars and restaurants situated in certain tourism sites and whose annual invoicing exceeds 500 current monthly minimum wages (MCIT, Resolutions No. 347 and No. 348 of 2007).

[274] Law No. 1.101 of 2006, Article 2, and Decree No. 1.036 of 2007.

[275] Decree No. 1.036 of 2007, Article 2.

[276] MCIT and National Planning Department (2011).

[277] Law No. 1.101 of 2006, Articles 4-6, and Decree No. 1.782 of 2007.

[278] MCIT and National Planning Department (2011).

[279] Law No. 300 of 1996, Article 25.

219. Colombia has signed tourism cooperation agreements with Chile, Cuba, Jamaica, Mexico, Romania and Spain.[280]

[280] Online information from MCIT, "*Documentos internacionales*". Viewed at: https://www.mincomercio.gov.co/minturismo/publicaciones.php?id=12190.

REFERENCES

Bank of the Republic (2011a), *Informe sobre Inflación* (Inflation report), September. Viewed at: http://banrep.gov.co/documentos/publicaciones/inflacion/2011/septiembre.pdf.

Bank of the Republic (2011b), *Reporte de Mercados Financieros: Tercer trimestre de 2011* (Financial markets report: Third quarter of 2011), October. Viewed at: http://banrep.gov.co/documentos/informes-economicos/pdf/Reporte%20de%20Mercados_jul-sep_2011.pdf.

Bank of the Republic (2011c), *Reporte sobre Estabilidad Financiera* (Financial stability report), September. Viewed at: http://banrep.gov.co/documentos/publicaciones/report_estab_finan/2011/septiembre.pdf.

World Bank (2005), *Reporte de evaluación del sistema de adquisiciones públicas Colombiano* (Colombian public procurement system assessment report). Viewed at: http://www.wds.worldbank.org/external/default/WDSContentServer/WDSP/IB/2005/08/08/000160016_20050808170408/Rendered/PDF/332600CO0CPAR01090August1501public1.pdf.

Colombian Chamber of Infrastructure (CCI) (2009), *Conectividad: Gestión en Infraestructura Aeroportuaria* (Connectivity: Airport infrastructure management), November. Viewed at: http://www.infraestructura.org.co/PRESENTACIONESCONGRESOCCI/SEXTO/JUEVES/fernando%20sanclemente.pdf.

Bogotá Chamber of Commerce (undated), *Instrumentos de promoción de exportaciones* (Export promotion instruments). Viewed at: http://camara.ccb.org.co/documentos/3725_instrumentos promociondeexportaciones.pdf.

Communications Regulatory Commission (CRC) (2010), *Análisis del sector TIC en Colombia: Evolución y Desafíos* (Analysis of the ICT sector in Colombia: Development and challenges), December. Viewed at: http://www.crcom.gov.co/?idcategoria=56571#.

National Economic and Social Policy Council (CONPES) (1993), *Plan de expansión portuaria 1993-1995* (Port expansion plan 1993-1995), CONPES document No. 2680, November. Viewed at: http://biblioteca.dnp.gov.co/.

CONPES (1994), *Reordenamiento Institucional y Plan de Expansión del Sistema Aeroportuario* (Institutional reorganization and airport system expansion plan), CONPES document No. 2727. Viewed at: http://www.dnp.gov.co/Portals/0/archivos/documentos/Subdireccion/Conpes/2727.pdf.

CONPES (2002), *Una Política de Estado para la Transparencia y Eficiencia en la Contratación Pública* (A State policy for transparency and efficiency in government procurement), CONPES document No. 3186, July. Viewed at: http://biblioteca.dnp.gov.co/.

CONPES (2003), *Política de Contratación Pública para un Estado Gerencial* (Government procurement policy for a managerial State), CONPES document No. 3249, October. Viewed at: http://biblioteca.dnp.gov.co/.

CONPES (2004), *Optimización de los instrumentos de desarrollo empresarial* (Optimization of business development instruments), CONPES document No. 3280, April. Viewed at: http://www.dnp.gov.co/Portals/0/archivos/documentos/Subdireccion/Conpes/3280.pdf.

CONPES (2007), *Lineamientos para el control de la mercancía y la seguridad en los nodos de transferencia de comercio exterior* (Guidelines for merchandise control and safety in foreign trade transfer nodes), CONPES document No. 3469, April. Viewed at: http://www.dnp.gov.co/Portals/0/archivos/documentos/Subdireccion/Conpes/3469.pdf.

CONPES (2008a), *Bases de un plan de acción para la adecuación del sistema de propiedad intelectual a la competitividad y productividad nacional 2008-2010* (Basis for an action plan to align the intellectual property system with national competitiveness and production), CONPES document No. 3533, July. Viewed at: http://www.dnp.gov.co/Portals/0/archivos/documentos/Subdireccion/Conpes/3533.pdf.

CONPES (2008b), *Estrategia para la optimización y modernización del transporte de carbón por los puertos marítimos del municipio de Ciénaga y la bahía de Santa Marta* (Strategy for optimizing and modernizing the transportation of coal via seaports in the municipality of Ciénaga and the bay of Santa Marta), CONPES document No. 3540, August. Viewed at: http://www.imcportal.com/contenido.php?option=shownews&newsid=2848&render=page.

CONPES (2008c), *Política Nacional de Competitividad y Productividad* (National competitiveness and productivity strategy), CONPES document No. 3527, June. Viewed at: http://www.dnp.gov.co/Portals/0/archivos/documentos/Subdireccion/Conpes/3527.pdf.

CONPES (2008d), *Política Nacional Logística* (National logistics policy), CONPES document No. 3547, October. Viewed at: http://www.dnp.gov.co/Portals/0/archivos/documentos/Subdirección/Conpes/3547.pdf.

CONPES (2009a), *Importancia Estratégica del Proyecto "Aeropuerto del Café"* (Strategic importance of the "Coffee Airport" project), CONPES document No. 3586, 11 May. Viewed at: http://www.dnp.gov.co/Portals/0/archivos/documentos/Subdireccion/Conpes/3586.pdf.

CONPES (2009b), *Plan de Expansión Portuaria 2009-2011: Puertos para la competitividad y el desarrollo sostenible* (Port expansion plan 2009-2011: Ports for competitiveness and sustainable development), CONPES document No. 3611, September. Viewed at: http://www.dnp.gov.co/LinkClick.aspx?fileticket=FryOzFAHAzY%3D&tabid=907.

CONPES (2010a), *Fortalecimiento de la estrategia del Estado para la prevención y atención de controversias internacionales de inversión* (Reinforcement of the State's strategy for preventing and tackling international investment disputes), CONPES document No. 3684, October. Viewed at: http://www.dnp.gov.co/LinkClick.aspx?fileticket=3K9mgifm1wo%3d&tabid=1063.

CONPES (2010b), *Metodología para la determinación de la contraprestación económica aplicable a los puertos carboníferos* (Methodology for determining economic compensation applicable to coal ports), CONPES document No. 3679, July. Viewed at: http://www.dnp.gov.co/LinkClick.aspx?fileticket=u9q5-oQjMOU%3d&tabid=1063.

Office of the Comptroller General of the Republic (2009), *Zonas francas: herramientas para el desarrollo productivo* (Free zones: Tools to develop production), 31 August. Viewed at: http://200.93.128.205/c/document_library/get_file?&folderId=15848373&name=DLFE-21153.pdf.

National Planning Department (2010a), *Guía Metodológica para el Seguimiento de las Empresas Industriales y Comerciales del Estado* (Methodological guide for the monitoring of State industrial and commercial enterprises), August. Viewed at: http://www.dnp.gov.co/LinkClick.aspx?fileticket=_PufGF4M4LM%3D&tabid=268.

National Planning Department (2010b), *Plan Nacional de Desarrollo 2010-2014: Prosperidad para Todos* (National development plan 2010-2014: Prosperity for all). Viewed at: http://www.dnp.gov.co/PND/PND20102014.aspx.

Directorate of Taxes and National Customs (DIAN) (2009), *Declaración del impuesto sobre las ventas - IVA* (Sales tax (VAT) declaration). Viewed at: http://www.dian.gov.co/descargas/Formularios/2009/iva_2009.pdf.

Dueñas, R. (2008), *Introducción al sistema financiero y bancario* (Introduction to the financial and banking system), Politécnico Grancolombiano, June. Viewed at: http://crear.poligran.edu.co/publ/00008/SFB.pdf.

Agricultural Sector Financing Fund (FINAGRO) (2012), *Manual de Servicios* (Services manual). Viewed at: http://www.finagro.com.co/html/cache/manual/SIN-MAN-001_MANUAL_DE_SERVICIOS_DE_FINAGRO_CAP_5.doc.

International Monetary Fund (IMF) (2011), *IMF Country Report No. 11/224, Colombia, 2011 Article IV Consultation - Staff Report; Public Information Notice on the Executive Board Discussion; and Statement by the Executive Director for Colombia.* Viewed at: http://www.imf.org/external/pubs/ft/scr/2011/cr11224.pdf.

Gómez Restrepo, H.J., Botiva León, M.A., and Guerra Forero, A.M. (2010), *Institucionalidad y estrategias para el desarrollo exportador y la innovación en Colombia: diagnóstico inicial* (Institutional framework and strategies for export development and innovation in Colombia: Initial diagnosis), ECLAC, March. Viewed at: http://www.eclac.org/publicaciones/xml/2/38982/W294_institucionalidad_estrategias_desarrollo_exportador_Colombia.pdf.

Guerra, M.R. (2009), *Las Tecnologías de la Información y las Comunicaciones y la Competitividad* (Information and communication technologies and competitiveness), Ministry of Information and Communications Technology (MTIC), 29 September. Viewed at: http://www.cccc.com.co/news/wpcontent/uploads/docs/DESAYUNO%20MINCOMUNICACIONES.pdf.

Colombian Agricultural Institute (ICA) (2005), *Guía para Importación y Exportación de Animales, Vegetales y Productos Agropecuarios* (Guide to importing and exporting animals, plants and agricultural products). Viewed at: http://www.ica.gov.co/getattachment/e187d1fc-07b6-4144-a4f0-ba175aa7f650/Publicacion-16.aspx

Institute of Political Science (2009), *Cesión del IVA en licores a cargo de las licoreras departamentales e impuesto al patrimonio* (Elimination of VAT on spirits payable by departmental distilleries, and wealth tax), Bulletin No. 145, November. Viewed at: http://www.icpcolombia.org/archivos/observatorio/boletin_145.

Lizcano Ortiz, C. (2010), *Aspectos regulatorios de TIC en convergencia y el rol de la CRC* (Regulatory aspects of ICT convergence and the role of the Communications Regulatory Commission (CRC)), Communications Regulatory Commission (CRC)), 26 March. Viewed at: http://www.regulatel.org/eventos/2010/IRG/Manaos/SEGUNDO%20DIA/PANEL%202/Christian%20Lizcano.pdf.

Ministry of Agriculture and Rural Development (2010a), *Cartilla Política Agropecuaria 2010-2014* (Agricultural policy primer, 2010-2014). Viewed at: http://www.minagricultura.gov.co/archivos/cartilla_politica_agropecuaria_2010.pdf.

Ministry of Agriculture and Rural Development (2010b), *Reglamento Técnico para la Adjudicación del Incentivo Sanitario para Flores y Follajes* (Technical regulations on the granting of sanitary incentives for flowers and foliage). Viewed at: http://www.minagricultura.gov.co/archivos/reglamento_tecnico.pdf.

Ministry of Agriculture and Rural Development and FINAGRO (2011a), *Guía básica para el empresario afectado por la ola invernal* (Basic guide for producers affected by the cold spell). Viewed at: http://www.minagricultura.gov.co/archivos/guia_empresarios_Ola_Invernal.pdf.

Ministry of Agriculture and Rural Development and FINAGRO (2011b), *Portafolio de Servicios* (Portfolio of services). Viewed at: http://www.finagro.com.co/html/cache/Portafolio_Servicios_2011_2.pdf.

Ministry of Commerce, Industry and Tourism (2003), *El Sistema Generalizado de Preferencias (SGP) de la Federación de Rusia* (The Generalized System of Preferences (GSP) of the Russian Federation), 23 May. Viewed at: https://www.mincomercio.gov.co/descargar.php?id=57993.

Ministry of Commerce, Industry and Tourism (2008a), *Manual de Licencia Previa* (Prior licensing manual). Viewed at: https://www.mincomercio.gov.co/descargar.php?id=24459.

Ministry of Commerce, Industry and Tourism (2008b), *Plan Sectorial de Turismo 2008-2010: Colombia, destino turístico de clase mundial* (Sectoral plan for tourism 2008-2010: Colombia, a world-class tourist destination), June. Viewed at: https://www.mincomercio.gov.co/minturismo/publicaciones.php?id=1313.

Ministry of Commerce, Industry and Tourism (2010), *Manual para presentación de solicitudes de declaratoria de zonas francas* (Manual on submitting applications for the declaration of free zones), June. Viewed at: http://www.dnp.gov.co/PortalWeb/Portals/0/archivos/documentos/DDE/Manual-ZF.pdf.

Ministry of Commerce, Industry and Tourism (2011a), *El turismo en el Plan Nacional de Desarrollo* (Tourism in the national development plan). Viewed at: https://www.mincomercio.gov.co/minturismo/publicaciones.php?id=655.

Ministry of Commerce, Industry and Tourism and National Planning Department (DNP) (2011b), *Plan Sectorial de Turismo 2011-2014: Turismo: factor de prosperidad para Colombia* (Sectoral plan for tourism 2011-2014: Tourism, a factor in Colombia's prosperity), June. Viewed at: https://www.mincomercio.gov.co/minturismo/publicaciones.php?id=657.

Ministry of Finance and Public Credit (2010), *Estrategia económica y fiscal 2010-2014* (Economic and fiscal strategy 2010-2014), November. Viewed at: http://www.minhacienda.gov.co/portal/page/portal/MinHacienda/haciendapublica/politicafiscal/informacionfiscal/marcofiscalmedianoplazo/Libro%20strategiaEconYFiscal.pdf.

Ministry of Finance and Public Credit (2011), *Marco Fiscal de Mediano Plazo 2011* (Medium-term fiscal framework 2011), June. Viewed at: http://www.minhacienda.gov.co/portal/page/portal/MinHacienda/haciendapublica/politicafiscal/informacionfiscal/marcofiscalmedianoplazo/Documento%20MFMP%202011.pdf.

Ministry of Mining and Energy (2011), *Documento de Política: Precios de los Combustibles* (Policy document: Fuel prices). Viewed at: http://www.minminas.gov.co/minminas/downloads/UserFiles/File/hidrocarburos/DOCUMENTO%20GENERAL%20PRECIOS%20DE%20LOS%20COMBUSTIBLES.pdf.

Ministry of Transport (2009), *Memorias al Congreso 2008-2009* (Report to Congress 2008-2009). Viewed at: http://www.mintransporte.gov.co/descargar.php?id=398.

Mondragón, J.C. (2010), *Transformación productiva: la apuesta para el futuro* (Transforming production: an investment for the future), October. Viewed at: http://www.cnzfe.gov.do/documentos/presentacionesconferencia/JuanCarlosMondragon.pdf.

Organization for Economic Cooperation and Development (OECD) (2011), *Competition Issues in the Air Transport Sector: Contribution from Colombia*, Latin American Competition Forum, 13-14 September 2011, Bogotá, 30 August. Viewed at: http://www.oecd.org/officialdocuments/publicdisplaydocumentpdf/?cote=DAF/COMP/LACF%282011%297&docLanguage=En.

Olivera, M., Cabrera, P., Bermúdez, W., and Hernández, A. (2011), *El impacto del transporte aéreo en la economía colombiana y las políticas públicas* (The impact of air transport on the Colombian economy and public policies), Cuadernos Fedesarrollo, No. 34, April. Viewed at: http://www.fedesarrollo.org.co/wp-content/uploads/2011/08/Cuaderno-de-Fedesarrollo-No-34-Final.pdf.

World Trade Organization (WTO) (2006), *Trade Policy Review - Colombia*, Geneva.

World Intellectual Property Organization (WIPO) (2010), *Policies, Measures and Experiences Regarding Intellectual Property and Genetic Resources*, 7 May. Viewed at: http://www.wipo.int/edocs/mdocs/tk/en/wipo_grtkf_ic_16/wipo_grtkf_ic_16_inf_23.pdf.

World Tourism Organization and Ibero-American General Secretariat (2009), *Estudio de la oferta y la demanda de formación de los recursos humanos en el sector turístico en América Latina* (Study on human resource training supply and demand in the Latin American tourism sector), October. Viewed at: http://segib.org/documentos/esp/Informe%20Final%20SEGIB-OMT_051009%5B2%5D.pdf.

PricewaterhouseCoopers and Proexport (2010), *Doing Business and Investing in Colombia*, June. Viewed at: http://www.pwc.com/co/es/doing-business/assets/doing-business-10-en.pdf.

Proexport (2010a), *Sector Agroindustrial Colombiano* (The Colombian agro-industrial sector), December. Viewed at: http://www.inviertaencolombia.com.co/Adjuntos/087_Perfil%20Sector%20Agroindustrial.pdf.

Proexport (2010b), *Turismo en Colombia: una oportunidad de inversión* (Tourism in Colombia: an investment opportunity). Viewed at: http://www.inviertaencolombia.com.co/Adjuntos/086_Brochure%20INV%20Turismo%20ESP-web.pdf.

Proexport, Brigard & Urrutia Lawyers, and Brigard & Castro S.A. (2010), *Guía Legal para hacer Negocios en Colombia* (Legal guide on doing business in Colombia), June. Viewed at: http://www.bu.com.co/BUP/Archivos/guia_legal_para_hacer_negocios_en_colombia.pdf.

Ramos, J. and Rodríguez, K. (2011), *Zonas francas en Colombia: beneficios tributarios en el impuesto de la renta* (Free zones in Colombia: income tax concessions), Borradores de Economía No. 657, Bank of the Republic, May. Viewed at: http://www.banrep.gov.co/docum/ftp/borra657.pdf.

Ríos Plata, J. (2011), *Avances en la implementación del reglamento sanitario internacional* (Progress in the implementation of international health regulations), Ministry of Social Welfare (Port Health Unit), May. Viewed at: http://www.mexico.icao.int/Meetings/CAPSCA/RAMPHT3SCM3/CAPSCA%20Avances%20en%20la%20Implementacion%20del%20RSI%20Aerop.pdf.

Ports and Transport Supervisory Authority (2011), *Movimiento de carga en los puertos marítimos colombianos: Informe Consolidado Año 2010* (Freight handling at Colombian seaports: Consolidated report 2010), January. Viewed at: http://www.supertransporte.gov.co/super/phocadownload/Estadisticas/Puertos/InformeConsolidado%202010%20Definitivo_1.pdf.

Colombian Financial Supervisory Authority (2011), *Actualidad del Sistema Financiero Colombiano* (Current situation of the Colombian financial system), November. Viewed at: http://www.superfinanciera.gov.co/ComunicadosyPublicaciones/comsectorfinanciero112011.pdf.

APPENDIX TABLES

Table AI.1
Merchandise exports (f.o.b.) by product, 2005-2011
(US$ million and per cent)

Description	2005	2006	2007	2008	2009[a]	2010[a]	2011
Total (US$ million)	**21,190**	**24,391**	**29,991**	**37,626**	**32,853**	**39,820**	**56,954**
			(% of exports and re-exports)				
Total primary products	62.3	61.0	58.1	65.8	67.8	72.7	77.6
Agriculture	21.7	20.2	19.5	17.8	18.2	14.5	12.4
Food	17.2	15.8	15.3	14.4	14.8	11.2	10.0
0711 Coffee, not roasted, whether or not decaffeinated; coffee husks and skins	7.0	6.1	5.8	5.1	4.7	4.7	4.6
0573 Bananas (including plantains), fresh or dried	2.4	2.2	1.9	1.7	2.5	1.9	1.4
0612 Other beet or cane sugar and chemically pure sucrose, in solid form	0.8	1.0	0.6	0.3	0.8	0.9	0.9
0713 Extracts, essences and concentrates of coffee and preparations with a basis of these products or with a basis of coffee; coffee substitutes and extracts, essences and concentrates thereof	0.7	0.6	0.5	0.5	0.7	0.6	0.5
0622 Sugar confectionery (including white chocolate), not containing cocoa	0.8	0.8	0.8	0.6	0.7	0.5	0.5
Agricultural raw materials	4.5	4.4	4.3	3.4	3.4	3.3	2.3
2927 Cut flowers and foliage	4.3	4.0	3.7	2.9	3.2	3.1	2.2
Mining	40.6	40.8	38.6	48.0	49.6	58.2	65.2
Ores and other minerals	0.8	1.7	1.7	1.6	1.3	1.2	0.9
Non-ferrous metals	0.5	0.7	0.6	0.4	0.3	0.3	0.3
6812 Platinum and other metals of the platinum group (including metals clad with platinum or other metals of the platinum group), unwrought, unworked or semi-manufactured	0.1	0.1	0.1	0.0	0.1	0.1	0.1
6842 Aluminium and aluminium alloys, worked	0.3	0.3	0.3	0.2	0.1	0.1	0.1
Fuels	39.2	38.4	36.3	46.0	48.0	56.7	64.1
3330 Petroleum oils and oils obtained from bituminous minerals, crude	19.0	18.6	18.5	24.7	24.5	33.6	40.4
3212 Other coal	11.5	11.5	11.1	12.2	16.0	13.9	13.8
334 Petroleum oils and oils obtained from bituminous minerals	7.1	7.3	5.8	7.3	5.8	7.2	8.0
3250 Coke and semi-coke (including char) of coal, of lignite or of peat, whether or not agglomerated; retort carbon	0.7	0.4	0.6	1.2	0.5	1.2	0.9
3432 Natural gas, in the gaseous state	0.0	0.0	0.0	0.4	0.8	0.5	0.6
Manufactures	34.7	35.6	39.2	31.5	27.4	22.0	17.5
Iron and steel	4.9	5.7	6.5	3.3	2.9	3.1	1.9
6715 Other ferro-alloys (excluding radioactive ferro-alloys)	3.5	4.5	5.6	2.3	2.2	2.4	1.5
Chemicals	8.4	8.3	8.0	7.8	8.3	7.1	5.8
5751 Polymers of propylene or of other olefins	0.9	1.0	0.9	0.9	0.7	0.9	0.8
5731 Polyvinyl chloride	0.9	0.9	0.8	0.7	0.7	0.7	0.6
5429 Medicaments, n.e.s.	0.8	0.8	0.7	0.7	0.9	0.6	0.5
Other semi-manufactures	5.9	6.3	6.7	6.3	5.3	3.9	3.1
6429 Articles of paper pulp, paper, paperboard or cellulose wadding, n.e.s.	0.5	0.7	0.7	0.7	0.7	0.5	0.4
6673 Precious stones (other than diamonds) and semiprecious stones, whether or not worked or graded but not strung, mounted or set; ungraded precious stones (other than diamonds) and semiprecious stones	0.3	0.4	0.4	0.4	0.3	0.3	0.2
Machinery and transport equipment	6.0	6.2	7.4	5.0	4.3	3.2	3.0
Power-generating machinery	0.1	0.1	0.0	0.1	0.1	0.1	0.0
Other non-electrical machinery	0.8	0.8	0.8	1.0	1.2	0.6	0.5
Office machines and telecommunications equipment	0.3	0.2	0.1	0.1	0.2	0.1	0.1
Other electrical machinery	1.3	1.6	2.0	1.7	1.6	0.9	0.7
7781 Batteries and electric accumulators, and parts thereof	0.2	0.2	0.3	0.2	0.2	0.2	0.2
7752 Household-type refrigerators and food freezers (electrical and other)	0.4	0.4	0.5	0.5	0.4	0.2	0.1
Automotive products	3.1	3.1	3.8	1.4	0.8	0.9	0.7
7821 Motor vehicles for the transport of goods	0.6	0.3	0.5	0.3	0.2	0.3	0.2

Description	2005	2006	2007	2008	2009[a]	2010[a]	2011
7812 Motor vehicles for the transport of persons, n.e.s.	2.0	2.3	2.6	0.7	0.1	0.2	0.2
Other transport equipment	0.5	0.5	0.6	0.6	0.5	0.6	1.0
7924 Aeroplanes and other aircraft, mechanically-propelled (other than helicopters), of an unladen weight exceeding 15,000 kg	0.0	0.0	0.0	0.0	0.0	0.4	0.9
Textiles	1.7	1.6	2.1	2.3	1.9	1.0	0.9
6552 Other knitted or crocheted fabrics, not impregnated, coated, covered or laminated	0.3	0.3	0.4	0.6	0.5	0.2	0.1
Clothing	4.3	3.9	4.5	3.2	1.8	1.6	1.1
8414 Men's or boys' trousers, bib and brace overalls, breeches and shorts, of textile fabrics, not knitted or crocheted	1.1	0.9	0.8	0.6	0.3	0.3	0.2
Other consumer goods	3.6	3.5	4.1	3.5	2.9	2.0	1.6
8931 Articles for the conveyance or packing of goods, of plastics; stoppers, lids, caps and other closures, of plastics	0.4	0.4	0.4	0.3	0.4	0.3	0.3
8921 Books, pamphlets, maps and globes, printed (not including advertising material)	0.6	0.6	0.6	0.5	0.4	0.3	0.2
Other	3.0	3.4	2.7	2.8	4.8	5.4	4.9
Gold	3.0	3.4	2.7	2.7	4.7	5.3	4.9

a Includes re-exports amounting to US$181 million in 2009 and US$344 million in 2010.

Source: WTO Secretariat estimates based on data from the Comtrade database (SITC Rev.3) and the authorities.

Table AI.2
Merchandise imports (c.i.f.) by product, 2005-2011
(US$ million and per cent)

Description	2005	2006	2007	2008	2009	2010	2011
Total (US$ million)	**21,204**	**26,162**	**32,897**	**39,669**	**32,898**	**40,683**	**54,675**
				(% of imports)			
Total primary products	15.6	16.3	16.5	18.6	17.0	18.2	19.3
Agriculture	10.4	10.3	10.5	11.5	11.5	11.0	10.5
Food	8.7	8.7	9.2	10.1	10.2	9.7	9.3
0449 Other maize, unmilled	1.5	1.8	2.0	2.3	2.0	2.0	1.7
0412 Other wheat (including spelt) and meslin, unmilled	1.1	1.0	1.1	1.3	1.0	0.9	1.0
0813 Oilcake and other solid residues (except dregs), whether or not ground or in the form of pellets, resulting from the extraction of fats or oils from oil-seeds, oleaginous fruits and germs of cereals	0.7	0.7	0.8	1.0	1.1	0.9	0.8
4211 Soya bean oil and its fractions	0.4	0.4	0.4	0.6	0.4	0.5	0.6
0989 Food preparations, n.e.s.	0.5	0.5	0.5	0.4	0.6	0.5	0.4
0371 Fish, prepared or preserved, n.e.s.; caviar and caviar substitutes prepared from fish eggs	0.3	0.3	0.3	0.3	0.4	0.3	0.3
Agricultural raw materials	1.6	1.6	1.4	1.3	1.2	1.4	1.2
2631 Cotton (other than linters), not carded or combed	0.2	0.3	0.2	0.2	0.2	0.3	0.3
Mining	5.2	6.0	6.0	7.1	5.6	7.1	8.8
Ores and other minerals	0.5	0.5	0.6	0.7	0.3	0.3	0.3
Non-ferrous metals	2.1	2.8	2.6	1.9	1.5	1.7	1.4
6824 Copper wire	0.5	0.7	0.8	0.6	0.5	0.6	0.5
6842 Aluminium and aluminium alloys, worked	0.4	0.5	0.5	0.4	0.3	0.3	0.3
Fuels	2.6	2.6	2.8	4.6	3.8	5.1	7.0
334 Petroleum oils and oils obtained from bituminous minerals	1.1	1.9	1.8	1.6	3.8	5.0	6.9
Manufactures	83.2	82.3	82.1	80.2	81.7	80.4	79.6
Iron and steel	5.1	4.8	5.5	6.3	4.5	4.8	5.0
6791 Tubes, pipes and hollow profiles, seamless, of iron or steel	0.4	0.5	0.7	0.8	0.8	0.8	0.9
6793 Other tubes and pipes (e.g., welded, riveted or similarly closed), having internal and external circular cross-sections, the external diameter of which exceeds 406.4 mm, of iron or steel	0.0	0.0	0.1	0.3	0.2	0.1	0.6
Chemicals	20.8	20.0	18.5	18.7	18.6	18.3	16.8
5429 Medicaments, n.e.s.	1.4	1.5	1.4	1.4	1.9	1.6	1.4
5416 Glycosides; glands or other organs and their extracts; antisera, vaccines and similar products	0.5	0.6	0.7	0.7	1.2	1.2	1.0
5111 Acyclic hydrocarbons	1.4	1.5	1.2	1.3	0.7	1.0	0.8
Other semi-manufactures	6.5	6.7	6.5	6.2	6.5	6.5	6.4
6252 Tyres, pneumatic, new, of a kind used on buses or lorries	0.5	0.5	0.4	0.4	0.5	0.5	0.6
6251 Tyres, pneumatic, new, of a kind used on motor cars (including station wagons and racing cars)	0.4	0.4	0.3	0.3	0.3	0.4	0.4
Machinery and transport equipment	40.4	40.2	41.3	39.2	41.8	40.0	40.7
Power-generating machinery	1.3	1.3	1.3	1.4	1.6	1.4	1.2
7165 Generating sets	0.4	0.2	0.2	0.4	0.3	0.4	0.3
Other non-electrical machinery	8.9	8.8	9.8	10.0	10.8	9.6	9.7
7232 Mechanical shovels, excavators and shovel-loaders, self-propelled	0.5	0.6	0.8	1.0	1.2	1.0	1.0
Agricultural machinery and tractors	0.3	0.2	0.3	0.3	0.4	0.2	0.3
Office machines and telecommunications equipment	13.1	12.0	11.2	10.5	9.1	10.1	8.5
7643 Transmission apparatus for radio	5.7	4.8	2.9	2.3	1.2	1.8	1.7
7522 Digital automatic data-processing machines, containing in the same housing at least a central processing unit and an input and output unit, whether or not combined	0.5	0.5	1.0	1.1	1.4	1.5	1.3
7611 Television receivers, colour (including video monitors and video projectors), whether or not incorporating radio-broadcast receivers or sound- or video-recording or reproducing apparatus	1.0	1.1	1.0	1.1	1.3	1.5	1.2

Description	2005	2006	2007	2008	2009	2010	2011
Other electrical machinery	3.1	3.2	3.3	3.2	3.0	3.1	2.8
Automotive products	9.0	11.0	11.8	8.9	7.8	9.7	11.6
7812 Motor vehicles for the transport of persons, n.e.s.	4.1	4.7	5.3	4.1	3.8	5.2	5.1
7821 Motor vehicles for the transport of goods	1.9	3.0	3.0	2.7	2.0	2.4	3.1
Other transport equipment	5.0	3.9	4.0	5.3	9.5	6.1	6.9
7924 Aeroplanes and other aircraft, mechanically-propelled (other than helicopters), of an unladen weight exceeding 15,000 kg	1.9	1.1	0.9	1.9	5.7	3.5	4.4
Textiles	3.4	3.3	3.0	2.5	2.5	2.7	2.8
6513 Cotton yarn, other than sewing thread	0.3	0.4	0.4	0.3	0.2	0.3	0.3
Clothing	0.6	0.6	0.8	0.8	0.9	1.0	1.2
Other consumer goods	6.4	6.7	6.5	6.4	6.9	7.1	6.7
8722 Instruments and appliances used in medical, surgical or veterinary sciences (including sight-testing instruments but excluding electro-diagnostic and radiological instruments and apparatus)	0.5	0.5	0.5	0.5	0.5	0.5	0.5
8996 Orthopaedic appliances (including crutches, surgical belts and trusses); splints and other fracture appliances; artificial parts of the body	0.3	0.3	0.4	0.4	0.5	0.5	0.4
Other	1.2	1.4	1.4	1.2	1.3	1.5	1.1

Source: WTO Secretariat estimates based on data from the Comtrade database (SITC Rev.3) and the authorities.

Table AI.3
Merchandise exports (f.o.b.) by trading partner, 2005-2011
(US$ million and per cent)

Description	2005	2006	2007	2008	2009[a]	2010[a]	2011
Total exports (US$ million)	**21,190**	**24,391**	**29,991**	**37,626**	**32,853**	**39,820**	**56,954**
			(% of exports and re-exports)				
America	77.5	74.2	72.4	76.6	72.3	71.5	70.9
United States	41.8	40.8	35.4	38.0	39.9	43.1	38.5
Other America	35.7	33.4	37.0	38.7	32.3	28.5	32.3
Canada	1.4	1.1	0.9	0.9	1.2	1.3	1.1
Chile	1.4	1.1	1.3	2.3	1.9	2.3	3.9
Panama	1.2	1.1	0.8	0.8	0.9	2.4	3.4
Ecuador	6.3	5.1	4.3	4.0	3.8	4.6	3.4
Bolivarian Republic of Venezuela	9.9	11.1	17.4	16.2	12.3	3.6	3.1
Aruba	0.6	0.9	0.0	0.1	0.1	0.2	3.0
Peru	3.4	2.8	2.7	2.3	2.4	2.8	2.5
Brazil	0.7	0.8	1.6	1.7	1.8	2.6	2.4
Trinidad and Tobago	0.9	0.8	1.1	1.4	1.2	0.6	1.8
Mexico	2.9	2.4	1.7	1.6	1.6	1.6	1.2
Europe	14.7	17.4	18.8	16.0	18.7	15.4	18.6
EU(27)	13.4	14.4	15.2	12.8	14.4	12.6	15.6
Netherlands	2.1	2.1	2.8	2.0	4.1	4.1	4.4
Spain	1.6	2.1	1.9	1.7	1.5	1.4	3.0
United Kingdom	1.5	1.6	1.4	1.8	2.3	1.7	2.1
EFTA	0.8	2.4	3.0	2.6	3.2	2.2	1.7
Switzerland and Liechtenstein	0.7	2.3	3.0	2.5	3.2	2.1	1.7
Other Europe	0.6	0.6	0.5	0.6	1.1	0.7	1.2
Turkey	0.5	0.5	0.4	0.5	1.0	0.5	1.0
Commonwealth of Independent States (CIS)	0.4	0.3	0.3	0.3	0.3	0.3	0.2
Russian Federation	0.3	0.2	0.2	0.2	0.2	0.2	0.2
Africa	0.2	0.4	0.6	0.2	0.5	0.9	0.6
Côte d'Ivoire	0.0	0.0	0.0	0.0	0.0	0.5	0.3
Nigeria	0.0	0.0	0.0	0.0	0.0	0.0	0.1
Middle East	1.1	0.9	0.7	0.6	0.7	0.9	1.3
Israel	0.9	0.8	0.6	0.5	0.5	0.7	1.2
Asia	4.3	5.0	5.3	4.8	6.6	10.3	7.2
China	1.1	1.9	2.6	1.2	2.9	4.9	3.5
Japan	1.6	1.3	1.3	1.0	1.0	1.3	0.9
Six East Asian Traders	1.3	1.4	1.0	2.5	1.0	2.9	1.4
Singapore	0.1	0.1	0.2	1.2	0.3	1.1	0.5
Republic of Korea	0.6	0.8	0.4	0.3	0.3	0.9	0.5
Chinese Taipei	0.4	0.4	0.2	0.9	0.1	0.5	0.2
Hong Kong, China	0.1	0.1	0.1	0.1	0.2	0.2	0.1
Thailand	0.1	0.1	0.0	0.1	0.1	0.1	0.1
Malaysia	0.0	0.0	0.0	0.0	0.0	0.1	0.0
Other Asia	0.3	0.5	0.4	0.2	1.7	1.2	1.5
India	0.0	0.3	0.3	0.0	1.4	0.9	1.3
Australia	0.1	0.1	0.1	0.1	0.1	0.1	0.1
Indonesia	0.0	0.0	0.0	0.0	0.1	0.1	0.1
Other	1.8	1.9	2.0	1.5	0.9	0.6	1.1
Free zones	1.8	1.9	2.0	1.4	0.9	0.5	0.6
Areas not elsewhere specified	1.8	0.0	0.0	0.0	0.0	0.0	0.5

a Includes re-exports amounting to US$181 million in 2009 and US$344 million in 2010.

Source: WTO Secretariat estimates based on data from the Comtrade database (SITC Rev.3) and the authorities.

Table AI.4
Merchandise imports (c.i.f.) by trading partner, 2005-2011
(US$ million and per cent)

Description	2005	2006	2007	2008	2009	2010	2011
Total imports (US$ million)	**21,204**	**26,162**	**32,897**	**39,669**	**32,898**	**40,683**	**54,675**
				(% of imports)			
America	63.3	63.5	60.0	58.8	57.5	56.3	57.8
United States	28.5	26.6	26.2	29.2	28.9	25.9	25.0
Other America	34.9	36.9	33.7	29.6	28.6	30.4	32.8
Canada	1.8	1.9	2.0	2.0	2.1	2.0	1.8
Mexico	8.3	8.8	9.3	7.9	7.0	9.5	11.1
Brazil	6.5	7.2	7.3	5.9	6.5	5.8	5.0
Argentina	1.9	2.2	2.2	2.3	3.2	3.7	3.4
Ecuador	2.5	2.7	2.2	2.0	2.1	2.1	1.9
Peru	1.7	2.0	1.8	1.8	1.9	1.9	1.9
Chile	1.8	2.0	2.0	1.8	1.8	1.8	1.6
Trinidad and Tobago	0.8	0.4	0.9	0.8	0.5	0.9	1.1
Bolivarian Republic of Venezuela	5.7	5.7	4.2	3.0	1.7	0.7	1.0
Europe	15.0	14.5	13.7	14.8	17.1	15.2	14.9
EU(27)	13.8	13.3	12.4	13.5	15.7	14.0	13.7
Germany	3.6	3.6	3.7	3.9	4.1	4.1	4.1
France	1.8	1.6	1.6	2.3	4.6	2.9	3.3
Italy	1.6	1.5	1.6	1.5	1.6	1.6	1.5
EFTA	1.1	1.0	1.1	1.1	1.2	1.1	0.9
Switzerland and Liechtenstein	1.0	1.0	1.0	1.0	1.1	1.0	0.8
Other Europe	0.1	0.1	0.1	0.2	0.2	0.1	0.2
Turkey	0.1	0.1	0.1	0.2	0.1	0.1	0.2
Commonwealth of Independent States (CIS)	0.9	0.7	0.5	0.8	0.8	0.6	0.7
Russian Federation	0.7	0.5	0.3	0.5	0.5	0.4	0.5
Ukraine	0.3	0.2	0.2	0.2	0.1	0.1	0.1
Africa	0.4	0.4	0.4	0.5	0.2	0.2	0.3
South Africa	0.2	0.1	0.1	0.1	0.1	0.1	0.1
Middle East	0.5	0.6	0.6	0.5	0.7	0.8	0.5
Israel	0.5	0.5	0.5	0.4	0.7	0.7	0.3
Asia	18.1	19.8	21.4	21.4	20.6	23.7	25.1
China	7.6	8.5	10.1	11.5	11.3	13.5	15.0
Japan	3.3	3.6	3.7	2.9	2.5	2.8	2.6
Six East Asian Traders	5.1	5.4	5.2	4.9	4.3	4.8	4.7
Republic of Korea	2.8	2.9	2.7	2.3	2.1	2.3	2.3
Chinese Taipei	1.1	1.1	0.9	0.9	0.9	0.8	0.9
Thailand	0.4	0.5	0.6	0.7	0.7	1.0	0.8
Malaysia	0.4	0.5	0.5	0.4	0.3	0.3	0.4
Singapore	0.2	0.2	0.2	0.2	0.2	0.2	0.2
Hong Kong, China	0.2	0.2	0.3	0.3	0.2	0.2	0.1
Other Asia	2.0	2.2	2.3	2.2	2.4	2.5	2.8
India	1.2	1.3	1.4	1.3	1.5	1.7	1.8
Indonesia	0.5	0.5	0.4	0.3	0.3	0.3	0.4
Other	1.7	0.7	3.6	3.2	3.1	3.2	0.9
Free zones	0.6	0.7	3.6	3.2	3.1	3.2	0.9

Source: WTO Secretariat estimates based on data from the Comtrade database (SITC Rev.3) and the authorities.

Table AII.1
Overview of free trade agreements, 1 January 2006 - 12 March 2012

Trade agreements in force	
Colombia-Chile[a]	
Parties	Colombia and Chile
Date of signature/ entry into force	27 November 2006/ 8 May 2009
Transition period for full implementation	2012
Duty-free lines	98.3% (2011) and 100% (2012); the Andean price band system (SAFP) is applied.
Goods-related provisions	Under the tariff elimination programme, Colombia liberalized (0%) 98.9% of tariff lines in 2009 (ACE No. 24). The remaining tariff lines were liberalized on 1 January 2012.[b] Colombia maintains parafiscal contributions in respect of coffee and emeralds, and controls on imports of used and imperfect goods, remains, scrap, waste and residues, and motor vehicles.
Services covered	Yes
WTO document series	WT/REG272
Colombia-Cuba	
Parties	Colombia and Cuba
Date of signature/ entry into force	Second Additional Protocol, 1 February 2008/ Second Additional Protocol, 6 November 2008
Transition period for full implementation	No transition period, this is a Fixed Preferences Agreement.
Duty-free lines (2011)	Some 330 Cuban tariff lines and around 200 Colombian tariff lines have a 100% preference. This is an agreement with fixed tariff preferences.
Goods-related provisions	Supersedes Annex I (Preferences granted by the Republic of Colombia to the Republic of Cuba) and Annex II (Preferences granted by the Republic of Cuba to the Republic of Colombia) of ACE No. 49. Also includes provisions on sanitary and phytosanitary measures, technical standards and conformity assessment procedures, rules of origin, market access (incorporation of new products and broadening of existing preferences) and dispute settlement. The tariff elimination programme covers 1,900 tariff lines, and preferences range from 40% to 100%.
Services covered	No
WTO document series	Not notified to the WTO
Colombia-Northern Triangle of Central America (El Salvador, Guatemala and Honduras)	
Parties	Colombia and El Salvador, Guatemala and Honduras
Date of signature/ entry into force	9 August 2007/ 12 November 2009 (Guatemala) / 1 February 2010 (El Salvador) / 27 March 2010 (Honduras)
Transition period for full implementation	Up to 20 years
Duty-free lines (2011)	64% with El Salvador, 63% with Guatemala and 76% with Honduras
Goods-related provisions	Progressive tariff elimination for agricultural and industrial products (Annexes 3.4 and 3.04). Under the partial scope agreements signed with El Salvador and Honduras in 1984, Colombia continues to grant preferential treatment to 15 tariff lines for El Salvador and 6 tariff lines for Honduras. Colombia maintains parafiscal contributions in respect of coffee and emeralds (Annex 3.11), controls on imports of used goods, vehicles, and coffee exports (Annex 3.3), and actions authorized by the WTO Dispute Settlement Body (Annex 3.3).
Services covered	Yes
WTO document series	Not notified to the WTO
Colombia-Mexico	
Parties	Colombia and Mexico (Protocol to the Agreement between Colombia and Mexico which entered into force on 1 January 1995)
Date of signature/ entry into force	11 June 2010/ 2 August 2011
Transition period for full implementation	2020
Duty-free lines (2011)	Around 95%
Goods-related provisions	Trade liberalization under the original agreement for both parties is around 95% when the full transition period is considered. The Protocol amends/supplements the original agreement and improves market access. In Mexico's case, tariffs are eliminated for a further 57 tariff lines, while in Colombia's case, they are eliminated for 45 tariff lines. The tariff elimination programme varies from immediate elimination upon the entry into force of the agreement, to a maximum transition period of 10 years for other products, which will be exempt from levies by 2 August 2020.

Trade agreements in force	
Services covered	Yes
WTO document series	WT/REG289
Colombia-European Free Trade Association (EFTA)	
Parties	Colombia and Iceland, Liechtenstein, Norway and Switzerland
Date of signature/ entry into force	25 November 2008/ 1 July 2011 (Switzerland and Liechtenstein)[c]
Transition period for full implementation	17 years until 2027
Duty-free lines (2011)	67.41%
Goods-related provisions	Progressive tariff elimination programme for processed agricultural products (Annex III), fishery and other marine products (Annex IV), industrial products (Annex VIII) and agricultural commodities.[d] Preferential treatment and/or reductions applied to the base rate of 5%, 10%, 15% and 20%. Colombia excludes from tariff elimination 84 tariff lines under HS Chapters 29, 33, 35, 38, 41, 43 and 50-53 (Annex II). Colombia maintains parafiscal contributions in respect of coffee and emeralds (Annex IX), controls on imported goods (e.g. import licensing for used, imperfect, repaired, rebuilt or refurbished goods), vehicle imports and coffee exports, and measures relating to the taxation of alcohol (Annex X).
Services covered	Yes
WTO document series	WT/REG299
Colombia-Canada	
Parties	Colombia and Canada
Date of signature/ entry into force	21 November 2008/ 3 August 2011
Transition period for full implementation	2032 (Colombia); 2027 (Canada)
Duty-free lines (2011)	66.89%
Goods-related provisions	Progressive tariff elimination programme for agricultural and industrial products (Annex 203); certain agricultural products are excluded from tariff elimination. Contains an agricultural transversal clause applicable to tariff lines under HS Chapters 02, 07, 17 and 22 (Annex 203). Colombia will eliminate tariffs on beef (high quality, standard quality, offal and entrails) and beans in 12 equal annual stages; certain specific quantities will, however, remain duty-free in any calendar year (Annex 203). Colombia may apply agricultural safeguard measures in the form of an additional tariff (120% or 150% of the tariff quota) to imports of beef (high quality, standard quality, offal and entrails) and beans (Annex 217). Colombia maintains parafiscal contributions in respect of coffee and emeralds (Annex 210), controls on imported goods (e.g. import licensing for used, imperfect, repaired, rebuilt or refurbished goods), vehicle imports and coffee exports, measures relating to the taxation of alcohol, and actions authorized by the WTO Dispute Settlement Body (Annex 202).
Services covered	Yes
WTO document series	WT/REG301
Signed trade agreements	
Colombia-United States	
Parties	Colombia and the United States
Date of signature/ entry into force	22 November 2006/ not in force
Transition period for full implementation	The agreement has not yet entered into force. United States 15 years; Colombia 19 years
Duty-free lines (2011)	73%
Goods-related provisions	Progressive tariff elimination programme for agricultural and industrial products and textiles (Annex 2.3). Colombia may apply agricultural safeguard measures in the form of an additional tariff (120%, 130% or 140% of the tariff quota) to imports of standard quality beef, poultry at the end of its productive cycle, chicken leg quarters, dry beans, and rice (Annex 2.18). Colombia maintains parafiscal contributions in respect of coffee and emeralds (Annex 2.11), controls on imports of used goods and vehicles and coffee exports, measures relating to the taxation of alcohol, and actions authorized by the WTO Dispute Settlement Body (Annex 2.2).
Services covered	Yes
WTO document series	Not notified to the WTO, although a preliminary announcement of the signing of the agreement has been made.

Trade agreements in force	
Colombia-European Union	
Parties	Colombia and the European Union
Date of signature/ entry into force	24 March 2011/ not yet in force
Transition period for full implementation	Mainly 10 years; 17 years for other products
Duty-free lines (2011)	60.7%
Goods-related provisions	Progressive tariff elimination programme for agricultural, industrial and fishery products (Annex 1). Reduction applied to the base rate. Colombia may apply agricultural safeguard measures in the form of an additional tariff (20% of the tariff quota) to imports of tariff lines under HS Chapters 04 and 19 (Annex 4).
Services covered	Yes
WTO document series	Not notified to the WTO

a The Free Trade Agreement (FTA) forms Additional Protocol No. 9 to the Economic Complementarity Agreement (ACE No. 24) between Colombia and Chile which entered into force on 6 December 1993. The FTA annuls Articles 1, 7-9, and 11-40 of ACE No. 24; however, Articles 3-6 and 10, Annexes 1-5, and the additional protocols to ACE No. 24 remain in effect.

b Between September 2004 and August 2006, Colombia suspended concessions granted to Chile (HS subheadings 0808.10.00.00, 0808.20.10.00, 0806.10.00.00, 2106.90.20.10, 2204.21.00.10, 2402.20.20.00 and 8704.21.00.10) in response to the restriction imposed by Chile on sugar and mixtures of sugar from Colombia (Decrees No. 3.146 of 2004, No. 3.234 of 2004 and No. 2.777 of 2006).

c Not ratified by Norway or Iceland.

d Trade in agricultural commodities is covered by complementary agreements to the FTA.

Source: WTO Secretariat based on information from the WTO Regional Trade Agreements Information System, viewed online at: http://rtais.wto.org/UI/PublicMaintainRTAHome.aspx; information from the Ministry of Commerce, Industry and Tourism, "*Comercio Exterior*" (Foreign trade), viewed online at: http://www.mincomercio.gov.co/eContent/minihome.asp?idcompany=7; information from the Ministry of Commerce, Industry and Tourism, "*Tratado de Libre Comercio: Acuerdo Colombia-Cuba*" (Free Trade Agreement: Colombia-Cuba), viewed online at: https://www.mincomercio.gov.co/publicaciones.php?id=1888; information from the Latin American Integration Association (LAIA), "*Integración y Comercio: Acuerdos: Disposiciones de Internalización, Sumarios y Textos: Acuerdos Actuales: Colombia*" (Integration and trade: Agreements: Internalization provisions, summaries and texts: Current agreements: Colombia), viewed online at: http://www.aladi.org/nsfaladi/textacdos.nsf/vpaises/colombia; information from the Organization of American States, "*Foreign Trade Information System: Trade Policy Developments: Andean Countries - European Union*", viewed online at: http://www.sice.oas.org/TPD/AND_EU/AND_EU_e.ASP; WTO document WT/REG289/1 of 9 January 2012; and information provided by the Colombian authorities.

Table AIII.1
Import modalities and other regimes

Import modality	Description
Duty-free importation	Total or partial exemption from customs duties under a treaty, agreement or law. Goods remain in restricted circulation unless otherwise specified in the relevant rules. Where goods are left in free circulation, the importer is required to pay the exempted customs duties.
Reimportation after outward processing	Reimportation of goods exported temporarily for manufacturing, repair or processing; customs duties are payable only on the value added abroad, including costs relating to such operations, for which the rates corresponding to the tariff subheading of the reimported finished product are applied. In cases duly justified before the customs authority, the importation of compensating products (i.e. products obtained abroad or in a free zone during or as a consequence of the manufacturing, processing or repair of goods exported temporarily for outward processing) may be authorized, without requiring the prior exportation of the goods that are to be repaired, processed or manufactured.
Reimportation in the same state	Temporarily or definitively exported goods in free circulation may be imported without paying customs duties provided that they have not been modified abroad, they are clearly the same goods that were exported, the internal taxes have been cancelled and the profits obtained through exportation repatriated (e.g. exemption from income tax through export contracts and tax reimbursement certificates (CERT)). Goods imported in this way remain in free circulation.
Importation under a guarantee	Duty-free importation of goods that have been repaired abroad under a manufacturer's or supplier's guarantee or which replace other previously exported goods that were found to be damaged, defective or unsuitable for the purpose for which they were imported. Free circulation of goods.
Temporary admission for re-exportation in the same state	Suspension of customs duties for certain goods that are to be re-exported within a specified period without having undergone any modification other than normal wear and tear. The circulation of such goods is restricted. Fungible goods cannot be imported under this procedure.
Temporary admission for inward processing	
Temporary admission of capital goods for inward processing	Temporary admission with suspension of customs duties for capital goods, parts and spares that are to be re-exported after repair or overhaul, for a period of no more than six months. The circulation of such goods is restricted. Where there is good cause, the customs authority may authorize an extension to the six-month period for a length of time not exceeding the period initially granted. DIAN decides which goods are subject to this import procedure. In order to ensure re-exportation within the established timeframe, the customs authority requires the lodging of a security amounting to 100% of the customs duties payable on the imported goods.
Temporary admission under the special import-export systems (SIEX)	Admission with total or partial suspension of customs duties for specific goods that are to be exported fully or in part within a certain timeframe after having undergone processing, manufacturing or repair, and the inputs required for such operations. The circulation of goods imported in this way remains restricted. Importers of such goods are required to demonstrate compliance with export commitments.
Temporary admission for industrial processing	Temporary duty-free admission for raw materials and inputs that are to be industrially worked, processed or manufactured by industries recognized as "high export users" or "regular customs users". Goods that have been industrially worked, processed or manufactured by a "high export user" are to be exclusively for export. At least 30% of goods that have been industrially worked, processed or manufactured by "regular customs users" are to be exported.
Importation for processing or assembly	Importation of goods for processing or assembly, by industries recognized for that purpose and authorized by DIAN. The circulation of such goods is restricted.
Postal traffic and urgent shipments	Letter-post items, items arriving in national territory via the official postal network, and urgent deliveries, provided that their value does not exceed US$2,000 and they require rapid delivery to their addressee. Imported goods remain in free circulation.
Urgent deliveries	If necessary, DIAN may authorize, without any prior formality, the direct delivery of certain goods to the importer when admitted as aid for disaster or accident victims or when of a special nature or meeting a pressing need. In the last two cases, the relevant customs duties will be incurred and Customs, where considered appropriate, will require the lodging of a security to guarantee the completion of the relevant import formalities.
Travellers	Travellers entering the country are entitled to bring accompanied baggage of a total value of up to US$1,500, or the equivalent thereof, without an import registration or licence and duty-free. Travellers entering the country having spent a minimum of five calendar days abroad are entitled to bring as accompanied or unaccompanied baggage, without an import registration or licence and upon payment of a one-off duty of 15%, up to three units of each of the following goods: items for domestic use, whether or not electrical; sports equipment; and items pertaining to their activity or occupation, up to a total value of US$2,500 or the equivalent thereof.

Import modality	Description
Special Customs Zones	
Free port of San Andrés, Providencia and Santa Catalina	Imports are duty-free and only liable to a consumption tax of 10% of their c.i.f. value. The Department collects, administers and supervises these revenues. The following are exempt from the tax: food items; building materials; machinery and items used to provide public services in the Department; machinery, equipment and spare parts used to promote local industry and fishing activity; electric generators in non-commercial quantities; medicines; vessels for transporting ordinary or mixed cargo and passengers which operate a scheduled service to the free port; and foreign goods arriving in transit for future shipment to foreign ports. No import registration or licence or any other authorization or certification is required, except when importing alcoholic beverages, which must be accompanied by the relevant health certificate.
Special Customs Zones of the region of Urabá, and of Tumaco and Guapí	Imports entering the zone are only subject to sales tax on the customs value of the goods, upon the presentation and acceptance of a simplified import declaration. No vehicles, household appliances, spirits or cigarettes may be imported under this regime. No import registration or licence, or other permit, authorization or certificate is required.
Special Customs Zones of Maicao, Uribia and Manaure	Imported goods are only subject to an entry tax of 4% of the customs value. Imports of capital goods, machinery, equipment and parts thereof for the construction of public infrastructure and works for economic and social development, and capital goods for establishing new industries or expanding existing ones, for use exclusively within the zone, are exempt from the tax. This regime does not apply to imports of vehicles, which are subject to the relevant customs duties and the ordinary import regime.
Special Customs Zone of Leticia	Imports of consumer goods are exempt from customs duties and import licensing and registration requirements. A simplified import declaration is required under the duty-free modality when the f.o.b. value of the goods exceeds US$1,000.
Inírida - Guainía, Puerto Carreño, La Primavera and Cumaribo	Imports of goods destined for municipalities in the zone will remain exempt from custom duties until 28 October 2015. Sales tax is payable on the customs value of the goods.

Source: Decree No. 2.685 of 26 December 1999 (and amendments thereto) and information provided by the Colombian authorities.

Table AIII.2
Main SPS measures in force

Product	Summary of the measure	Legislative text
Animals (including aquatic animals), products and by-products. External Circular No. 037/11 lists the products subject to this requirement	Animal health import document (*Documento Zoosanitario de Importación* - DZI) valid for 90 days. Physical inspection and issuing of health inspection certificate. The Colombian Agricultural Institute (ICA) is responsible for animal health controls at the point of entry into the country. Resolution No. 3.336/04 establishes the animals and products of animal origin that do not require a DZI	ICA Resolution No. 1.558 of 07/05/10
Animals used for fur; semen and embryos	Prior sanitary import permit issued by the ICA. Animals from countries where exotic diseases are present must comply with pre-quarantine requirements in the country of origin and quarantine requirements upon arrival in Colombia	Ministry of Agriculture Resolution No. 361 of 19/07/84
Terrestrial or aquatic animals and the products thereof or other products posing a risk to the country's animal health	Foreign establishments exporting to Colombia must register with the ICA.	ICA Resolution No. 000004 of 04/01/05
Animals and animal products	Airports, seaports, river ports and border crossings authorized for the importation of these products	ICA Resolution No. 003365 of 09/09/09
Animals, products and by-products	Pest risk analysis	ICA Resolution No. 01277 of 09/06/04
Birds for breeding, first-generation commercial birds and fertile eggs for incubation	Registration of importer and products with the ICA, valid for three years	ICA Resolution No. 3.019 of 17/12/99
Live "spent" poultry	Importation prohibited	ICA Resolution No. 000003 of 04/01/05
Bovine animals, bovine semen and embryos, milk and dairy products, hides and skins, gelatine and collagen, protein-free tallow, dicalcium phosphate, food for cats and dogs, meat and meat products	Specific sanitary requirements	ICA Resolution No. 1.281 of 13/04/10
Meat of bovine animals and products thereof from Canada	Export safety certificate issued by the Canadian Food Inspection Agency (CFIA). Products must be fit for human consumption. Packing, packaging, labelling and transport requirements	Decree No. 3.525 of 15/09/09
Meat of bovine animals, goats, sheep and poultry, and products and by-products thereof	Sanitary inspection in the country of origin conducted by official Colombian veterinarians	ICA Resolution No. 2.418 of 07/09/06
Fresh poultry meat, live poultry, eggs for incubation and consumption, and poultry meat products from Canada	Importation prohibited. ICA Resolution No. 01103 of 09/06/04 provides for a number of exceptions	ICA Resolution No. 00554 of 24/03/04
Fresh poultry meat, live poultry, eggs for incubation and consumption, and poultry meat products from the United States	Importation prohibited. ICA Resolution No. 00957 of 18/05/04 provides for a number of exceptions	ICA Resolution No. 00374 of 27/02/04
Crustaceans and molluscs for human consumption	Importation prohibited unless heat-processed at a temperature of at least 60°C for 30 minutes	ICA Resolution No. 01104 of 10/06/04
Bovine Spongiform Encephalopathy (BSE). Live bovine animals for breeding from Canada	Specific animal health requirements	ICA Resolution No. 003274 of 02/09/09
BSE. Live bovine animals for breeding from the United States	DZI certifying compliance with certain sanitary requirements; quarantine requirements	ICA Resolution No. 002118 of 22/06/2010
BSE. Meat meal, blood meal, steamed bone meal, meat and bone meal and mammalian offal meal	The country of origin must prove the existence and operation of an official system established specifically for the continuous monitoring of BSE	ICA Resolution No. 00991 of 01/06/01
Foot-and-mouth disease. Animals and products from Paraguay capable of transmitting or carrying the virus	Suspension of imports	ICA Resolution No. 3.683 of 20/09/11 (in force until 20/03/12)

Product	Summary of the measure	Legislative text
Foot-and-mouth disease. Animals, products and by-products entering free zones with or without vaccination	Sanitary requirements aimed at preventing the introduction of the virus into the country. Temperature requirements for meat products. Quarantine requirements	ICA Resolution No. 001729 of 20/08/04
Foot-and-mouth disease. Bovine animals, swine and products from Uruguay	Suspension of imports	ICA Resolution No. 00986 of 30/05/01
West Nile fever. Wild and ornamental birds from Spain and Italy	Suspension of imports	ICA Resolutions No. 3.695 and No. 3696 of 21/09/11 (in force until 20/03/12)
Bovine livestock for genetic enhancement	ICA approval	Ministry of Agriculture Resolution No. 0632 de 11/08/92
Eggs and young larvae of silkworms	Certificate issued by the competent body in the country of origin. Registration of importer with the ICA (Articles 2 and 7)	ICA Resolution No. 2.587 of 18/05/93
Ferrets, rabbits, chinchillas, hamsters, guinea pigs and gerbils	Official health certificate issued in the country of origin. Animal health import document issued by the ICA. Sanitary inspection before entry into Colombian territory. Post-entry quarantine	ICA Resolution No. 000842 of 22/02/10
Avian influenza. Poultry and fertile eggs	Sanitary requirements. Monitoring at ports, airports and border crossings	ICA Resolution No. 003655 of 28/09/09
Avian influenza. Live birds, eggs from the Netherlands	Suspension of imports	ICA Resolution No. 00747 of 26/03/03
Avian influenza. Birds and eggs from Belize, El Salvador, Guatemala, Honduras, Mexico and Nicaragua	Suspension of imports	ICA Resolution No. 00950 of 07/05/02
Avian influenza. Birds and bird products from the State of Connecticut (United States)	Importation prohibited	ICA Resolution No. 00748 of 26/03/03
Dried milk and milk substitutes	Animal health permit issued by ICA animal inspection and quarantine offices	ICA Resolution No. 2.475 of 06/05/1993
Seminal material and embryos	Registration of importer with the ICA. Registrations will be issued through a resolution and remain valid indefinitely	ICA Resolution No. 02820 of 11/10/01
Contagious Equine Metritis. Horses from the State of Arizona (United States)	Importation prohibited (Article 1)	ICA Resolution No. 3.231 of 10/08/11
Velogenic Newcastle disease. Birds and bird products at risk of transmitting the virus, from the State of Zulia (Bolivarian Republic of Venezuela)	Suspension of imports	ICA Resolution No. 01182 of 29/05/02
Newcastle disease. Poultry and fertile eggs	Sanitary requirements to prevent the introduction of the virus into the country	ICA Resolution No. 003654 of 28/09/09
Poultry products from Ecuador	Official certification from the exporting country's health authority confirming that the means of transport and packaging used have been cleaned and disinfected with products suitable for combating hepatitis	ICA Resolution No. 02455 of 13/10/98
Cane or beet sugar in solid form	Sanitary approval issued by the Colombian Institute for the Surveillance of Food and Drugs (INVIMA)	INVIMA Resolution No. 016.563 of 05/08/02
Coffee beans	Phytosanitary import requirements. The moisture content must not exceed 9%. Imported shipments of coffee must be fumigated with phosphine and the treatment must be recorded in the phytosanitary certificate of the country of origin. The packaging used must be new and must identify the country of origin and the provenance of the product	ICA Resolution No. 000293 of 09/02/07
Natural rubber	Phytosanitary permit issued by the ICA	Postal Circular SOI No. 067 of 03/09/84. Colombian Foreign Trade Institute (INCOMEX)
Barley for malting or for brewing beer (1003.00.9010)	Certificate of traceability issued by an international quality control body	Decree No. 2.222 of 05/07/06

Product	Summary of the measure	Legislative text
Citrus fruits from countries where the disease citrus leprosis is present	Phytosanitary certificate from the country of origin confirming that the products have undergone a selection, brushing, washing and waxing process	ICA Resolution No 3.182 of 05/11/96
Wood packaging material	ICA inspection at ports, airports and border crossings	ICA Resolution No. 01079 of 03/06/04
Beans of the genera Phaseolus spp. and Vigna spp. for consumption or industrial use	Phytosanitary certificate issued by the official agricultural health authority in the country of origin. New and unused containers	ICA Resolution No. 1.743 of 24/07/98
Fresh fruit from Brazil which is host to Bactrocera	Phytosanitary certificate containing an additional declaration that the products come from areas free of Bactrocera	ICA Resolution No. 1.934 of 22/09/99
Germplasm and banana reproduction material	Importation prohibited from countries that have reported the presence of the fungus Fusarium oxysporum f. sp. cubense race 4 and Chinese Taipei	ICA Resolution No. 2.398 of 31/03/11
Live plant material from the Netherlands Antilles, Saudi Arabia, Australia, Belize, China, the Philippines, Grenada, Guyana, Hawaii, Hong Kong, China, India, Indonesia, the British Virgin Islands, Puerto Rico, the Bolivarian Republic of Venezuela, Saint Lucia, and Trinidad and Tobago	Measures to prevent the introduction into Colombia of the pink hibiscus mealy bug, *Maconellicoccus hirsutus* (Green). ICA inspection at the point of entry into the country	ICA Resolution No. 00121 of 16/01/03
Nursery stocks of oil palm plants	Registration of importer with the ICA	ICA Resolution No. 000395 of 10/02/05
Ornamental plants, cut flowers, foliage and propagation material	Registration of importer with the ICA	ICA Resolution No. 000492 of 18/02/08
Plant products	Phytosanitary import permit. Inspection by the Inspection and Quarantine Unit of the ICA Plant Health Department	ICA Resolution No. 1.412 of 19/06/98
Plant products	Pest risk analysis	ICA Resolution No. 01277 of 09/06/04
Plant products	Airports, seaports, river ports and border crossings authorized for the importation of these products	ICA Resolution No. 003365 of 09/09/09
Plant products. External Circular No. 037/11 lists the products subject to this requirement	Phytosanitary import document issued by the ICA prior to shipment, valid for one shipment only and for 90 days. Physical inspection and issuing of sanitary inspection certificate. ICA phytosanitary control upon entry into the country	ICA Resolution No. 1.558 of 07/05/10
Wheat for sowing, consumption or industrial use from India	Importation prohibited	ICA Resolution No. 1.891 of 10/07/96
Clonal fruit-tree propagation material	Registration of importer with the ICA	ICA Resolution No. 2.713 of 10/10/06
Forage plant and vegetable seed	Registration of importer with the ICA	ICA Resolution No. 1.881 of 10/07/92
Seed for sowing and seedlings of forest species	Registration of importer with the ICA	ICA Resolution No. 002457 of 21/07/10
Seed	Quality certificate issued in the country of origin showing the quality standard, indicating whether the product is a genetically modified organism, and confirming compliance with quality and phytosanitary standards. Registration of importer with the ICA	ICA Resolution No. 970 of 10/03/10
Alcoholic beverages	Sanitary registration of the product with the Ministry of Health. Certificate of free sale issued by the health authority in the country of origin. Registration of importers with the Ministry of Health. Labelling requirements	Decree No. 3.192 of 21/11/83, as amended by Decrees No. 761/93 and No. 365/94
Alcoholic beverages	Sanitary registration of the product with the Ministry of Health. Certificate issued by the health authority of the exporting country showing that the product is legally authorized for human consumption and freely on sale in that country	Ministry of Health Decree No. 2.742 of 09/12/91, as amended by Decree No. 2.311 of 19/12/96.
Energy drinks for human consumption	Registration of importer with INVIMA	INVIMA Resolution No. 13.710 of 13/05/10

Product	Summary of the measure	Legislative text
Hydrating energy drinks for sport	Sanitary registration of product with the Ministry of Health. Maximum permissible mineral levels	Ministry of Health Resolution No. 02229 of 02/04/94
Alcoholic drinks and liquids	INVIMA approval	External Circular No. 0075 of 29/12/06. Colombian Foreign Trade Institute and INVIMA. Amended by External Circulars No. 018/07 and No. 007/11
Bio-inputs for pest control	Registration of product with the ICA. Certificate of free sale in the country of origin. Registration of importer	ICA Resolution No. 698 of 04/02/11
Dieldrin, chlordane, dodecachloride, pentachlorophenol, dicofol, DDT, BHC, heptachlor, lindane and compounds related thereto	Importation prohibited	Ministry of Public Health Resolution No. 10.255 of 09/12/93
Dimetridazole	Importation prohibited	ICA Resolution No. 00991 of 19/05/04
Semi-formulated or finished fertilizers and soil conditioners	ICA approval. Registration of importer with the ICA (Article 8)	ICA Resolution No. 00150 of 21/01/03, as amended by ICA Resolution No. 968/010
Maneb and zineb fungicides and compounds related thereto	Importation prohibited	Ministry of Health Resolution No. 09913 of 06/12/93
Inoculants for leguminous plants	Registration of importer with the ICA	ICA Resolution No. 2.713 of 10/10/06
Lindane-based pesticides	Importation prohibited	Ministry of Health Resolution No. 04166 of 12/11/97
Agricultural pesticides and raw materials for the formulation thereof	Sales licence for marketing in the country, issued by the ICA	ICA Resolution No. 425 of 03/03/93
Agricultural pesticides	Registration of importer with the ICA. Sales licence issued by the ICA	ICA Resolution No. 2.713 of 10/10/06
Chemical pesticides for agricultural use	Registration of importer and product with the ICA. Certificate of free sale and use issued by the competent authority in the country of origin	ICA Resolution No. 03759 of 16/12/03, as amended by Resolution No. 000026 of 25/01/05
Chemical pesticides for agricultural use	ICA registration and control of the product	Decree No. 502 of 05/03/03, as amended by Decree No. 2.404 of 15/07/05
Pesticides	Registration of product with the Ministry of Health and permit for use in the country	Ministry of Health Decree No. 1.843 of 22/07/91, as amended by Decree No. 1.482 of 31/07/98
Pesticides	Product registration issued by the ICA	Law No. 9 of 24/01/79. Health Code
Pesticides	Approval issued by INVIMA or sanitary registration as indicated in the Annex to the legislative text	INVIMA External Circular No. 0075 of 29/12/06, as amended by External Circulars No. 018/07 and No. 007/11
Physiological regulators and adjuvants for agricultural use	Registration of importer with the ICA. Certificate of free use in the country of origin	ICA Resolution No. 2.713 of 10/10/06
Cosmetics	Sanitary registration of product issued by INVIMA. Certificate of free sale in the country of origin	Ministry of Public Health Decree No. 219 of 30/01/98
Homeopathic medicines	Sanitary registration of product issued by INVIMA, valid for ten years. Certificate of free sale in exporter's country of origin. Certificate of good manufacturing practices (GMP) issued by INVIMA	Decree No. 3.554 of 28/10/04, as amended by Decree No. 1.861 of 09/06/06
Homeopathic medicines	Laboratories importing homeopathic medicines must present GMP certification issued by the health authority of the country of origin	Decree No. 1.861 of 09/06/06
Medicines and cosmetics (with exceptions established for each product)	Approval issued by INVIMA or sanitary registration as indicated in the Annex to the legislative text	INVIMA External Circular No. 0075 of 29/12/06, as amended by External Circulars No. 018/07 and No. 007/11

Product	Summary of the measure	Legislative text
Medicines	Certificate of compliance with good manufacturing practices (CCGMP), valid for three years. Medicines without a CCGMP are not allowed into the country	Ministry of Health Decree No. 549 of 29/03/01, as amended by Decrees No. 162 of 22/01/04 and No. 2.086/10
Medicines; cosmetics; pharmaceutical preparations based on natural resources; hygiene products	Sanitary registration of product issued by INVIMA. Sanitary registration and renewals thereof will be valid for five years	Decree No. 677 of 26/04/95, as amended by Decrees No. 341/97, No. 2.091/97, No. 1.792/98, No. 822/03, No. 2.510/03, No. 426/09 and No 2.086/10
Absorbent personal hygiene products	Sanitary registration of product issued by INVIMA. Certificate of free sale issued by the competent authority of the country of origin	Ministry of Health Decree No. 1.545 of 04/08/98
Phytotherapeutic products	Sanitary registration of product issued by INVIMA	Decree No. 2.266 of 15/07/04, as amended by Decree No. 3.553 of 28/10/04
Genetically modified organisms (GMOs)	Registration of importer with the ICA	ICA Resolution No. 1.063 of 22/03/05
Live genetically modified organisms	Registration of importer with the ICA. For marketing purposes, the words "genetically modified organism" must be clearly displayed on the labelling of live genetically modified organisms	ICA Resolution No. 000946 of 17/04/06, as amended by Resolution No. 32 of 17/01/12
Food additives used in the production of food for human consumption	Registration of importer with INVIMA	INVIMA Resolution No. 20.072 of 01/07/10
Food for human consumption originating in or shipped from certain Japanese prefectures in view of the risks arising from the accident at the Fukushima nuclear power station	ICA approval. Maximum levels of radioactive contamination. Certification signed by the competent authority	ICA Resolution No. 3.231 of 10/08/11
Slaughtered birds, whole, cut in pieces and/or boneless, marinated	Composition and quality requirements. Sanitary registration issued by INVIMA	Ministry of Health Resolution No. 00402 of 10/04/02
Meat, edible meat products and meat by-products, including of wild species, for human consumption	Countries interested in exporting to Colombia must submit an export application to INVIMA. After establishing feasibility, INVIMA will conduct an "international audit" with a view to authorizing the country to export the product. INVIMA, together with the ICA, will inspect imports and issue a health inspection certificate for entry into national territory	Ministry of Social Welfare Decree No. 1.500 of 04/05/07, as amended by Decrees No. 2.965/08 and No. 2.380/09
Chocolate and chocolate products for human consumption	Maximum levels of heavy metals and contaminants. Physico-chemical and microbiological requirements	Ministry of Social Welfare Resolution No. 1.511 of 06/05/11
Powdered milk and powdered dairy by-products	Sanitary approval issued by INVIMA	INVIMA Resolution No. 1.679 of 25/01/02
Natural honey for human consumption	Physico-chemical and microbiological health requirements. Inspection conducted by INVIMA	Ministry of Social Welfare Resolution No. 1.057 of 23/03/10
Panela cane sugar for human consumption (1701.11.10.00)	Sanitary requirements. Conformity assessment certificate issued by INVIMA	Ministry of Social Welfare Resolution No. 000779 of 17/03/06
Agricultural, agri-food and agro-industrial products	Administrative procedures for the drafting, adoption and implementation of SPS measures in the agri-food sector	Decree No. 4.003 of 30/11/04
Food products and raw materials for food	Sanitary registration of product issued by INVIMA. Certificate of free sale in the country of origin. Health certificate issued by the country of origin	Decree No. 3.075 of 23/12/97, as amended by Decree No. 1.270 of 17/06/02
Food products	Sanitary inspection at the point of entry into the country and laboratory analysis for obtaining the health inspection certificate for inward customs clearance. Laboratory analysis	Decree No. 3.075 of 23/12/97, as amended by Decree No. 1.270 of 17/06/02
Food products	INVIMA approval or sanitary registration as indicated in the Annex to the legislative text	INVIMA External Circular No. 0075 of 29/12/06, as amended by External Circulars No. 018/07 and No. 007/11

Product	Summary of the measure	Legislative text
Products and by-products of animal origin for human consumption	Official health certificate from the country of origin attesting to the washing, sterilization and cooking processes carried out to ensure product safety	Ministry of Agriculture Resolution No. 361 of 19/07/84
Preserved sardines (1604.13.00.00)	Sanitary requirements. Conformity certificate issued by INVIMA	Ministry of Social Welfare Resolution No. 000337 of 07/02/06
Dietary supplements	Certificate issued by the health authority of the exporting country. Sanitary registration of product issued by INVIMA (valid for ten years, renewable for the same length of time)	Decree No. 3.249 of 18/09/06, as amended by Decree No. 3.863/08

Source: SICE.

Table AIII.3
State-owned enterprises

Sector	Enterprise	State holding (%)	EICE	SEM	Regulation	Control
Agriculture and rural development						
	ALMAGRARIO S.A.	64.62		X	..	..
	Banco Agrario de Colombia S.A.	99.99	X			
	Central de Abastos de Cúcua S.A.	75.14		X		
	Empresa Colombiana de Productos Veterinarios (VECOL) S.A.	82.82		X		
	FIDUAGRARIA S.A.	95.68	X			
	Fondo para el Financiamiento del Sector Agropecuario (FINAGRO)	78.24		X		
Mines						
	ECOPETROL S.A.	89.90		X	Energy and Gas Regulatory Commission (CREG)	Companies Supervisory Authority
Energy						
	Central Hidroeléctrica de Caldas S.A. E.S.P.	80.58		X	Energy and Gas Regulatory Commission (CREG)	Companies Supervisory Authority; Public Services Supervisory Authority
	Centrales Eléctricas de Nariño (CEDENAR) S.A. E.S.P.	99.98	X			
	Centrales Eléctricas de Norte de Santander S.A. E.S.P.	92.05	X			
	Centrales Eléctricas del Cauca S.A. E.S.P.	100.00	X			
	Corporación Eléctrica de la Costa Atlántica (CORELCA) S.A. E.S.P.	99.99	X			
	Electrificadora de Santander S.A.E.S.P.	96.86	X			
	Empresa de Energía del Amazonas S.A. E.S.P.	100.00	X			
	Electrificadora del Caquetá S.A. E.S.P	72.35		X		
	Electrificadora del Huila S.A. E.S.P	99.93	X			
	Electrificadora del Meta S.A. E.S.P	72.38		X		
	Empresa Colombiana de Generación Eléctrica (ISAGEN) S.A. E.S.P.	70.61		X		
	Empresa de Energía de Boyacá (EBSA) S.A. E.S.P.	99.00	X			
	Empresa de Energía de Cundinamarca S.A. E.S.P.	97.95	X			
	Empresa Distribuidora del Pacífico (DISPAC) S.A. E.S.P.	99.99	X			
	Empresa URRA S.A. E.S.P.	99.38	X			
	Empresa de Energía del Quindío S.A. E.S.P.	99.57	X			
	Financiera Energética Nacional (FEN) S.A.	100.00	X			
	Generadora y Comercializadora del Energía del Caribe (GECELCA) S.A. E.S.P.	99.99	X			
	Gestión Energética (GENSA) S.A. E.S.P.	90.93	X			
	Interconexión Eléctrica (ISA) S.A. E.S.P.	56.73		X		
Information and communication technology						
	Canal Regional de Televisión del Caribe (TELECARIBE)	100.00	X		Communications Regulatory Commission	Companies Supervisory Authority
	Colombia Telecomunicaciones S.A. E.S.P.	100.00	X			
	Empresa Metropolitana de Telecomunicaciones (METROTEL) S.A.	99.99	X			
	Radio Televisión Nacional de Colombia (RTVC)	100.00	X			
	Servicios Postales Nacionales S.A	100.00	X			
	Sociedad Canal Regional de Televisión (TEVEANDINA Ltda.) – Canal 13	100.00	X			
	Sociedad de Televisión de Caldas, Risaralda y Quindío Ltda. (TELECAFÉ Ltda.)	100.00	X			
	Empresa de Telecomunicaciones de Bucaramanga (TELEBUCARAMANGA)	99.99	X			

Sector	Enterprise	State holding (%)	EICE	SEM	Regulation	Control
Social welfare						
	Administradora Colombiana de Pensiones (COLPENSIONES)	100.00	X		National Council for Social Security in Health; Health Regulatory Commission	National Health Supervisory Authority
	Caja de Previsión Social de Comunicaciones (CAPRECOM)	100.00	X			
	Instituto de Seguros Sociales (ISS)	100.00	X			
	Centro Dermatológico Federico Lleras Acosta	100.00	X			
	Instituto Nacional de Cancerología	100.00	X			
	Sanatorio de Agua de Dios E.S.E.	100.00	X			
	Sanatorio de Contratación E.S.E.	100.00	X			
Defence						
	Caja Promotora de Vivienda Militar (CAPROVIM)	100.00	X		..	..
	Corporación de la Industria Aeronáutica Colombiana (CIAC) S.A.	100.00	X			
	Industria Militar (INDUMIL)	100.00	X			
	SATENA S.A	100.00	X			
	Sociedad Hotelera Tequendama S.A.	100.00	X			
Justice						
	Imprenta Nacional de Colombia	100.00	X		..	..
Trade, industry and tourism						
	Artesanías de Colombia S.A.	97.43	X		..	Supervisory Authority for Industry and Trade (SIC)
	Banco de Comercio Exterior de Colombia (BANCOLDEX) S.A.	99.72	X			
	Fiduciaria de Comercio Exterior S.A.	89.10		X		
	Fondo Nacional de Garantías S.A.	99.97	X			
	Leasing Bancoldex S.A. – Compañía de Financiamiento Comercial	99.93	X			
Transport						
	Centro de Diagnóstico Automotor de Cúcuta Ltda. (CEDAC)	100.00	X		..	..
Financial sector						
	Central de Inversiones (CISA) S.A.	99.99	X		..	Financial Supervisory Authority
	Fiduciaria La Previsora S.A.	99.99	X			
	Financiera de Desarrollo Territorial (FINDETER) S.A.	99.75	X			
	La Previsora Seguros S.A.	99.71	X			
	Positiva Compañía de Seguros S.A.	99.97	X			
	Sociedad de Activos Especiales S.A.S. (SAE)	99.90	X			

.. Not available.

Note: EICE: State industrial and trading enterprise. SEM: Semi-public company.

Source: Information provided by the Colombian authorities.

Table AIV.1
Air transport agreement modalities, 1974-2012

Countries	Transport	Date	5th freedom	7th freedom	Cabotage	Designation	Withholding	Capacity	Tariffs	Cooperative arrangements	Exchange of statistics
Signed between 2006 and 2012											
Aruba	Passengers	2009	Yes	No	No	Multiple	..	FD/PD[a]	COO	Yes	No
Singapore	Passengers and cargo	2009	Yes	No	No	Multiple	..	PD	COO	Yes	No
Barbados	Passengers and cargo	2010	No	No	No	Multiple	..	PD	..	Yes	Yes
Iceland	Passengers and cargo	2010	No	No	No	Multiple	..	PD	COO	Yes	Yes
Panama	Passengers and cargo	2010	Yes	No	No	Multiple	..	FD	COO	Yes	Yes
Paraguay	Passengers and cargo	2010	No	No	No	Multiple	..	FD	COO	Yes	Yes
Costa Rica	Passengers and cargo	2011	Yes	No	No	Multiple	..	FD	COO	Yes	Yes
El Salvador	Passengers and cargo	2011	Yes	No	No	Multiple	..	FD	COO	Yes	Yes
United Arab Emirates	Passengers and cargo	2011	Yes	No	No	Multiple	..	FD	COO	Yes	Yes
Israel	Passengers and cargo	2011	Yes	No	No	Multiple	..	FD	COO	Yes	Yes
Qatar	Passengers	2011	Yes	No	No	Multiple	..	FD	COO	Yes	Yes
Turkey	Passengers	2011	Yes	No	No	Multiple	..	PD	COO	Yes	Yes
	Cargo	2011	No	No	No	Multiple	..	PD	COO	Yes	Yes
Reviewed between 2006 and 2012											
Belgium	Passengers and cargo	2007	No	No	No	Multiple	..	PD	COO	Yes	Yes
Chile	Passengers	2007	Yes	No	No	Multiple	..	FD	COO	No	No
Netherlands Antilles (Curaçao)	Passengers and cargo	2008	No	No	No	Multiple	..	PD/FD[b]	DA	No	No
United Kingdom	Passengers	2008	Yes	No	No	Single	..	PD	DA	Yes	No
Germany	Passengers	2010	Yes	No	No	Multiple	SOEC	PD	DA	Yes	No
Argentina	Passengers	2010	Yes	No	No	Multiple	..	PD	DA	Yes	No
United States	Passengers and cargo	2010	Yes	No	No	Multiple	SOEC[c]	PD/FD[d]	DA[e]	Yes	No
Mexico	Passengers and cargo	2010	No	No	No	Multiple	..	FD	DA	Yes	Yes
Brazil	Passengers and cargo	2011	Yes	No	No	Multiple	..	PD	COO	Yes	Yes
Ecuador	Passengers and cargo	2011	Yes	No	No	Multiple	..	FD	COO	Yes	No
Dominican Republic	Passengers	2011	Yes	No	No	Multiple	..	FD/PD[f]	COO	Yes	Yes
Spain	Passengers	2012	Yes	No	No	Multiple	..	PD	COO	Yes	Yes
Cuba	Passengers and cargo	2012	Yes	No	No	Multiple	..	PD	COO	No	No
Netherlands	Passengers and cargo	2012	Yes	No	No	Multiple	..	PD	COO	Yes	Yes
Luxembourg	Passengers and cargo	2012	Yes	No	No	Multiple	..	PD	COO	Yes	Yes

Countries	Transport	Date	5th freedom	7th freedom	Cabotage	Designation	Withholding	Capacity	Tariffs	Cooperative arrangements	Exchange of statistics
Agreements prior to 2006											
Suriname	Passengers and cargo	1974	Yes	No	No	Single	..	PD	DA	No	No
Italy	Passengers and cargo	1980	No	No	No	Single	SOEC	PD	COO	Yes	No
Bolivarian Republic of Venezuela	Passengers and cargo	1993	Yes	No	No	Multiple	SOEC	FD	COO	Yes	No
Portugal	Passengers and cargo	1997	No	No	No	Single	SOEC	PD	DA	No	No
Switzerland	Passengers and cargo	2000	Yes	No	No	Single	SOEC	PD	DA	Yes	No
Uruguay	Passengers and cargo	2001	Yes	No	No	Multiple	..	PD	DA	Yes	No
Plurinational State of Bolivia	Passengers and cargo	2004	No	No	No	Multiple	..	FD	COO	Yes	No
Peru	Passengers and cargo	2004	Yes	No	No	Multiple	..	FD	COO	Yes	No
Republic of Korea	Cargo	2004	No	No	No	Multiple	..	FD	..	No	No
France	Passengers and cargo	2005	Yes	No	No	Multiple	SOEC	PD	DA	Yes	Yes

.. Not available.

a Free determination (FD) for flights between Colombia and Aruba, and Aruba and Colombian tourist destinations (Armenia, Cartagena, San Andrés and Santa Marta, but not Barranquilla). Pre-determination (PD) for flights between Aruba and other Colombian cities.

b Free determination for flights between the Netherlands Antilles and Colombian tourist destinations (Armenia, Cartagena, San Andrés and Santa Marta, but not Barranquilla).

c Except for foreign investment from countries with open skies agreements.

d FD from 1 January 2013.

e Tariff freedom applied from 1 January 2013.

f Pre-determination for flights from/to the two capitals.

Note: FD: free determination; PD: pre-determination; SOEC: substantial ownership and effective control; COO: country of origin; DA: double approval. The table only covers provisions relating to passenger traffic.

Source: WTO Secretariat and information provided by the Colombian authorities.

PART C

REPORT BY COLOMBIA

CONTENTS

COLOMBIA: MACROECONOMIC, TRADE AND INVESTMENT ENVIRONMENT

I. OVERVIEW: WHERE DO WE STAND AND WHERE ARE WE HEADED?

1. In November 2006, on the occasion of the third Trade Policy Review of Colombia, WTO Members were informed of the rationale and objectives of Colombia's Democratic Security Policy, designed to enhance physical safety and improve investor confidence in order to stimulate economic growth and reduce poverty.

2. For the four-year period from 2010 to 2014, the Colombian Government has planned to bolster security, social cohesion and investor confidence, and to make significant progress in its democratic prosperity policy, "Prosperity for All".

3. To achieve this goal, Colombia will act in three main areas in accordance with its national development plan, "Prosperity for All": it will continue to focus on security; it will consolidate growth; and it will create more jobs and reduce poverty rates.

4. Job creation is directly linked to economic growth and vitality, and is a prerequisite to improving the welfare of the people. In an effort to achieve that objective, the Government has singled out five so-called "locomotive" sectors: agriculture and rural development; housing and friendly cities; development and expansion of mining and energy; transport infrastructure; and new innovation-based sectors. Given the driving potential of these sectors, the Government hopes to be able to boost productivity, growth and employment.

5. The fight against poverty requires a cross-cutting strategy that involves both direct and indirect action. The direct action is linked to the economic growth strategy designed to increase household income, while the indirect action includes the Social Protection System, the Social Welfare component, and the *Red Unidos* (United Network) strategy to lift 350,000 families out of extreme poverty.

6. On the international front, the Colombian Government is pursuing its objective of becoming more integrated into the markets of Latin America and the Caribbean, Europe and Asia, and strengthening its participation in multilateral organizations. To that end, it has reinforced its efforts to internationalize its economy by: (i) adjusting its tariff policy to promote the transformation of production; (ii) negotiating, implementing and administrating international trade agreements; (iii) promoting investment; and (iv) facilitating trade.

7. None of this could have been achieved without concrete steps to consolidate good governance by applying the principles of transparency, efficiency, effectiveness and accountability, as well as the adoption of the Anti-Corruption Statute contained in Law 1474 of 2011, which updates the legislation and provides for a stricter disciplinary system for public officials and government contractors.

II. SOUND AND COMPETITIVE ECONOMIC GROWTH

(1) OVERVIEW

8. Colombia's GDP grew at an annual average rate of 4.8 per cent from 2005 to 2011, exceeding the average rate for Latin America and the Caribbean (according to ECLAC, 4 per cent). The main driving force behind this growth was investment, whose share in GDP increased by 8 percentage points to above 28 per cent in 2011.

9. This surge in investment is attributable to the positive growth outlook for the economy and the country's sound fiscal accounts, which attracted both domestic and foreign investors. Foreign direct investment (FDI) in Colombia rose from US$6.056 billion in 2006 to US$13.234 billion in 2011, a historical peak for Colombia.

10. The Government is committed to ensuring that public spending is rooted in a sound legal foundation of fiscal responsibility. The Government's legislative initiatives in that area include the enactment of the Tax Adjustment Law, the Fiscal Sustainability Legislative Act and the Fiscal Rule Law.

11. Preliminary figures for the close of the fiscal year 2011 show a consolidated public sector deficit of 2.2 per cent of GDP instead of the predicted 2.9 per cent. This good performance was due mainly to the improvement in the central government fiscal balance, to less budgetary spending in the regions, and to a decrease in the deficit of the Fuel Price Stabilization Fund. The plan for 2012 is to continue reducing the consolidated public sector deficit to 1.8 per cent of GDP, and the central government deficit to 2.8 per cent of GDP.

12. In 2011, inflation reached 3.7 per cent, exceeding the midpoint of the long-term target range established by the Bank of the Republic (3 per cent ± 1 per cent). However, this was the lowest rate among the leading economies of the region. According to the Central Bank's inflation expectations survey of March 2012, private operators expect inflation to decrease in 2012 to 3.5 per cent.

13. Colombia's sovereign debt recovered its investment-grade credit rating by the leading risk-rating agencies between March and July 2011, 12 years after losing it. That rating can be expected to be lifted once again: the rating agency Dominion Bond Rating Service, one of the four agencies currently rating Colombia, upgraded the country's outlook from stable to positive in February. It took the same amount of time for the Colombian economy to revert to one-digit unemployment rates, with 9.3 per cent for the fourth quarter of 2011 and 10.8 per cent for the entire year.

14. The encouraging trend in employment and the positive results of the Government's programmes[1] to increase the coverage and quality of different basic services, together with the introduction of programmes to reduce extreme poverty, have resulted in a fall in the poverty rate from 45 per cent in 2005 to 37.2 per cent in 2010 and 36 per cent between September and December of 2011.

15. In 2011, GDP grew by 5.9 per cent. The sectors that contributed most to this growth were: mining (14.3 per cent), transport, storage and communications (6.9 per cent), trade and hotels (5.9 per cent), finance (5.8 per cent), construction (5.7 per cent), the manufacturing industry (3.9 per cent), and agriculture (2.2 per cent).

16. These results show that sectors identified as the "locomotive" sectors - mining and energy, transport, housing, and agriculture and rural development - are performing satisfactorily, and are expected to continue to do so throughout 2012. Petroleum production, in particular, has grown steadily over the past months, and with the discovery of new fields and a policy aimed at attracting foreign investment, Colombia is beginning to play a strategic role on the regional energy stage.

[1] Consolidation of the Social Protection System, strengthening of the Social Promotion component, and the United Network strategy.

17. The agricultural sector has performed well, with a 3 per cent increase in sowing and 4.6 per cent increase in agricultural production. At the same time in the housing sector, there were 181,888 housing starts (cumulative, year-on-year up to the third quarter of 2011), a historical record. Of these, 85,351 correspond to interest subsidy housing.

18. On the employment front, the sectors that most contributed to creating new jobs were trade, accounting for 26.4 per cent; services, at 19 per cent; agriculture, at 18.1 per cent; and the manufacturing industry at 13 per cent.

(2) COMPETITIVENESS AND GROWTH IN PRODUCTIVITY

19. One of the fundamental strategies for strengthening competitiveness has been the promotion of the so-called "locomotive" sectors. Innovation, the strengthening of competition and business formalization are essential to achieving the proposed goals.

20. Efforts in this area have notably included the strengthening of 71 technological research and development centres through which the knowledge and innovation needed to transform production can be promoted, and the allocation of resources for entrepreneurship through mechanisms such as loans to micro, small and medium enterprises guaranteed by the National Guarantee Fund (FNG) to the tune of 7.3 billion Colombian pesos (US$3.95 billion), and disbursements by the Colombian Foreign Trade Bank - Bancoldex - amounting to 2.96 billion Colombian pesos (US$1.601 billion) for the purpose of boosting productivity and competitiveness of micro, small and medium enterprises.

21. In December 2010, Law 1429 on Formalization and Employment Creation was enacted for the purpose of encouraging formalization at the initial stages of enterprise creation, increasing the benefits and reducing the costs in relation to subsequent formalization. One year after the introduction of this law, 290,703 enterprises had taken advantage of some of the benefits offered, and 181,843 new jobs had been registered, exceeding the target for 2011 by 43 per cent.

22. The Colombian Government has adopted a three-pronged strategy for supporting the competitiveness of local producers: (i) access to financial services; (ii) improvement of the business environment; (iii) private-sector participation in the supply of public goods.

23. The first prong of the strategy focuses on the positive relationship between access to formal financial services and economic growth. One of the first results has been the registration of 19,230 agent banks, ensuring access to financial services throughout the country. At the same time, efforts have been made to promote economic and financial education. In 2011, a number of design and innovation workshops were organized to foster business competitiveness, providing non-financial support to 509 micro, small and medium-sized enterprises, 92.5 per cent higher than the annual target.

24. The second prong of the strategy consists of improving the business and entrepreneurial environment in order to ensure more flexible and efficient procedures for setting up and formalizing companies. The implementation of the strategy of streamlining the formalities and regulations involved in the life cycle of a company has been reflected in the World Bank's "Doing Business" indicator for Colombia between 2005 and 2010, when it ranked 39th of 183 countries. With the inclusion of the "getting electricity" component in 2011, the general ranking changed and Colombia ended up in 47th place.

25. Colombia's reforms earned it the distinction of "top ten reformer", and moved it up five places in the general rankings to 42nd place. Thus, Colombia improved in relative terms, and has maintained

its third place in Latin America and its status as one of the 12 economies that have most improved their ease of doing business ranking.[2]

26. The third prong of the strategy targets the active involvement of the private sector in the process of overcoming the problems - productive and social - encountered in the different sectors. This involves the organization of events to promote the public-private dialogue for competitiveness at the regional and national levels.

New innovation-based sectors

27. Spearheading the innovation efforts are a series of measures to transform production in knowledge-intensive sectors. The Government is seeking to boost its exportable production of innovative and high value-added products by developing an action plan which provides for:

(a) Tools to help boost competitiveness. To that end, the Bancoldex Development Unit was created to encourage more entrepreneurs to become involved in high-impact processes emphasizing innovation, job creation and formalization. The idea is to support technology-based companies, to provide funds for business modernization and innovation, to encourage the creation of research and development centres in Colombian companies, and to support the development of projects through regional clusters.

(b) strengthening of the Productive Transformation Programme (PTP) launched in 2010[3] with a view to implementing a focused sectoral economic development model whose methodology calls for a common language, and public-private alliance as well as inter-institutional coordination in defining targets and objectives, the aim being to encourage and stimulate the development of Colombian goods and services in certain sectors while ensuring that progress on the domestic front is compatible with integration in the global economy.

The PTP involves new and emerging sectors with the potential to become "world-class sectors". Public-private initiatives have focused on four cross-cutting aspects: (i) human capital formation; (ii) infrastructure; (iii) rules and regulations; (iv) strengthening of industry and promotion.

A first stage covered eight industrial and services sectors[4], followed by four agro-industrial sectors.[5] In 2011, four new innovation sectors were added to the programme: (i) metalworking, iron and steel; (ii) dairy products; (iii) fruit and vegetables; (iv) nature tourism. As a result the value of PTP exports in 2011 rose to US$6.308 billion, exceeding the target of US$5.500 billion.

---

[2] *Doing Business* - World Bank (2012). Doing business in a more transparent world: Comparing regulation for domestic firms in 183 economies.

[3] CONPES 3678 of 2010: *Política de Transformación Productiva: un modelo de desarrollo sectorial para Colombia.*

[4] Business process outsourcing and offshoring (BPO&O); software and IT services; health tourism; cosmetics and toiletries; auto parts and vehicles; electrical energy and services and related goods; textiles and clothing; design and fashion; and graphic communication industry.

[5] Cocoa, confectionery and chocolate; palm, other vegetable fats and oils; shrimp farming; and bovine meat.

(c) Redirecting of investment promotion instruments towards free zones so that they can contribute to the development of scientific and technological capacity and innovation.

(d) Coordination of investments in science, technology and innovation with entrepreneurial demands. In the course of 2011, 206 companies benefited from instruments for the promotion of innovation, and eight regional innovation platforms were supported by *Colciencias* (Colombian Innovation Agency). *Colciencias* is working together with the National Learning Service (SENA), the Ministry of Information Technology and Communications (MINTIC), Ecopetrol, *Cerrejón*, *Codensa-Emgesa*, *Corpoica* and the Ministry of Industry, Commerce and Tourism, to promote the transformation of production in the "locomotive" and strategic sectors.

(e) Finally, bilateral cooperation in science and technology is being fostered in an effort to turn Colombia into a country of knowledge. To that end, Colombia is endeavouring to strengthen its bilateral cooperation with the United States, Brazil, France, Russia, Germany and Switzerland.

III. TRADE POLICY: CURRENT SITUATION AND OUTLOOK

(1) Overview

28. For Colombia, increased internationalization of the economy and the transformation of domestic production are fundamental to achieving greater economic development and reducing poverty.

29. Since the last Trade Policy Review, Colombia has continued with its successful development and implementation of a strategy for integration into the global economy. This strategy has been introduced in a context in which a number of different integration processes are taking place simultaneously, ranging from slow and complex multilateral integration processes to regional integration, the conclusion of a considerable number of bilateral agreements, and unilateral market opening.

30. In this context, Colombia's trade policy is focused on improving participation in the value chains by increasing and diversifying foreign trade in goods and services and foreign direct investment flows. It should be possible, in 2014, to exceed the 2011 figures for goods and services exports. As a minimum, this should include US$22 billion worth of non-mining/energy exports and US$6.2 billion worth of services exports, while the amount of foreign direct investment attracted should exceed US$14.4 billion.

(2) Multilateral, Regional and Bilateral Developments

31. In the course of 2001, Colombia improved its integration and strengthened its position on the international scene. It managed to: (i) diversify its markets by implementing new agreements; (ii) strengthen its relations with Latin America and the Caribbean; (iii) enhance its participation in multilateral organizations through acceptance in the OECD Investment Committee; (iv) develop border integration and development strategies; (v) strengthen international cooperation; (vi) develop strategies for rapprochement with Asia and the Pacific; (vii) maintain a dynamic and constructive presence in the WTO.

(2.1) Multilateral sphere

32. Colombia continues to participate actively at the multilateral level, and to stick to its commitments under the WTO and the GATT when it comes to applying the agreements and developing trade relations with the different partners. It is confident that the multilateral trading system can be strengthened and stands ready to continue working constructively to reactivate the negotiations. Colombia strongly supports an early and balanced completion of the Doha Round on the basis of the advances already made, maintaining as the central plank the reform of agriculture.

33. For the Colombian Government, the ideal forum to advance the trade integration process is the WTO. However, given that the rate at which decisions are taken and implemented at the WTO has not kept up with the requirements of globalization, Colombia has opted for regional and bilateral negotiations with its priority partners.

34. Holding regional and bilateral negotiations has become the best available way to complement Colombia's serious engagement at the multilateral level. At the Eighth Ministerial Conference, our Minister of Commerce, Industry and Tourism stated that Colombia was "seeking open trade within a transparent, predictable and inclusive multilateral system, which is complemented by regional and bilateral efforts. We believe in the importance of bringing Latin America closer to the Asia-Pacific Basin and to Africa".

(2.2) Regional and bilateral spheres

35. At the regional level, the natural integration framework for Colombia is the Andean Community (CAN). In July 2011, Colombia assumed the *pro tempore* presidency of the CAN for one year, and in that capacity, it developed a work plan focusing on four main objectives: prioritization of the Andean Strategic Agenda; institutional development; deepening of the subregional market in other areas; and cooperation between promotion agencies and development banks. Once that period is over, it will continue to participate actively and to pursue its efforts to strengthen integration.

36. To date, the CAN has produced decisions relating to migration statistics, harmonized balance-of-payments statistics and financial vulnerability indicators; the updating of the NANDINA Common Nomenclature; statistics on tourism; rules for the registration, control, marketing and use of veterinary products, and trade facilitation in customs. Work has also been done on: identifying elements of complementarity and differences with a view to future convergence of the CAN, MERCOSUR and UNASUR; fostering regional energy integration to make full use of a region's potential; and supporting the restructuring of the Andean Integration System.

37. After six years of inactivity, the Committees of Export Promotion Authorities and of Aeronautical Authorities were revived, and a meeting of the development banks of the CAN countries was held.

38. Aware of the importance of expanding and strengthening its ties with Latin America, Colombia decided, as from the beginning of 2011, to push for the Pacific Alliance, an initiative which calls for the creation of an area of deep integration in which goods, services, capital and persons can circulate freely between Colombia, Chile, Peru and Mexico. Panama and Costa Rica are participating as observers. It is hoped that the framework agreement establishing this alliance will be concluded in June 2012.

39. The technical work has focused on: (i) the movement of business persons and facilitation of transit migration, including police cooperation; (ii) trade and integration, including trade facilitation and customs cooperation; (iii) services and capital, including the possibility of integrating the stock exchanges; and (iv) cooperation and dispute settlement mechanisms.

40. Efforts to diversify bilateral relations began to take concrete form in 2011 with the entry into force of the free trade agreements (FTAs) with Switzerland and Liechtenstein in the framework of the European Free Trade Association (EFTA) in July and with Canada in August, the signature of the FTA by the United States Government in October 2011, and the approval by the European Commission of the trade agreement with the European Union.

(3) INTEGRATION OF PRODUCTION INTO WORLD MARKETS

41. The development of a comprehensive trade policy based on the competitiveness of Colombian enterprises abroad, the conditions governing foreign trade, and foreign direct investment (FDI) has produced positive results. At the end of 2011, the value of exports reached US$56.954 billion, 43 per cent higher than 2010. The main exports were mining and energy products (petroleum and petroleum products, coal, ferro-nickel, gold and emeralds) which totalled US$40.396 billion - a growth of 56 per cent - and accounted for 71 per cent of total exports during the period. Exports of goods other than mining and energy products increased by 19 per cent.

42. Colombia's main trading partners were the United States (38 per cent), the European Union (15.6 per cent), Chile (4 per cent) and China (3.5 per cent). Of these four countries, the sharpest increase in Colombian exports was with Chile (104 per cent) and the European Union (77 per cent). It should be also be noted that in the course of 2011, exports to Venezuela increased by 23 per cent, reflecting the improvement in bilateral trade relations between the two neighbours after a fall in sales of more than 60 per cent in 2010.

43. Meanwhile, FDI reached US$13.234 billion in 2011 - 4 per cent of GDP - exceeding the 2010 figure by 91.8 per cent. Of this, US$5.083 billion went to the petroleum sector (38.4 per cent of the total). This was followed by mining and quarrying, with US$2.621 billion (19.8 per cent of the total); commerce, restaurants and hotels with US$2.264 billion (17.1 per cent of the total); transport and communication with US$1.421 billion (10.7 per cent of the total); electricity, water and gas with US$585 million (4.4 per cent of the total); and the manufacturing sector with US$533 million (4 per cent of the total).

44. At the same time, the flow of direct investment from Colombia reached US$8.289 billion, 26.3 per cent higher than in 2010. This increase is the result of the new investments in the Latin American pensions market and the expansion plans in Central and South America.

45. International integration strategies focus on three main areas:

(a) The legal environment

46. Pursuing its trade agenda, approved by the Higher Council for Foreign Trade, Colombia has continued with the negotiation of new agreements as well as the consolidation of some of the existing agreements. The target for 2014 is to complete the negotiation of a total of 18 trade agreements (nine more than currently exist). The Partial Scope Agreement with Venezuela, which defines the preferential treatment that applies to trade in products originating in the two countries, has already been concluded. By the end of the first half of 2012, the negotiation of free trade agreements with South Korea and Turkey should be completed, and negotiations with Panama and Israel should be

concluded by the end of the year. The negotiating agenda includes Japan - with which a task force has been set up to outline the negotiation of an economic association agreement - Costa Rica, the Dominican Republic and Australia.

47. Inclusion in different forums in Asia and the Pacific continues to be one of Colombia's goals. In 2011, a Colombian delegation toured Asia, visiting members of APEC and ASEAN in order to progress towards membership in APEC, and to establish a mechanism for political dialogue with the member countries of ASEAN and conclude trade and bilateral cooperation agreements.

48. Thanks to these efforts, Colombia (i) was invited as a non-member country to attend the APEC working groups on tourism, SMEs, energy, mining, telecommunications, and customs procedures; (ii) participated in the APEC Business Summit where it reiterated its interest in joining APEC once the moratorium was lifted; (iii) became regional coordinator of the Forum for East Asia-Latin America Cooperation (FEALAC) for 2011-2013, with the challenge of finding new horizons for FEALAC and organizing the first Business Forum in 2012.

49. Of the 18 agreements that Colombia aims to have negotiated by 2014, those with the United States, the European Union, Venezuela, Panama, Korea, Turkey and Israel should be fully operational by the end of this year. If we add the agreements with Canada and with Switzerland and Lichtenstein in the framework of EFTA, which entered into force recently, the total number of fully operational agreements will be 13. This means that Colombian exports will have preferential access to a market of 1.512 billion people.

50. On the investment front, the negotiation of international investment agreements, whether Reciprocal Investment Promotion and Protection Agreements or as part of a more comprehensive agreement - for instance the sections on investment in the trade agreements - is central to Colombia's strategy of minimizing legal risks and improving the investment climate.

51. Colombia hopes to have 20 international investment agreements in force by 2014, i.e. 14 more than the six currently in force. The new countries with which it hopes to establish stable investment regulations are; India, the United States, China, the United Kingdom, Panama, Korea, Kuwait, Japan, the United Arab Emirates, Turkey, and two others for which negotiations have not yet started.

52. Approximately 65 per cent of inward foreign investment in Colombia comes from the countries with which it has, or is currently negotiating, an investment agreement, while 66 per cent of Colombian investment abroad is in countries with which it has, or is currently negotiating, an investment agreement. The planned negotiations should therefore enable Colombia to achieve the right balance between the benefits of FDI in the country and the cost that could arise from the possibility granted to foreign investors of filing lawsuits against Colombia in international courts.

53. Worth noting in this connection is the creation of the National Legal Defence Agency, which began to operate as a Special Administrative Unit in March 2012. Its role is to coordinate, organize and structure the country's defence, and where possible, to avoid damage to the State's assets while at the same time promoting respect for fundamental rights.

54. At the same time, taking advantage of the recent momentum, efforts are being made to formulate a public policy for Colombian investment abroad, which in 2011 amounted to US$8.289 billion. The plan is to create mechanisms to help Colombian investors to enter foreign markets and position themselves in strategic sectors in which they are competitive. This also involves

identifying any obstacles that are currently preventing Colombian investors from entering other markets.

55. As part of the general strategy aimed at improving the investment climate with a view to acceding to OECD, coordinated by the President of the Republic, in 2011 the Ministry of Commerce, Industry and Tourism set out to adhere to the Declaration on International Investment and Multinational Enterprises and hence to become a permanent member of OECD Investment Committee.

56. Accordingly, in October 2011, Colombia's investment policy was subjected to a Peer Review with the OECD's Investment Group. The outcome was successful and the Group recommended that the General Council invite Colombia to adhere to the OECD Declaration on International Investment and Multinational Enterprises. Colombia formally subscribed to the Declaration in December 2011. The OECD's final report on investment policy in Colombia was revised and is currently being translated into Spanish. It will be made available during the first half of 2012.

(b) Management and promotion

57. The Colombian government is committed to reforming its programs and initiatives in order to manage and take full advantage of the better access conditions available to it under the trade agreements signed and in force. This will involve activities such as organizing the administrative commissions as well as information and export and investment facilitation seminars. Efforts are also being made to design and implement a policy to support Colombian investment abroad, as mentioned earlier, and a programme to facilitate and promote services exports.

(c) Trade facilitation and institution building

58. Colombia has undertaken to facilitate foreign trade formalities and procedures, to keep improving the Single Foreign Trade Window, to provide for simultaneous inspection of goods and the adoption of non-intrusive technology for these processes, and to ensure digitization and recognition in other countries of import and export documents such as certificates of origin.

59. Significant progress has also been made in rationalizing the tariff structure, in developing software to facilitate access to trade defence instruments, and in monitoring commitments under trade and investment agreements. These are measures that improve the transparency of trade transactions.

60. The tariff reform has aimed to reduce average tariff dispersion, streamline customs administration and bolster the Government's efforts to prevent the peso from becoming too strong.

61. Thanks to the measures that were adopted, the average tariff was brought down from 12.2 per cent to 8.3 per cent, which unquestionably led to a reduction of the anti-export bias and an improvement in the competitiveness of domestic production by substantially lowering tariffs on raw materials and capital goods.

62. Inter-institutional coordination on the part of both the customs and health authorities has been a key to progress in removing the obstacles blocking access by Colombian exporters to other markets.

63. In this connection, the Colombian Customs Statute was specially altered to be bring its procedures into line with the current dynamics of foreign trade. Measures were adopted to streamline customs operations, with a guarantee that the international trade facilitation standards contained in the Framework of Standards of the World Customs Organization (WCO) would be applied.

64. The new Customs Statute seeks to ensure that customs users comply with their obligations by introducing information technology, non-intrusive inspection equipment, and security devices to help reduce the time required and the operational costs while strengthening control mechanisms to counteract illegal practices.

65. Progress has been made in the health field as well, with improved coordination among the competent authorities in an effort to treat the requirements for domestic production and imported products in a comprehensive and balanced manner, and technical cooperation programmes to achieve greater recognition of technical standards and regulations in the export destination countries.

66. It is worth noting in this connection that in 2010, the National Institute for the Surveillance of Food and Drugs (INVIMA) was designated by the Pan-American Health Organization as a reference National Regulatory Authority (NRA) for Latin America. Only the health agencies of Argentina, Brazil and Cuba have thus far received this certification. On the basis of this recognition, the four agencies concluded a cooperation agreement with each other and with other agencies to strengthen and recognize local capacities, raise the region's regulatory standards and practices to world level, and ensure that they are known as internationally recognized good practices.

67. Similarly, it should be noted that Colombia has been making progress as regards the improvement of its health status. Proof of this is that it received OIE recognition as a country free of foot and mouth disease with vaccination in 2009 and as a country with a "negligible risk" of bovine spongiform encephalopathy last month. In addition, Colombia implements an institutional strengthening programme aimed at ensuring effective technical and scientific evaluation in sanitary risk assessment. Work has also begun on creating a single window to simplify and streamline agricultural input registration procedures.

68. Moreover, the Global Competition Review (GCR), which administers the only world ranking of competition authorities, has just nominated the Supervisory Authority for Industry and Trade (SIC) for its annual award in the category "best competition authority in America", together with its counterparts in United States, Mexico and Chile. This is a tribute to the SIC's successful efforts in the area of protection of free competition during 2011.

IV. CONCLUSIONS

69. The sound economic growth achieved over the past few years, the fall in the rate of unemployment and in the consolidated public sector deficit, the success in maintaining the lowest level of inflation in the region, and the figures for goods and services exports and for foreign direct investment provide clear evidence of the Colombian Government's commitment to boosting the growth rate in order to create more jobs, reduce poverty and bring greater prosperity to all Colombians.

70. According to private-sector economic analysts, in 2012 most of the countries of Latin America will grow at a slower rate than in 2011 owing to the slowdown in the world economy and the fall in international commodity prices. Colombia, however, should grow faster than the average for the economies of the region, and should in fact achieve one of the highest growth rates.

71. The Government's growth forecast for this year is approximately 5 per cent. The challenge is to continue working to achieve faster growth, to create new jobs so that unemployment can be reduced to a single digit, and to move forward with the formalization of the economy. At the same time, it is hoped that infrastructure can be improved through productive investment of the resources

from the new royalty distribution scheme, from private sector contributions and from the efficient use of resources from the country's general budget.

72. Efforts will also be made to maintain the recovery of the industrial sector accomplished thanks to the revival of the economy and of foreign trade, the momentum achieved in areas such as construction, the availability of credit, and the efforts and achievements of companies in the areas of innovation, internationalization, marketing, and diversification of products and export destinations.

73. In other words, the challenge is to consolidate Colombia's integration in international goods and services markets in order to be able to participate successfully in global value chains and to continue improving the country's competitiveness through development of infrastructure, education, formalization, information technologies and innovation.

74. To achieve all of this, the government will continue to work resolutely to strengthen the country's institutions and improve its economic and trade policies so that it can offer its own citizens and foreigners a friendly investment and business environment with a view, ultimately, to providing higher standards of living.